Horace Maloy

D1292249

EXEMPLARS OF
SOCIAL RESEARCH

EDITORS

PHILLIP FELLIN
TONY TRIPODI
HENRY J. MEYER
THE UNIVERSITY OF MICHIGAN

 F. E. PEACOCK PUBLISHERS, INC.
ITASCA • ILLINOIS

Acknowledgements

Exemplars of Social Research is the outgrowth of a concern on the part of the editors with the potential contribution empirical research can make to social practice. As a consequence of this concern, our goal in this volume and the complementary work, *The Assessment of Social Research,* is to facilitate the consumption of empirical research reports. Many of the ideas we have developed in regard to the assessment of social research were the result of our reading and reflecting upon the studies included in this volume. In addition, the direct and indirect contributions of our colleagues and students are equally appreciated. Our thinking about the assessment of social research has been particularly stimulated by associations with: David Fanshel, Samuel Finestone, Ernest Greenwood, James Bieri, Martin McCarthy, Edgar Borgatta, Edwin Thomas, Eugene Litwak, Irwin Epstein, Rosemary Sarri, and John Tropman.

We are grateful to Fedele F. Fauri, Dean, and Robert D. Vinter, Associate Dean, of the School of Social Work, University of Michigan, for fostering the intellectual climate among the faculty which sustained our enthusiasm during the preparation of this volume. Among the administrative and secretarial staff of the School of Social Work, we express our special appreciation to Roy Gaunt, Marian Iglesias, Diane Etzel, Sande Smith, and Betty Ring.

We thank the following graduate assistants for their help: Roslyn Weinberger, Elizabeth MacIntyre, Anne Springer, Ben Hemke, John Ford, Carol Lee Wortman, Tai K. Shin, and David Dillman. We appreciate the suggestions and constructive reactions by students in our classes on research methods.

The consent of authors and publishers to reprint materials is gratefully acknowledged here, and specifically recognized where the materials are reproduced.

We thank F. E. Peacock, our publisher; his associate, Thomas LaMarre, Editor; Joyce Usher, Managing Editor; and members of our families, Carol Lee Tripodi, Phyllis Fellin, and Suzanne Meyer, for their helpful advice and constant encouragement.

Contents

ONE | # The Assessment of Social Research

INTRODUCTION

The major objective of this book is to facilitate the consumption of empirical research reports. To become a proficient consumer, the research reader must learn how to assess published studies and he must have practice in doing so. For these purposes, this book offers guidelines for the assessment of social research and provides examples of research studies which may be used to develop skill in the assessment of major types of social research.

Assessment of research requires standards for judging how well a study has been done and how useful it can be. Evaluation and utilization are crucial features of assessment, and these in turn are facilitated by the classification of a study in terms of its purposes and research methods. It is helpful to view the processes of classification, evaluation, and utilization with respect to their relations to knowledge. Research is classified to place it within the context of the goals of research for seeking knowledge.

The evaluation of research involves a determination of the extent to which a researcher has been able to accomplish his objectives, as well as a consideration of alternative procedures that might have been used to approximate more closely the objectives of the research. Finally, utilization of research includes a determination of the level of knowledge achieved in the research, and then a consideration of the potential application of the findings to specific areas, such as social work practice.

Assessment of empirical research is a significant activity of the social scientist and the social practitioner. They both seek to understand phenomena in the social world, to assimilate new knowledge into frameworks of previously obtained knowledge, and to utilize research procedures and knowledge in the conduct of research or in the application of knowledge to problems of practice.

In recognition that effective consumption of research depends on skill in reading and assessing research as reported in the literature, this volume includes published studies of different types of research. Selections have been made from journals of social work, psychology, and sociology. Moreover, bibliographies of additional research articles are included so that students and instructors of courses in social research can have a ready source of studies to assess. These references, and the selections reproduced in this book, also provide a foundation for the discussion of research methods and hence can be used in conjunction with basic research methods courses in social work and social science.

The consumer of research should be prepared, after the exercise of assessing studies selected for this book, to pursue his own directions of interest in the literature. Our selections have been made from the literature of social work, sociology, and psychology because these are the fields of our own greatest experience and also because their substantive content is a major source of knowledge for social workers. However, we believe that the guidelines for assessment can be applied to research reports from other disciplines.

The principles and criteria that underlie these guidelines are fully developed in *The Assessment of Social Research: Guidelines for the Use of Research in Social Work and Social Science* (Tripodi, Fellin, & Meyer, 1969). The research reader may find it particularly helpful to examine the narrative assessments of three research reports included in that book. These assessments may be used as models for the reader engaged in assessing the studies reproduced herein. So that *Exemplars of Social Research* may be used as an independent as well as a complementary work, this section summarizes the viewpoint taken in the development of guidelines for the classification, evaluation, and utilization of social research.

CLASSIFICATION OF RESEARCH

Research is the application of systematic procedures for the purpose of developing, modifying, and expanding knowledge which can be communicated and verified by independent investigators. Research in the social sciences and related disciplines involves the use of a variety of available methods to obtain relatively unbiased observations of human behavior, and such research is concerned with logical alternatives for approximating degrees of relative certainty in the attainment of knowledge. Based on the objectives of the research investigation and the use of different strategies and methods, research studies can be classified into three broad categories: experimental, quantitative-descriptive, and exploratory (Weinberger and Tripodi, 1968). *Experimental studies* have the general purpose of producing empirical generalizations, i.e., verified hypotheses. Such studies attempt to establish cause-effect relationships by minimizing the influence of variables other than those specified in the hypothesis being tested through the use of such devices as random assignment of subjects to experimental and control groups. *Quantitative-descriptive studies* have a range of objectives from the production of facts to the determination of correlations among selected variables and the testing of hypotheses through approximations to rigorous experimental designs. Unlike experimental and quantitative-descriptive studies, *exploratory studies* have as their major purpose the articulation of concepts and the development of hypotheses. A variety of research procedures such as techniques for interviewing and participant observation may be used, but the systematic application of research procedures to establish accurate quantitative relations among variables is a secondary concern.

Within the three major categories, the classification system includes sub-types which are identified below, and further defined in later sections. An outline of the classification system is as follows:

    I. Experimental Studies
        1. Laboratory Experiments
        2. Field Experiments
    II. Quantitative-Descriptive Studies
        1. Hypothesis Testing
        2. Program Evaluation
        3. Population Description
        4. Searching for Variable Relationships
    III. Exploratory Studies
        1. Combined Exploratory-Descriptive
        2. Use of Specific Data Collection Procedures
        3. Use of Experimental Manipulations

This classification system is intended for use with empirical research reports, and it is not applicable for categorizing non-empirical studies, such as historical and bibliographical research. Furthermore, only reports of single research investigations can be usefully classified in this scheme. Although they may be concerned with research, essay reviews of one or more research studies cannot be classified in these categories. Likewise outside the scope of the scheme are studies which use findings from research investigations to develop practice implications or to support theoretical notions, such as discussions of research strategies and methodological issues.

Assumptions regarding knowledge which serve as the foundation for this classification system are most clearly postulated by Eaton (1958), who states that knowledge about a particular phenomenon is not absolute although it can be approximated by relative degrees of certainty through the scientific approach. In addition, when assessing studies it is important to consider the forms in which knowledge comes to us, i.e., concepts, hypotheses, empirical generalizations, and theory (Greenwood, 1960; Thomas, 1964). Different approaches in social research are contingent on the form of knowledge sought, which ranges from clarification of concepts to the testing of hypotheses derived from theory. Thus, the potential utility of research can be enhanced if consumers of research consider both the form and the degree of relative certainty of the knowledge produced by research studies. The classification system has been developed to assist the research reader in this endeavor.

To facilitate classification, we suggest general steps to be followed in classifying any particular research study:

1. First read the article quickly in order to obtain an overview of the research study. Then read the study carefully, paying particular attention to the objectives of the study and the methods employed to accomplish the objectives. It is important to note that objectives may be included throughout the presentation of the study, as well as in sections devoted to problem formulation and to the conclusions of the research.

2. List the explicit and implicit objectives of the study, and arrange the objectives into a hierarchy of importance for the investigation. Hierarchy of importance refers to a rank ordering of objectives in terms of what was done in the research. If most of the study is devoted to describing a particular population, then that may be the most "important" objective.

3. List the specific research methods and procedures used in the study, and determine which procedures were used to accomplish each objective listed above.

4. Do not accept an author's classification of his study. Look for the

necessary criteria that place the study in the classification scheme here presented.

5. In order to classify the study it is useful to begin with the most explicitly defined category, experimental studies. Determine whether or not the study can be classified as experimental. If the study is experimental, then decide whether it should be categorized as a field experiment or as a laboratory experiment.

6. If the study is not experimental, then determine whether it can be categorized as a quantitative-descriptive study. If the study is quantitative-descriptive, decide to which one of the four sub-types the study could be assigned. The study should be categorized by that sub-type which is most representative of the research.

7. If the study is not quantitative-descriptive, determine whether or not it can be regarded as an exploratory study. If the study is exploratory, decide on its appropriate sub-type.

The foregoing suggestions are by no means meant to limit the research reader in the formulation of his own, individually developed mode of proceeding to the point where he can distinguish various types of research on the basis of their purposes and methods. Indeed, with experience, he will discover that these suggestions merely outline the initial activities that must engage his thinking as he proceeds to assess research reports. The crucial point is that assessment must begin with a determination of purposes and methods of the research, and this is aided by a framework in which to differentiate the study from those with other purposes and methods. Classification of research studies is not an end in itself; deciding that a study is a "field experiment" or "combined exploratory-descriptive research" is useful only because it allows more clarity in the total process of assessing the research. The process includes evaluating the study and judging its utility, as well as determining its purposes and methods.

EVALUATION OF SOCIAL RESEARCH

Guidelines for evaluation call for a systematic assessment of the major aspects of an empirical research investigation, i.e., problem formulation, research design and data collection, and data analysis and conclusions. Our review of the literature produced no set of guidelines which focused on these major aspects of the research process in the context of both purposes and methods of research. Yet, differentiation of context when evaluating research appears necessary in order to achieve maximum utilization of research knowledge.

Guidelines for evaluation are usefully formulated with reference to the three major aspects previously noted: problem formulation, research design and data collection, and data analysis and conclusions. A typical research study, if properly reported, contains information about each of these interrelated aspects of the research process. Problem formulation and research design involve the articulation of the precise problem to be investigated and the specification of the logical approach used to answer the questions posed for study. The sampling procedures are indicated, and appropriate methods of gathering data relevant to the research problem are considered. Data are analyzed by quantitative and qualitative devices, and there is a consideration of the extent to which conclusions can be reached regarding answers to the major questions of the investigation. Basic to our perspective on evaluation is the position that different standards should be used for different levels of scientific inquiry. Most available guidelines for evaluating research are devoted primarily to research which has the purpose of producing empirical generalizations, with the implication that all research studies are to be judged by their achievement of absolute certainty. Since most studies fall short of this achievement, readers may be tempted to conclude that no research is useful. It is particularly erroneous for the reader to apply criteria for evaluating experiments to exploratory studies which have different purposes from those of verifying hypotheses. Studies should not be evaluated without first determining their specific purposes and methods. If such a determination is not made, the possibility of differential assessment is minimized and conclusions from different research studies may erroneously be regarded as equivalent.

Some additional problems may face the research reader in his evaluation of studies. The research report may not contain sufficient information and detail to allow for evaluation. Sufficient information for understanding the major objectives of the study, the methods employed to reach the objectives, and the use of data in forming conclusions should be included in the research report. Secondly, not all research reports will be clearly presented. To the extent that the written report is not systematic, clear, and internally consistent, it will be difficult for the reader to classify and evaluate the research study. Thirdly, the classification and evaluation of research presumes a minimum level of sophistication in research methodology. The reader must be familiar with the major and commonly accepted concepts utilized in discussing scientific research. In addition, the greater the degree of substantive knowledge of the area under investigation possessed by the reader the greater the potential for assessing the research study.

Early in the reading of the research report, the evaluator should be sensitive to alternative strategies which might have been pursued with regard to the study being evaluated. It is useful for the reader to consider the relative advantages and disadvantages of alternative designs vis-a-vis the purposes of the study.

UTILIZATION OF SOCIAL RESEARCH

Our focus on utilization has been developed mainly within the context of the usefulness of research knowledge for social work practice. Unlike questions about classification and evaluation, questions about utility for social work practice require the reader to consider relevance of the research to the professional objectives of the social worker or of the social work profession. In this context the research reader should consider the kinds of knowledge that may be gained from the research. Three kinds of knowledge can be distinguished: empirical knowledge, conceptual knowledge, and methodological knowledge. Considerations of these kinds of content are also applicable to the research reader not concerned with practice, but acting purely in the role of the social scientist. However, the research reader's assessment of the utility of the knowledge will differ somewhat, depending on whether he wants to apply the knowledge to practical problems in social welfare, education, social planning, and so forth, or whether he seeks to use the knowledge for research or other endeavors which do not call for engineering the knowledge to solve practical social problems.

For both the social scientist and the social practitioner, the consideration of knowledge content is necessary in assessing the utility of the research. Empirical research investigates some aspect of the observable world. What is investigated is the empirical referent of the research and what is reported about the empirical referent is the empirical content of the research. The study may be about mental retardates, or about race riots, or about groups of boys at a settlement house. It may be about what social workers do or about rates of mental illness or about families where marriage partners are in conflict. Some kind of behavior, some social condition, some set of events is looked at through the concepts and methods of research, resulting in empirical research findings.

Empirical research studies also provide conceptual knowledge. The empirical phenomena are always viewed through concepts; concepts are often related to one another in hypotheses which may be explicitly or implicitly linked together into theories; generalizations about the empirical phenomena may be established or suggested. The level of conceptual content that the reader can make use of is dependent on the purpose and methods of the research (and hence its type) and also on the success with which the research achieves its purpose (and hence on an evaluation of it). For the social practitioner, all levels of knowledge may be useful, each in different ways allowing him to deal with problems in his practice with increased awareness of the nature of the phenomena he works with and his own ways of working. Thus the reader should determine not only what level of knowledge the research provides, but also what level is most useful to him in relation to particular interests he brings from his practice.

Experimental research may allow the reader to consider the applicability to his practice of the empirical generalizations it demonstrates; it may allow him also to consider the applicability of hypotheses tested and the concepts that have been used. The conceptual content of an exploratory study on the other hand will not include empirical generalizations; the knowledge it offers may be limited to hypotheses and concepts.

The research reader may gain useful methodological knowledge from a research study. We refer here not only to knowledge about how to use methods to carry on research, but also to possible uses of the research methods in social practice. For instance, the test or questionnaire developed to collect data for a study of role conflict in marriage may be useful, or adaptable for use, in diagnosis of cases involving marital conflict. A method of identifying community leaders for the study of community power may be useful for identifying community leaders for the board of a new agency.

For the practitioner, the usefulness of a research study will depend both on the soundness, or validity, of its contribution to the reader's knowledge (determined by a systematic evaluation of the research) and on the extent to which the knowledge is engineerable, or capable of being put into use for practice.

Therefore, it is not the achievement of the ideal characteristics of useful research but the recognition of potential usefulness of the research that is important for the research consumer. It is equally important for him to judge what the research may contribute and where its limits are. Different kinds of research are differentially useful, and usefulness is a judgment arising from the research reader's recognition of the broadest range of social practice or academic interests. In formulating guidelines, two questions frame the problem of utilization for the social practitioner: "What knowledge does the research offer?" and "What activities of social practice does it bear on?"

PLAN OF THE BOOK

In accordance with the conviction that assessment of social research requires initially the differentiation of purposes and methods of the research, we have included in this book a section on each of the three major research types that have been distinguished: experimental studies, quantitative-descriptive studies, and exploratory studies. In each section, a definition is first provided of the major research type and its sub-types. Secondly, questions are presented to serve as guidelines for the classification, evaluation, and utilization of research studies. These guidelines are applicable to the assessment of studies from the research literature of social work, sociology, and psychology that are reproduced as the third part of each section. The guidelines are stated as general questions, however, so that they may be applied not only to the journal articles presented in this book but also to the published reports listed in a bibliography of research studies of each type that comprise the fourth part of each section. References of the bibliography were selected from a review of principal journals to exemplify major approaches of research and because they were deemed relevant to social practice, particularly to social work.

THE USE OF GUIDELINES

When suggesting steps to follow in classifying a research study, we cautioned the user of this book not to be limited by the suggestions but to be led by them to more specific, and more personal, formulations that fit the particular study under consideration and the particular interests and style of the research reader. This injunction bears repeating here because the sets of guidelines presented in each of the three sections that follow are essentially the same. This is the case because the emphases, but not the criteria, vary as one assesses different types of research. The same criteria come to have different consequences when applied, for example, to an experimental study seeking to test a specific hypothesis and to a study seeking to explore how some concept may illuminate a problem. One asks whether each of these studies is well-designed for its purpose, how reliable and valid the data are in each study, how accessible to the influence of the practitioner the variables of each study are, and many other questions. Each study in its own terms receives answers to the questions but the questions themselves will not change. Hence, suggested guidelines can be stated in general terms to serve each of the three types of research that we distinguish and present in the separate sections of this book.

The statement of guidelines in general terms should encourage the research reader to avoid their mechanical application. It is our intent, and our hope, that stated guidelines will be transformed by practice into habitual modes of critical response to the potential contributions of empirical research to social practice. Such a critical response recognizes what may be gained as well as what cannot be accepted as an addition to the reader's state of knowledge. Such a critical response is, we believe, the mark of sophistication of the social practitioner who wants to base his practice as much as possible on tested knowledge.

TWO | # Experimental Studies

Definitions

In the classification scheme followed in this book, there are several requirements that a research study must fulfill before it can be classified as experimental.

1. *There must be an explicit or implicit hypothesis that is being investigated.* An explicit hypothesis is one that is specified in the formulation of the problem for research. Implicit hypotheses are those not articulated precisely in the formulation of the problem but implied, nevertheless, in the overall research study. An example is a report of the evaluation of a tutorial program devised to increase the reading skills of students in the program. Although hypotheses might not be specifically stated in a research evaluation of the program, the research design may involve the random assignment of students either to an experimental group for tutoring or to a control group which does not receive tutoring. In addition, measurements may be obtained from both groups with respect to reading skills before and after the experimental group receives tutoring. The implicit hypothesis is that tutoring will increase the reading skills of students.

2. A second requisite for studies to be classified as experimental is that the *variables in the hypotheses of the study must be operationally defined so that measurement is possible.* This is necessary so that quantitative descriptions among variables can be ascertained in order to provide evidence for establishing an association between the independent and dependent variables.

3. A third requisite is that *the independent variable must be manipulated by the experimenter.* This is done in experimental studies to assure that the independent variable occurs prior in time to the dependent variable.

4. The fourth requisite is that *one or more control groups must be employed* to provide a basis for contrasting the results obtained in the presence of the experimental variable (the independent variable) to those results obtained in the absence of the experimental variable.

5. The fifth requisite is that *randomization procedures must be employed*

in the assignment of subjects to experimental and control groups. This is a minimum requirement for experiments; it provides some assurance of the equivalence among experimental and control groups, and it provides the basis for the use of tests of statistical inference in the interpretation of results. The reader is referred to Edwards' text on *Experimental Design in Psychological Research* (pp. 13-27, 1960) for a discussion of the importance of randomization in the execution and interpretation of experiments.

In summary, experimental studies may be defined in the following manner:

Experimental studies are empirical research investigations which have as their primary purpose the testing of hypotheses concerned with cause-effect relationships. All of these studies use experimental designs which include control groups, randomization procedures, and the manipulation of independent variables in order to control pertinent factors to as great a degree as possible. Relevant variables are specified so they can be described quantitatively. These studies may employ rigorous sampling techniques to increase the generalizability of the experimental findings.

Two subtypes of experimental studies are identified: laboratory experiments and field experiments. Both types must satisfy the requirements of the definition for experimental studies. The chief distinction between laboratory and field experiments is the degree of control maintained by the experimenter in the setting in which the experiment is conducted. Since there is an environment artificially created by the experimenter in laboratory experiments, the possibility for the control of influential variables other than those postulated in the hypothesis is increased. The field experiment which takes place in the natural environment poses relatively more obstacles to experimental control. Field experiments may be used for testing hypotheses linked to theory and for testing hypotheses which are relatively more pertinent to practical situations, while laboratory experiments are used predominantly in testing theoretical propositions. The reader is referred to Kerlinger (1967), French (1953) and Festinger (1953) for detailed discussion regarding the conduct of laboratory and of field experiments.

Definitions of laboratory and field experiments are presented below.

Laboratory experiments are experimental studies in which the investigator creates an isolated situation in an artificial setting with hypothetically constructed variables. Relationships among variables are tested by the manipulation of one or more independent variables and by the control of the potential influence of variables which are extraneous to the hypothesis being tested.

Field experiments are experimental studies which involve the manipulation of one or more independent variables in a natural setting in order to determine causal relationships. These studies may attempt to control the influence of environmental constraints on the relationship between independent and dependent variables. They do not rely exclusively on natural conditions of the environment in that the independent variables are manipulated by the experimenter. Field experiments typically have less rigorous control features than laboratory experiments.

Guideline Questions

The guideline questions suggested for the assessment of experimental studies are grouped into three major categories: classification, evaluation, and utilization. The guideline questions are not to be considered exhaustive and are not to be applied mechanically, since consuming research is an active and creative process. As the reader gains experience in assessment of questions, the guidelines that follow are intended to stimulate the reader in this direction.

CLASSIFICATION:

1. What is (are) the specific purpose(s) of the study?
2. What research methods do the authors use to accomplish their purpose?
3. Why is the study classified as experimental? How does it differ from exploratory and quantitative-descriptive studies?
4. Should the study be sub-typed as a field experiment or as a laboratory experiment?

EVALUATION:

I. PROBLEM FORMULATION

1. How does the author utilize the literature in conceptualizing the problem for study?
2. What major concepts are formulated for the study and how well are they defined conceptually and operationally?
3. What hypotheses are proposed for test in the experiment? What is the rationale for the inclusion of concepts in the hypothesis and for the prediction made in the hypothesis?
4. What assumptions are made by the author in regard to the selection of variables for study?
5. What contingent variables are recognized by the author, and how are they handled, i.e., through assumptions or controls?

6. What methodological issues are raised by the author which are believed to be relevant to the testing of the hypothesis, and how does the author propose to handle the issues?
7. What are the independent and dependent variables proposed within the hypothesis, and are they conceptually and operationally distinct?
8. Are there conditions which prevent the manipulation of the independent variable or the measurement of its effects on the dependent variable?
9. To what extent is the experimental design appropriate for investigating the problem of the study?

II. RESEARCH DESIGN AND DATA COLLECTION

1. In what ways does the experimental design include provisions for maximizing the internal validity of the experiment?
2. What assumptions are made in the design?
3. What variables are not controlled for, but considered relevant to the study?
4. What alternative experimental designs might have been employed?
5. What sampling procedures were employed in the study? How were assignments made to experimental and control groups?
6. How were the data collected? To what degree were the data reliable and valid?
7. To what extent does the experimental design maximize external validity?
8. Was the independent variable manipulated successfully, and to what extent were the effects of measurement controlled or handled?

III. DATA ANALYSIS AND CONCLUSIONS

1. Do the data provide evidence for testing of the study hypothesis?
2. Are the statistical tests employed appropriate to the design of the study and the problem under investigation?
3. To what extent are the hypotheses supported by the data?
4. Are the author's claims for the findings consistent with the data?
5. What are the author's principal conclusions, and are they consistent with the findings?
6. What are the implications of the study as defined by the author?
7. To what extent did the researcher accomplish the purposes set forth for the study?

UTILIZATION:

1. What objects of social work interest are addressed by the research (recipients, the process of serving, purveyance of services) ?

2. To what extent is the research relevant to the social work purposes of treatment, enhancement, and prevention?
3. On what levels does the research view the objects of social work interest? Is it concerned with individuals, groups, organizations, communities, or society?
4. Is the level of knowledge achieved by the research useful to social work primarily as empirical findings ("facts" or empirical generalizations), conceptual contributions (concepts, hypotheses, theories), or methods (for diagnostic or treatment procedures), potentially applicable to practice?
5. After evaluation, how valid is the research judged to be?
6. How engineerable are the variables identified in the research?
    a. How available (accessible and manipulable) are the variables for possible control by practitioners?
    b. How much difference in the practice situation will it make if the variables are manipulated?
    c. How feasible is it to manipulate variables of the research in the practice situation (economic feasibility, ethical suitability, organizational constraints)?
7. What types of use can be made of the research (direct application, indirect or complementary application, general stimulation of ideas)?

Exemplars

Seven examples of experimental studies are reproduced in this section. These studies include both laboratory and field experiments and they have been selected because their form of presentation and their content allow the reader a range of research reports which can be assessed by using the suggested guidelines. If the research reader treats his assessment of these studies as exercises for the development of skills in reading this type of research, he should find that his own formulation of guiding questions will emerge. Then he can, with greater confidence and increasing sophistication, move further into the research literature of social work and social science as reflected not only in the bibliography of references which concludes this section, but especially in the specific areas of professional interest and competence he wishes to inform with research-based knowledge.

WILLIAM C. BERLEMAN, THOMAS W. STEINBURN

I | *The Execution and Evaluation of a
Delinquency Prevention Program**

While increasing emphasis is being put upon community youth projects
aimed at "delinquency prevention," it is nonetheless "extremely rare to
find written into an experimental project in this field a provision for
even the most elementary kind of evaluation."[1] This would certainly
seem to be the case if by *delinquency prevention* is meant the provision
of a social service to children who are not yet officially adjudged delinquent and who therefore partake of the service without coercion and if by
evaluation is meant an exhaustive and rigorous assessment of the service
and the experimental design underlying that service. The Cambridge-
Somerville Youth Study[2] still stands, thirty years after its inception, as
the most rigorous evaluative study of delinquency prevention techniques
applied in the open community among voluntary subjects. Because few
projects since that study have applied a similar kind of scientific examination in assessing their service, it is safe to say that there is only the
beginning of a tradition of astute evaluation in delinquency prevention
projects.[3]

*Reprinted from *Social Problems*, Vol. XIV, No. 4 (Spring, 1967), pp. 413–23, by
permission of the journal, the authors, and The Society for the Study of Social Problems.
1 United Nations Consultative Group on the Prevention of Crime and the Treatment of Offenders, "Methods Used for the Prevention of Juvenile Delinquency,"
Geneva: The United Nations, MSOA, 61/SD 4, December, 1961, p. 4. mimeo.
2 Edwin Powers and Helen Witmer, *An Experiment in the Prevention of Delinquency:
The Cambridge-Somerville Youth Study*, New York: Columbia University Press, 1951;
William McCord, Joan McCord, and Irving Kenneth Zola, *Origins of Crime: A New
Evaluation of the Cambridge-Somerville Youth Study*, New York: Columbia University
Press, 1959.
3 By *astute evaluation* is meant reliance upon some form of the experimental design
—that is, the comparison of an experimental, or treated group, with a control, or untreated group—in assessing the effectiveness of the delinquency prevention service. Other
than the Cambridge-Somerville Youth Study, completed delinquency prevention projects
utilizing the experimental design and engaging subjects who voluntarily participated in
proferred services have been: (1) the Midcity Project (see Walter B. Miller, "The Impact of a Community Group Work Program on Delinquency Corner Boys," *Social Service
Review*, 31 [December, 1957], pp. 390–406, and Walter B. Miller, "The Impact of a
'Total-Community' Delinquency Control Project," *Social Problems*, 10 [Fall, 1962], pp.
181–91); (2) the Maximum Benefits Project (see C. Downing Tait, Jr., M.D., and Emory
F. Hodges, Jr., M.D., *Delinquents, Their Families and the Community*, Springfield:
Charles C. Thomas, 1962); (3) The New York City Youth Board's validation study of the
Glueck Prediction Scale (see Maude M. Craig and Philip W. Furst, "What Happens after
Treatment: A Study of Potentially Delinquent Boys," *Social Service Review*, 39 [June,

In 1962, the Seattle Atlantic Street Center, a small settlement house situated in Seattle's central area, undertook to evaluate its social work services to acting-out boys. With the aid of a National Institute of Mental Health grant, the Center commenced a five-year study. The study's second year, 1963-64, was designated as a pretest phase in which selection procedures, social work service, recording instruments, and evaluative techniques would be put into operation and refined. The remaining time, 1964 through 1967, would be devoted to the test phase proper.

The pretest phase was governed by an experimental design parallel to that planned for the test phase. In each phase, carefully screened seventh-grade junior high school boys would comprise a high-risk population, i.e., boys considered likely to act out in an antisocial way in excess of their peers. Acting out was defined simply as the objective evidence of a boy's social misbehavior as reported in police and school disciplinary files. By random selection boys in the high-risk population would be assigned to experimental and control groups. Those in the experimental group would be offered the Center's services; those in the control group would not.

The Center has now completed its pretest phase and has done an analysis of the pretest data to assess the impact of service. Major emphasis will be given the Center's procedural and evaluative methods rather than service and service impact. While the analysis reveals a trend suggesting a positive service impact, the reader is cautioned against making inferences about service effectiveness. The data fail to meet conventional criteria for the rejection of the null hypothesis. In addition, the number of treated pretest subjects was too small to support generalizing service impact to larger, more representative populations.

The pretest's importance lies in the rigor of its design and execution. Prior community based, delinquency prevention experiments have not collected and assessed sufficient data to speculate about the accuracy of their selection procedures or to contrast the experimental and control subjects' levels of acting out with that established by the remainder of the peer group from which the study's subjects were initially selected. Rates of service attrition have not been elucidated nor have the levels of acting out for attrition subjects been reported. Indeed, forms of "treatment," while often given elaborate theoretical underpinnings, have not been adequately explained in terms of kinds and amounts of simple attention shown experimental subjects by service agents, presumably because no consistent efforts have been made to collect such baseline data. Such

---

1965], pp. 165–71) ; and (4) the Youth Consultation Service (see Henry J. Meyer, Edgar F. Borgatta, and Wyatt C. Jones, *Girls at Vocational High: An Experiment in Social Work Intervention,* New York: Russell Sage Foundation, 1965).

deficiencies the Center's procedures attempted to overcome. What follows is an elaboration of the Center's pretest procedures. Particular attention will be given to (1) the selection of the pretest high-risk population, (2) an outline of the service with attention given the amount of time experimental boys were exposed to the service, and (3) the evaluation of service impact.

SELECTION OF THE HIGH-RISK BOYS

High-risk boys chosen for the pretest phase were Negroes who in the 1962-63 school year passed from one of Seattle's six most racially segregated elementary schools into the seventh grades of Seattle's two central area junior high schools. The population from which the high-risk boys were drawn numbered 167. The problem was to order the population along a continuum ranging from low-risk, or boys least likely to act out, through high-risk, or boys most likely to act out.

Two assumptions guided the placing of a boy in a risk category. The first assumption was that past misbehavior is predictive of future misbehavior. A record search was done on each boy to see if there was evidence of delinquent behavior in his career through the sixth grade, i.e., behavior judged delinquent by law, or acting-out behavior, i.e., antisocial behavior which had not been legally designated as being delinquent but was sufficiently serious to be found in official records. The Center's research staff carefully noted whether or not a boy's name appeared in juvenile court, police, school guidance, and school disciplinary files. In this manner the population was arrayed from those boys having no records—low-risk boys—through those having both community and school records—extreme high-risk boys.

The second assumption was that there might be other factors, in addition to the actual evidence of acting out, which could be predictive of acting-out behavior. It was assumed that the seventh-grade boys most likely to act out during their junior high school years would be those with backgrounds most closely resembling the backgrounds of boys who were then in the ninth grade and who had acted out while in junior high school. This required a search for factors, identifiable prior to the end of the sixth grade, that were associated with acting-out behavior by the end of the ninth grade. Factors closely associated with acting out could then be utilized in categorizing current seventh-grade boys into risk groupings. An exhaustive record search of boys in both groups was then conducted. Data regarding school grades, citizenship patterns, school attendance, home composition, health records, were collected and analyzed. If factors were found in the career of a seventh-grade boy which closely resembled factors found in the careers of acting-out ninth-grade boys, then it was "predicted" that the seventh-grade boy would act out while in junior high school.[4]

Once the actual and predicted acting-out data had been compiled, it was possible to construct a matrix which crossed a boy's actual evidence of acting out with the prediction of his acting out in the future so that the population arrayed itself from the nonacting-out boys (those who had not acted out in the past and were predicted not to act out in the future) to the highest acting-out boys (those who had acted out in the past and were predicted to continue doing so). Since predictions of antisocial behavior are rightfully held suspect,[5] the Center refused to consider for selection those boys placed in the high-risk category by prediction alone. Also eliminated from consideration for selection were those boys who had acted out in the past but who were predicted not to act out in the future. For selection, then, the high-risk boys were confined exclusively to those who in the past had exhibited antisocial behavior and who were predicted to continue doing so. Antisocial behavior tended to break down into two categories: misbehavior in both the community and school[6] and misbehavior in the school alone. Table 1 illustrates the distribution of the population into risk categories.

It will be noted that the high-risk boys occupy four cells of the matrix and that these cells can roughly be equated to types of severity, i.e., Type I, evidence of acting out in school only and predicted to continue doing so, being least severe, and Type IV, evidence of acting out in the community and school and predicted to continue doing so, being the most severe. Selection was weighted against the Center's social workers by assigning a higher proportion of the most serious types to the experimental group than to the control while the reverse was true for the least serious types. Table 1 shows this distribution by types. Once the number

---

4 This is a simplified account of an extremely complex prediction procedure. Essentially this was an application of multiple regression prediction techniques, utilizing 43 criterion measures made available from police, school and court records, and 76 predictor measures made available from the same sources. The data were analyzed by extensive computer processing utilizing IBM Fortran programs written especially for the prediction problem. This procedure proved excessively costly and cumbersome considering the results obtained. See Bruce Bloxom, "Use of Predictor Accretion Selection Techniques in the Prediction of Acting-Out Behavior," Seattle: Seattle Atlantic Street Center, June, 1964, mimeo; and Herbert Costner, "Commentary on the Prediction Device Developed for the Atlantic Street Center," Seattle: Seattle Atlantic Street Center, June, 1964, mimeo.

5 Elizabeth Herzog, "Identifying Potential Delinquents," *Juvenile Delinquency, Facts and Facets,* No. 5 (Washington, D.C.: Children's Bureau, U.S. Department of Health, Education and Welfare, 1960).

6 Since it was exceedingly rare for a boy to have exhibited acting-out behavior in the community while not also being a problem in school, there was not a distinct acting-out-in-community-only category.

TABLE 1

DISTRIBUTION OF POPULATION INTO RISK CATEGORIES AND OF HIGH-RISK BOYS INTO
EXPERIMENTAL AND CONTROL BOYS

Prediction of Acting-Out 7th-9th Grade	Actual Evidence of Acting-Out Prior to 7th Grade			Total
	Neither	School Only	Community and School and Community Only	
Neither	49	15	6	70
School Only	22	30	3	55
		11 Exp. 19 Con. (High Risk Type I)	3 Exp. 0 Con. (High Risk Type III)	
Community and	11	15	13	39
School and Community Only		6 Exp. 9 Con. (High Risk Type II)	8 Exp. 5 Con. (High Risk Type IV)	
Total	82	60	22	164a

a The original population numbered 167; three boys were dropped because they had moved away.

from each type to be assigned to the experimental group had been
determined, the required number of specific cases was selected
randomly.

TABLE 2

DISPOSITION OF HIGH-RISK BOYS DURING PRETEST PHASE

High-Risk Category	Experimental Boys		Control Boys		Total
	In Service	Attrition	Control	Attrition	
Type IV	6	2	5	0	13
Type III	2	1a	0	0	3
Type II	5c	1	6	3	15
Type I	8	3	15	4	30
Total	21	7	26	7b	61

a This boy moved out of the community; all other experimental attrition boys refused to participate.
b These boys were not in attendance at the two central area junior high schools.
c One of these boys did not participate in the service himself but his mother did receive 18 hours of service from the worker.

The more serious high-risk boys were deliberately assigned to the
workers in order to hedge against attrition. It would have been unrealistic to suppose that all 28 high-risk boys assigned to the experimental
group would wish to partake of the Center's services. If the experimental
and control groups had been apportioned equally and if the expected
refusals had been concentrated in the experimental Type III and Type
IV boys, then it would have been questionable if the experimental and
control groups were sufficiently similar to make valid comparisons. By
concentrating the Type III and Type IV boys in the experimental group
there would be little question but that the experimental boys might
reasonably be anticipated to be as "bad," assuming no effective preventive treatment, as the control boys. Table 2 illustrates that 21 of the 28

experimental boys were engaged in service and that these boys could be considered acting-out equivalents for their control counterparts with only 19 percent of the control group as opposed to 38 percent of the experimental group coming from the two "worst" types.

RECORDING SERVICE AND
ATTENTION GIVEN SUBJECTS

The staff for the pretest phase consisted of three trained male social workers. Through random assignment from each of the four high-risk categories two workers received the names of nine boys; one worker received the names of ten boys.[7] Boys comprising the control group were not made known to the workers so long as service was being given.

The workers then sent personal letters, one to the boy and one to the boy's parents or parental surrogates, inviting the boy to join a "club." Next, the workers arranged home visits. Depending upon the degree of recognition of a problem by the boy and his parents, the worker's interpretations ranged from the general, e.g., expressing the need for more constructive youth services in the central area, to the specific, e.g., recognizing the particular social difficulty in which the boy was involved.

Eventually the workers formed three groups composed of seven boys each. Each group met once a week at the Center for approximately two-and-a-half hours. Once the groups were established, the workers deliberately broadened their activity. Increasingly boys and their parents were seen in the schools and homes, usually as a result of chronic or emerging problems, such as delinquent behavior, school problems, or parent child disagreements.

In order to keep an accurate account of these many contacts, the Center's social work and research staff devised a unique recording system by means of which the workers noted their activities in numerical code form.[8] This coded system allowed for the orderly accumulation of (1) the dates of a worker's contacts with a person in the client system, (2) the exact persons contacted, (3) the mode of contacts, (4) the duration of the

---

[7] The assignment of ten boys to one worker was the result of an error. Rather than the planned for 27 experimental boys, 28 boys were actually so designated. As Table 2 shows, attrition reduced the experimental population to 21 boys.

[8] The Center's recording procedure avoids many of the difficulties posed by each worker keeping process records in his own discursive style. By having all workers use a Recording Manual in which types of problem situations encountered are listed, grouped under theoretical headings and given code numbers, the consistency among workers is enhanced while the codes permit rapid computer tabulation and analysis. See James R. Seaberg, "Case Recording by Code," *Social Work* 10 (October, 1965), pp. 92–98 and Roy P. Wakeman, "Using Data Processing to Analyze Worker Activity," in *Social Work Practice, 1965*, New York: Columbia University Press, 1965, pp. 54–64.

contacts, (5) the problems encountered and the theoretical context into which those problems fell, and (6) the worker's response to those problems.

While an analysis of the data accumulated by this method cannot be presented here, one aspect of the worker's service—time spent with or on behalf of experimental subjects—deserves elaboration. This fundamental dimension of service has generally been so poorly documented in past delinquency prevention experiments that it is difficult to assess to what extent experimental subjects were in fact exposed to service agents. The scanty evidence suggests that in most experiments the subjects enjoyed only minimal contact with project staff.[9] Consequently, it remains unclear whether treatment methods have been ineffective or whether they have never really been tried.

It might be argued that the Center's pretest phase was deficient in that the experimental boys and the significant others were exposed to the workers for only five months (February, 1964 through June, 1964). During that time, however, the workers sought to provide intensive service. Of the 21 experimental boys considered permanently engaged in the pretest phase, the least time any boy was in direct contact with his worker was 45½ hours; the most was 100 hours. Table 3 gives the total amounts of direct and indirect contact time the three workers had with the 21 boys and their significant others.

The median amount of service time a boy and his significant others received during the pretest was slightly in excess of 75 hours. In short, although the span of the pretest phase was brief, the service within that time was intense.

EVALUATION OF IMPACT

Two sources of data were available which reflected acting-out behavior: (1) the two junior high schools' disciplinary files[10] and (2) police records.[11] Data from school disciplinary files and police records were first

---

[9] A review of the literature pertaining to previous delinquency prevention experiments regarding the exposure of experimental subjects to service agents suggests that exposure was generally minimal, that is, probably less than two contacts per month over the span of service. See William C. Berleman and Thomas W. Steinburn, "Delinquency Prevention Experiments and Attention Given Experimental Subjects," Seattle: Seattle Atlantic Street Center, 1965, mimeo.

[10] Because procedures for collecting disciplinary data from schools other than the two central area schools were not established during the early phases of the experiment, the data that follow are based only on the records of boys in attendance at these two schools. Seven boys who moved to other schools are excluded for this reason.

[11] Juvenile Court records were also available. However, court records revealed so few contacts with the pretest population that no reliable index of acting-out behavior could be constructed from court data. The court records tended to reflect, only to a lesser degree, what was in the more comprehensive police records.

obtained shortly after the close of the pretest service in June, 1964. One year after the end of service, in June, 1965, data were again collected from the schools and police. What follows is the procedure used for evaluating these data. In the interest of brevity, only school data will be used for illustrative purposes. While the police data were analyzed in the same manner, the fewer police contacts make police data more unstable as measures of service impact.

The data were analyzed in four time periods:

TABLE 3

HOURS OF DIRECT AND INDIRECT CONTACT TWENTY-ONE EXPERIMENTAL BOYS AND SIGNIFICANT OTHERS HAD WITH THREE WORKERS FEBRUARY 1, 1964 THROUGH JUNE, 1964

	Experimental Boys	Families	Others	Total
Direct Contact (face-to-face) [a]	1377.50	127.00	11.75	1516.25
Indirect Contact (telephone, letters)	16.25	55.50	.50	72.25
Hours of Contact..........	1393.75	182.50	12.25	1588.50

a Direct contact includes group meetings, individual interviews, interviews with subgroups, and family interviews.

1. The Pre-Service Period: Since service did not begin until February, 1964, junior high school disciplinary records which accumulated from September, 1963 through January, 1964 were available for evaluation of school performance in the period just prior to service. All police contacts earlier than February, 1964 were included in the pre-service police data.[12] Data for this period are included to provide a before-service base for comparison of the different groups.
2. The Service Period: February, 1964 through June, 1964.
3. First Post-Service Period: July, 1964 through December, 1964.
4. Second Post-Service Period: January, 1965 through June, 1965.

In order to summarize the offenses which had accumulated in the school disciplinary and police records, judgments concerning the relative seriousness of every recorded offense were obtained from the Center's professional staff. These judgments were averaged and converted into weights and the resulting weights were then used to score each boy's record. Because school and police data are products of two quite different institutional and referral systems, school and police data were weighted and processed separately.[13]

___

12 Police offense data for these boys, most of whom were 12 or under prior to the pretest, were practically nonexistent in the six month period preceding service. This necessitated the accumulation of all prior police offense data. Police data relating to dependency were not considered.

13 The school disciplinary items were weighted from one for minor infractions, such as chewing gum or eating candy in class, through thirty for major infractions, such as

School and police data were gathered on the population of 164 Negro seventh grade boys from which the high-risk boys were drawn. Scores were generated for each time period for each of the boys in the four groups into which this population was then divided: (1) the experimental group, (2) the control group, (3) the service-attrition group, i.e., those boys selected for service but who refused to participate, [14] and (4) the low-risk group, i.e., those boys not designated as high-risk in the selection process. Data on the last two groups have been included to enlarge the scope of the analysis. For example, inclusion of the attrition boys, even though a small group, sheds light on the possible biases introduced by refusals to accept service. The low-risk group provides data on the success of the selection procedure in identifying acting-out boys. These two groups and especially the low-risk group, also provide second level control groups for assessing general trends in school disciplinary and police contact activity. In most instances these two groups and the control group change in parallel.

Four indices derived from the school and police data were used to evaluate the performance of the pretest boys:

1. The first index gives the average offense score per boy in each of the four groups. This was derived by summing all offense scores accumulated by boys in each group and then computing an average score per boy per group. This index indicates the total performance of the group, and consequently is the most important of the four indices. (Table 4)
2. The second index reveals what percentage of boys within each group actually generated the total offense score for each group. This index serves as a corrective to the first index in that it would show if a few highly acting-out boys in any particular group were responsible for the average score borne by each boy in each group. It would be expected, for example, that a significantly higher percentage of boys would act out among the high-risk boys than among the low-risk boys. (Table 5)
3. The third index shows the average severity of offenses committed by boys in each group. This was derived by dividing the sum of offense scores accumulated by each group by the number of offenses recorded. This index shows whether the boys engaged in "petty" offenses or in more serious offenses. (Table 6)

---

breaking and damaging school property. Police contacts were weighted in a similar manner. It should be noted that this weighting procedure was not used in the initial selection of high-risk boys. At the time of selection, it was simply noted whether or not a boy had a community and/or school record. (See selection above.) The use of a record/no record procedure for selection purposes and a graduated weighting procedure for evaluation purposes created some discrepancies; notably, that certain types of police contacts and many school guidance contacts, which figured in the selection procedure, were not used for evaluative purposes. Nonetheless, it was still evident that the two methods of identifying acting-out boys produced essentially the same results.

[14] A fifth group composed of boys who moved out of the community could also be designated. This "area attrition" group could not be evaluated since they did not accumulate records in the designated schools or local police files, and so had to be eliminated from consideration.

4. Finally, the fourth index gives the average severity score for those boys in each group who compiled records. This was derived by dividing the sum of offense scores accumulated by the number of boys who actually committed the offenses. This index, coupled with the second, shows whether the overall performance of a group stems primarily from the extensiveness or the intensiveness of acting-out behavior of its members. (Table 7)

TABLE 4
AVERAGE SCHOOL DISCIPLINARY SCORE PER BOY IN EACH GROUP[a]

	Pre-Service (5 months)	Service (5 months)	First Post-Service (4 months)	Second Post-Service (6 months)
Attrition	48	66	116	52
Experiment	24	18	22	31
Control	19	27	18	25
Low Risk	6	15	11	22

a The total number of boys in each group for each period was: Attrition—4, 3, 3, 4; Experiment—21, 21, 19, 19; Control—26, 26, 26, 26; Low Risk—88, 88, 85, 85.

TABLE 5
PERCENT OF BOYS WITH SCHOOL DISCIPLINARY RECORDS

	Pre-Service (5 months)	Service (5 months)	First Post-Service (4 months)	Second Post-Service (6 months)
Attrition	75.0	100.0	100.0	100.0
Experiment	47.6	47.6	57.9	84.2
Control	57.7	65.4	53.8	53.8
Low Risk	27.3	34.1	40.5	38.8

TABLE 6
AVERAGE SERIOUSNESS PER DISCIPLINARY CONTACT[a]

	Pre-Service (5 months)		Service (5 months)		First Post-Service (4 months)		Second Post-Service (6 months)	
Attrition	22	(9)	14	(14)	14	(24)	17	(12)
Experiment	18	(28)	14	(27)	14	(29)	15	(39)
Control	15	(33)	14	(49)	16	(29)	15	(44)
Low Risk	11	(46)	14	(98)	15	(64)	15	(71)

a Figure in parentheses is the number of contacts for that period.

TABLE 7
AVERAGE SCORE PER BOY WITH A SCHOOL DISCIPLINARY RECORD

	Pre-Service (5 months)	Service (5 months)	First Post-Service (4 months)	Second Post-Service (6 months)
Attrition	65	66	116	52
Experiment	51	37	37	37
Control	33	42	34	46
Low Risk	21	45	29	31

In terms of the average score per boy in the groups (Table 4), the service-attrition group in the pre-service period was double the average score of the next highest group, the experimentals. In one sense, the service-attrition group represented a failure of the service, that is, a failure to engage those boys whose acting out was the greatest. On the other hand, even though these boys were excluded from the experimental boys for this analysis, the experimental boys still had a score about one-third higher than the control boys in the pre-service period, indicating that in spite of the biasing effect of attrition, the experimental group was still at least as "bad" as the controls. The low-risk group had an average score of only a third that of the controls. The other indices (Tables 6 and 7), except for the percentage of boys with school disciplinary records (Table 5), show essentially the same pattern.

In the service period, while the average disciplinary score per boy increased for the attrition, the control and the low-risk groups, it decreased for the experimental boys. Although the percentage of boys with records did not decrease for experimental boys, it did remain constant in the face of increases for the other three groups. In general, the remaining two indices also show experimental group values decreasing while the other three groups register increases.

In the first post-service period, the direction of changes for the groups was somewhat more mixed. The experimental group went back up toward the level of performance of the pre-service period, while the other groups moved down toward their pre-service levels. To show this relative performance, the data on the experimental and control groups were converted to ratios.[15] These data appear in Figure 1.

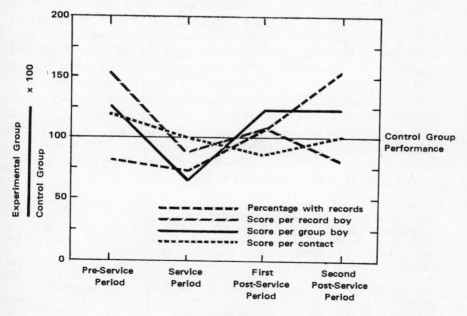

FIGURE 1
School Disciplinary Contacts

In the pre-service period, on all but one index, the experimental group was performing at a poorer level than the control group. With the initiation of service, the experimental group improved its performance relative to the control group on every index, with the least improvement occurring in the percentage with records. It must also be noted that in the service period, the experimental group did as well as the control group or even better on all four indices. In the first post-service period, performance of the experimental group on three of the indices again became worse than that of the control group with a continued slight improvement in the score per contact index. In the last period, the average score per boy remained steady, the percentage with records and the score per contact both worsened and the average score per boy with a record improved relative to control group performance.

From these data, it can be seen that the experimental group initially was performing in school at a somewhat poorer level than the control group, that with service, the experimental group performed at a better level; and, with termination of service, the group reverted back toward the same relative level of performance it had prior to service.[16]

SUMMARY

The Seattle Atlantic Street Center's pretest phase involved the execution of a delinquency prevention experiment in the open community among voluntary subjects. Because the pretest study was severely circumscribed in time and population serviced, the pretest phase did not represent a test of service, but rather the opportunity for implementation of rigorous procedural and evaluative techniques not generally employed in this kind of experiment. By collecting offense data on the entire at-risk population from which control and experimental subjects were drawn, questions concerning the accuracy of selection, rates of attrition and levels of acting-out behavior exhibited by low- through high-risk groups could begin to be answered. In addition, a coded recorded system used by service agents supplied such baseline data as which subjects were actually receiving service in what amounts and forms.

---

15 These data were standardized around the control group performance by the following formula: Ratio = (100) (EXPERIMENTAL)/(CONTROL)

16 Statistical tests of changes in performance for the experimental and control groups between the pre-service and service period, and the service and first post-service periods were made utilizing *Student's t*. The probability of the null hypothesis being true in the first comparison was between .10 and .05 ($t = 1.57$, $df = 45$). The probability of the null hypothesis being true in the second comparison was between .10 and .05 ($t = 1.64$, $df = 43$). Both tests are one-tailed tests. Although the data fail to meet conventional criteria for rejection of the null hypothesis, the joint probability of both null hypotheses being true lies between .01 and .0025. Because they were so few, data on police contacts were not tested for statistical significance; they tended to show, however, essentially the same patterns as the school data.

While no in-depth analysis of the accumulated data is presented, the advantages of these or similar procedural methods and evaluative techniques are evident. Most generally, they suggest that a tidying of the experimental social laboratory is possible for more exact evaluations of intervening variables. With more complete data, inappropriate criticisms of prior delinquency prevention experiments, such as the tendency to castigate service or the theories undergirding service when it is not at all clear that service was actually given, can be avoided.

ROBERT C. DAY, ROBERT L. HAMBLIN

2 *Some Effects of Close and Punitive
Styles of Supervision**[1]

INTRODUCTION

Close supervision was originally isolated and studied as a style or dimension of supervision by teams of researchers connected with the Survey Research Center at the University of Michigan and led by Daniel Katz.[2] In an early study of female workers in a large metropolitan insurance firm, Morse reported that workers subjected to a close supervision style were less satisfied with the supervisor's ability to handle people, less satisfied with the reasonableness of her expectations, and generally less satisfied with the rules she enforced.[3] These findings suggest a specific hypothesis that aggressive feelings are instigated by close supervision. Katz and Kahn reported finding this relationship between close supervision and aggressive feelings of workers in a tractor plant.[4] Furthermore, if lowered productivity is taken as a form of retaliatory aggression toward the supervisor, data reported earlier by Katz and his associates[5] are also consistent with this hypothesis. Gouldner produced evidence, from an illuminating study of a gypsum factory, that further supports the close supervision-aggression hypothesis.[6]

In the present study, close supervision is conceptualized as one end of a

* Reprinted from the *American Journal of Sociology*, Vol. LXIX, No. 5 (March, 1964), pp. 499–510, by permission of The University of Chicago Press and the authors.

1 This research was supported in part by a contract with the Office of Naval Research Nonr 816 (11), and the computer analysis was supported in part by a grant from the National Science Foundation, No. G-22296. The authors also wish to thank Professor Alvin W. Gouldner for his encouragement, suggestions, and criticisms.

2 D. Katz and R. L. Kahn, "Some Recent Findings in Human-Relations Research in Industry," in G. E. Swanson, T. M. Newcomb, and E. L. Hartley (eds.), *Readings in Social Psychology* (2d ed.; New York: Holt, Rinehart & Winston, Inc., 1952), pp. 650–65; D. Katz and R. L. Kahn, "Leadership Practices in Relation to Productivity and Morale," in D. Cartwright and A. Zander (eds.), *Group Dynamics* (2d ed.; Evanston, Ill.: Row, Peterson Co., 1960), pp. 554–70; D. Katz, N. Maccoby, G. Gurin, and Lucretia G. Floor, *Productivity, Supervision and Morale among Railroad Workers* (Ann Arbor: Survey Research Center, University of Michigan, 1951); and D. Katz, N. Maccoby, and Nancy C. Morse, *Productivity, Supervision and Morale in an Office Situation*, Part 1 (Ann Arbor: Survey Research Center, University of Michigan, 1950).

3 Nancy C. Morse, *Satisfactions in the White Collar Job* (Ann Arbor: Survey Research Center, University of Michigan, 1953).

4 Katz and Kahn, "Leadership Practices . . . ," *op. cit.*

5 Katz and Kahn, "Some Recent Findings . . . ," *op. cit.*

6 A. W. Gouldner, *Patterns of Industrial Bureaucracy* (Glencoe, Ill.: Free Press, 1954).

continuum that describes the degree to which a supervisor specifies the roles of the subordinates and checks up to see that they comply with the specifications. However, there are two other points of this continuum worth noting. The opposite extreme to close supervision might appropriately be termed "anomic supervision," as it would involve no specifications (that is, no expectations or norms) and no checkups. Somewhere in the middle area of this theoretical continuum, the general style of supervision can be postulated; it involves a moderate number of specifications and checkups, at least enough to let the workers know what they are supposed to do. Thus, in close supervision the attempt is to structure completely the workers' behavior, and in general supervision, to structure it only to the point where the worker does not feel at a loss as to what to do; in anomic supervision no attempt is made at all to structure the behavior. Although it would have been interesting, anomic supervision was not included in the present investigation because of the limits of time.

To account for the relationship between close supervision and aggressive feelings or actual aggression, a softened version of the frustration-aggression hypothesis can be used,[7] since close supervision apparently is frustrating to the subordinate. To the extent that it is frustrating, then, the subordinate should be instigated to aggress against the supervisor as the agent of frustration and, in some cases, perhaps actually to translate his impulses into direct aggression, such as angry words, or indirect aggression, such as a conscious retaliatory slowdown in productivity.

However, an important point to grasp here is that close supervision is not in itself aggression. For to be aggression, a manifest intention in applying it would necessarily be to hurt or injure the subordinate. But as Gouldner has suggested, the manifest intention involved in using the close style of supervision is probably to increase productivity.[8] The supervisor may not even be aware that his close supervision is frustrating, thus producing psychological pain or injury. In terms of intention or awareness, the close style of supervision may be contrasted with a second style, "punitive" supervision, which involves the intentional, conscious use of aggression to gain the compliance of subordinates.

To the extent that a supervisor enforces work specifications or rules by aggressing against those subordinates who depart from or violate the rules, he is using a punitive style of supervision. When the punitive supervisor uses aggression (most often in the form of angry, ego-lacerating reprimands), he is attempting to reinforce the avoidance of behavior that violates work rules. Thus, he is usually aware that his aggression is

---

[7] N. E. Miller, "I. The Frustration-Aggression Hypothesis," *Psychological Review*, XLVIII (1941), 337–42.

[8] *Op. cit.*

painful to the subordinate, and is in effect saying to him, "I know this hurts, but it is your own doing. If you want to avoid it in the future, follow my rules." Because it is so painful, he is probably aware that his aggression instigates subordinates to counteraggress, but because of his authority to hire, fire, promote, or demote, he evidently also assumes ultimate victory in any aggressive exchange. Furthermore, since the workers are aware of his superior power, he counts upon their not wanting to start an aggressive exchange by counteraggressing.

Yet, unresolved tensions have a way of being channeled into more subtle forms of indirect aggression that are not easily detected or eliminated, as, for example, when workers channel their aggressive impulses into conscious, retaliatory slowdowns in production. If artfully practiced, this form of aggression can hurt the supervisor badly while making it most difficult for him to fix blame or take active corrective measures. This evidently happened with railroad section gangs studied by Katz and his associates, who found that foremen of low-producing gangs tended to use a punitive style of supervision.[9]

Thus far, we have postulated that aggression is the over-all result of both the close and the punitive styles of supervision because both styles, whether intentionally or not, are painful to subordinates. Specifically, we have mentioned two forms of aggression: angry words and a conscious, retaliatory slowdown in production. But these may not be the only manifestations of aggression that result from the frustrations inherent in the close and punitive styles of supervision. Negative emotions often become displaced, and consequently could magnify out of proportion the aggression that sometimes accompanies routine conflicts among workers. Furthermore, these emotions might also be displaced to magnify any incipient dissatisfaction with the work situation itself. Thus, in hypothesizing that both the close and the punitive styles of supervision result in increased aggression, we are actually predicting that they both result in (1) an increase in the amount of verbal aggression toward the supervisor, (2) a decrease in productivity, (3) an increase in verbal aggression toward co-workers, and (4) an increase in dissatisfaction with the work situation. However, in making our predictions we should note that Pepitone and Reichling found that relationships based on displacement are usually weaker than the others.[10]

Although the close supervision-aggression hypothesis has been generally supported in a number of investigations, evidently the strength of the relationship is quite variable. Again, if lowered productivity is taken

---

[9] Katz, Maccoby, Gurin, and Floor, *op. cit.*

[10] A. Pepitone and G. Reichling, "Group Cohesiveness and the Expression of Hostility," *Human Relations*, VIII (1955), 327–37.

as an indication of indirect aggression, the data reported by Katz and his associates in 1950 show that a strong relationship exists where the close versus general styles are used by second-line supervisors in their relations with section heads, but only a moderate relationship in relations between section heads and their subordinates.[11] Data from a second study in 1951 by Katz and associates indicate no relationship at all between close versus general supervision and worker aggression.[12] These variations seem to indicate that a third variable mediates the relationship between close supervision and aggression. In this instance, the mediator is probably a characteristic of the subordinate that influences the amount of frustration he experiences when he is subjected to close and perhaps punitive supervision. The rationale for suggesting self-esteem as the mediating variable is best understood in the context of Goffman's dramaturgical theory of social behavior.[13]

Using the theoretical metaphor extensively, Goffman views the behavior of persons in social contexts as a sequence of carefully guided performances serving to create a "front" or an impression. In attempting to create and maintain a satisfactory self-image, the individual tries to define the situation in such a way that he is able to guide and control the impressions that others obtain of him in the situation. The individual's concern, then, is to put his act over successfully, to maintain by various techniques a favorable, creditable self-image. Thus, in a bureaucratic situation the workers may be viewed as striving to project a self-image to the supervisor and to co-workers, "and the characteristic issue, the crucial concern, is whether it [the self-image] will be credited or discredited."[14]

From the assumption that the workers are attempting to project a creditable self-image, it follows that the close and punitive styles of supervision would be frustrating for two reasons. First, the styles imply a lack of competence, a lack of skill on the part of the worker. Second, they imply a lack of motivation on his part to do the right thing or, in fact, a kind of malicious motivation to do the wrong thing. Thus, when a subordinate is subjected to either of these two styles of supervision, his self-image may be discredited severely. Furthermore, he may be able to do very little to change the situation so that he can create a more favorable impression.

However, and this is the critical assumption, not all subordinates may

11 Katz, Maccoby, and Morse, *op. cit.*

12 Katz, Maccoby, Gurin, and Floor, *op. cit.*

13 We wish to express our appreciation to Alvin W. Gouldner for suggesting Goffman's theory as the conceptual context in which to discuss self-esteem as a mediating variable (E. Goffman, *The Presentation of Self in Everyday Life* [Garden City, N.Y.: Doubleday & Co., 1959]).

14 *Ibid.*, p. 253.

be equally concerned with maintaining the front, with presenting a creditable self-image. Specifically, our assumption is that some individuals have such strong, favorable self-images, such high *self-esteem*, that they are relatively *unconcerned* with impression management, whereas other individuals have such ambiguous, ambivalent self-images, such low *self-esteem*, that they are *highly concerned* with impression management, with maintaining a front and thus projecting a creditable self-image. If so, the amount of frustration an individual experiences when subjected to close or punitive supervision should vary inversely with his self-esteem. Furthermore, since the strength of the postulated relationship between either style of supervision and aggression should be a function of the amount of frustration experienced,[15] the strength of the relationship should also be a function of the self-esteem of subordinates. Perhaps a simpler statement is: The association between the two styles of supervision and the various aggression variables should be relatively weak among subordinates who have high self-esteem, but relatively strong among those with low self-esteem.

METHOD

THE EXPERIMENTAL GROUPS

Twenty-four groups, each consisting of four women recruited from undergraduate classes and dormitories at Washington University, were used in the experiment. Controls were applied for age (17-19 years) and years of schooling (Freshmen and Sophomores).

THE EXPERIMENTAL SITUATION

At an appointed time each group arrived at the laboratory and was ushered into an experimental room designed to simulate reasonably well an industrial work station. Here the subjects were given a pre-experimental questionnaire and then task instructions. After these were completed, each group worked at the task for a period of 40 minutes, and then completed a post-experimental questionnaire. The 40-minute experimental session included 10-minute periods with a supervisor (a trained member of the experimental staff) in the room and two intervening 5-minute periods during which the supervisor left the room for the expressed purpose of evaluating the workers' production. Her absence, however, was designed to give the subjects a chance to be alone and thereby some freedom to express any aggressive feelings toward the supervisor or the experiment. Her exits and entrances were timed precisely with a stopwatch that she held in her hand and that, in addition to

---

15 Miller, *op. cit.*

accurate timing, provided a note of precision and authority. As in a factory setting, an impersonal buzzer was used to signal the beginning and end of the work period.

The task consisted of assembling models of molecules using pegs, springs, and various colored balls provided in Sargent Kits, which are often used in university chemistry classes. Drawings of elaborate, complicated molecular structures were provided as "blueprints" for molecule construction. These models seemed to be novel and complex enough to interest and involve the subjects for the required 40-minute work period. The fact that the task was complex and naturally suited for assembly-line procedures contributed to making this a natural situation where various styles of supervision could be used. (In any experiment it is important that the manipulation not be external to the situation and thus relatively obvious to the subjects, who usually are interested in guessing "what they're after." The general assumption is, of course, that subjects cannot systematically fake behavioral effects unless the goals of the experimenters are obvious.) In addition to providing a natural environment for the manipulations, the kits for molecule construction afforded a rather simple but reliable quantitative measure of productivity.[16]

To simulate an industrial setting, the member of the experimental staff who took the role of supervisor was introduced simply with, "This is Miss Bradshaw, your supervisor during the work period." To heighten the impersonality of the situation, subjects were not introduced to the supervisor, but were addressed by numbers conspicuously displayed at each of their work stations. In addition, words such as "supervisor," "worker," "blueprint," "material bin," "work efficiency," "production unit," "subassemblies," and "production line" were used to convey the atmosphere of an industrial situation. However, in order to promote interaction, the situation was designed to be different from the usual production line in one important way: The subjects were stationed around an oval table that permitted each subject to view all co-subjects during the work period.

---

[16] Several considerations went into the decision to set up a production line. First, it was desirable to standardize and keep constant the over-all sequence of operations for all groups. To this end, subjects were given definite subtasks to perform; that is, the groups did not determine their own division or non-division of labor. Second, it was undesirable either for the final combinations of operations to be so inefficient or slow that tension would be generated by the task itself, or for each worker to be allowed to proceed to construct whole models by herself in relative isolation, with no interdependence with the others. Although the latter procedure would have maximized productivity in the time allotted to the task, intersubject conflict would have been virtually absent even in high-tension situations. Consequently, although the sequence of operations chosen was efficient enough to keep frustrations at a minimum, it included enough interdependence among subjects to make some conflict inevitable.

THE EXPERIMENTAL DESIGN

Technically, the experiment involved a two-by-two factorial design with high-low manipulations of the two independent variables, that is, the close and punitive styles of supervision. Using a table of random numbers, six of the twenty-four groups were assigned to each of the four "cells," as shown in Figure 1.

	Close Supervision	General Supervision
High Punitive Style	6 Groups	6 Groups
Low Punitive Style	6 Groups	6 Groups

FIGURE I

To operationalize the four styles of supervision, two lists of remarks were drawn up for use by the supervisor. To operationalize closeness of supervision, a set of clear, concise instructions (role definitions) was developed. In the general supervision situations, the eight most essential of these instructions were used by the supervisor to give a minimum definition of the situation. In the close supervision situations, forty instructions were used; also, certain amounts of obvious hovering and watching as well as repetitions of previous instructions were used as checkup techniques.

To operationalize the punitive style in both the close and general situations, a list of sarcastic, negative, status-deflating remarks was developed for the supervisor to use as punitive sanctions. In the high-punitive situation, she made forty such remarks; in the low-punitive situation, she made none at all.

Two members of the staff who observed verbal aggression by the subjects also counted the supervisor's punitive remarks. The experimenter kept a count of the instructions and checkups, and a system of lights informed the supervisor when she had given the required number of remarks for each situation.

Fourteen practice sessions were required to standardize and internalize the multiple facets of the supervisor's role.[17] All extraneous remarks had to be identified and inhibited, and important non-verbal gestures (facial

---

17 The supervisor's role demanded a person who could combine a certain ability to act with emotional stability, maturity, and general interpersonal insightfulness. The role was taken by a recent graduate in nursing who had a major in psychiatric nursing and whose past experience in therapeutic role-playing with mental patients and hospital-ward supervision constituted an excellent background for the job.

and body) had to be standardized. She had to learn to recognize and "control" subjects who were skilled at becoming dependent on the supervisor through asking for support. To help the supervisor control and minimize support-giving, observers registered all supportive remarks by the supervisor during this training period. Finally, she had to practice giving instructions that were devoid of aggressive connotations.

MEASUREMENT

Self-esteem.—The measure of self-esteem used in this experiment was developed by de Charms and Rosenbaum[18] and was based in part on an earlier measure by Janis.[19] The subjects were instructed to choose an answer ranging from "strongly agree" through "strongly disagree" that best characterized their usual reactions. (In listing these and other items in this section, the numbering and order are appropriate to this presentation and consequently depart from the format used in the questionnaire.)

1. I feel capable of handling myself in most social situations.
2. I seldom fear my actions will cause others to have a low opinion of me.
3. It doesn't bother me to have to enter a room where other people have already gathered and are talking.
4. In group discussions I usually feel that my opinions are inferior.
5. I don't make a very favorable first impression on people.
6. When confronted by a group of strangers, my first reaction is always one of shyness and inferiority.
7. It is extremely uncomfortable to accidentally go to a formal party in street clothes.
8. I don't spend much time worrying about what people think of me.
9. When in a group, I very rarely express an opinion for fear of being thought ridiculous.
10. I am never at a loss for words when I am introduced to someone.

Agreement with items 1, 2, 3, 8, and 10 and disagreement with items 4, 5, 6, 7, and 9 probably indicate high self-esteem or self-confidence and little concern with the presentation of self, that is, with the management of the image presented to others. On the other hand, opposite responses to these items indicate low self-esteem and low self-confidence and a great deal of concern and anxiety about the presentation of self in everyday situations.

Aggressive feelings.—To measure covert aggressive feelings toward the supervisor, that is, those aggressive feelings which did not erupt into overt behavior, the following items were used:

1. How often did you become annoyed with the supervisor?

---

18 R. de Charms and M. E. Rosenbaum, "Status Variables and Matching Behavior," *Journal of Personality,* XXVIII (1960), 492–502.

19 I. L. Janis, "Personality Correlates of Susceptibility to Persuasion," *Journal of Personality,* XXII (1954), 504–18.

2. How often did you become irritated with the supervisor?
3. If you were to participate in this group again, how would you feel about having the supervisor replaced?

On the first two items, the subjects were asked to make responses on a six-point scale ranging from "continually" to "never"; for the third item, a seven-point scale was used ranging from "extremely favorable" to "extremely unfavorable." The responses provided an estimate of the frequency with which each subject experienced aggressive feelings toward the supervisor during the work period.

Two sets of items similar to these were used to measure aggressive feelings toward co-workers and dissatisfaction with the task. The first set was identical with the above items except that the term "co-workers" was substituted for "supervisor." The response alternatives were the same except for the third item; here the subjects were asked to indicate the actual number of co-workers they would prefer to have replaced. In measuring dissatisfaction with the task, only the first two of the above items were used, but they were used twice, first with the term "molecules" and second with the phrase "job in general" substituted for the term "supervisor." Ranging from "continually" to "never," the response alternatives were the same as before.

Overt aggression.—As may be recalled, we assumed that overt aggression might be expressed directly as verbal aggression or indirectly as a conscious slowdown in production. Two rather complex measures thus were required.

After two female observers had reached a level of competence where they could reliably code verbal aggression as it occurred during the experimental-work period, they independently entered marks on forms each time a subject (a) antagonistically criticized the supervisor or used indirect sarcasm with definite negative content in reference to the supervisor; *(b)* antagonistically criticized or used sarcasm about her co-worker; or (c) antagonistically criticized or joked about the task or the experimental situation. In general, the observers were asked to perceive and evaluate each remark simultaneously along two dimensions: objective content and affective content. All remarks that were negative in objective meaning were counted as verbal aggression regardless of affective content. Remarks that were not objectively negative but tended to carry negative affective connotations were more difficult to categorize reliably. However, 85 percent agreement of two observers was obtained throughout the experiment on items, not just cell totals.

The production-line arrangement of work required to encourage interdependence in interaction among subjects virtually precluded the possibility of taking accurate or even meaningful measures of each subject's production rate. Consequently, a measure based on the group's total production was used. This was calculated as the sum of the model components (the colored balls, pegs, and springs) completed per 40-minute work period, minus errors and omissions.

Factor analysis.—Data from each of the scales administered in the pre- and post-experimental questionnaires were factor-analyzed using the principal axis method. The obtained factor weights were used, together with standardized scores for each of the subjects, to obtain indexes for each of the above-mentioned dimensions[20] (Table 1).

RESULTS

Analysis of the results began with group data and the testing of basic hypotheses for the stable effects. Then individual scores and a smaller number of independent variables selected on the basis of the initial analysis were used to test the more complex hypotheses involving the mediating variable, that is, the psychological dimension of self-esteem.

THE BASIC HYPOTHESES TESTED WITH GROUP DATA

Results relevant to the basic hypotheses are presented in Tables 2 and 3. For all the basic hypotheses, the analysis-of-variance results in Table 2 gives significance as well as explained variance. In Table 3 the means are given where significant relationships were found.

From Tables 2 and 3 it is apparent that close supervision produced a significant and large increment in aggressive feelings toward the supervisor. The data also indicate a moderate and near-significant increment in aggressive feelings toward co-workers. On the other hand, close supervision was not significantly related to dissatisfaction with the task, to

TABLE 1

FACTOR ANALYSIS WEIGHTS* FOR PRE- AND POST-EXPERIMENTAL QUESTIONNAIRE SCALES

Scale	Item Number									
	1	2	3	4	5	6	7	8	9	10
1. Self-esteem	0.77	0.42	0.74	—0.50	—0.42	—0.75	—0.35	0.38	—0.65	0.58
2. Aggressive feelings, supervisor	.94	.96	.78	—	—	—	—	—	—	—
3. Aggressive feelings, co-workers	.97	.95	.64	—	—	—	—	—	—	—
4. Dissatisfaction, task	0.90	0.89	0.88	0.92	—	—	—	—	—	—

* These weights were extracted using the principal axis method. A separate analysis was done for each scale, and in each case the weights given are those obtained on the first factor.

verbal aggression against the supervisor or co-workers, or to verbal dissatisfaction with the task. Finally, the data indicate that close supervision results in a significant and rather substantial decrease in productivity.

---

[20] These procedures are outlined in detail in M. J. Hagood and D. O. Price, *Statistics for Sociologists* (New York: Holt, Rinehart & Winston, Inc., 1952), pp. 526–30.

TABLE 2

SUMMARY OF TWO-WAY ANALYSIS OF VARIANCE USING DATA TABULATED BY GROUPS

	Close Supervision		Punitive Supervision		Interaction	
Dependent Variable	F-Value*	Explained Variance[a]	F-Value	Explained Variance	F-Value	Explained Variance
1. Aggressive feelings, supervisor[b]	10.3	.24	10.9	.25	3.0	.07
2. Aggressive feelings, co-workers	4.0	.16	0.0	.00	0.4	.02
3. Dissatisfaction, task.	.6	.03	0.2	.01	0.1	.01
4. Verbal aggression, supervisor	1.8	.04	20.3	.48	0.9	.02
5. Verbal aggression, co-workers	2.8	.11	2.2	.09	0.1	.00
6. Verbal dissatisfaction, task	2.0	.09	1.4	.06	0.0	.00
7. Productivity	5.2	.17	4.2	.14	1.1	.04

* Results are significant at the 0.10 level if F is equal to or greater than 3.0; at the 0.05 level if F is equal to or greater than 4.4.
a The measure of explained variance is η.
b Using Bartlett's test, the variance of all dependent variables was tested for homogeneity. All variances were homogeneous except for this particular variable. To achieve homogeneity, the scale was transformed using the following formula: $\frac{1}{4}(X - 100/50)$. We wish to thank Keith Miller for helping us find this and other transformations used later.

TABLE 3

CELL MEANS FOR TWO-WAY ANALYSIS OF VARIANCE

	Means			
Dependent Variable	General Non-punitive Style	Close Non-punitive Style	General Punitive Style	Close Punitive Style
1. Aggressive feelings, supervisor*	0.73	1.14	1.15	1.27
2. Aggressive feelings, co-workers*	1.84	2.07	1.70	1.84
3. Dissatisfaction, task*	1.90	2.06	1.64	2.01
4. Verbal aggression, supervisor[a]	0	4.5	10.8	11.7
5. Verbal aggression, co-workers[a]	5.2	14.0	15.2	19.2
6. Verbal dissatisfaction, task[a]	9.3	17.8	16.5	24.5
7. Productivity[b]	335	252	258	226

* These measures of aggressive feelings are based on standard scores which have little obvious meaning. However, the means are included here to give an idea of the relative magnitude of the effects of close and punitive supervision.
a All of these verbal measures are in terms of the number of aggressive or negative remarks.
b In terms of the number of correct connections of the pegs, springs, and balls completed during the work period.

Tables 2 and 3 also indicate that the punitive style of supervision resulted in a large, significant increment in aggressive feelings toward the supervisor. However, in this case the relationships between punitive supervision and aggressive feelings toward co-workers or dissatisfaction with the task are both small and insignificant, as are the relationships between punitiveness and verbal aggression toward co-workers or verbal dissatisfaction with the task. Unlike close supervision, however, punitive supervision resulted in a large, significant increase in verbal aggression toward the supervisor. Finally, it is evident that punitive supervision also resulted in a relatively large decrease in productivity—a decrease which, because of a small N, is of borderline significance.

Thus far the data have not supported all of the basic hypotheses. The results with respect to direct verbal aggression and the displacement of aggressive feelings toward co-workers and the task were variable. Consequently, the more detailed analysis will be limited to two dependent variables: aggressive feelings toward the supervisor and productivity.

TABLE 4

SUMMARY OF THREE-WAY ANALYSIS OF VARIANCE INVOLVING CLOSE SUPERVISION, PUNITIVE SUPERVISION, AND SELF-ESTEEM, USING DATA TABULATED IN TERMS OF INDIVIDUAL SCORES

Source of Variation	Aggressive Feelings, Supervisor*		Productivity	
	F-Value[a]	Explained Variance[b]	F-Value	Explained Variance
1. Close supervision	9.3	.08	23.7	.17
2. Punitive supervision	11.3	.10	18.0	.13
3. Self-esteem[c]	0.3	.00	0.1	.00
Close style × punitive style....	2.7	.02	4.0	.03
Close style × self-esteem	5.0	.04	1.1	.01
Punitive style × self-esteem ...	1.0	.01	0.7	.00
1 × 2 × 3	0.0	.00	0.7	.01

* Using Bartlett's test, the variance of this dependent variable was tested for homogeneity with negative results. The unhomogeneous variance was corrected using a log x transformation.
a Results are significant at the 0.10 level if F is equal to or greater than 2.79; at the 0.05 level if F is equal to or greater than 3.96.
b The measure used for explained variance is η.
c Because of unequal cells, the approximate method for analysis of variance was that presented in Helen M. Walker and Joseph Lev, *Statistical Inference* (New York: Holt, Rinehart & Winston, Inc., 1953).

HYPOTHESES INVOLVING SELF-ESTEEM

AND ANALYSIS IN TERMS OF

INDIVIDUAL SCORES

The results relevant to the mediating hypotheses are found in Tables 4, 5, and 6. Table 4 gives the results of an analysis of variance, with significance levels and explained variance; Tables 5 and 6 show the means involved in the significant interactions. Before turning to these interactions, note that the relationships between punitive or close supervision, on the one hand, and aggressive feelings toward the supervisor or productivity, on the other, are much stronger in this than in the preceding analysis. This reflects the difference between group and individual data—largely the difference between an N of 24 (groups) and an N of 96 (individual subjects).

In Table 4 the findings indicate a significant interaction between closeness of supervision and self-esteem with respect to feelings of aggression toward the supervisor, but not with respect to productivity. In Table

5, the means indicate that this significant interaction is precisely the one that was predicted. The relationship between close supervision and aggressive feelings toward the supervisor is much stronger among subjects with low than among subjects with high self-esteem. In fact, the difference between the means for subjects with high self-esteem is nil. In other

TABLE 5

MEANS INVOLVED IN SIGNIFICANT INTERACTION BETWEEN CLOSE SUPERVISION AND SELF-ESTEEM WITH RESPECT TO AGGRESSIVE FEELINGS TOWARD SUPERVISOR

Means	Aggressive Feelings, Supervisor
General style, low self-esteem	1.54
Close style, low self-esteem	1.74
General style, high self-esteem	1.64
Close style, high self-esteem	1.66

words, the over-all relationship observed between closeness of supervision and aggressive feelings toward the supervisor is due primarily to the subjects with low self-esteem. Yet, at the level of indirect aggression apparently no difference existed, since the interaction between close supervision and self-esteem with respect to productivity involved very little variance and was insignificant as well. In the close supervision variations, the subjects with high self-esteem evidently engaged in indirect aggression through lowered productivity as readily as did those with low self-esteem. The difference apparently was in their emotional state; that is, whether or not aggressive feelings, perhaps anger, accompanied their decision to decrease productivity. However, it should be noted that this pattern could be an artifact of the group productivity scores.

In Table 4 it is apparent that the interactions between punitive supervision and self-esteem with respect to both aggressive feelings and productivity are insignificant. Apparently the experience of being aggressed against in the form of punitive supervision produces aggressive feelings as well as indirect aggression equally in subjects with high and low self-esteem. We can make this assumption with some confidence because the variance involved in the relevant interactions is very low and because we have seen that the measure of self-esteem is sensitive enough to detect rather precise effects.

Finally, are the effects of the two supervisory styles a simple additive function? If they are, the interactions between close and punitive supervision with respect to any of the aggression variables will be insignificant. It is apparent in Table 4 that the interaction between the close and punitive styles of supervision with respect to aggressive feelings toward the supervisor only approaches significance at the 10 percent level. However, the interaction with respect to productivity is significant, even though a modest amount of variance is involved. This result, of course, implies something more than a simple additive effect with respect to productivity. Apparently the effects of punitive and close supervision with respect to productivity are less than would be expected on the basis of the effects of close supervision alone and punitive supervision alone. As can be noted in Table 6, close supervision by itself reduces productivity by 25 percent and punitive supervision reduces it by 23 percent. Together they do not reduce it by 48 percent as would be expected if the effects were a simple additive function, but only by 33 percent. Since the decrease in productivity, indicating as it does an increase in aggression, is less than might be anticipated, we will refer to the phenomenon apparent in this interaction as the dampened-increment effect.

TABLE 6

MEANS INVOLVED IN SIGNIFICANT INTERACTION BETWEEN CLOSE AND PUNITIVE SUPERVISION WITH RESPECT TO PRODUCTIVITY

Means	Productivity	
	No. of Units	Percentage Reduction
General style, non-punitive..............	84	100
Close style, non-punitive................	63	75
General style, punitive..................	65	77
Close style, punitive....................	56	67

This dampened-increment effect might have occurred for one of two reasons. First, productivity in the experimental situation might have been very difficult to reduce below some minimal level regardless of aggressive feelings or impulses to reduce it still further. Second, the aggressive feelings themselves might not have been additive. In other words, double frustration may not lead to double aggressive feelings, but to something much less than double. As can be seen from the first line in Table 3, the data are consistent with this latter interpretation. The scores indicating aggressive feelings toward the supervisor are increased (from .73) 41 points by close supervision alone and 42 points by punitive supervision alone. Together, however, they increase the score only 54 points, as compared with an increment of 83 points that would be predicted if the effects were not dampened. These data, showing as they do a dampened-increment effect, are remarkably consistent with the data in the previous paragraph which showed a similar effect with respect to productivity.

DISCUSSION

Over-all, the results present an interesting pattern that is laden with implications. The lack of support for a number of the hypotheses matters very little, as these involved displacement which usually vitiates the strength of aggressive phenomena. But the interesting thing is that in the close supervision situations a certain amount of displacement evidently did occur. The subjects by and large expressed more than usual aggressive feelings against one another as co-workers. It is this tendency to displace, plus the absence of verbal aggression toward the supervisor, which distinguishes the close from the punitive supervision situations. In the latter, the tendency to displace aggressive feelings was conspicuously absent and verbal aggression toward the supervisor conspicuously present. Why should such a difference obtain?

A number of explanations are possible, but the one that suggests itself involves the generic distinction between close and punitive supervision made in the theoretical section, that of intention. Our argument there was that with close supervision the *intention* is simply to increase production; the resulting psychological pain is unanticipated, unintentional, and possibly even an unknown consequence. Therefore, close supervision was characterized as frustrating rather than aggressive. On the other hand, with punitive supervision, the pain-producing activities are used intentionally because the pain presumably reinforces the desired avoidance responses. Since activities used with the intention of producing pain or injury are by definition aggression, we pointed out that punitive supervision is a form of aggression. Thus, at a more generic level, the close supervision-aggression hypotheses tested here are simply variants of the basic frustration-aggression hypothesis, whereas the punitive supervision-aggression hypotheses are basically aggression-aggression hypotheses. Phrased this way, these hypotheses may appear to be circular, but they are not. What really is meant is: "To the extent that A frustrates B, B will be instigated to aggress against A," and "To the extent that A aggresses against B, B will be instigated to aggress against A." In other words, genuine causal relationships are involved in the hypotheses because the hypotheses involve an exchange between two individuals.

If this distinction is valid, then the difference in response patterns to close and punitive supervision may actually represent a more generic difference in response patterns to frustration and aggression. Evidently, when A either frustrates B or aggresses against B, the unvarying result is the instigation of aggressive feelings in B. Furthermore, if an indirect avenue of aggression is available, such as decreasing productivity, then in either case B will use this indirect aggression against A. However, a basic difference evidently arises at the level of direct verbal aggression. Although they recognized that the pain they felt was not intended, those subjects who were frustrated by the close supervision practices had a difficult time expressing their aggressive feelings directly at the verbal level, whereas those subjects who felt the aggression inherent in punitive supervision, perhaps because they recognized it as intentional, retaliated openly in kind. Apparently because the latter subjects were able to verbalize their aggressive feelings directly, they were not led into displacing the feelings as were the subjects who experienced the frustrations of close supervision.

Before concluding, we must pay tribute to the women who were subjects in this investigation. While their behavior was not predicted precisely, it was not entirely unpredictable, as we sometimes feared it would be. They probably reacted to the various styles of supervision in much the same way as men would have reacted; most differences probably would be a matter of degree. However, our empirical impression is that women suppress their tendencies to overt aggression, particularly verbal aggression, more than do men. Rather than express their negative feelings in words, they tend to express them more in nervous laughter, or alternatively to withdraw more than do men. In other words, if the experiment were duplicated using men, we think any change in results would be with respect to verbal aggression: verbal aggression would be much more frequent in the punitive situation, and a significant relationship might obtain between close supervision and verbal aggression.

HENRY J. MEYER, EDGAR F. BORGATTA,
WYATT C. JONES

3   *An Experiment in Prevention through
Social Work Intervention**

INTRODUCTION

This report describes a portion of a study of the consequences of providing social work services to high school girls whose record of earlier
performance and behavior at school revealed them to be potentially
deviant. Over the course of four years girls with potential problems who
entered a vocational high school in New York City were identified from
information available to the school. From this pool of students a random
sample of cases was referred to an agency where they were offered casework or group counseling services by professional social workers. A
control group was also selected at random from the same pool of potential problem cases in order that a comparison could be made between
girls who received service and similar girls who did not. Since all these
girls were identified as potential problem cases, they may be considered
latent or early detected deviants. Services to them consisted of efforts to
interrupt deviant careers.

Youth Consultation Service (the agency in which this research was
located) is a nonsectarian, voluntary social agency, in New York City,
that has specialized in offering services to adolescent girls through a
highly trained staff of caseworkers and group therapists for more than 50
years. The characteristic problems that bring troubled girls between the
ages of 12 and 25 to YCS are out-of-wedlock pregnancy, school behavior
problems, chronic truancy, unmanageability at home, "immoral conduct," incorrigibility, and "runaway." At the time this research was
undertaken, the agency served approximately 200 clients each year of
whom about two-fifths were unmarried mothers.

The major service offered to clients is casework, but since about 1952
the agency has developed a supplementary group-therapy program and
has pioneered in group methods of treatment for unmarried mothers and
adolescent girls with other behavior problems. In addition to the regular
complement of psychiatric consultants, group-therapy consultants have
been provided.

* Reprinted from Edwin J. Thomas (ed.), *Behavioral Science for Social Worker*.
Copyright © 1967 by The Free Press, a Division of the Macmillan Company, with permission of the authors, The Free Press and the Russell Sage Foundation.

The research arose from a problem the agency had been concerned with for some time, namely, how to serve effectively the adolescent girl with types of problems that got her into difficulties at school and elsewhere. Previous experience had led the social workers to believe that intervention earlier than they had heretofore been able to achieve with similar clients might facilitate the establishment of meaningful treatment relationships that would, hopefully, decrease the likelihood of serious difficulties later. It was recognized that a preventive effort would present novel issues: general rather than specific presenting problems, uncertainty about and diversity of treatment objectives, the need for special efforts to involve girls who were not yet in severe difficulties, development of ways of working with the school that was the referral source, and uncertainty about criteria of effectiveness. But it seemed to attempt a preventive effort and to investigate its effects carefully.

THE RESEARCH DESIGN

The basic plan of the research was a simple experimental design requiring random assignment of adolescent girls with potential problems (1) as clients of Youth Consultation Service to constitute an experimental sample, that is, to receive treatment, and (2) as members of a group of control cases, with no treatment provided by YCS. The comparison of these two groups of cases after the former was exposed to the services of the agency will constitute a test of the effects of that service, since in other respects the two groups may be assumed to begin equally and to differ in experiences only to the extent that the control cases have not had the services of YCS. It is to be noted that these are assumptions and therefore require some empirical examination if they are to be accepted with confidence.

In order to check these assumptions, as well as to provide information additional to the experimental test, it was arranged that the total school population from which experimental and control cases were chosen would be tested prior to random assignment, and again periodically throughout the study, so that equivalence could be examined and change differentials noted. Similarly, it was arranged that the total school population, as well as the experimental and control cases, would be observed at a determinate follow-up point according to criteria that reflected a range of objectives contemplated by YCS in its services to the experimental sample.

Through additional procedures, including clearance with the Social Service Exchange and direct inquiry from both experimental and control subjects, an effort would be made to estimate whether YCS service did, in fact, constitute the primary variation in experience of the two groups of cases, or whether, for example, similar or comparable services might have been provided elsewhere for the control cases. In the strictest sense, therefore, the experimental test was not one of provision of service vs. withholding of service, but rather the known provision of service vs. unknown experiences excluding these specific services. This is a severe test of the impact of such services. But it is also a powerful one and the sort of question that is, in effect, asked of social agencies: "Have your services benefited clients more than no services or services provided on a casual and haphazard basis?"

IMPLEMENTATION OF THE RESEARCH DESIGN

SELECTION OF EXPERIMENTAL AND CONTROL CASES

The cooperating school—here called Vocational High—agreed with the agency that the girls selected for referral would be encouraged to accept the help of Youth Consultation Service and that the necessary home permission for the girls to go to the agency would be sought by the school in cooperation with YCS. Vocational High also agreed that the girls selected could fit into their school-day schedules the required appointments with caseworkers at the agency and (as group procedures developed) the scheduled group meetings. The school also accepted the condition that the project would continue through four years in order that the requisite numbers could be referred and observed throughout their high school years, normally the time between entrance and graduation from the school (tenth, eleventh, and twelfth grades).

It was established practice at Vocational High to review each entering student's prior record to assess academic preparation and plan programs, and also to identify problems that might require special planning by the school. The social workers at YCS and the researchers concurred that these records could be used to note aspects of the student's school behavior, personal characteristics, and home situation indicative of possible future difficulties. In this way an inclusive pool of girls with potential problems was identified from which referral and control cases could be designated. This procedure was relatively superficial but it represented the use of kinds of information the agency would have accepted as warranting referral for at least further diagnostic study. When subsequently asked, "Do you feel this client was really in need of treatment when she was referred?," the social worker answered "not at all or slightly" for only 6 percent of the cases referred to YCS; 36 percent were rated "somewhat or quite a bit" in need of treatment, and 58 percent were judged to need treatment "to a considerable extent or very much."

The records of four entering cohorts of girls at Vocational High were screened and potential problem cases identified for each. Only those entering in the fall term were included in order to provide as long a time for treatment as possible. Approximately one-fourth of each cohort was included in the potential problem cases and from this pool a random procedure was used to select those to be referred to YCS, the number depending on the capacity of the agency to accept additions to its case-load. At the same time, and by the same random procedure, the control group was selected from the potential problem cases. Over the course of four years, 189 referrals and 192 control cases were selected and included in the experimental and control samples.

Referral from the School

When YCS indicated that it could accept a number of clients for the project, the names of those selected were drawn from the pool and given both to the school guidance department and to the agency. Neither the school nor the agency was given the names of other girls who had been selected as control cases, and they were not informed of the students who constituted the rest of the potential problem cases.

The girls selected for referral had to be approached with an explanation of the program and invited to accept help from YCS. They had to obtain parental permission to leave the school premises during school hours and arrange appointments with the agency within their school schedules. In addition, they had to be given some rationale for this unusual attention directed toward them. Furthermore, in keeping with the design of the research, the entire entering class of girls, including the potential problem cases, was given a series of tests and asked to fill out questionnaires so that uniform information would be available to describe the experimental and control samples.

The specific act of referral was handled in various ways by the Guidance Department. In general, it consisted in telling the girls individually that they had been selected because the school thought that they deserved the opportunity to have the extra assistance that YCS could give them with problems high school girls usually have. They were told that such opportunity was available only to a few of the students and they were encouraged to take advantage of it. There is little doubt that the warm and friendly interest of the administrative assistant in charge of guidance was a factor in conveying a positive attitude toward referral even if, as the caseworkers subsequently reported, some girls were uncertain and confused about the basis of their selection and expressed the fear that they were thought "crazy" or otherwise invidiously identified. The school's interest was emphasized by its willingness to permit the girls to go to YCS on school time and this, also, undoubtedly entered into the success with which referral was achieved. Whatever doubts the referred girls entertained, they did, for the most part, voluntarily accept the invitation and subsequently make contact with the agency. Of the 189 girls who were designated for referral, only 3 percent failed to have at least one service contact with a social worker at YCS in addition to the interview in which the girl was invited. The median number of casework interviews or group counseling sessions that the total experimental group had with YCS workers was 16. Approximately 25 percent of the girls had 36 or more scheduled treatment contacts, 50 percent had between 7 and 35 contacts, and 25 percent had 6 or fewer contacts.

ACCEPTANCE AT THE AGENCY

Just as the school had no choice, under the design of the project, with respect to which students among those in the pool of girls with potential problems it could refer to YCS, so, too, the agency relinquished its freedom to decide by its own criteria which of these girls it wished to accept and endeavor to treat. This restriction was accepted to protect the validity of the experimental results from unknown selective processes that would affect the equivalence of the experimental and control cases. In the interest of the preventive goal of the project, it is also to be noted that the agency thereby accepted clients without the overt presenting problems customary for its intake, which is a novel situation for a voluntary social agency. However, this constituted not only a challenge but a fruitful professional experience.

Although the agency agreed that the pool of potential problem cases consisted of the kinds of girls they wanted to try to help through preventive intervention, the requirement of arbitrary referral and acceptance created an experimental population that could be expected to differ in unknown ways from the usual clientele of the agency. One might speculate that Vocational High students were less motivated to accept help than clients who came entirely on their own initiative. However, adolescent girls were often seen by YCS under conditions not likely to encourage positive motivation. Despite the acute difficulties they often were experiencing, few of the usual clients were self-referrals; they were frequently brought in by parents or sent by schools, community agencies, or professional persons. They often had attitudes resistant or even hostile to adult help. When it had facilities, YCS attempted to work with such clients as long as it was deemed possible and useful. With project clients, the social workers were obligated to attempt service persistently and hence may have continued to see some girls they felt unable to benefit. Like other clients, Vocational High referrals were free to discontinue contact when they wished but the agency, on its part, undertook to see the girls as long as they were willing to come and considered in need of treatment.

Many of the arbitrary referrals from Vocational High might not have been as visibly in need of help as some of the usual clients of YCS. However, as previously indicated, the preventive objective of the project accepted this as the major question to examine: could help before problems were clearly visible prevent them from developing? It was not the effectiveness of the agency with its usual clients that was in question, therefore, but rather the effectiveness of its special effort with a determinate clientele in an experimental project.

RESEARCH DATA OBTAINED FOR THE STUDY

With the focus of the research on evaluation of effectiveness by comparing referred and control samples, data on criteria of success and change were required.

For experimental and control cases alike, information was obtained about school performance and behavior. Did the student finish school or drop out? Was she ever suspended or expelled from school? Was she truant from school? Did she pursue the vocational training program provided for her? Was her attendance at school good or poor? Was her school conduct satisfactory or unsatisfactory? Did she receive honors, awards, and good ratings for school service? Did teachers regard her as outstanding or as presenting a serious problem to them?

Some out-of-school behavior also is indicative of getting into trouble, but this was more difficult to obtain without resources for an extended field follow-up. Out-of-wedlock pregnancy, however, was one event that became known to the school and represented unsatisfactory behavior, and it was included among the criteria. Also, getting into trouble with police or becoming known through delinquent acts was a relevant negative behavioral criterion, and an effort was made to obtain information about this for experimental and control cases through use of the Social Service Exchange, in which contact with juvenile authorities as well as social agencies is recorded. In general, it might be expected that out-of-school serious trouble for a girl would result in her removal from school or impairment of her school record, so that school continuity was considered a reflection, at least in part, of the out-of-school situation.

It may be asked whether such objective criteria of appropriate adolescent behavior can be expected to reflect the type of treatment offered by an agency such as YCS. From one viewpoint, the agency is not directing its primary effort to achieving school continuity and good behavior, but rather is seeking to achieve optimal functioning, healthy personalities, satisfactory interpersonal relations, and the like. Therefore, a number of clinical criteria of success were included.

Two direct measures of personality change were used, the Junior Personality Quiz[1] and the Make A Sentence Test.[2] The JPQ is a questionnaire containing items that have been selected through factor analysis to reflect 12 personality dimensions. This personality test was expressly developed for use with young adolescents between 12 and 16 years of age. Its dimensions have meaningful relationship in content to the more fully developed 16 Personality Factor Test that has been widely used in studies of adult personality.

An alternative method of reflecting personality was sought. It appeared that the sentence-completion form had more advantages and fewer liabilities than other projective tests. Responses to sentence-completion test items are capable of content analysis by standardized techniques, and such surface interpretation of content appears to be an important part of even the more subtle uses of projective tests. Other projective test approaches—the TAT and Rorschach, for example—appeared too demanding of language ability for group administration and prohibitive in individual administration. Therefore, the MAST was adopted after considerable developmental work. The scoring categories have been used reliably and have been shown to be correlated with apparently similar dimensions as measured by a number of objective personality tests.[3]

It may be argued that the type of treatment to which the adolescent girls referred to YCS were exposed cannot be expected to affect fundamental personality characteristics such as those presumably measured by these tests. Persons may not change basically from limited contact with social workers. This may very well be true but it is an open question and one on which light may be shed by examining these measures. Plausible differences to be expected from so-called healthier, more normal, less disturbed, better functioning persons may readily be hypothesized in terms of the categories of these tests. Therefore, they may suggest differences between treated and control cases that are in directions accepted as indicative of successful treatment.

A more superficial but nevertheless clinically meaningful level of

---

1 Test developed by R. B. Cattell, J. Beloff, D. Flint, and W. Gruen, Institute for Personality and Ability Testing, Champaign, Ill. For a description, see R. B. Cattell and H. Beloff, "Research Origin and Construction of the I.P.A.T. Junior Personality Quiz: The J.P.Q.," *Journal of Consulting Psychology,* 17 (1953), 436–42.

2 Test developed by Edgar F. Borgatta and Henry J. Meyer. For description, see Edgar F. Borgatta in collaboration with Henry J. Meyer, "Make a Sentence Test: An Approach to Objective Scoring of Sentence Completions," *Genetic Psychology Monographs,* 63 (1961), 3–65; also Edgar F. Borgatta and Henry J. Meyer, "The Reliability of an Objective Sentence Completion Scoring Technique," *Journal of Social Psychology,* 58 (1962), 163–66; Edgar F. Borgatta, "The Make a Sentence Test (MAST): A Replication Study," *Journal of General Psychology,* 65 (1961), 269–92.

3 Edgar F. Borgatta in collaboration with Henry J. Meyer, *op. cit.,* pp. 27–46.

change for successfully treated girls might be expected. Therefore, a number of questionnaires were administered that sought to reflect general feelings the girls might have about themselves and their problems, their sense of the dynamics of behavior and the value of getting help from others, and their outlook for the future.

Another behavioral measure was used that might possibly have some relationship to changes induced by treatment and hence become available as an interpretable criterion of successful preventive treatment. This was a general sociometric questionnaire asking the student to list classmates who are "friends of yours, whom you pal around with." Several alternative hypotheses bearing on successful treatment experience might be investigated with such sociometric data. First, it might be hypothesized that casework treatment might reduce perception of social isolation at school or increase gregariousness. Second, it might be hypothesized that the healthier girls would be more often chosen than those with more manifest problems. Third, the hypothesis might be proposed that composition of the friendship circle might change, for successfully treated girls, toward greater association with those showing positive rather than negative characteristics. Thus, successfully influenced clients might be expected to have fewer "bad associates." In particular, changes through the years in the type of choices made and received might reflect trends in positive or negative directions that could be indicative of beneficial influence from YCS.

VALIDITY OF THE EXPERIMENTAL ASSUMPTIONS

Data were analyzed on social and family background characteristics of the total population of high school girls involved in the study, on some of their attitudes, and on their measured personality characteristics, in order to test the assumptions that experimental and control samples were initially equivalent and that both—constituting the pool of potential problem cases—differed from the remaining girls in their cohorts, the residual cases. Differences observed between potential problem cases and residual cases were generally in keeping with the intention of the project to identify for treatment a group of girls for whom future school and personal difficulties could be anticipated. It is clear that this intention was achieved, and it is to be noted that potential problem girls dropped out of school in greater proportion than their peers who were not so identified.

The data also indicate that the random procedure for selecting experimental and control cases among the potential problem population resulted in generally similar groups on which to examine effectiveness of social work intervention.

TREATMENT EXPERIENCES

The primary data for observations and judgments about the character of treatment experiences are the case records of the workers and the group records of the therapists. These individual and group records were reviewed regularly by the supervisors and served as the basis for periodic discussions with the appropriate consultants. The reports of these consultations were also incorporated into the permanent records of each case and group. In preparing summaries of this material for research purposes, a supervisor and the director of casework read the complete records of all individual cases. The senior group therapist and the group-therapy consultant read all of the group records. Each of these readers prepared an extensive analysis of the cases involved.

INDIVIDUAL TREATMENT

Insofar as the experimental setting would permit, the 53 cases referred for individual treatment in the first phase of the project were handled within the framework of the agency's normal intake processes. When these were not effective in reaching a girl, more intensive efforts were directed toward making contact with her and finding some way to involve her in the agency's program. In six of these cases, such efforts were of no avail and the girls were not seen at all. When the caseload was reviewed by the director of casework, a little more than half of the girls who were seen, 27, were not considered to be involved in treatment to any appreciable degree. The other 20 girls were judged by their caseworkers to have been treated significantly.

The 27 cases considered not appreciably involved in treatment were seen from 1 to 19 times by the caseworkers, but little or no progress was reported toward motivating the clients to use the agency's services constructively. Three of the girls were seen once, 1 was seen twice, 4 were seen 3 times, and 4 were seen 4 times. In contrast to these 12 short-term cases, 11 girls had from 5 to 8 interviews and 4 girls had from 11 to 19 individual sessions.

The other 20 cases referred for individual treatment were judged by the caseworkers to have been sufficiently involved in the relationship for it to have had some significant effect upon them. The number of interviews with these clients ranged from 1 client who was seen only 5 times, 15 who were seen from 10 to 15 times, and 4 who were seen from 60 to 90 times. The average for this group was about 35 interviews. This figure is approximately 1 per week for a school year of 9 months.

FROM GROUP TO CASEWORK TREATMENT

In the later years of the project, girls were referred from groups to the casework department for individual treatment when the group therapist and consultant thought this might be the preferred treatment technique, when there were special or unusual problems requiring individual attention and handling, or in order to clear the case for official closing by the agency for whatever reason. In the course of the project, 72 cases were so referred.

GROUP TREATMENT

The decision to try large unselected observation groups as a referral technique was made in the spring of 1957 when one group was activated. Four others were activated early in the next fall term and continued through the school year. With a change in group-therapy consultants, the entire group treatment program was reevaluated the following year and the decision was made to continue working with general discussion groups which, however, should be smaller in size—composed of 7 or. 8 members instead of 13 as in earlier groups. The girls already in the program and the new referrals coming from the short-term orientation groups were reassigned to one or another of the specialized treatment groups designed to meet their particular needs.

In contrast with similar girls in individual casework, the girls in these groups were seen by the social workers as less tense and apprehensive and better able to ventilate their feelings, whether hostile or not, about unhappy and depressing facts in their lives. Whenever they did so, they seemed to gain reassurance by noting that others had similar problems. Each week a different girl emerged, presenting her own particular problems, and most of the girls in the group could relate to the material.

Although these first groups were large and unselective, the staff felt that a certain kind of constructive change occurred among the girls. The staff felt, however, that in unstructured groups of that size, many girls who might benefit from more deliberately structured group therapy could not be reached in a meaningful way. An attempt was made to meet this situation by developing new principles for the formation of groups. The new groups consisted of fewer members and an attempt was made to be selective about their composition.

The new series of small, selective groups was introduced by reassigning girls from the earlier unselective groups and adding new members from the current orientation screening groups that were subsequently formed for all new referrals. During the remaining part of the project, 13 selective groups, averaging seven members each, were formed. These consisted of five Observation Groups, two Family Life Education Groups, three Interview Treatment Groups, two Protective Groups, and one Activity Group. All of these were not in existence at one time, and many of the girls were in more than one group. Generally, girls who were placed first in the Activity Group were later put in other groups or referred for individual treatment.

In the most general terms, the group program tried to help adolescent girls who face crises "to add significantly to their repertoire of reality-based problem-solving techniques and thus improve their crisis-coping capacity for the future."[4]

OBJECTIVE CRITERIA OF EFFECTS

The experimental and control cases were, as intended, essentially alike at the beginning of the experimental project. This was to be expected from the random procedure of assigning potential problem cases to experimental and control groups. The potential problem group itself (including both experimental and control cases) differed from the remaining girls in their school classes (residual cases) in the "negative" ways one would expect from the deliberate selection of potential problem girls to constitute the pool from which experimental and control cases were chosen. For example, a significantly smaller proportion of potential problems than of residual cases remained throughout the three high school years. We may be reasonably confident therefore, that the therapeutic program for experimental cases among the potential problem group was offered to girls who were less promising, girls who were, for the most part, "in need of treatment," as the social workers saw them. Almost all of the girls (95 percent) received some treatment services, and half of these had 17 or more treatment contacts with social workers. The experimental cases as a group were clearly well exposed to the therapeutic program. In short, the experimental cases consisted of high school girls more likely to get into trouble, recognized by social workers as needing treatment, and actually receiving treatment.

Measures of effect are provided by the periodic testing procedures at the end of each school year and by the collection of terminal data about each potential problem case three school years after entrance into high school or as of a cutoff date in the summer of 1960. Four cohorts were subject to the experimental program, beginning with the cohort entering in September, 1955. Therefore, the normal three-year period of the high school had elapsed for the first three of the cohorts by the terminal date in 1960. For the fourth cohort, only two years had elapsed. In the analysis of effects, where criteria are appropriately applied only to cases with the longer time span (for example, graduation from high school), the first three cohorts taken together will be examined. This group of cases had the longest exposure to the therapeutic program. Where lapse of time is

---

[4] Gerald Caplan, *Prevention of Mental Disorders in Children: Initial Explorations* (New York: Basic Books, 1961), p. 12.

less relevant (school grades or behavior ratings), the fourth cohort will be included and the total potential problem sample examined. For all cohorts the random selection procedure resulted in equivalent duration of time for experimental and control cases when measures of effect were taken.

The samples used in the analysis may be summarized as follows:

TABLE 1

AMOUNT OF ELAPSED TIME FROM SCHOOL ENTRANCE, FOR
EXPERIMENTAL AND CONTROL CASES

Elapsed Time from School Entrance to Terminal Date	Experimental Cases	Control Cases	Total Cases
Cohorts with three years elapsed time......	129	132	261
Cohorts with two years elapsed time.......	60	60	120
All cohorts	189	192	381

COMPLETION OF SCHOOL

School status at the end of the project.—Identical proportions of all experimental and control cases had graduated from high school by the termination of the project: 29 percent of each. Equal proportions had left school without graduation or were in school, either in their normal grades or below normal grade. Success—in the sense of graduation or achieving normally expected grade—was the school status of 53 percent of both experimental and control cases, and lack of success—in the sense of dropping out of school or being behind normal grade in school—was the school status of 47 percent. [For purposes of brevity, where the text is relatively explicit, tables have been selectively omitted.—Editor's note.]

When only those girls are considered who could be observed over three full school years, 48 percent of both the experimental and the control cases had graduated or were in normal grade. By way of contrast, 65 percent of the residual cases who could have graduated actually did finish high school.

Clearly the treatment program had no discernible impact with respect to the criterion of graduation from high school.

Highest school grade completed.—Graduation is the formal symbol of completion of high school. Nevertheless, girls who complete their senior year of high school, whether they formally graduate or not, represent a higher level of success when compared to those who do not remain in school as long. Each successive grade completed is that much more education. Proportionately more of the experimental cases than of the control cases completed higher grades of school, although the differences between the two groups are not statistically significant.[5] Among experimental cases, 49 percent completed the senior year whether they graduated or

---

[5] The .05 level of significance has been accepted for this study.

not, compared to 42 percent among control cases. Seventy-three percent of the experimental cases and 64 percent of the control cases completed at least the junior year. None of the experimental cases, compared to 4 percent of the control cases, failed to complete at least the freshman year of high school.

Concerning the number of years attended by those girls who might have attended any high school at least four years by the terminal date of the project, 56 percent of the experimental cases and 49 percent of the control cases attended four or more years of high school, and 83 percent, compared to 75 percent, attended at least three years. The distribution for residual cases indicates that significantly more of them (73 percent) than either experimental or control cases attended high school four or more years.

A smaller percentage of experimental cases (52 percent) than of control cases (56 percent) were suspended or discharged from school during the period of the project but, again, the difference is not statistically significant. When the reasons for suspension and discharge are classified into nonpunitive and punitive, slightly more of the control than the experimental cases were removed from school for nonpunitive reasons, such as poor health, employment, transfer, or other circumstances not reflecting misbehavior or poor academic performance. This difference hints at the possibility that the services given to girls by the social agency helped those with circumstantial problems somewhat more than it helped those with behavior problems. This is only the barest of speculations, of course, in view of the minimal difference observed, but it may be worth noting when considering benefits of service programs to high school girls with potential problems.

Taken together, the findings with respect to completion of school can be said to support only an extremely cautious suggestion that the treatment program had any effect. At most, it can be said that extremely small differences in staying in school favor the experimental cases. Since the differences are not statistically significant, only their consistency permits even this cautious conclusion.

ACADEMIC PERFORMANCE

Grades earned in vocational and academic subjects.—The number of failures can be taken as one indication of academic performance. If the treatment program had any effect, it should be most evident after it had been in operation some time, either because of cumulative influences or because, selectively, students who perform better stay in school. We know that similar proportions of experimental and control cases drop out. Therefore, unless some factor is operating to differentiate them, similar proportions ought to show failures.

The trends of failures for both vocational and academic subjects are essentially similar. Decreasing proportions of both experimental and control cases are found to have failures between their first and third years, but the decrease is greater for experimental cases. Thus, for vocational subjects, 40 percent of the experimental cases had one or more failures their first year but only 16 percent their third year, and this difference is statistically significant. On the other hand, for control cases there were 31 percent with one or more failures the first year and 20 percent the third year, a substantial decrease to be sure but the difference does not reach statistical significance. The corresponding trend for academic subjects is to be noted: a statistically significant decrease from 39 to 24 percent for experimental cases, compared to a smaller decrease, not statistically significant, from 31 to 20 percent for control cases. It is further to be noted that the record of experimental cases is not as good as that of control cases in the initial year (although the difference is not statistically significant), whereas it is better or equal to that of the control cases in the third year.

The finding is not so clear when academic performance is measured by the number of A and B grades recorded. Such high grades are about equally found for experimental and control cases at each year, with slight tendencies for proportionately fewer A's and B's in the later years, except for a minor countertrend among experimental cases in vocational subjects. None of the differences is statistically significant.

If one is to interpret these findings as evidence of an effect of the treatment program, it must be seen as an effect mediated through the selection process. Rather than conclude that academic performance, as reflected in grades, is directly improved by the program available to experimental cases, it is more exact to say that girls who would earn better grades (especially fail fewer subjects) were helped to remain in school. Such a positive selective effect is, nevertheless, a constructive, if modest, achievement to be attributed to the treatment program.

Advancement with class and assignment to cooperative work-study program.—Associated with performance in subjects, but dependent as well on additional evaluations by the teachers, the promotion or detention of a student at the end of each school year and the decision to assign, at the normal time, to the cooperative work-study program are further indications of general academic performance.

A slightly greater proportion of experimental cases than of control cases advanced normally with their classes. Thus, 74 percent of all the experimental cases, compared to 70 percent of the control cases, remained in their normal class, whereas 24 percent of the former and 28 percent of the latter were held back or reclassified to lower-standing vocational programs, and the same proportion of both groups (2 percent) were advanced above the normal level for their classes. None of these differences is statistically significant. They can only be taken as a possible suggestion of better performance by experimental cases.

At this high school, students are placed in work-study jobs in the industry for which they are trained when their work is adequate and they are deemed responsible by teachers of vocational subjects and by the guidance counselors. This is a prized assignment since it provides on-the-job experience, apprentice wages, and potential access to the job market after graduation. Assignments are normally made for the second semester of the junior year and continued throughout the last year of high school. Occasionally, students will be assigned for the first time at the beginning of their senior year if they have shown improvement deemed to warrant it, and occasionally they will be dropped from the work-study program if they do not perform adequately in it.

No differences of significance are found between experimental and control cases in the pattern of assignment. For both groups, 48 percent were never selected. Slightly more of the control than the experimental cases (48 and 45 percent, respectively) were assigned in their junior year, but a few more of the latter were assigned later. Altogether, half of each group (51 percent of the experimental and 49 percent of the control cases) participated in the *co-op* training program.

Honors and awards and service ratings.—Slightly greater percentages of control cases than experimental cases had entries in their records of awards and honors, but in both groups the numbers were few. Only 14 percent of the former and 9 percent of the latter were so recognized. Similarly, more of the control cases (65 percent) than the experimental cases (59 percent) had at least one service rating, but this difference also is not statistically significant. Such minor differences hardly bear interpretation.

In recapitulation of the findings with respect to the several measures of academic performance, we note the positive selective effect of the treatment program in reducing failing grades in academic subjects.

SCHOOL-RELATED BEHAVIOR

Attendance.—No consistent or significant differences were found between the attendance records of experimental and control cases. Calculation of the unexcused-absence rate shows that slightly more than one-third of both groups were absent on the average one day a month or less in their initial year; nearly half the cases in school three years later had this low rate of absences. Experimental cases show a slightly better rate for the latter year (49 percent compared to 43 percent with less than ten days, not a statistically significant difference). The decrease in unexcused absences in excess of this rate was more substantial for experimental cases than for control cases. It fell from 40 percent in the first year to 23 percent in the third year, a statistically significant difference for those with 18 or more days of unexcused absences. This decrease occurs primarily between the second and third years, when a lesser decrease for control cases is also apparent.

As was pointed out in the discussion of academic performance, differences through time for such measures as attendance may be taken as a positive selective effect of the treatment program provided for experimental cases, but since these cases do not differ significantly from the control cases on these measures one must make no claim for direct effects.

Truancy.—There were 107 problem-potential cases who were truant during the project; 62, or 58 percent of these cases, were control cases and 45, or 42 percent, were experimental cases. The difference between experimental and control cases shows the former to have the better record and is substantial enough to take note of, although it does not quite reach the criterion of statistical significance adopted in this analysis. Instances of truancy occur for experimental cases disproportionately in the year of cohort entry, when 42 percent of them are reported. Truancies in later years are disproportionately greater for control cases: 74 percent, compared to 58 percent for experimental cases, but with such small numbers of truancies reported this noticeable difference is not quite statistically significant.

We are probably justified in a cautious conclusion that experimental cases were less truant than control cases as an effect of the social work program. This is an effect that might be expected in view of the weekly schedule of interviews or group sessions, attendance at which was of immediate and constant concern to the social workers. Since these scheduled contacts with the social workers took place during the school day, encouragement to meet the appointment with the caseworker or group leader was tantamount to encouragement to come to school. It is perhaps surprising that more favorable truancy and school-attendance records were not found for the experimental cases. Nevertheless, the effect that does appear must be accepted as a positive achievement of the treatment program.

Conduct Marks.—Each student's official school record includes, for each term, a teacher's rating on *conduct,* that is, on appropriate behavior or misbehavior that may or may not subject the student to some form of discipline. We might expect such behavior to be affected favorably as a result of the therapeutic attention to which the experimental cases were subjected.

In each year, the difference between experimental and control cases was minimal and there were no consistent trends that change the relationship between the distributions of conduct marks for the two groups of cases. Significant decreases occurred between the first and third years in the proportions of both experimental and control cases that received unsatisfactory marks for conduct. The selective process operated with equal effect whether the girls did or did not participate in the therapeutic program. However, the major decrease for experimental cases with unsatisfactory conduct marks occurred between the initial and the second years, whereas for the control cases the decrease between each year was more even.

When conduct marks were used as a criterion, no interpretable effect from the treatment program was found for the experimental cases.

Teacher Ratings for Character Traits and Work Traits.—For each term the student's homeroom teacher, on the basis of reports from all the student's teachers, rated the student on a number of character traits and work traits, and these ratings became part of the official record of the student. Ratings were on a scale from 1 (very poor) to 5 (excellent). The character traits rated were interest, industry, initiative, courtesy, cooperation, self-control, appearance, dependability, and health habits. The work traits were care of tools and equipment, "follows instructions," neatness, speed, attitude, use of English, safety, and workmanship. The records were not entirely consistent in the extent to which all traits were rated but there were usually four or five of each list that were rated. So far as we were able to determine from discussing the ratings with school staff, the teachers varied not only in the meanings and standards they applied but also in the extent to which students were known well enough for judgments to be made. This accounts in part for incomplete ratings for some students and full ratings for others. It is likely that behavior that was noticeably deviant—either negatively or positively—would call the student sufficiently to the teacher's attention so that traits would be rated for her.

With these reservations, the utility of such ratings is obviously limited. Nevertheless, one may assume that students who made up the experimental and control cases had equal opportunities to be rated in the same manner and, hence, any differences that they exhibited had equal chances of being reflected in the ratings. We have averaged the ratings for each year for the comparison of experimental and control cases.

Essentially, the findings for teacher ratings parallel those for conduct marks: no significant differences appear between experimental and control cases, but the latter tend to have slightly higher ratings. Average ratings for both experimental and control cases shift significantly upward between the first and third years, but the shift is approximately the same for both groups of cases. There is no evidence, therefore, of an effect of the treatment program so far as this measure is concerned.

We may summarize the findings on all the measures that have been grouped together as school-related behavior by noting that none of them supplies conclusive evidence of an effect by the therapeutic program. However, the relatively better showing of experimental cases with respect to truancy suggests that the surveillance that accompanies the rendering of treatment services tends to have some effect. This is by no means a trivial achievement, if further research shows that it does indeed occur. Other deviant forms of behavior have often been observed to be concomitants of truancy. An additional conclusion is suggested by the findings with respect to trends on the measures here examined through the three years observed: that there is some tendency for a favorable differential to develop for experimental cases through the selective process. It would appear that if girls remain in school, those with the benefit of the treatment program exhibit somewhat less negative school-related behavior. From the point of view of the school a less deviant population remains and, possibly, educational objectives might more readily be achieved for them. Likewise, a student body resulting from such favorable selective processes might constitute a more favorable context for students who are not deviant in the ways exhibited by the problem-potential segment of the school population.

OUT-OF-SCHOOL BEHAVIOR

Entries on Health Record.—Matters of health arising from acute circumstances, as well as the results of periodic health examinations by the school nurse and physicians serving the school, are recorded for each student on a health record. Such information covers a broad range of observations, including overweight and underweight, allergies, psychosomatic complaints, and emotional or psychological difficulties. It was considered possible that a treatment program addressed in major part to more positive mental health attitudes and self-understanding might be reflected in such school health records. Since we believed that the records were not sufficiently detailed for refined diagnostic categories, we have taken the frequency of all entries as a rough index of health status. Experimental and control cases were compared on this basis.

Somewhat fewer entries on the health records are found to be made for experimental cases, but the difference from control cases is not statistically significant. There are significant decreases for both groups of cases between the year of cohort entry and the last year observed. It is likely that, in addition to the effects of selection, the older ages of the girls constituting the latter cases would affect this measure. The school health personnel might be less likely to make note of minor health problems for 16- to 18-year-old than for 13- to 15-year-old girls, and the girls themselves might be less likely to bring such problems to the attention of school personnel.

Attention of Authorities and Agencies.—To see whether experimental and control cases might differ in the extent to which they had come to the attention of the police, courts, and other agencies of community control, the potential problem cases were cleared through the Social Service Exchange at the terminal date of the project. However, the appearance of any entries, especially those with explicit reference to the girls themselves, was so infrequent that it is meaningless to compare experimental and control cases on this measure.

When a girl became involved in court proceedings for some offense, and it was known to the school, a notation was kept and this was taken as a further indication of deviant out-of-school behavior. We cannot accept the information as accurate under the more or less informal manner it was recorded, but the data available do not differentiate experimental and control cases in any event. Thirteen of the former (7 percent) and nine of the latter (5 percent) were noted to have been involved in court cases.

Out-of-wedlock Pregnancy.—Because premarital pregnancy is cause for suspension from school, and a rule made it mandatory that resumption of schooling for unmarried mothers must be in a different school, somewhat more reliable information was available about out-of-wedlock pregnancy than other forms of nonschool deviant behavior. For all the potential problem cases (except five for which data were not available), out-of-wedlock pregnancy was reported for 41 girls, or 11 percent. Of these 41 girls, 23 (56 percent) were control cases and 18 (44 percent) were experimental cases, a difference that favors the latter but is not statistically significant.

On the very limited measures of out-of-school behavior available, we may note, in summary, that only the slightest advantage was found for experimental cases. We find very little evidence, therefore, of effect on these measures of the therapeutic program.

OTHER CRITERIA OF EFFECTS

PERSONALITY TESTS

The Junior Personality Quiz was the personality test used throughout the series of test periods in the research. On only two factors was there the suggestion that experimental and control cases differed significantly or meaningfully.

Compared to control cases, scores on the factor designated as Will Control vs. Relaxed Casualness change toward the higher pole of the dimension for experimental cases. Thus we may conclude that the treatment program promoted personality-test responses indicating greater self-control, and persistent, orderly behavior. These traits did not increase for the comparable control cases.

Although not statistically significant, slight numerical trends with respect to the factor designated as Adventurous Cyclothymia vs. Withdrawn Schizothymia occur in opposite directions for experimental and control cases. The former increase in boldness, whereas the latter increase in shyness, aloofness, lack of confidence. This is a suggestive difference in keeping with the objectives of the treatment program to which the experimental cases were exposed.

On the other ten factors that make up this personality test no interpretable differences appear between experimental and control cases. We must conclude, therefore, that the treatment program had only the barest effect on personality changes insofar as this instrument detects them.

The Make A Sentence Test failed to reveal interpretable differences and therefore the data will not be presented.

Thus with the use of two standardized measures of personality—one objective and the other projective—only the barest evidence of an experimental effect of the treatment program can be found.

QUESTIONNAIRE RESPONSES

Three questionnaires were used to detect possible effects at the level of expressed attitudes. The first of these questionnaires asked about general feelings. The minimal differences between experimental and control cases suggest that those girls who had the benefit of treatment may respond slightly less negatively to several questions intended to reflect general self-assessments of their personal situations.

After reviewing data from a second questionnaire that sought to reflect psychological insight and reactions to help, we may report that girls in the treatment program clearly recognized the opportunity to discuss their problems with an adult and, in contrast to the control cases, did not feel that they had been limited in doing so. Experimental cases did not, however, especially attribute benefits to themselves from this opportunity in significantly greater proportions than the control cases. From responses to a number of questions, there was weak evidence to suggest that participation in the treatment program was associated with somewhat greater psychological insight. It is always possible that a superficial attitude questionnaire would fail to reflect so subtle a difference as heightened insight. Indeed, small measured differences might even reflect much greater actual differences.

On a third questionnaire, which asked seniors about their situations and their futures, the major difference between experimental and control cases was the greater recognition by girls who had been in the program that they had been helped by a social worker.

The scant findings from these questionnaires can support only the slightest indication of effect. At best we may cautiously suggest that the pattern of response tends to be somewhat less negative if viewed from the objectives of the treatment program.

SOCIOMETRIC DATA

Sociometric choices were analyzed for those students who remained in school throughout the four testing periods and these data will be considered here. Between the first and fourth test periods, the percentages of control and residual cases naming one or more serious problem students decreases, whereas a greater proportion of experimental cases named one or more serious problem students. Even so, the difference between the experimental, control, and residual cases is not large enough to be statistically significant.

When the sociometric data are considered with respect to outstanding students named by and choosing experimental, control, and residual cases, the trends are similar for both of the potential problem samples (experimental and control cases) ; no significant differences appear between them. Whether naming or chosen by outstanding students, increased proportions of such students are found at the fourth test period when compared to the first period, and these differences are statistically significant. This is merely evidence, of course, that all students become better known as they remain in school. This phenomenon does not appear differentially to any meaningful degree for experimental and control cases. The same trend, however, is sufficiently greater for residual cases than for either of the potential problem samples so that the differences found between the residual and the experimental and control cases, taken together at the fourth test period, are statistically significant. Although they are not differentiated from one another, both the experimental and the control cases are found to be less likely to name or be named by outstanding students than the residual cases. Slightly fewer of the experimental than the control cases at the fourth testing period are found to name or be chosen by outstanding students, but the differences are small and cannot constitute evidence of a negative result of the treatment program.

With respect to sociometric volume—that is, the total number of students named by or choosing girls in the several samples of the research population—there are no important differences between experimental, control, and residual cases. The trend is for each of the three groups of cases to name more students at the fourth than at the first test period. Likewise, they are chosen by more at the later period, with the residual cases somewhat more likely to be chosen, but not to a statistically significant degree.

The sociometric data do not show evidence of effect from the treatment program. Insofar as the hypothesis that the program would reduce the undesirable associations of the experimental cases is concerned, there is no evidence to support such a conclusion. Nor has there been an evident effect on the level of general popularity of experimental as compared to control cases.

The personality tests, questionnaire responses, and sociometric data have failed to detect substantial differences between experimental and control cases. We must conclude that, with respect to all the measures we have used to examine effects of the treatment program, only a minimal effect can be found.

CONCLUSION

The measures of effect that have been examined here are objective, in the sense that they are observations external to the girls we studied, as well as self-reports or responses on tests. Such measures constitute, therefore, fairly severe tests of an experimental effect of the treatment program. On these tests no strong indications of effect are found and the conclusion must be stated in the negative when it is asked whether social work intervention with potential problem high school girls was effective in this instance.

However, the evidence is not wholly negative. With due recognition of the very low magnitude of any relationship between experimental or control status of the cases and any of these criteria measured, it may be noted that the direction of many of them tends to favor girls who had the benefit of the treatment program. This may be little basis for enthusiasm, in view of the tireless efforts of able social workers and the splendid cooperation of school personnel in an attempt to help the girls with potential problems, but it is not entirely discouraging. It testifies to the difficulty of changing deviant careers, a difficulty that is apparent whenever serious evaluative assessments have been undertaken. This is certainly not surprising to social workers who have struggled to find ways to be helpful. And it should caution those who like to believe that ways are already known, if but tried, to meet the serious problems of adolescents in their high school years.

ROGER R. MILLER

4 | *An Experimental Study of the*
*Observational Process in Casework**

I feel . . . well, I still say, "Why in hell did it happen to have to be me?" You see? I mean, I've never been able to live another way. It's been economic.[1]

From a flow of communication such as this, the caseworker draws inferences, institutes activities, and gauges results. The verbal material is vague, loosely organized, and incomplete. The meanings of the words are modified or amplified by complex and transient behavior. As a further complication, the caseworker himself actively affects the presentation of his client. Not only are the data slippery and elusive, but the very method by which they are elicited would appear to prevent their systematic study.

We are all familiar with the complexities of interview data. Nevertheless, most of us would agree that the skilled caseworker does achieve a workable understanding of his client through the interview. The therapeutic objectives he attains are themselves a tribute to his competence in interpersonal perception. Moreover, the reliability of casework judgments has been given impressive statistical support through the development and extension of the Movement Scale.[2] But *how* does the interviewer accomplish this impressive feat? How are reliable judgments made from a communicative stream which appears to defy conventional objective scientific methodology?

There is no very satisfactory explanation at hand to account for the observational success of the interviewer. The processes which occur within the observer appear to constitute part of the "art" of our practice. Empirically developed methods have here outstripped the development of theory. Our ability to perform exceeds our ability to explain that performance.

The research to be summarized in this paper was initiated to learn something more about one of our most basic practice skills—our ability

* Reprinted with permission of the National Association of Social Workers from *Social Work*, Vol. 3, No. 2 (April, 1958), pp. 96–102, and the author.

1 Excerpt from an interview used in the present research.

2 J. McV. Hunt and Leonard S. Kogan, *Measuring Results in Social Casework* (New York: Family Service Association of America, 1950), pp. 10–11; and Margaret Blenkner, "Predictive Factors in the Initial Interview in Family Casework," *Social Service Review*, Vol. 28, No. 1 (March, 1954), p. 68.

to understand our clients. More certain knowledge than we presently hold about our observational accomplishments should aid in the refinement of that skill. Such knowledge might also pave the way for the measurement of casework skill.

THEORETICAL FRAMEWORK

Clinical observation is a special form of a universal social process; in the course of normal living, every person makes judgments about others. As would be expected, the subject of interpersonal perception has been widely studied. Some of the characteristics of the good judge of others have been identified, and some headway has been made in distinguishing productive observational methods.[3] However, these studies clearly fail really to explain the process of observation. For an explanation, one must move beyond established knowledge into the less certain realm of theory.

In preparation for this study, a search was made for a formulation of the observational process which would be consistent with research findings and which would fit with actual experience. Of the formulations considered, one presented by Theodor Reik seemed to us most promising. In his book, *Listening with the Third Ear*,[4] Reik sets forth, implicitly, a model of the observational process. In brief, Reik suggests that perception occurs preconsciously and that only a portion of the percepts ever become conscious. The perceptions which do not attain immediate consciousness, but which are nevertheless received and noted, are believed to contribute most to psychological understanding. It is suggested that in normal interpersonal communication extensive use is made of such preconscious material. These perceptions are said to be assimilated into the unconscious ego of the observer by means of a special form of incorporation.

From a transient introjection of the impulses of the subject into the unconscious ego of the observer, an unconscious sharing of emotion is said to occur. This in turn produces changes in the observer; the assimilated emotions become, temporarily, the observer's own. As these impulses seek outlet, the observer may become consciously aware of them. Foreign emotions may then be noted and reprojected onto the subject. The inferences derived from such self-awareness, along with the data apprehended consciously, are then subjected to logical scrutiny. The resulting conscious psychological comprehension of the subject is thus the product of rational thought, selection, and logical classification.

---

3 *Cf.*, Jerome S. Bruner and Renato Tagiuri, "The Perception of People," in Gardner Lindzey, ed., *Handbook of Social Psychology* (Cambridge, Mass.: Addison-Wesley Publishing Company, Inc., 1954), pp. 634–654.

4 New York: Farrar, Straus and Cudahy, Inc., 1948.

From these assumptions, Reik derives a number of hypotheses about observational technique. It follows from his assumptions about the value of preconscious perception that the observer should not restrict himself chiefly to the sharp and accurate observation of whatever may be presented to consciousness. Instead, he must find observational methods which facilitate the purposeful utilization of data which ordinarily do not attain immediate consciousness. Reik's analysis of observational methods, appropriate for clinical purposes, is built around the concept of attention.

Reik divides the attention of the observer into an active and a passive *form*. Active, or "voluntary," attention is described as a selective, focused, and specific receptivity to interview data. Passive, or "free-floating," attention is the antithesis of the voluntary form. It is conceived as a reactive, diffuse, nonselective receptivity to obtruding content. Free-floating attention may be thought of as a general state in which everything is noted equally.

While it is believed that every observer uses both forms of attention, it is hypothesized that the trained observer comes to rely too heavily on voluntary attention. Certain components of the interview are singled out for close inspection, so that other facets of the presentation may not be noted. Free-floating attention is regarded as valuable for the accumulation of potentially valuable but obscure data. It is believed that the trained observer tends to work too hard to derive meaning quickly from the client's presentation. Reik recommends an approach which only prepares for subsequent understanding. This is to prevent a "set" in the observer which may encourage a too-hurried attempt to understand content which can only be grasped by more passive, patient means.

Reik introduces a second dimension of the kind of attention used in interviewing, its *direction*. Both voluntary and free-floating attention are capable of direction to two sources of understanding. Attention may focus externally toward the communicative stream; or it may be steered internally toward the observer's own responses. Reik attaches greater importance to self-observation than to an externally directed attention. Self-observation is said to be essential for the purposeful tapping of preconscious material. The externalized "set" of the observer may encourage him to ignore or distrust his intuition or empathic understanding.

Reik's theory of clinical observation thus leads to an interesting hypothesis: *The adequacy of the observer's conscious psychological comprehension is said to be positively related to the extent to which he uses free-floating attention and the extent to which his attention is directed internally.* This central hypothesis offers a test of the predictive value of his theory.[5]

METHOD AND PROCEDURE

An experiment was designed to investigate the association between attention and understanding. In order to give all subjects similar interview content, a film[6] of an actual interview was used to provide a common "client." Since all observers were presented with an identical communicative stream, their attention and understanding could be compared.

For the investigation, the researcher hoped to influence the attention of observers in several ways; if successful, these variations in attention should affect the understanding of the observers in predictable ways. The method by which attention was to be shifted was simple. It was assumed that information about the *purpose* of the observation would influence the form and direction of the observer's attention. Accordingly, three experimental groups were set up:

1. *The Process Group* was told that a research objective was to *measure how accurately* caseworkers observed a client's presentation. They were told their responses would be collected after seeing the film and that they should be prepared to write a process record—a full, accurate step-by-step account of the material. It was expected that under these conditions the use of voluntary and external attention would be high. This is the distribution of attention which is said to contribute least to psychological comprehension.

2. *The Diagnostic Group* was told that the research was designed to *measure how well* caseworkers understand their client. They were told to be ready to write a diagnostic summary of the case material—a report organized to bring out what is really important rather than all the details. This set was expected to induce more reliance on voluntary and internal attention—a distribution which should create an intermediate level of understanding.

3. *The Empathic Group* was given the information that the research was not a study of individual performance and that there was no need for concern about their participation in the research. These subjects were encouraged not to expect too much of themselves but were asked instead to *respond to the client naturally* and to see what general feelings and

---

[5] This account represents the effort of the researcher to present Reik's ideas accurately. The theory is developed discursively, however, and is open to a range of interpretation.

[6] *The Clinical Picture of Claustrophobia, Psychotherapeutic Interviewing Series* (16 mm. black & white, sound, 30 minutes). Produced by Presentation Division, Veterans Administration, for Department of Medicine and Surgery, Veterans Administration. (VA Central Office Film Library, Washington, D. C.)

impressions developed during the interview. These instructions were designed to enable the observer to be free to use free floating and internally directed attention. The empathic set was expected to encourage the distribution of attention said to be most conducive to psychological understanding.[7]

Subjects. The experimental subjects were drawn from the casework students at the School of Applied Social Sciences of Western Reserve University. Since both first- and second-year students were used, the experimental groups were randomly composed, after stratification according to year of training and field work grade. The research was conducted in the late spring, so that all subjects were nearing completion of either one or two years of training. The obtained sample of 54 students represents 87 percent of the potential subjects. Their division into experimental groups was judged to be sufficiently randomized to allow the comparisons needed for the research; the groups appeared reasonably well matched.

In addition to the student subjects, 13 noncaseworkers were studied. These subjects, roughly comparable in age and level of education to the casework students, represented a variety of professional backgrounds which did not include training in interviewing. This group was given instructions almost identical to those for the Empathic Group.

Each of the experimental groups was divided into two sections which were scheduled separately for the experiment. By these means, it was hoped that the possible effects of unexpected conditions or the order of participation would be balanced. Prior to viewing the movie, all subjects were given identical orientation to the research. Without interruption, each group was given one of the special instructional sets, designed to influence its attention. Immediately after this, the participants were shown the 30 minute movie. Finally, the responses of each subject were collected. Except for the variation in instruction, the conditions for each experimental group seemed identical.

MEASUREMENT OPERATIONS

1. *The psychological understanding* of the subjects was investigated by Q-Technique. Thus, after observing the movie, each subject was given a set of 80 statements about the client, printed separately on small cards. The instructions were:

> Your task is to divide the cards so as to give your diagnostic understanding of the client. The statements on these cards all refer to the client in the movie.

---

[7] Not all possible combinations of form and direction were attempted. These three were selected in part to fit sets which people may actually experience in the practice of social work.

From among all of them pick out the two statements you want to stress most. Put these two on the far left. Then build up the second column by selecting the four statements you want to stress next to give your understanding of the client. On the far right, put the two statements you want to stress least in creating your picture of the client.

It was necessary for the subject to distribute the statements among 11 columns. This meant that a number of fine discriminations were required.

The statements themselves were brief phrases such as "has had bad luck," "worries constantly about his health," and "feels dissatisfied with himself." In choosing the statements, attention was given to the kind of observation the subjects were likely to consider. The 80 items were independently judged to reflect some features of the interview content. In operation, it was found that observers could rank the items in a meaningful way and could describe their impression of the client without a noticeable sense of distortion.

The criterion variable for measuring the understanding of each subject was provided by a panel of five caseworkers with a reputation for expertness. These practitioners (from the Cleveland area) observed the interview and were then asked to describe their diagnostic understanding of the client by arranging the 80 statements about the client[8] on the same scale used by the student-subjects. The individual scores for each statement were averaged, and the resulting set of means was taken as the criterion of "understanding." Each subject's array of statements was then compared with the pooled scores of the panel. The difference between a subject and the panel was used as a measure of the discrepancy of his understanding of the client from the criterion.

2. *The measure of emphasis of attention* was derived from the same operation which yielded the score for understanding.[9] The 80 statements were of four different types, preselected on the basis of their logical *a priori* connection with the conceptual dimensions of attention. Thus consciously intended objective communications, such as "is uncritical of others," were expected to be emphasized by subjects who depended more on voluntary and external attention. Conversely, content not consciously communicated relating to affective states of the client, such as "feels he has injured himself," were expected to provide an index of free-floating and internal attention. In describing the client, each subject gave greater or lesser weight to the four subgroups of statements. By looking at the

---

[8] The reliability of this instrument was evaluated by a study of the intercorrelations of the five panel members. In view of the fine discriminations involved, the correlations (.50 to .68) were regarded as impressive.

[9] Other instruments were used in the research. Since these were ancillary to the major research question, their description and the data obtained by their use are not reported here.

average score assigned such a block of statements, comparisons were made about the importance attached to categories of data—the operationalized components of attention.[10]

RESULTS

A. ADEQUACY OF UNDERSTANDING

1. *The effects of different experimental conditions.*—The criterion of understanding was provided by the combined judgment of a panel of five caseworkers generally accepted to be expert. For the research subject, adequacy of understanding was judged by how closely his distribution of statements approached that of the experts. A discrepancy score was derived for each subject, showing the size of his departure from the panel. These discrepancy scores, summarized in Table 1, are thus a negative measure of understanding; the higher the score, the less adequate the understanding.

The over-all difference in the measure of understanding was first investigated by analysis of variance. It was found that the scores of the experimental groups differed significantly $(F = 3.70; Pr. < .05)$. From inspection, it was evident that most of the difference was contributed by the relatively poor showing of the subjects in the Process Group. When the groups were compared by t-test, it was found that the Process Group differed strongly from each of the other two $(Pr. < .01)$. It will be recalled that the Process Group had been expected to show the least adequate understanding of the client.

While the performance of the Process Group conformed to the theoretical expectations, the Diagnostic Group did not. The test failed to reveal any meaningful difference between the Diagnostic and Empathic Groups. In fact, it was discovered that such slight variations as these were highly likely to occur in random samples drawn from a common population. The ambiguity of this finding led to certain further analysis to be reported below.

2. *The effects of level of training.*—The reader will note from Table 1 that in each experimental group the second-year students showed less discrepancy from the panel than did the first-year subjects. This difference approached significance by analysis of variance: $(F = 3.21; Pr. = .08)$. This result seems to indicate at the very least that greater training leads to a kind of understanding which is more similar to that of experts. The connection between level of training and quality of understanding

---

[10] The validity of the measure of emphasis of attention was judged by the capacity of the instrument to distinguish among populations which were believed to differ in patterns of attention. It was found that the measured emphasis of attention of non-caseworkers, students, and experts differed significantly in expected directions.

was further tested by comparison of the students with the group of untrained subjects. It was found that the first-year students achieved a

TABLE 1

THE UNDERSTANDING OF THE EXPERIMENTAL SUBJECTS, EXPRESSED AS THE MEANS OF THEIR ABSOLUTE DIFFERENCES FROM THE PANEL ON CARD TEST

| Level of Training | Experimental Groups | | | Total |
	Process	Diagnostic	Empathic	
First Year............	M = 142.73	M = 127.53	M = 129.47	M = 132.85
	N = 9	N = 11	N = 9	N = 29
Second Year..........	M = 133.32	M = 119.17	M = 121.12	M = 124.48
	N = 8	N = 7	N = 10	N = 25
Total	M = 138.30	M = 124.28	M = 125.07	M = 128.97
	N = 17	N = 18	N = 19	N =54

significantly more adequate understanding of the client than did the untrained observers (Pr. $<$ .05 by t-test) .[11]

B. KINDS OF ATTENTION USED BY THE EXPERIMENTAL SUBJECTS

In terms of Reik's theory, the Diagnostic subjects showed an unexpectedly good understanding of the client. In the hope of learning why these observers did so well, a check was made on the distribution of attention. It was important to learn how the instructions had influenced the form and direction of the attention of the experimental subjects. Here use was made of the structure of the card test which had been designed to get at the pattern of attention.

When the mean scores for categories of data were compared by experimental group, it was found that the Process Group gave evidence of using more voluntary and external attention than did the other groups (Pr. = .10 and .12 by T test) . The experimental instructions seemed to have affected these subjects in precisely the manner which had been hoped. On the other hand, the patterns of attention of the Diagnostic and Empathic Groups were almost identical. In fact, there was no evidence that the Diagnostic and Empathic Groups had differed from each other in the kind of attention used. One or both of the experimental sets given these subjects was apparently ineffective.

The investigation of kinds of attention suggests that the instructions tended to divide the subjects into only two groups: the Process Group was influenced to use relatively more voluntary and external attention and the remaining subjects tended to use relatively more free-floating and internal attention. The difference in levels of understanding followed the same line of division; the Process Group did conspicuously

---

[11] These findings are reminiscent of those reported by Hunt and Kogan, *op. cit.*, pp. 10–11.

poorly and the remaining subjects did comparatively well. The measurement of attention and understanding yielded associations which were entirely consistent with the theoretical predictions.[12]

DISCUSSION

This experiment indicates that the model proposed by Reik may continue to be entertained as a fruitful explanation for the process of observation in casework interviewing. The research supports the use of some concepts of clinical attention. At the most practical level, the variables of attention seem to provide a new and productive way of looking at a number of things about our work. In actual practice, is the attention of the caseworker influenced by such things as recording requirements? Does the time-limited diagnostic study or the administrative separation of study and treatment tend to induce a "set" which interferes with understanding, such as occurred with the Process Group? Should further study bear out the connections seen here between attention and understanding, any of our practice procedures could be reexamined for their influence upon casework observation.

The concepts of attention also appear to offer a toehold to the task of learning more about our chief professional resource—the caseworker himself. Knowledge about the stability or flexibility of his attention patterns and of the things which really affect these would be particularly useful. Additional insight into the processes which underlie observational skill could yield such practical rewards as the refinement of our ongoing educational efforts. The experience accumulated during this research encourages the belief that further investigations of these areas are well within the limits of current methodology.

---

12 This impression was reinforced when the attention patterns of all 54 student subjects were examined together. It was found that the students who used more than average free floating attention also gave evidence of a superior grasp of the client ($r_t = .72$; Pr. $< .01$). Similarly, the observers who directed more than an average amount of their attention internally demonstrated superior psychological comprehension ($r_t = .40$; Pr. $< .01$).

GORDON L. PAUL

5 *Insight Versus Desensitization in Psychotherapy Two Years After Termination*[*][1]

After a review of the difficulties of follow-up studies on psychotherapy, Sargent (1960) concluded that, "the importance of follow-up is equalled only by the magnitude of the methodological problems it presents." In the absence of a carefully designed outcome study on which to base follow-up investigations, the follow-up may be doomed from the start. Thus, in many studies, the methods of assessment at follow-up differ from those at pretreatment and posttreatment (e.g., Berle, Pinsky, Wolf, & Wolff, 1953; Cowen & Combs, 1950; Sinett, Stimput, & Straight, 1965). Other studies, especially of a retrospective nature, have used assessment procedures of questionable reliability and validity (e.g., Cooper, Gelder, & Marks, 1965; Sager, Riess, & Gundlach, 1964; Schmidt, Castell, & Brown, 1965). Still others have neglected to include appropriate no-treatment control groups for assessing change in the absence of treatment (e.g., Bookbinder, 1962; Fiske & Goodman, 1965; Rogers & Dymond, 1954). The follow-up also suffers, inherently, from the uncontrolled nature of client experiences during the posttreatment period. This is especially important when the time between treatment termination and follow-up is considerably longer than the duration of treatment; environmental experiences during the posttreatment period may have more influence on Ss' status at follow-up than a brief program of treatment some months or years in the past. The greatest confounding comes from the fact that many Ss receive additional treatment of unknown nature during the posttreatment period, thus invalidating the design for determining cause-effect relationships for the specific treatment under investigation. This practical problem has limited the value of many follow-up

* From: Gordon L. Paul, "Insight Versus Desensitization in Psychotherapy Two Years After Termination," *Journal of Consulting Psychology*, Vol. 31, No. 4 (August, 1967), pp. 333–48. Copyright 1967 by the American Psychological Association, and reproduced by permission.

1 Appreciation is expressed to the Graduate College Research Board of the University of Illinois whose support made this study possible. The earlier data used in this paper were drawn from a study supported in part by Public Health Services Fellowship 1 F1 MH-19, 873, 01 from the National Institute of Mental Health, and in part by the Cooperative Research Program of the Office of Education, United States Department of Health, Education and Welfare, Contract No. 4-10-080, Project 006.

Thanks are extended to Tom Brudenell for his aid in collating and analyzing FU_2 data. Correlational analyses were performed by the IBM-7090 computer of the University of Illinois Computer Science Laboratory.

studies (e.g., Braceland, 1966; McNair, Lorr, Young, Roth, & Boyd, 1964; Stone, Frank, Nash, & Imber, 1961).

Overshadowing all other problems of follow-up research is the practical difficulty of sample maintenance and attrition. Even adequately designed studies may not be able to obtain consistent follow-up data on treated Ss, let alone controls (e.g., Fairweather & Simon, 1963; Kogan, Hunt, & Bartelme, 1953; Lang & Lazovik, 1963). The problem of differential dropout and selective biasing of the sample cannot be ignored, since differences have been found between follow-up returnees and nonreturnees (Fiske & Goodman, 1965), and further, as May, Tuma, and Kraude (1965) point out, even if differences are not found, nonreturnees are clearly different in cooperation, mobility, or both. To highlight the magnitude of this problem, a thorough search of the literature failed to reveal a single study on individual treatment of noninstitutionalized adults which obtained data on all treated Ss two years or more after treatment termination, nor one which included an attempt to obtain such data on an appropriate group of control Ss.

The present study is a two-year follow-up of an earlier investigation which was presented as a model design for the controlled evaluation of comparative therapeutic outcome (Paul, 1966). In the earlier study, a modified form of Wolpe's (1961) systematic desensitization was found to be significantly more effective in reducing maladaptive anxiety than insight-oriented psychotherapy or an attention-placebo treatment. Additionally, all three treated groups were found to show significant improvement over untreated controls. Although these effects were found at termination of treatment, under stress-condition assessment, and were maintained at a six-week follow-up, the differing theoretical models from which the treatment techniques are derived make a long-term follow-up even more desirable than is usually the case.

Specifically, the disease-analogy model underlying the insight-oriented approach to psychotherapy would interpret the results obtained by systematic desensitization and attention-placebo treatments as suggestion or positive transference—in either case, results which would be regarded as merely symptomatic and temporary (e.g., Hendrick, 1958). According to this model, not only would Ss treated by either systematic desensitization or attention placebo be expected to show "relapse" after the "supporting contact with the therapist fades (Sargent, 1960)," but possibly harmful results would also be expected because of the necessary occurrence of symptom substitution (see Ullmann & Krasner, 1965). In fact, the minimal symptom-substitution effect expected would be an increase in anxiety, introversion, rigidity, or dependency (Fenichel, 1945). Additionally, some unsuccessful cases treated by insight-oriented psychotherapy might be expected to realize benefits at some time after treatment termination when their "insights" have had time to "consolidate" (Sargent, 1960). On the other hand, the learning model underlying systematic desensitization would predict no greater relapse for one group than another after treatment termination, since relapse would be expected to occur only on the occasion of unusual stress or if conditions favoring the relearning of anxiety were encountered. Further, this model would expect to find no change in behaviors that were not the specific focus of treatment, except through generalization or an increase in behavior previously inhibited by target behaviors. Thus, from the learning framework, if any change in anxiety, introversion, rigidity, or dependency were to occur at all after treatment termination, it would be in the opposite direction of that expected from the symptom-substitution hypothesis (Paul, 1966). Although the findings at six-week follow-up strongly favored the interpretation of the learning model, with none of the results expected on the basis of the disease model forthcoming, it is possible that the first follow-up period was too short to allow the expected processes to show their effects.

In the present study an attempt has been made to overcome the methodological and practical difficulties of follow-up research more adequately than previous attempts. By starting with a well-controlled outcome study, the same measures of assessment could be obtained from Ss at a consistent interval for long-term follow-up as were previously obtained at pretreatment and short-term follow-up. Persistent effort resulted in a greater return of data than has been reported before, not only for treated Ss, but for untreated controls as well. Additionally, specific frequency data were obtained to allow both the exclusion of Ss receiving additional treatment and the assessment of life stresses and possible symptom substitution during the posttreatment period. The major purpose of the present study was: (a) to determine the overall comparative effects of the different treatments from pretreatment to two-year follow-up and (b) to examine the relative stability of improvement from the six-week follow-up to the two-year follow-up, particularly with regard to the questions of differential relapse and symptom substitution versus generalization, as predicted from the conflicting theories on which the treatments were based.

METHOD

SUBJECTS

The Ss included in the present investigation consisted of three groups of 15 Ss each (10 males, 5 females) who received individual systematic desensitization, insight-oriented psychotherapy, or attention-placebo treatment and 44 Ss (32 males, 12 females) who composed an untreated control group. This included all Ss from the previous outcome study (Paul, 1966), except for a group of untreated controls who participated in a different therapy program in another context (Paul & Shannon, 1966). At pretreatment assessment all Ss were undergraduates *(Mdn =* sophomore) enrolled in a required public speaking course at the University of Illinois, ranging in age from 17 to 24 years *(Mdn = 19).* Each S was selected on the basis of indicated motivation for treatment, high scores on performance anxiety scales, and low falsification from a population of 380 students who requested treatment for interpersonal performance anxiety, as described in detail in the earlier report (Paul, 1966). Although the public speaking situation was reported to be the most stressful condition imaginable, anxiety was also reported in almost any social, interpersonal, or evaluative situation. As a group, the Ss also differed from the normal student population by obtaining higher general anxiety and emotionality scores and lower extroversion scores. The Ss' degree of anxiety in performance situations was strong to severe, and was reported to be of 2-20 years duration.

PROCEDURE

Pretreatment assessment consisted of the administration of a battery of personality and anxiety scales to the students enrolled in the speech course the week following their first classroom speech. The battery was constructed specifically to assess focal treatment effects and to show symptom substitution or generalization if such processes were operating. The battery thus included forms of *(a)* IPAT Anxiety Scale (Cattell, 1957); *(b)* Pittsburgh Social Extroversion-Introversion and Emotionality Scales (Bendig, 1962); *(c)* Interpersonal Anxiety Scales (speech before a large group, competitive contest, job interview, final course examination) of the S-R Inventory of Anxiousness (S-R; Endler, Hunt, & Rosenstein, 1962); *(d)* a scale of specific anxiety in a referenced speech performance (PRCS; Paul, 1966).[2] Following initial selection and prior to treatment assignment, Ss underwent stress-condition assessment in which they were required to give a four-minute speech before an unfamiliar audience which included four psychologists recording the presence or absence of 20 observable manifestations of anxiety during each 30-second period on a timed behavioral checklist. In addition, the palmar sweat index and pulse rate were obtained immediately before the stress speech, as was the Anxiety Differential (see Footnote 3). All Ss underwent stress evaluation except for an equated subgroup of controls initially used to evaluate the effects of the stress-condition assessment itself.

---

[2] The original battery also included a form of the Anxiety Differential (Husek & Alexander, 1963). This form was excluded from follow-up analysis since an additional stress administration was not obtained.

Following stress-condition evaluation the groups were formed, equating all groups on observable anxiety, with Ss randomly assigned to therapists. After a short screening interview, during which standard expectations were established, the treatments began—four weeks after pretreatment assessment. Five experienced psychotherapists (of Rogerian and Neofreudian persuasion) worked individually with three Ss (two males, one female) in each of the three treatment groups for five sessions over a six-week period. All three treatments were conducted concurrently, with missed sessions rescheduled during the same week. Within the week following treatment termination, a posttreatment stress-condition assessment was obtained on treated Ss and no-treatment controls, including the same measures used in the pretreatment stress condition. The first follow-up (FU₁) data were then obtained by a second administration of the test battery to all Ss six weeks after treatment termination. Attitudinal and improvement ratings were also obtained from treated Ss and therapists. The details of all aspects of procedure and results through FU₁ are reported in the earlier study (Paul, 1966).

The two-year follow-up (FU₂) procedure required tracking down the Ss for a third administration of the test battery which had been administered at pretreatment and FU₁. For FU₂ the test battery was augmented to obtain specific frequency data regarding the occurrence of stress during the post-treatment period; the frequency of external behaviors which might reflect predicted symptom-substitution effects of increased dependency, anxiety, or introversion; and information concerning additional psychological treatment or use of drugs which might affect Ss' behavior or response to the anxiety scales.

Information on external stress was obtained by requesting Ss to indicate the number of times each of a number of events occurred since the last contact (FU₁). These events covered five major areas of stress: (a) illness or death of loved ones; (b) conflict (with fiancé or spouse, with persons in authority); (c) change in family structure (engagement, marriage, separation, divorce, pregnancy, or birth); (d) personal illness or accident; (e) change in work or living arrangements (move to a different residence, move to a different city, take a new job, change vocational goals, leave college).

Behavioral frequencies regarding possible symptom substitution consisted of the following 13 items:

1. In the past *two weeks,* how many times did you seek advice, guidance or counsel from: friends?_____; spouse/fiance?_____; instructor/supervisor? _____; parents?_____; physician?_____; others (please specify)?_____

2. In the past *two weeks,* how many times was advice, guidance, or counsel *offered* which you did *not* seek from: (same as #1).

3. In the past *two weeks,* how many times did you *accept* advice, guidance, or counsel when it was provided from: (same as #1).
4. Of your close friends and relatives, with how many different people would you currently feel that you could discuss personal problems should the need arise?_____.
5. To how many clubs or organizations do you currently belong?_____.
6. How many dances, parties, or similar social events have you attended in the *past month?*_____.
7. In the *past month,* how many events have you attended as a "spectator" (such as concerts, meetings, sporting events, etc.)?_____.
8. How many times in the *past month* have other persons been to your home (or room) to visit you?_____.
9. In the *past month,* how many times have you visited or "gone-out" with another person?_____.
10. Of the *different people* you have visited, gone-out with socially, or who have visited you in the *past month,* how many were: males?_____; females?_____.
11. How many times have you participated in group discussion in the *past month?*_____.
12. In the past *three months,* how many times have you spoken or appeared before a group?_____.
13. How many *different* groups have you appeared before in the past *three months?*_____.

Additional information was requested regarding the date and audience size of public appearances in order to appropriately analyze the PRCS and S-R speech scales. The same self-ratings of specific and general improvement which were obtained from treated Ss at FU_1 were also included at FU_2.

The procedure for FU_2 contact ran as follows: 24 months from the date of treatment termination a packet containing the test battery, behavioral questionnaires, and rating scales was mailed to the last known address of each S. The packet was accompanied by a cover letter explaining the importance of participation for one last time and was otherwise designed to enlist cooperation, including an offer to furnish the results of the investigation. This letter set a date three weeks in the future by which the completed forms were to be returned in a stamped, self-addressed envelope which was provided. Those Ss not returning forms by the first due date were sent a personal letter which further stated the importance of their specific participation, and a new due date was set two weeks hence. The Ss not responding to the second letter were then sent a complete new packet by registered mail, as were those Ss for whom new addresses were necessary. Those Ss not responding to the third letter were personally contacted by telephone and reminded of the importance of returning the data, and a promise was elicited to do so immediately. An arbitrary cut-off date was set exactly 27 months after treatment termination, for determining "non-returnee" status of contacted Ss. Thus, although FU_2 was designated as a two-year follow-up, the actual time from termination was 25-27 months, closer to two years from FU_1 than from treatment termination.

RESULTS

RETURN RATE

Of first concern was the adequacy of the follow-up procedure for locating Ss and eliciting their cooperation. Even though the sample was highly mobile (64% no longer in the local area, and 27% out of state or out of the country) all treated Ss and all but three control Ss were located. Complete data were returned by 100% of the treated Ss $(N = 45)$, and 70% of the controls $(N = 31)$. Of the 13 nonreturning controls (ten males, three females), one was deceased, one was in a mental hospital, one flatly refused, seven failed to return after multiple contact, and three could not be located. Thus, the return rate was 79% for contacted controls who could return data, still significantly lower than the return rate for treated Ss $(p < .001$, Fisher exact probabilities test).

Since the purpose of the long-term follow-up was to determine the effects of the specific treatments included in the previous outcome study, Ss who received three or more sessions of psychological treatment during the posttreatment period were excluded from further analyses. On this basis, three Ss were excluded from the insight-oriented group, as were one each from systematic-desensitization and attention-placebo groups, and 12 returning controls; the difference between the proportion of treated Ss and controls receiving treatment during the follow-up period being highly significant $(\chi^2 = 9.87, df = 1, p < 01)$. Additionally, one desensitization S was excluded because she was undergoing chemotherapy for a thyroid deficiency at FU_2, and one control was excluded on the basis of an extreme falsification score. While argument could be made either for including Ss who received additional treatment or for counting all such Ss as relapses, the data available on such additional treatment is unclear. It appears that most of the treated controls, two of the treated insight Ss, and the attention-placebo S did seek treatment for anxiety-related difficulties, while the desensitization S and one insight S sought primarily vocational counseling.

Although data obtained at pretreatment and FU_1 revealed no significant differences between the treated Ss who obtained additional treatment and those who did not, there is no question that the retained controls constituted a biased subsample of the original control group. The nonreturning controls were found to differ from the retained controls in showing significantly greater increases from pretreatment to FU_1 (Pre–FU_1) on the general and examination anxiety scales, and a higher rate of academic failure over the follow-up period (78% versus 32%). Those controls excluded because they received treatment during the follow-up period also differed from retained controls by showing a greater Pre–FU_1 decrease in general anxiety, lower extroversion scores, and significantly greater increases on all specific anxiety scales. Even though there were no differences in demographic variables between retained controls and those lost or excluded, the retained controls appear to have improved more from pretreatment to FU_1, therefore raising the possibility that differences between treatment groups and controls at FU_2 may underestimate treatment effects. Likewise, if Ss excluded on the basis of additional treatment really were cases of relapse, the differential exclusion of these Ss would operate most in favor of the control group and, secondly, in favor of the insight-oriented group, while biasing results against systematic desensitization and attention-placebo treatments.

COMPARATIVE TREATMENT EFFECTS FROM PRETREATMENT TO FU_2 (Pre–FU_2)

The overall evaluation of treatment effectiveness is most reasonably made by a comparison of Pre–FU_2 changes between groups since Pre–FU_1 changes had been subjected to detailed analysis earlier. Two scales of the battery (PRCS and S-R speech) focus specifically on performance anxiety in the speech situation, the specific treatment target. Unlike pretreatment and FU_1 assessments, however, there was no common reference speech for PRCS, and the size of audiences to which Ss had been exposed varied so widely that the separate consideration of S-R speech was no longer meaningful. Therefore, these two scales were converted to T scores and combined to form a Speech Composite score before analyses were undertaken. While the Speech Composite provides evaluation of specific treatment effects, the additional S-R scales report on performance anxiety in three different interpersonal-evaluative situations, none of which were the specific focus of treatment. These latter scales, along with the general scales on Social Extroversion, Emotionality, and General Anxiety, provide information on generalization or, conversely, symptom substitution. Before carrying out the main analyses on the data, the possibility of systematic differences attributable to the five participating therapists was investigated. As was previously found on pretreatment and posttreatment stress-condition data and Pre–FU_1 analyses, in no instance for any measure were significant or suggestive Pre–FU_2 differences found among the overall (main) effects achieved by the five therapists or among the effects achieved by different therapists with the three different treatment procedures (interactions). Consequently, the Ss within treatment groups have been pooled in the following analyses.

The Speech Composite and each of the additional scales from the test battery were subjected to three-way analysis of variance (Treatments, Pre—FU_2, Subjects) on the scores of Ss retained at FU_2. Means and standard deviations for all assessment periods are presented in Table 1 for specific anxiety scales and in Table 2 for general scales.

TABLE 1

MEAN SCORES ON SPECIFIC ANXIETY SCALES AT PRETREATMENT, SIX-WEEK FOLLOW-UP (FU_1), AND TWO-YEAR FOLLOW-UP (FU_2) FOR SUBJECTS RETAINED AT FU_2

Treatment	Testing	Scale							
		Speech Composite		S-R Interview		S-R Examination		S-R Contest	
		M	SD	M	SD	M	SD	M	SD
Desensitization	Pretreatment	115.5	9.74	43.2	11.01	46.8	10.32	35.6	7.92
($N = 13$)	FU_1	85.0	16.10	37.4	8.82	43.2	10.81	35.5	7.28
	FU_2	82.5	16.07	31.5	8.79	36.5	9.28	30.5	6.68
Insight	Pretreatment	117.7	7.15	37.6	9.67	42.5	10.79	40.8	8.73
($N = 12$)	FU_1	103.4	14.18	35.6	11.94	42.2	12.01	39.1	10.24
	FU_2	95.2	18.70	31.3	9.42	39.0	8.99	36.3	10.77
Attention-	Pretreatment	110.7	11.98	34.8	7.34	40.6	9.79	36.9	9.69
Placebo	FU_1	86.4	12.47	32.1	7.22	35.9	12.23	34.0	9.75
($N = 14$)	FU_2	82.9	20.85	28.7	8.03	32.1	7.74	28.9	10.40
Control	Pretreatment	110.9	12.20	37.2	12.98	40.7	10.62	33.9	11.51
($N = 18$)	FU_1	104.3	14.21	34.7	10.16	41.9	11.29	36.3	8.19
	FU_2	99.2	21.66	32.2	10.98	38.4	11.07	33.2	8.11

These analyses indicate highly significant Pre—FU_2 changes ($p < .01$; $df = 1/53$), not only for the Speech Composite ($F = 82.70$), but for all other specific anxiety scales ($F = 35.94, 26.93, 10.39$ for S-R Interview, Examination, and Contest, respectively) and general scales ($F = 12.69$ and 15.21, respectively, for Extroversion and IPAT Anxiety Scale) except Emotionality, which only approached significance ($F = 3.05$, $p < .10$). More important, significant Treatment $\times$ Pre—FU_2 interactions ($df = 3/53$) were obtained for the Speech Composite ($F = 3.68$, $p < .05$) and for S-R Interview ($F = 5.14$, $p < .01$), S-R Examination ($F = 6.96$, $p < .01$), and IPAT Anxiety Scale ($F = 3.46$, $p < .05$), indicating differential changes among groups from pretreatment to the two-year follow-up. The nature of these changes may be seen in Figure 1, which presents the mean change for each group from pretreatment to FU_1 and FU_2 for all scales of the test battery. Unlike Pre—FU_1 changes, where significant overall effects were found only for speech anxiety and extroversion, the significant Pre—FU_2 main effects reported above reflect general trends in the improved direction for all scales at FU_2.

Of the significant Pre—FU_2 interactions, of most interest is the Speech Composite, which reflects change in the focal area of treatment. Inspection of Figure 1 reveals that all four groups maintained their relative positions from FU_1 to FU_2, with slight additional shifts in the direction of lower mean anxiety scores for all groups. As was the case with Pre–FU_1 comparisons, all three treatment groups were found to show significant improvement over controls ($t = 3.70$, 2.04, and 2.38 for desensitization, insight, and attention-placebo groups, respectively; $p < .05$), with no significant difference between the mean anxiety reduction achieved by the attention-placebo group and the insight group ($t < 1$). Also, like Pre–FU_1 comparisons, Ss treated by systematic desensitization showed significantly greater mean Pre–FU_2 reductions in anxiety on the Speech Composite than Ss who were treated by insight-oriented psychotherapy ($t = 2.09$, $p < .05$). However, even though the magnitude of the difference between mean anxiety-reduction scores of the desensitization group and the attention-placebo group for Pre–FU_2 comparisons was the same as that of Pre–FU_1 comparisons, these differences were no longer found to be significant at FU_2 ($t < 1$). This was the result of greater variability in the Pre–FU_2 change scores of the attention-placebo group, primarily due to a drop of 71 points for one attention-placebo S. The overall effects between these two groups may be seen better in the individual data presented below.

TABLE 2

MEAN SCORES ON GENERAL SCALES AT PRETREATMENT, SIX-WEEK FOLLOW-UP (FU_1), AND TWO-YEAR FOLLOW-UP (FU_2) FOR SUBJECTS RETAINED AT FU_2

Treatment	Testing	Scale					
		Extroversion-Introversion		Emotionality		IPAT Anxiety	
		M	SD	M	SD	M	SD
Desensitization	Pretreatment	14.1	7.58	19.8	6.03	40.7	10.69
($N = 13$)	FU_1	17.9	8.45	18.9	6.16	38.2	11.18
	FU_2	19.9	6.18	17.5	7.08	32.0	10.01
Insight	Pretreatment	16.4	6.57	17.2	5.59	33.7	10.09
($N = 12$)	FU_1	18.9	4.70	18.3	6.12	35.0	11.72
	FU_2	18.9	4.64	15.6	6.56	30.5	12.29
Attention-Placebo	Pretreatment	14.1	8.15	18.1	6.02	35.4	9.77
($N = 14$)	FU_1	17.1	7.68	16.8	7.01	30.7	11.74
	FU_2	16.1	7.01	17.1	6.75	28.2	12.12
Control	Pretreatment	17.9	5.53	17.9	5.92	37.7	16.91
($N = 18$)	FU_1	20.2	6.30	18.4	6.31	37.7	11.48
	FU_2	19.4	6.56	17.2	7.97	33.6	14.34

Having found essentially the same results to obtain for focal treatment effects at the two-year follow-up as at the six-week follow-up, the significant interactions between groups and Pre–FU_2 change scores on the other scales of the test battery become of interest. Of the additional specific anxiety scales and general scales, a significant interaction effect was found only for IPAT Anxiety in the earlier analysis of Pre—FU₁ data. The source of that interaction was found in significantly greater anxiety reduction for desensitization and attention-placebo groups than

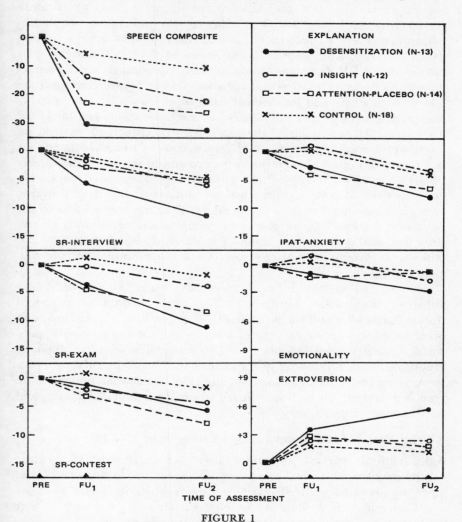

FIGURE 1

MEAN CHANGE FROM PRETREATMENT TO SIX-WEEK FOLLOW-UP (FU_1) AND TWO-YEAR FOLLOW-UP (FU_2) FOR Ss RETAINED AT FU_2

for controls. A significant overall increase in extroversion was also found on Pre—FU₁ analysis, but no significant interaction was obtained over that time period. As indicated above, significant Pre—FU₂ interactions were again found for IPAT Anxiety and, in addition, for S-R Interview and Examination anxiety scales. Inspection of the nature of these changes (Figure 1) showed continued improvement over the follow-up period for the desensitization group on the S-R Interview scale, such that the Pre—FU_2 reduction for the desensitization group was significantly greater than that for controls ($t = 1.75$, $p < .05$) and approached significance when compared with insight and attention-placebo groups (respectively, $t = 1.39$, 1.61; $p < .10$). The source of the significant Pre—FU_2 interaction for S-R Examination was found in significantly greater reductions for both desensitization and attention-placebo Ss over controls ($t = 2.44$, 1.75; $p < .05$) and for desensitization over insight ($t = 1.72$, $p < .05$). Figure 1 shows that the significant interaction obtained on IPAT Anxiety at FU_2 is a result of the combined FU_2 reduction obtained by the desensitization and attention-placebo groups as compared to insight and control groups, although the latter two groups improved sufficiently from FU_1 to FU_2 that individual between-group comparisons alone were no longer significant. By the two-year follow-up, the desensitization group had continued to show increased Social Extroversion scores to the point that the Pre—FU_2 increase in extroversion was significantly greater than that of the other three groups ($t = 2.06$, $df = 53$, $p < .05$). No other mean group comparisons approached significance from pretreatment to FU_2.

Although self-ratings of improvement by treated Ss had previously failed to discriminate between groups, direct ratings of perceived improvement were still included at FU_2 because of widespread usage in other follow-up studies. As before, in sharp contrast to the specific measures of anxiety reduction, no significant differences were found among groups on mean self-ratings of improvement. The Ss in all three treatment groups gave mean ratings ranging from "somewhat improved" to "much improved" for both specific reduction of performance anxiety and improvement in other areas.

INDIVIDUAL S IMPROVEMENT FROM PRETREATMENT TO FU_2

Since clinical workers are more often concerned with percentage improvement in individual cases than with mean group differences, and since negative treatment effects or symptom substitution would be more easily identified from data on individuals, all test data were further evaluated on the basis of individually significant Pre—FU_2 change scores. An individual case was classified as "significantly improved" on each scale if the Pre—FU_2 reduction in anxiety score or increase in extroversion score exceeded 1.96 times the standard error of measurement for the instrument (two-tailed .05 level, as previously determined from a population of 523, Paul, 1966). Likewise, an individual case was classified as "significantly worse" on each scale if a Pre—FU_2 increase in anxiety score or decrease in extroversion score exceeded 1.96 times the standard error of measurement for the instrument.

Overall Pre–FU$_2$ improvement rates presented in Table 3 again disclosed significant differences between groups not only for focal treatment effects from the Speech Composite, but for all other comparisons as well. Particularly striking was the finding that not a single case retained at FU$_2$ in any group showed a significant increase in performance anxiety. Additionally, the percentage improvement of groups was remarkably consistent with a similar classification made earlier on the basis of pre- to posttreatment change from stress-condition data. By comparing the percentage of improved Ss in the attention-placebo group with untreated controls, it was possible to estimate the percentage of Ss responding favorably to merely undergoing treatment, over and above the base-rate improvement from extratreatment experiences throughout the 2.5-year period—28%. Similarly, by comparing the percentage of Ss improved under attention-placebo with those improved under insight-oriented

TABLE 3

PERCENTAGE OF CASES SHOWING SIGNIFICANT CHANGE FROM PRETREATMENT TO TWO-YEAR FOLLOW-UP

Treatment	Significantly Improved	No Change	Significantly Worse
Focal Treatment (Speech Composite)[a]			
Desensitization	85%	15%	——
Insight	50%	50%	——
Attention-Placebo	50%	50%	——
Control	22%	78%	——
All Other Comparisons (Six Scales)[b]			
Desensitization	36%	64%	——
Insight	25%	71%	4%
Attention-Placebo	25%	70%	5%
Control	18%	74%	8%

Note.—$N = 13$, 12, 14, and 18, respectively, for desensitization, insight, attention-placebo, and control. Classifications derived by two-tailed .05 cut-offs on each individual change score (see text).
[a] $\chi^2 = 11.64$, $p < .01$.
[b] $\chi^2 = 8.11$, $p < .05$.

psychotherapy and systematic desensitization, it was possible to estimate the percentage of additional Ss receiving lasting benefit from either the achievement of "insight" or "emotional re-education," over and above the nonspecific effects of undergoing treatment. For Ss receiving systematic desensitization, these comparisons revealed an additional lasting improvement of 35% for focal effects and 11% for generalized effects over that improvement expected from attention placebo. Again, no differences were found between the effects achieved by insight-oriented psychotherapy and attention-placebo treatment, although both produced better improvement rates than untreated controls. The "other comparisons" in Table 3 also favored a generalization interpretation of the effects of desensitization for changes found in areas which were not the specific focus of treatment, without the slightest suggestion of symptom substitution. Symptom substitution would be reflected in higher percentages in the "significantly worse" category for both attention-placebo and desensitization groups.

COMPARATIVE RELAPSE AND SYMPTOM SUBSTITUTION

OVER THE FOLLOW-UP PERIOD

While overall Pre–FU_2 evaluations gave no suggestive evidence to support the symptom-substitution hypothesis, nor any evidence that more Ss treated by desensitization and attention-placebo programs became significantly worse in any area, no information on relapse can be obtained from Pre–FU_2 comparisons. Rather, cases of relapse must be identified as those cases showing a significant increase in anxiety as reflected on the Speech Composite from FU_1 to FU_2. Similarly, if a symptom-substitution process were operating, a higher percentage of change in the "worse" direction should be obtained from FU_1 to FU_2 on nonfocal scales for desensitization and attention-placebo Ss who maintained improvement on the Speech Composite. As noted above, the data presented in Figure 1 show no evidence of relapse or symptom substitution for the groups as a whole from FU_1 to FU_2.

Before concluding that the symptom-substitution effects and differential relapse predicted by the disease model had not occurred, a more sensitive analysis was made of the individual data from FU_1 to FU_2. A case was classified as significantly worse on each scale if from FU_1 to FU_2 an increase in anxiety on the Speech Composite (relapse) or other anxiety score (symptom substitution) or a decrease in extroversion score (symptom substitution) exceeded 1.65 times the standard error of measurement for the instrument (one-tailed .05 level cut-offs). The percentage of Ss maintaining status versus the percentage "getting worse" from FU_1 to FU_2 for each group is presented in Table 4. No significant differences between groups were found on any measure. In fact, as the figures for the Speech Composite demonstrate, there was not a single case which could be considered a relapse in any of the retained Ss from the three treatment groups. Additionally, the percentage of scores in the significantly worse direction, which would reveal symptom substitution, did not differ from the .05 level for any group. If Ss who received additional treatment during the follow-up period were to be included as cases of relapse, the figures would be even less in favor of the predictions based on the disease model, with 93% maintaining status for both desensitization and attention-placebo groups, as compared to 80% for insight and less than 40% for controls.

TABLE 4

PERCENTAGE OF CASES SHOWING RELAPSE OR SYMPTOM SUBSTITUTION FROM SIX-WEEK FOLLOW-UP TO TWO-YEAR FOLLOW-UP

Treatment	Maintained FU_1 Status	Significantly Worse
Focal Treatment (Speech Composite)		
Desensitization	100%	—
Insight	100%	—
Attention-Placebo	100%	—
Control	89%	11%[a]
All Other Comparisons (Six Scales)		
Desensitization	97%	3%[b]
Insight	96%	4%[b]
Attention-Placebo	94%	6%[b]
Control	93%	7%[b]

Note.—$N = 13$, 12, 14, and 18, respectively, for desensitization, insight, attention-placebo, and controls. Classifications derived by one-tailed .05 cut-offs on each individual change score (see text).
[a] "Relapse."
[b] "Symptom substitution."

The frequency data obtained from the 13-item behavioral questionnaire specifically constructed to reveal hypothesized symptom-substitution effects also failed to provide any support for the symptom-substitution hypothesis. Kruskal-Wallis one-way analyses of variance by ranks over the four groups on each item produced an $H < 3.66$ (p> .30) on all items but one. On that item—No. 9, frequency of social exchange—the value of H approached the .10 level of significance and was in favor of the desensitization group. In fact, a significant coefficient of concordance $(W = .47, p < .01)$ over all items was obtained, with the desensitization Ss receiving an equal mean rank with the insight Ss, both in the direction opposite to symptom-substitution effects. Similarly, Kruskal-Wallis analyses over the four groups for frequencies of each of the five areas of stress reported over the follow-up period failed to reveal significant differences between groups (all $H < 3.66, p > .30$; except C, "Change in family structure," where $H = 5.08, p < .20$). Thus while the occurrence of stress might be considered as evidence of symptom substitution or an external influence on relapse (Stone, et al., 1961), these questions need not be of concern in the present study, since no differences in the reported occurrence of stress approached significance between groups.

INTERRELATIONSHIPS AMONG VARIABLES

Since the earlier study assessed specific improvement through several different instruments, persons, and situations in addition to the instruments on which FU_2 data were obtained, information relating to both predictive and construct validity of improvement may be gained through the correlation of previous improvement scores with those obtained at FU_2. For systematic agreement across different instruments, positive correlations would be expected between all change scores for each measure of performance anxiety. FU_1 improvement ratings of Ss and therapists should be positively correlated with Ss' ratings at FU_2. Further, FU_1 ratings of improvement should be negatively correlated with $Pre-FU_2$ performance-anxiety change scores. Opposite relationships would be expected for therapist posttreatment ratings of prognosis, since these scales were reversed.

Table 5 presents the correlations of pre-to posttreatment stress-condition change scores, therapist posttreatment ratings, and FU_1 ratings of treated Ss with FU_2 ratings of treated Ss and $Pre-FU_2$ change on the Speech Composite and all other scales of the test battery. Specific FU_2 improvement data (Ss' ratings, $Pre-FU_2$ Speech Composite) were significantly correlated in the expected direction, with all indicants of specific improvement at posttreatment and FU_1, except for the relationship between the Physiological Composite and the Speech Composite. Previous analyses had also failed to find significant relationships between physiological and self-report data, although physiological change was significantly correlated with observable manifestations of anxiety under stress conditions as assessed by the behavioral checklist.

Of the correlations presented in Table 5, the relationship of the behavioral checklist with $Pre-FU_2$ assessments is of a special importance. The behavioral checklist was the most objective measure of all instruments used and was highly reliable (interrater reliability $= .96$). Additionally, checklist data were obtained in a situation where target behaviors were most likely to occur, and pre-to posttreatment checklist change was consistently related to all other prior indicants of specific anxiety reduction. The correlation of .61 between pre- to posttreatment change on the behavior checklist with $Pre-FU_2$ change on the Speech Composite is strong evidence for both the construct validity of focal improvement at FU_2 and for the predictive validity of observable posttreatment improvement.

Table 5 also reveals discriminative relationships in the correlations of therapist and subject ratings with $Pre-FU_2$ improvement. Therapist ratings of specific improvement and prognosis were significantly correlated with $Pre-FU_2$ Speech Composite change and with FU_2 ratings of improvement by treated Ss. Conversely, therapists' ratings of general improvement and prognosis were not significantly related to specific improvement, although "other prognosis" was related to $Pre-FU_2$ change in extroversion. Likewise, Ss' ratings at FU_1 were significantly related to

Pre–FU$_2$ change in a discriminative way, although "method factors" predominate in improvement ratings of Ss as they had earlier.

TABLE 5

CORRELATION OF PRIOR IMPROVEMENT SCORES WITH ALL CHANGE SCORES FROM PRETREATMENT TO TWO-YEAR FOLLOW-UP

Prior Improvement Data	Subject FU$_2$ Rating of Improvement		Pre–FU$_2$ Change						
	Specific	Other	Speech Composite	S-R Interview	S-R Exam	S-R Contest	IPAT Anxiety	Emotionality	Extroversion
Pre- to posttreatment stress-condition change									
Physiological composite	—.33*	—.31*	.11	.13	.32*	.22	.46a	.38a	—.09
Behavioral checklist....	—.34*	—.13	.61a	.07	.20	.17	.20	.15	—.25*
Anxiety differential....	—.33*	—.27*	.44a	.28*	.22	.26*	.46a	.23	—.34*
Standardized therapist posttreatment rating									
Specific improvement..	.30*	.15	—.51a	—.18	—.24	—.31*	—.38a	.04	.12
Other improvement....	.02	.03	.01	.07	.00	.02	.08	—.10	—.24
Specific prognosis......	—.35*	—.31*	.50a	.13	.30*	.11	.24	.02	—.17
Other prognosis	—.19	—.19	.25	.05	.01	—.11	.16	—.09	—.32
Subject FU$_1$ rating									
Specific improvement..	.68a	.47a	—.56a	—.04	—.30*	—.19	—.18	.03	.34*
Other improvement....	.56a	.65a	—.24	—.15	—.03	—.19	—.11	.08	.20

Note.—$N = 44$ for stress condition; $N = 39$ for ratings.
* $p < .05$.
a $p < .01$.

The correlation of specific improvement data from the earlier time periods with Pre–FU$_2$ change on the scales of the test battery which were not directed towards focal treatment effects also showed several significant relationships. Inspection of the prime correlations among all variables presented in Table 5 found the source of covariation in every instance to result primarily from increased relationships at posttreatment and FU$_2$, with several of the prime correlations also reaching the .01 level of significance. The significant correlations presented in Table 5 may be interpreted as evidence for the stability of improvement and generalization effects, rather than as a result of relationships existing before treatment began. Further, when the specific posttreatment and FU$_1$ improvement variables from Table 5 were correlated with FU$_1$–FU$_2$ change for test battery scales, several low, but significant, coefficients were obtained $(Mdn|r| = .31)$, all of which indicated that those Ss who showed greatest reduction in performance anxiety at posttreatment and FU$_1$ also showed greatest specific and generalized additional improvement over the period between FU$_1$ and FU$_2$. Since no significant correlations were obtained between pretreatment scores on the three general scales and change on the specific anxiety scales from Pre–FU$_1$, FU$_1$–FU$_2$, or Pre–FU$_2$, the slight additional improvement from FU$_1$ to FU$_2$ may be interpreted as the continuing effects of changes taking place during the treatment period, rather than as a function of pretreatment personality dimensions.

Further information concerning the stability of scores for each scale of the test battery over treatment and follow-up periods may be seen in the test-retest correlations from Pre–FU$_1$, Pre–FU$_2$, and FU$_1$–FU$_2$ (Table 6). The greater stability of Speech Composite scores from FU$_1$ to FU$_2$, as compared to Pre–FU$_1$ and Pre–FU$_2$ relationships, again indicated the influence of treatment effects obtaining after pretreatment assessment, with Ss holding relative positions in a reliable manner over the two years following FU$_1$. However, it appears that relatively greater position changes in Extroversion and IPAT Anxiety occurred over the follow-up period than over the treatment period.

Intercorrelations of FU$_2$ scores for all scales of the test battery revealed essentially the same relationships as those reported earlier for FU$_1$ scores. Significant intercorrelations were obtained among all scales ($Mdn\ r = .51$), except Extroversion which was significantly related only to the Speech Composite ($r = -.27, p < .05$). While the combined relationships reported above and in the earlier study support the assumption that FU$_2$ measures were internally consistent, the reliability of the Pre–FU$_2$ change for the primary measure can be directly estimated. The Pre–FU$_2$ changes for PRCS and S-R Speech (the scales which were converted to T scores and summed to obtain the Speech Composite) correlated .64, from which the reliability of the Speech Composite change can be estimated (by Spearman-Brown formula) at .78.

TABLE 6

INTERCORRELATIONS OF EACH TEST BATTERY SCALE OVER THE THREE TESTING PERIODS
FOR SUBJECTS RETAINED AT FU$_2$

Scale	Stability Coefficient[a]		
	Pre–FU$_1$	Pre–FU$_2$	FU$_1$–FU$_2$
Speech Composite	.27	.29	.68
S-R Interview	.57	.53	.63
S-R Examination	.50	.52	.51
S-R Contest	.47	.43	.64
IPAT Anxiety	.76	.44	.63
Emotionality	.80	.64	.72
Extroversion	.82	.59	.71

Note.—$N = 57$; $p = .05$, $r = .22$; $p = .01$, $r = .31$.
a Pearson r's.

Although no differences between groups were found for the 13 items of the behavioral questionnaire, indirect support for the validity of the items was obtained through correlational analyses. Moderate but significant correlations were found among the items, which clustered in the following way: Nos. 1, 2, and 3, ($Mdn\ r = .53$); Nos. 6, 9, and 10 ($Mdn\ r = .43$); Nos. 3, 5, 8, 11, 12, 13 ($Mdn\ r = .35$). Only No. 7 was unrelated to other items. Numerous significant correlations ($Mdn|r| = .32$) were found between the items of the second and third clusters and all scales of the FU$_2$ test battery, indicating that Ss obtaining lower anxiety scores and higher extroversion scores also tended to report having more close friends, belonging to more organizations, attending more social events, entertaining more, "going out" more, and more frequent group discussions and public appearances. Similarly, of the five areas of stress on which frequency data were obtained, all but one (change in family structure) were significantly intercorrelated $(Mdn \ r = .35)$. With one exception, no significant correlations were found between reported stress frequencies and items of the behavioral questionnaire, nor between either FU_1–FU_2 or Pre–FU_2 change for any scale of the test battery and stress frequencies. The exception was a significant relationship between the reported frequency of occurrence of change in family structure and FU_1–FU_2 change in extroversion $(r = -.42, \ p < .01)$; that is, those Ss increasing in extroversion from FU_1 to FU_2 tended to report less change in family structure over the same time period.

One last check on the symptom-substitution hypothesis was carried out by correlating Pre–FU_2 change on the Speech Composite with all other data. Several significant correlations were obtained between Pre–FU_2 Speech Composite change and items from the behavioral questionnaire, but all were in the opposite direction predicted by the disease model and favored a generalization interpretation. Intercorrelations of Pre–FU_2 change scores among all seven scales of the test battery revealed positive correlations between change on the Speech Composite and change on all other anxiety scales $(Mdn \ r = .34)$ and a negative correlation with change in Extroversion $(r = -.30)$. Similar relationships were found among the other scales, with positive correlations among all anxiety and emotionality change scores and negative correlations between the latter and change in Extroversion. Of the 15 correlations, 10 achieved statistical significance $(Mdn \ |r| = .29)$.

DISCUSSION

In general, the combined findings from individual and group data as well as correlational analyses showed the relative gains in focal treatment effects found earlier to be maintained over the two-year follow-up period. Some additional relative improvement in related areas was found for Ss treated by systematic desensitization and, to a lesser extent, for those treated by attention placebo. Like the findings at six-week follow-up, in no instance were the long-term effects achieved through insight-oriented psychotherapy significantly different from the effects achieved with attention-placebo treatment, although both groups showed significantly greater treatment effects than untreated controls. As a group, the systematic desensitization Ss continued to show greater positive treatment effects than any other group, with evidence of additional generalization, and no evidence even suggestive of symptom substitution. In fact, the comparative findings at two-year follow-up are so similar to the findings at post-treatment and six-week follow-up that the detailed discussion of results in relation to previous research, theoretical hypotheses concerning factors and effects within treatments, and methodological implications for research and clinical practice which were presented earlier (Paul, 1966, pp. 71–99) require no modification and need not be reiterated here.

The finding that effects of systematic desensitization are maintained over the follow-up period with evidence of additional improvement through generalization is consistent with the results of the only other controlled follow-up of systematic desensitization therapy (Lang & Lazovik, 1963) and with the suggestive findings from follow-up reports of accumulated case studies (Lazarus, 1963; Wolpe, 1961). Although all previous long-term follow-up studies have suffered considerably from the methodological problems described at the beginning of this report, the general trend of results for psychological treatment of noninstitution-alized adults has been for treatment effects to be maintained or slightly improved over the follow-up period (Stone et al., 1961). Consistent with this trend, the present investigation found no relapse for any of the retained treated Ss, no matter what treatment they had received.

While these findings were somewhat surprising for systematic desensi-tization and insight-oriented psychotherapy, the stability of improvement resulting only from the non-specific effects of attention-placebo treatment was almost completely unexpected. This was especially true since pre-vious studies of placebo responsiveness had not only found relapse on three–six-month follow-up (Gliedman, Nash, Imber, Stone, & Frank, 1958), but further, that Ss who improved most at the time of their initial placebo experience were more likely to relapse than those who improved least (Frank, Nash, Stone, & Imber, 1963). The difference between the latter effects of pure placebo (inert medication) and lasting effects of the attention-placebo treatment of the present investigation may lie in changes in attitudes and expectancies resulting from the interpersonal relationship with the therapist functioning as a "generalized reinforcer" (Krasner, 1955). Stone et al. (1961) point out that the long-term success of any form of treatment depends in large part on the extent to which changes that are accomplished are supported by the client's subsequent life experiences. This fact might be extended to suggest that no matter how change is brought about, it is likely to be maintained in a supportive environment which reinforces resulting behavior, and it is not likely to be maintained if the resulting behavior is not reinforced or if new aversive consequences or extreme stress reinstitute negative emotional responses. While systematic desensitization produced a more direct modification of the emotional reactions associated with interpersonal performance situations, resulting in significantly higher improvement rates, the emergent behaviors of Ss experiencing anxiety reduction from all three treatments were likely to be regarded as socially appropriate and were likely to be rewarded, independently of the manner in which change initially came about.

The usual concern with "spontaneous remission" rates from other populations need not be considered in this investigation, since an untreated control group from the same population was assessed on the same instruments as were the treatment groups. Even though results were favorably biased towards the controls, due to differential loss of Ss, superior long-term effects for all treatment groups were still obtained. Additionally, the 22% "improved" without treatment at the two-year follow-up for a favorably biased untreated subgroup seriously questions the "two-thirds spontaneous remission" rate so frequently quoted (e.g., Eysenck, 1966). Of course, Lesse (1964) notes:

> The concept of anything that is labeled as "spontaneous" must be considered in the light of the fact that it is spontaneous only because we do not understand the causes for the change or are at the present time unable to measure various factors that influence it. In all probability, therefore, so-called spontaneous remissions are probably not spontaneous at all [p. 111].

There is no reason to believe that factors other than the same environmental influences which maintained improvement for treated Ss were involved in the improvement and stability of untreated controls. In fact, processes similar to desensitization may take place through environmental interaction in the absence of formal treatment (Stevenson, 1961), and considerable nonspecific therapy may be expected without contacting a socially designated psychological helper (Goldstein, 1960).

While this investigation was able to overcome methodological difficulties more adequately than previous attempts, it still suffered from difficulties inherent in the nature of follow-up studies. The tight control procedures maintained during the earlier outcome study were not possible once Ss were "turned loose" after the six-week follow-up. When control is not possible, attempts at assessment are a second-best choice. Although Ss were asked to indicate whether or not treatment had been received during the follow-up period, only 5 indicated that they had, when a total of 17 were actually identified as having received treatment through a survey of clinics and therapists. Considering the high return rate for this investigation, the problem of Ss not reporting additional treatment in other studies could be astronomical. Even though a higher return rate was obtained than in previous follow-up studies, total assessment of cause-effect relationships for treatment groups was not possible due to the necessity of *S* exclusion. Additionally, the untreated controls were known to be a favorably biased subgroup which may have under- estimated treatment effects and overestimated (un)spontaneous remis- sion. Although the assessment instruments used possessed adequate reli- ability and validity for determining effects, the mobility of the sample precluded use of the instrument which was known to provide the most objective evaluation (i.e., the behavioral checklist).

These inherent difficulties have led some investigators to question the value of long-term follow-ups. May et al. (1965) point out:

> . . . Formal, controlled studies are doomed to depreciate progressively with the passage of time from the end of the controlled treatment period with much of their discriminating power being eroded by contamination. . . . It is inevitable that the longer the follow-up, the more all treatments approximate the same end result [p. 762].

On the basis of their own research, Stone et al. (1961) state further that, "evaluation of different forms of psychotherapy should be primarily in terms of their immediate results [p. 420]." In essential agreement, the stability of treatment effects over the two-year follow-up period in the present study, combined with the failure to find a single case which could be considered evidence of relapse or symptom substitution for any treated *S*, suggests that the short-term follow-up provided adequate evaluation of comparative treatment effects. Thus, for the evaluation of psychological treatment with noninstitutionalized adults, more scientifically useful information is likely to be obtained if future efforts are directed towards short-term follow-ups, in which total sample assessment of treated *S*s may be obtained, rather than longer follow-ups, which suffer from differential attrition and the effects of uncontrolled environmental influences. The number and timing of follow-ups should be determined by the nature of the population and problem, rather than preconceived theoretical notions (Paul, in press).

However, the methodological difficulties of follow-up studies should not overshadow the major findings of the present investigation. Namely, that modified systematic desensitization produced significant and lasting reductions in maladaptive anxiety, not only on an absolute level, but also in comparison with other treatment and control groups. None of the effects predicted on the basis of the traditional disease-analogy model were forthcoming, while considerable evidence was found for a learning model. Results as consistent as these are rare in the psychotherapy litera- ture and require not only replication, but also an extension of evalua- tions across differing populations of clients, therapists, and problems, as well as parametric investigations of the mechanics involved.

REFERENCES

BENDIG, A. W. Pittsburgh scale of social extroversion-introversion and emotionality. *Journal of Psychology*, 1962, 53, 199–210.

BERLE, B. B., PINSKY, R. H., WOLF, S., & WOLFF, H. E. Appraisal of the results of treatment of stress disorders. *Research Publications Association for Research in Nervous and Mental Disease*, 1953, 31, 167–77.

BOOKBINDER, L. J. Follow-up versus discharge status of psychiatric inpatients. *Journal of Clinical Psychology*, 1962, 18, 501–03.

BRACELAND, F. J. (ed.) Special section: Follow-up studies. *American Journal of Psychiatry*, 1966, 122, 1088–1124.

CATTELL, R. B. *The IPAT Anxiety Scale.* Champaign, Ill.: Institute for Personality and Ability Testing, 1957.

COOPER, J. E., GELDER, M. G., & MARKS, I. M. Results of behavior therapy in 77 psychiatric patients. *British Medical Journal*, 1965, 1, 1222–25.

COWEN, E. L., & COMBS, A. W. Follow-up study of 32 cases treated by nondirective psychotherapy. *Journal of Abnormal and Social Psychology*, 1950, 45, 232–58.

ENDLER, N. S., HUNT, J. McV., & ROSENSTEIN, A. J. An S-R inventory of anxiousness. *Psychological Monographs*, 1962, 76(17, Whole No. 536).

EYSENCK, H. J. *The effects of psychotherapy.* New York: International Science Press, 1966.

FAIRWEATHER, G. W., & SIMON, R. A further follow-up of psychotherapeutic programs. *Journal of Consulting Psychology*, 1963, 27, 186.

FENICHEL, O. *The psychoanalytic theory of neuroses.* New York: W. W. Norton & Co., Inc., 1945.

FISKE, D. W., & GOODMAN, G. The posttherapy period. *Journal of Abnormal Psychology*, 1965, 70, 169–79.

FRANK, J. D., NASH, E. H., STONE, A. R., & IMBER, S. D. Immediate and long-term symptomatic course of psychiatric outpatients. *American Journal of Psychiatry*, 1963, 120, 429–39.

GLIEDMAN, L. H., NASH, E. H., IMBER, S. D., STONE, A. R., & FRANK, J. D. Reduction of symptoms by pharmacologically inert substances and short-term psychotherapy. *A.M.A. Archives of Neurology and Psychiatry*, 1958, 79, 345–51.

GOLDSTEIN, A. P. Patient's expectancies and non-specific therapy as a basis for (un)spontaneous remission. *Journal of Clinical Psychology*, 1960, 16, 399–403.

HENDRICK, I. *Facts and theories of psychoanalysis.* New York: Alfred A. Knopf, Inc., 1958.

HUSEK, T. R., & ALEXANDER, S. The effectiveness of the Anxiety Differential in examination situations. *Educational and Psychological Measurement*, 1963, 23, 309–18.

KOGAN, L. S., HUNT, J. McV., & BARTELME, P. *A follow-up study of the results of social casework.* New York: Family Service Association of America, 1953.

KRASNER, L. The use of generalized reinforcers in psychotherapy research. *Psychological Reports*, 1955, 1, 19–25.

LANG, P. J., & LAZOVIK, A. D. Experimental desensitization of a phobia. *Journal of Abnormal and Social Psychology*, 1963, 66, 519–25.

LAZARUS, A. A. The results of behaviour therapy in 126 cases of severe neuroses.

Behaviour Research and Therapy, 1963, 1, 69–79.

LESSE, S. Placebo reactions and spontaneous rhythms: Their effects on the results of psychotherapy. *American Journal of Psychotherapy*, 1964, 18(Monogr. Suppl. No. 1), 99–115.

MAY, P. R. A., TUMA, A. H., & KRAUDE, W. Community follow-up of treatment of schizophrenia—issues and problems. *American Journal of Orthopsychiatry*, 1965, 35, 754–63.

McNAIR, D. M., LORR, M., YOUNG, H. H., ROTH, I., & BOYD, R. W. A three-year follow-up of psychotherapy patients. *Journal of Clinical Psychology*, 1964, 20, 258–63.

PAUL, G. L. *Insight vs. desensitization in psychotherapy: An experiment in anxiety reduction.* Stanford: Stanford University Press, 1966.

PAUL, G. L. Behavior modification research: Design and tactics. In C. M. Franks (ed.), *Assessment and status of the behavioral therapies and related developments.* New York: McGraw-Hill Book Company.

PAUL, G. L., & SHANNON, D. T. Treatment of anxiety through systematic desensitization in therapy groups. *Journal of Abnormal Psychology*, 1966, 71, 124–35.

ROGERS, C. R., & DYMOND, R. F. (eds.) *Pyschotherapy and personality change.* Chicago: University of Chicago Press, 1954.

SAGER, C. J., RIESS, B. F., & GUNDLACH, R. Follow-up study of the results of extramural analytic psychotherapy. *American Journal of Psychotherapy*, 1964, 18(Monogr. Suppl. No. 1), 161–73.

SARGENT, H. D. Methodological problems of follow-up studies in psychotherapy research. *American Journal of Psychotherapy*, 1960, 30, 495–506.

SCHMIDT, E., CASTELL, D., & BROWN, P. A retrospective study of 42 cases of behavior therapy. *Behaviour Research and Therapy*, 1965, 3, 9–19.

SINETT, E. R., STIMPUT, W. E., & STRAIGHT, E. A five-year follow-up study of psychiatric patients. *American Journal of Orthopsychiatry*, 1965, 35, 573–80.

STEVENSON, I. Processes of "spontaneous" recovery from the psychoneuroses. *American Journal of Psychiatry*, 1961, 117, 1057–64.

STONE, A. R., FRANK, J. D., NASH, E. H., & IMBER, S. D. An intensive five-year follow-up study of treated psychiatric outpatients. *Journal of Nervous and Mental Disease*, 1961, 133, 410–22.

ULLMANN, L. P., & KRASNER, L. (eds.) *Case studies in behavior modification.* New York: Holt, Rinehart & Winston, Inc., 1965.

WOLPE, J. The systematic desensitization treatment of neuroses. *Journal of Nervous and Mental Disease*, 1961, 132, 189–203.

OTTO POLLAK

6 *Worker Assignment in Casework with Marriage Partners**

Family Service of Philadelphia initiated in 1956 a research program intended to adapt the method of scientific inquiry to questions of practice which concerned the staff in the course of their daily operations. The first project selected by the staff, in cooperation with the administration and the writer, was a study of criteria for assigning cases in which two or more family members are seen. The primary question was whether one or two workers should be assigned in cases in which both marital partners are involved in treatment.

Even the first attempts to plan the research design revealed theoretical implications.[1] It became immediately apparent that the question of assigning one or two caseworkers to a family in which more than one family member was seen became relevant only when caseworkers were ready to return to a family focus not only in diagnostic orientation but also in therapeutic intervention. The research project was carried out, therefore, in the context of the concern with family diagnosis and family therapy that has been characteristic of casework and psychiatry in the last decade.[2]

Our specific question was studied, not through logical deductions or clinical analysis, but through statistical investigation of differences in the outcome of two methods of worker assignment applied, not on the basis of therapeutic conviction, but on the basis of randomization. This decision was not meant to indicate that we had no therapeutic preferences, but to state unequivocally that the research project was designed to test the validity of our preferences instead of defending or propagating them.

The project was designed to protect clients from our biases rather than to protect us from disappointment. Our research proved the wisdom of that decision, for our basic hypothesis and conviction, that family members needing a unifying experience would benefit from having one caseworker rather than two, proved to be diametrically opposed to the find-

---

* Reprinted from the *Social Service Review*, Vol. XXXVII, No. 1 (March, 1963), pp. 41–53, by permission of the University of Chicago Press and the author.

[1] Mary E. Macdonald, "Compatibility of Theory and Method: An Analysis of Six Studies," in *Use of Judgments as Data in Social Work Research*, ed. Ann W. Shyne (New York: National Association of Social Workers, 1959), p. 22.

[2] See Appendix II for references on family diagnosis.

ings. Our data suggest very strongly that even two marriage partners who need to come closer to one another are better served if each spouse has a caseworker of his own. Family therapy with marriage partners, in the practice pattern of Family Service of Philadelphia, does not seem to be enhanced by the assignment of one caseworker to both marriage partners. The methods of casework treatment offered to the clients are, by and large, supportive treatment and clarification. Insight therapy is rarely used. When clarification is used, it is directed to helping the spouses become aware of their patterns of behavior which cause the difficulties in the marriage relationship and to modify these patterns when possible. The practice of the agency follows the classical pattern of having each husband and wife seen in individual interviews. Joint interviews are not routinely arranged. If held, they are usually scheduled as part of the study period in intake. Workers are free, however, to use joint interviews more frequently.

It should be emphasized that these findings go against the earlier convictions of the writer, the director of casework, and the district directors. That effectiveness statistics thus proved us incorrect is an important, albeit painful, result. The only comfort left is the possibility that our results are applicable only to this agency and that different treatment methods in different settings may still lend support to our previous theoretical conviction.

The second major theoretical implication of the research was the discovery that we had to start our work with a clarification and elaboration of treatment goals for family casework. In a profession in which many members believe that a non-judgmental attitude toward the person of the client requires a non-judgmental attitude toward his future, this was a difficult step, but apparently a much-needed one. We therefore developed a model of healthy family relationships, in which we tried to outline in detail what we considered to be healthy family relationships between spouses, between parents and children, and between siblings and thus the goals of casework treatment when such relationships seemed to be disturbed. This model, which constituted our first report on the project,[3] met with a response that convinced us that the requirement of thinking out a research design can confront one with practice needs and requirements for theory-building which, though relevant to the profession, are often blurred under the pressure of daily work. It seems that only when focused by the uncompromising demands of designing an evaluative study does theory-building receive the attention that it merits.

---

[3] Otto Pollak, with an appendix by Ralph Ormsby, "Design of a Model of Healthy Family Relationships as a Basis for Evaluative Research," *Social Service Review*, XXXI (December, 1957), 369–76.

The need for theoretical clarification was also apparent when writing instructions to judges who were to evaluate family relationship improvement. We had to gain clarity about the dimensions of improvement or deterioration which we wanted to have assessed. In long discussions we finally settled on "communication" and "cooperation" as the two dimensions to be observed. To visualize degrees of improvement required further elaboration and classification of the phenomena of interaction which the two concepts of communication and cooperation covered.

METHODOLOGY

The problem.—The question of whether a case in which more than one family member is to be seen in therapeutic contacts should be assigned to one or to more than one caseworker obviously has to be answered in terms of an underlying principle. Otherwise there is no protection against its being answered with variations, according to the untested preference of a district director who makes the assignment or in accordance with the limitation created by the lack of staff. Such a principle may be developed in terms of deductive thinking or in terms of generalizations derived from clinical experience. In either case, it should be tested.

The basic hypothesis.—It was our basic hypothesis that members of a family who require a unifying experience will benefit from being seen by the same caseworker and that members of a family who require a separating experience will benefit from being seen by different caseworkers. It was, in turn, necessary to be clear about what family relationships in the concrete instance required unification and what family relationships required separation. We expected that in cases of family disturbances we were likely to encounter individuals whose personality expressions separated them from one another, against or beyond normal developmental tendencies, or persons who were entrapped in such closeness that they were prevented from establishing their own identities within the family relationship. The former we expected to encounter mostly in cases in which the spouses were too immature to shift from seeking human resource quality in parents or friends to seeking it in the marriage partner. The latter, on the other hand, we expected to find in situations in which parents could not permit their children to achieve independence commensurate with their age, or in which children were not ready to avail themselves of appropriate opportunities for seeking human resources other than their parents. We were prepared, however, to encounter also family relationship disturbances of a reverse character. Marriage partners might monopolize one another to the degree of depriving themselves of contact with other people altogether, or children might be so separated from their parents as to find no resource quality in them at all.

Integration of this view of family relationship disturbances in terms of "relationship tendency reversals" or "relationship tendency exaggerations" with our traditional understanding of personality development[4] suggested to us that current conditions requiring unification within the family might be caused by the persistence of former unresolved relationships. An unresolved oedipal attachment of a spouse might, for example, prevent him from achieving unity with his marriage partner; or unresolved sibling rivalry might prevent a mother from establishing closeness with her child. For this reason, we expected to find elements of undue psychological closeness associated with undue psychological separateness. We foresaw that such a combination might present difficulties in deciding whether two individuals needed a separating or a unifying experience. Hence we emphasized in our instructions to staff that, for our purposes, a diagnosis of the nature of a family relationship was concerned only with unity or separateness of the persons whom we had accepted for regular therapeutic contact. The unresolved psychological attachments of these persons to other family members, however, were recognized as important for an understanding of their psychological make-up and for the clarification of the type of casework treatment appropriate to help them.

Design.—Initially we considered using matched pairs of closed cases that met our criteria but had been assigned to one or two workers. If we had found sufficient numbers of such pairs of cases and had been able to compare the degree of family relationship improvement in them, we might have been able to forget about the problem of bias resulting from the very fact that a study was being made.[5] In the end, however, we decided against this method because after a great investment in record-reading we might have been left with an insufficient number of cases in one or the other category.

We decided, therefore, to establish our experimental and control groups from current cases on the basis of randomization.[6] The first step was to divide all marital and parent-child problem cases in which two family members needed to be seen in continued casework treatment into two groups, as follows: (1) those that required a unifying experience and, therefore, according to our hypothesis, needed a one-worker assignment; and (2) those that needed a separating experience and, therefore, accord-

---

4 Otto Pollak, *Integrating Sociological and Psychoanalytic Concepts* (New York: Russell Sage Foundation, 1956), pp. 47, 86, 87, 152.

5 Joseph W. Eaton, "Science, 'Art,' and Uncertainty in Social Work," *Social Work,* III (July, 1958), 9.

6 In making this decision, we had the benefit of advice and support from Margaret Blenkner, to whom we express our warm gratitude.

ing to our hypothesis, required a two-worker assignment. Within each of these two groups we planned to establish, by randomization, two sub-groups—an experimental group, in which the assignment was made according to our hypothesis, and the control group, in which assignment was made contrary to our hypothesis. The original design thus foresaw four groups, two testing the effect of one- and two-worker assignment upon family relationships requiring unification, and two groups testing the effect of one- and two-worker assignment upon family relationships requiring a separating experience. We aimed at 30 cases in each group.

It soon became apparent that very few of the marital situations which came to our agency seemed to require a separating experience. Two months after the start of sample collection, 30 cases requiring a unifying experience had been selected, but only four cases requiring a separating experience. Apparently the married couples seeking help from the agency suffered from remoteness more than from being tied too closely together, a phenomenon in harmony with the increasing frequency of appearance of character disorders in the caseloads of family agencies. Second, many of the parent-child problem cases coming to the agency seemed to require referral to other service sources, such as child-guidance clinics. We would have been delayed beyond all reason if we had insisted on establishing a universe of sixty cases requiring help with separating experiences. Hence, we restricted our design, after eight months, to an investigation of the hypothesis that the marriage partners whose relationships suffered from undue remoteness would benefit more from the experience of having one worker than from having two workers.

Therapeutic conviction versus randomization.—Although the staff accepted the statistical test of our hypothesis as a legitimate form of inquiry within the professional ethics of social work, we remained aware that, in individual cases, therapeutic conviction about the more appropriate worker assignment might produce considerable conflict for the assigning person. We therefore removed temptation to influence case assignment by centralizing the randomization procedure in the central office of the agency and by vesting it in an administrative secretary who could be presumed not to be burdened by personal convictions about what would be the more appropriate type of assignment in an individual case.

The following procedure of randomization was developed. The directors of the agency's four district offices were asked to have each intake worker obtain in the first interview information that would permit a decision about whether or not a couple needed a unifying experience. When it was impossible for the district director to make the necessary diagnostic decision on the basis of the information obtained by the intake worker, the intake study was to be continued until such a decision became possible. The district directors were asked, further, to specify those changes in the underlying need-frustration constellation of the marriage which would represent an increase in closeness between the two marriage partners and to list them as treatment goals on a research card which was to be started, in duplicate, as the case came to the district director. After the completion of intake, cases having complicating factors of unemployment, acute physical or mental health problems, alcoholism, or conflict with public authorities were to be excluded from the research project. There was no formal review of the decisions of the district directors, but we found later that when a district director seemed to have doubt about whether a case fell in any one of these categories of cases she checked with the director of casework or the research director. Furthermore, a number of cases considered eligible by the district directors were later excluded because they fell in one or another of these categories. We can assume, therefore, that there was not undue loss of cases. A certain loss, of which we were aware, occurred because of the obligation to assign to field work students some marital-conflict cases which would have been eligible for the project.

Each case was sent to the central office for assignment, and the district director was informed whether it was to be assigned to one or two workers. Originally we had foreseen that only caseworkers in classifications II and III should carry research cases. As the research procedure continued over several years, however, it was occasionally necessary to give a research case to a caseworker in classification I in order to provide him with experience necessary for professional development. Recording of the names of the caseworkers permitted us to establish smaller subsamples of greater equality in probable quality of casework service rendered.

Sample collection.—The period of sample collection lasted from September 2, 1958, to February 3, 1961. In the beginning we had expected that one-worker and two-worker cases would become eligible for judgment in about an equal length of time. Actually, for a time cases in which two workers had been assigned tended to drop out before having achieved the necessary minimum of five interviews with each marriage partner. It appeared that one-worker assignments held both spouses in treatment much better than two-worker assignments. Hence we occasionally had to interrupt alternate assignment and to assign all cases to the two-worker category until the samples were of equal size again. We felt entitled to make these shifts in the method of randomization because the principle of randomization was not violated; whether for a period we alternated assignment or for a period assigned cases to only one group, the cases were protected against assignment based on therapeutic conviction rather than on chance. At a later stage, one-worker cases seemed to be terminated more frequently. On final comparison, there seemed to be no significant difference in case mortality in the two groups.

Another difficulty arose from the frequent inequality of husband and wife in keeping appointments. Our original decision had been to judge cases only after each marriage partner had had at least five interviews after the study period and before the case was closed, or after each marriage partner had had a minimum of twenty interviews if the case was still open. Because of lapse of time, we decided to consider all open cases eligible for judging in which at least one marriage partner had been seen in twenty interviews, intake interviews included, and the other had received at least five interviews after intake. Because of expected loss of cases, we decided to build up an extra margin of eligible cases. In the end, we closed our sample collection after 34 cases in each group had come in for judging.

USE OF JUDGMENTS

Although we were greatly helped by the basic work of J. McVicker Hunt and the advances in refinement of techniques of measuring movement achieved by the Community Service Society of New York, we had to make certain changes in preparing our judgment procedure. Perhaps the most basic was a shift in what was being measured. While the theoretical and technical concern with therapeutic effectiveness in the Community Service Society group, and among other researchers, had been centered on changes in the individual client or patient, our concern was with change in a two-person relationship. Our therapeutic goal was improvement in family relationships. In consequence, an individualistic frame of reference, whether from learning psychology or from ego psychology, seemed inappropriate for our purposes. Our first step had been the development of a model of healthy family relationships. This orientation to family relationships we made the frame of reference for our assessment of differences in the effectiveness of the two casework methods. The phenomena which had to be judged on the basis of our recordings therefore were not individual capacities or habits, aptitudes, or environmental circumstances but the interaction patterns between the family members who were in treatment. The nature of these patterns was compared at two points of time— (1) at the opening and (2) at the closing of the case, or at the time at which at least one client had had twenty interviews (those of the intake study included) and the other at least five interviews, exclusive of intake. In some cases in which workers failed to send in the cases after the twentieth interview the judges found it hard to decide whether changes had taken place by the time of the twentieth interview or later.

Personnel.—Altogether, we employed four judges but subjected every case to only three judgments. Two judges judged every case. In addition, each case was judged by one of two district directors of the agency. The employment of two district directors as judges made it possible to have no case judged by the director of the district in which it had been carried. All judges were administrators concerned with exploring differential effectiveness and with putting findings to use. They had, therefore, a professional interest in the outcome of the study. They all were, or had been, significantly engaged in the design and administration of the project and thus were acquainted with all its facets. What we tried to do, in essence, was to employ judges who combined high caliber as practitioners with professional investment in the research project itself.[7]

Their findings were, of course, not completely alike, but they were close, with only a few reconciliation conferences necessary. Even before these conferences took place, all judges produced ratings pointing in the same direction, disproving our hypothesis. Reconciliation conferences were held only when the divergence between judgments exceeded one step on the scoring scales.

Instructions.—We started with the concept that a family relationship is an association between human beings with different needs and capacities that represent opportunities for mutual need satisfaction. Need for case-work services occurs when the relationship between two family members is interfered with by lack of capacities or lack of predisposition to act as need satisfier for the other, or through the monopolistic aspirations that drive one family member to deny the other any access to legitimate resource persons outside of the specific family relationship. The mutual need-resource constellation of two such family members—that is, in our project, between spouses—was visualized as operating in two dimensions and as expressing itself in various degrees of satisfaction.

The dimensions of spouse interaction in which we asked our judges to identify improvement or deterioration of the relationship were "communication" and "cooperation." "Communication improvement" was to be assumed if at least one marriage partner had begun to convey verbally to the other his concern over needs formerly unmet in the family and if the other recognized the claim to satisfaction instead of rejecting this claim. In other words, the gain in the ability of one spouse to let the other know about his concerns was not to be considered as a communication improvement unless it met a positive response. Talking, alone, was not considered enough, even if it followed silence. Content had to be considered. A quarrel is not a relationship improvement.

---

[7] The two who judged all cases were Martha Grossman, director of casework, Family Service of Philadelphia, and Beulah Winstel, director of Montgomery County Mental Health Clinic, a former staff member of Family Service. Harriet Guignon and Esther Venner were the two district directors.

"Cooperation improvement" was assumed to start as soon as one marriage partner began to meet needs that were of concern to the other, and did so with non-masochistic enjoyment. Assumption of martyrdom is no improvement of cooperation.

In summary, "communication" was defined in our instructions as an expression of concern over unmet needs which led to agreement between the spouses about the justification of this concern. "Cooperation" was defined as activation of the resource quality of one spouse for the satisfaction of needs about which the other felt concern.

In order to make it possible for our judges to rate improvement as "little," "some," or "considerable," we established within each of the two dimensions an ordinal scale with a partial order tie.[8]

The criteria for placing the improvement noted in one of those categories are shown in Appendix I. A deterioration in communication was to be scored if, during casework treatment, one or both partners had stopped conveying to the other concern over unmet needs which they had expressed verbally or non-verbally to one another at the beginning of contact with the agency and which were still unmet at the point of judgment. A deterioration in cooperation was to be scored if a family need formerly satisfied by one or both marriage partners was found not to be satisfied any longer and the stoppage had occurred during the casework treatment process.

In order to make this type of scoring possible, it was necessary for the district director, in cooperation with the caseworker assigned to the case, to make a notation of the needs unmet in the family at the beginning and for this record to be brought up to date if, in the course of treatment, other unmet needs were discovered. These unmet needs were listed in the form of specific goals. Thus in our instrument we attempted to keep abstraction at a minimum in the effort to avoid the intrusion of the judges into the situation.[9] Most important, however, we provided a definite quantitative basis for judgment.

Improvement in communication and deterioration in cooperation or vice versa were not considered to be incompatible. It is at least theoretically possible that improvement would occur in one and deterioration in the other. We therefore instructed judges to score improvement or deterioration in each area independently.

Scores on communication ranged from 1 for "little improvement" to 3 for "considerable improvement." Improvement in cooperation was scored from 2 for "little" to 6 for "considerable," because we believed on theoretical grounds that cooperation meant more for a family relationship than communication within every degree of improvement.

---

[8] Robert R. Bush, "The New Look in Measurement Theory," in Shyne, *op. cit.*, pp. 90–91.

[9] Genevieve W. Carter, "The Nature of Judgment Data," in Shyne, *op. cit.*, p. 20.

Deterioration in communication was scored −2 and in cooperation was scored −4. No attempt was made to establish degrees of deterioration. To do so would have required an enumeration of all needs being met at the time of application, a burden which we could not impose on our staff.

FINDINGS

The findings presented here relate to two matters—the judged changes in family relationships during the periods of treatment studied and the relationship between improvement in verbal communication and improvement in cooperation.

It should be noted that our findings are presented, first, for the total sample of 34 cases in each group and, second, for a subsample of cases carried by caseworkers in classification III—23 cases in the experimental (one-worker) group and 14 cases in the control (two-worker) group.

Table 1 presents the sum totals of the scores for the 34 cases in each subgroup. Scores are listed separately for the judges who rated every case

TABLE 1

TOTAL SCORES OF FAMILY RELATIONSHIP IMPROVEMENT IN ONE-WORKER AND TWO-WORKER CASES, BY JUDGE

Item	Total Scores		
	Judge A	Judge B	Judges C or D
Communication:			
One worker ....,......................	27	26	30
Two workers	31	27	39
Cooperation:			
One worker	50	44	54
Two workers	66	64	74

TABLE 2

AVERAGE FAMILY RELATIONSHIP IMPROVEMENTS IN CASES CARRIED BY ADVANCED WORKERS

Item	Average Scores		
	Judge A	Judge B	Judges C or D
Communication:			
One worker	.91	.91	.96
Two workers	1.07	1.00	1.29
Cooperation:			
One worker	1.48	1.30	1.65
Two workers	2.00	2.14	2.00

and are combined for the two district directors who shared the task of judging. Differences between the improvements associated with the two methods are of unequal size, but they invariably point in the same direction and favor the two-worker assignment over the one-worker assignment.

The size of the scores may impress some readers as very small. One might ask, for instance, how it could happen that a total of 34 cases showed an improvement score of only 27 in communication. The answer is twofold. It lies, first of all, in the arbitrarily determined numerical values assigned to the steps in the scales. Second it must be remembered that scores for deterioration were deducted. In a number of cases in which no movement occurred, changes in communication as well as in cooperation had to be scored as zero.

Table 2 presents the average scores of improvement in the cases carried by caseworkers in classification III (advanced workers). Since these workers had participated in unequal numbers of cases in the one-worker and in the two-worker group, only averages permit comparisons. For both communication and cooperation, improvement averages point without exception in the same direction and show greater improvements for the cases with a two-worker assignment.

In order to enable the reader to evaluate the scoring plan, Table 3 shows the frequency distribution of different scorings for the total sample. Apart from its explanatory value for an understanding of our scoring results, this table also shows the severity of the judges in evaluating family relationship change. Furthermore, it shows a very interesting phenomenon regarding the relationship of communication improvement and cooperation improvement. Except for judges C and D in the one-worker cases, all judges found that more situations showed improvement in cooperation than in communication. For example, Judge A found communication improvement in 18 one-worker cases and cooperation improvement in 20 one-worker cases. In the two-worker cases, this showing becomes stronger and consistent for all judges.

The scores for cases carried only by workers in classification III show similar relationships between the number of cases showing improvement in communication and the number showing improvement in cooperation, as shown in Table 4.

Apparently some clients are non-verbal to the degree that they cannot express to one another concern or acceptance even when they can feel it and act accordingly. If this should be corroborated by evidence available to others, the nature of the casework intervention, as distinguished from that in psychotherapy, might find an interesting elucidation. It might be conceived as including in its range help in relationship improvement for largely non-verbal clients.

In historical perspective, it may be of interest to the profession to learn that, as an afterthought in planning, all judges were asked to note any personality change observed in the clients. This was done in the expectation that even when no relationship change had occurred some intrapsychic developments might have been brought into existence which might have made it possible for the client to live more comfortably with himself, if not with others.

The findings show that relationship improvement was much more frequently achieved than positive personality change. In only 13 of the 68

TABLE 3

DISTRIBUTION OF SCORES IN ONE-WORKER AND TWO-WORKER CASES: TOTAL SAMPLE

Scores		One-Worker Cases			Two-Worker Cases		
		Judge A	Judge B	Judges C or D	Judge A	Judge B	Judges C or D
Communication:							
Deterioration	−2	1	1	2	2	2	2
No change	0	15	18	11	11	13	8
Little change	1	8	5	11	9	6	12
Some improvement	2	7	9	7	10	13	5
Considerable improvement	3	3	1	3	2	—	7
Total number of cases improved		18	15	21	21	19	24
Cooperation:							
Deterioration	−4	3	3	3	2	2	3
No change	0	11	15	11	7	9	5
Little change	2	13	7	10	13	10	14
Some improvement	4	4	8	7	12	13	7
Considerable improvement	6	3	1	3	—	—	5
Total number of cases improved		20	16	20	25	23	26

cases was personality improvement noted. However, there was not a single instance in which more than one judge noted personality improvement. This seems to us of tremendous theoretical and practical importance. It suggests, first of all, that people can gain from casework greater competence in interpersonal relations without change in personality structure. They can learn to perceive the needs of the other marriage partner better than they have before and they can learn to meet these needs without having to undergo personality change. It indicates, furthermore, the advisability of greater realism in the setting of goals. Caseworkers have often felt that they failed their clients if they could not help them to undo developmental impairments such as arrests in various phases of psychosocial growth or strengthening of superego formation. This self-blame has been largely based on the assumption that without repair of developmental impairment clients could not be helped to improve in their interaction with other people of significance in their life space. Our research suggests very strongly what is being increasingly observed also in other agency settings, that limited goals short of personality change can fully justify the casework effort.

IMPLICATIONS FOR FURTHER RESEARCH

In spite of the scientific thrill of having found that our careful design of a quantitative study can protect caseworkers against their own beliefs and preferences, we cannot conceal from ourselves or others that our findings did not attain our goal of establishing criteria for assigning a case of marital conflict either to one or to two caseworkers. At best it could be said that if staff were available in sufficient numbers, two-worker assign-

TABLE 4

DISTRIBUTION OF SCORES OF ONE-WORKER AND TWO-WORKER CASES: CASES CARRIED BY ADVANCED CASEWORKERS ONLY

Scores		One-Worker Cases			Two-Worker Cases		
		Judge A	Judge B	Judges C or D	Judge A	Judge B	Judges C or D
Communication:							
Deterioration	−2	1	1	2	0	0	0
No change	0	10	10	6	6	6	5
Little change	1	4	2	7	2	2	4
Some improvement	2	5	9	5	4	6	1
Considerable improvement	3	3	1	3	2	0	4
Total number of cases improved		12	12	15	8	8	9
Cooperation:							
Deterioration	−4	3	3	3	0	0	1
No change	0	6	7	7	4	4	2
Little change	2	8	6	4	6	5	7
Some improvement	4	3	6	6	4	5	3
Considerable improvement	6	3	1	3	0	0	1
Total number of cases improved		14	13	13	10	10	11

ment would give a greater statistical chance of success than one-worker assignment. Sufficient staff, however, is frequently not available and a statistical probability can never be fully accepted as a basis for clinical decisions.

It may be possible, however, to use the case material worked up on our project cases for a further search for such criteria. Almost one-third of the one-worker cases showed "some" or "considerable" improvement in communication, and about one-quarter showed such improvements in cooperation. On the other hand, about one-third of the two-worker cases showed no improvement in communication and close to one-quarter showed no improvement in cooperation. Herein lies the challenge for further research. In what respect do the cases differ? Do the differences lie in the clients or in the workers or in the constellations composed of workers and clients? Did the differences in waiting periods screen out different types of clients from the experimental and the control groups?

If we knew the answers to these questions, we might be considerably closer to establishing criteria for worker assignment. So far, our research has helped us only to say that, for the type of treatment rendered at Family Service of Philadelphia, the nature of the therapeutic goal is not a sufficient criterion for a decision between two types of assignment, and that, if in doubt, two-worker assignment is preferable.

APPENDIX

CRITERIA FOR JUDGING IMPROVEMENT IN COMMUNICATION AND CO-OPERATION BETWEEN MARRIAGE PARTNERS

Communication

Little

> One spouse conveys verbally to the other concern over at least one need* and at the most not all needs unmet in the family at the time of application to the agency for service, and the latter recognizes their claim to satisfaction.

Some

> One spouse conveys verbally to the other concern over all needs unmet in the family, and the latter recognizes their claim to satisfaction;

> or

> Both spouses convey verbally to one another their concern over at least one such need, but at best still not all such needs unmet in the family, and each meets with positive response from the other.

Considerable

> One spouse conveys verbally to the other concern over all needs unmet in the family to the other, and the latter conveys verbally to him in turn a concern over at least one need unmet in the family, with mutual recognition of their claims to satisfaction.

Cooperation

Little

> One spouse has begun to meet at least one need* but at best not all needs unmet in the family at the time of application to the agency for service, and enjoys doing so.

Some

> One spouse is doing something to satisfy all needs unmet in the family, and enjoys doing so;

> or

> Both spouses are doing something to satisfy at least one such need, but at best still not all such needs unmet in the family, and enjoy doing so.

Considerable

One spouse is doing something to satisfy all needs unmet in the family, and enjoys doing so; while the other is doing something to satisfy at least one need in the family, and enjoys doing so.

* The term "need" is defined throughout in accordance with our family health model.

ADDITIONAL REFERENCES ON FAMILY DIAGNOSIS

ACKERMAN, NATHAN W., M.D. *The Psychodynamics of Family Life: Diagnosis and Treatment.* New York: Basic Books, 1958.
FRIEND, MAURICE R., M.D. "Family Diagnosis and Treatment: Points of Reference for the Analysis of Family Processes," in *Casework Papers, 1957.* New York: Family Service Association of America, 1957, pp. 19–32.
GOMBERG, M. ROBERT. "Family Diagnosis: Trends in Theory and Practice," *Social Casework,* XXXIX (March, 1958), 73–83.
———, and LEVINSON, FRANCES T. (eds.). *Diagnosis and Process in Family Counseling.* New York: Family Association of America, 1951.
GROTJAHN, MARTIN, M.D. *Psychoanalysis and the Family Neurosis.* New York: W. W. Norton & Co., 1960.
GROUP FOR THE ADVANCEMENT OF PSYCHIATRY. *Integration and Conflict in Family Behavior.* Report No. 27. New York, August, 1954.
POLLAK, OTTO. "A Family Diagnosis Model," *Social Service Review,* XXXIV (March, 1960), 19–28.
SCHERZ, FRANCES H. "What Is Family-centered Casework?," *Social Casework,* XXXIV (October, 1953), 343–49.
SPIEGEL, JOHN P., M.D., and BELL, NORMAN W. "The Family of the Psychiatric Patient," in *American Handbook of Psychiatry,* ed. Silvano Arieti, M.D. New York: Basic Books, 1959, pp. 114–49.
WEISS, VIOLA W., and MONROE, RUSSELL R., M.D. "A Framework for Understanding Family Dynamics: Part I," *Social Casework,* XL (January, 1959), 3–9.
———, "A Framework for Understanding Family Dynamics: Part II," *Social Casework,* XL (February, 1959), 80–87.

LEE SECHREST, RONALD GALLIMORE,
PAUL D. HERSCH

7

*Feedback and Accuracy of
Clinical Predictions**

The generally low level of accuracy of clinical predictions, whether by experts or novices, is by now so well known as not to need documentation. However, what remains is the important question why accuracy is so low, and the consequent of its answer, a recommendation for improvement in clinical prediction.

Meehl (1954) exposed the poverty of clinical psychology in the predictive field by showing the generally equal or greater accuracy of mechanical or actuarial methods. However, Holt (1958) has suggested that a fundamental deficiency in Meehl's comparisons was that in all instances rather highly refined psychometric devices especially constructed for the purpose for which they were being employed were being matched against clinicians who had not had the opportunity to sharpen their skills by the systematic development and cross-validation of them against the criterion to be predicted. In addition, Holt believes, the clinicians were often attempting to predict a criterion with which they were not familiar and whose nature they did not understand. Therefore, Holt concluded that the comparisons made by Meehl were probably irrelevant to the question whether clinicians were necessarily inferior to actuarial methods. Other writers (e.g., Luft, 1950) have also pointed to the necessity for clinicians to experience feedback concerning the correctness of their predictions so that a corrective element may enter their systems.

This paper presents the results of three investigations concerned with the general efficacy of feedback in improving clinical prediction. In the studies to be reported, "clinician" populations consisted of naïve college undergraduates, and the prediction task is somewhat artificial but not totally unlike many clinical tasks. Since the clinical material to be given judges (*J*s) in the investigations below consist of brief incomplete-sentence protocols, it is relevant to point out that Jackson (1962) found that in making judgments about anxiety from sentence completions, naïve *J*s and expert clinicians were influenced in about the same degree by the same parameters of the response protocols.

* From: Lee Sechrest, Ronald Gallimore, and Paul D. Hersch, "Feedback and Accuracy of Clinical Predictions," *Journal of Consulting Psychology*, Vol. 31, No. 1 (February, 1967), pp. 1–11. Copyright 1967 by the American Psychological Association, and reproduced by permission.

With respect to the effect of feedback on predictions, these investigations clearly belong in the tradition of the many "knowledge-of-results" experiments on the basis of which Ammons (1956) concluded that knowledge of results (or feedback) almost universally results in a more rapid learning and a higher level of performance. In a study by Murray and Deabler (1958) which is directly relevant to the potential effect of feedback on improvement in clinical judgments, 15 psychologists attempted to "match" figure drawings with five diagnostic labels. After making his judgments for a set of drawings, the clinician was shown the correct diagnoses and given time to study the materials and to attempt to understand his errors. Then predictions were made for the next set of five drawings. Over a series of 20 sets of drawings, the results indicated clear progress in learning. Unfortunately the experiment had not been directed specifically at the question of feedback, and there was not a control group to justify the conclusion that it was feedback *per se* which contributed to improvement in performance. Oskamp (1962) did find some evidence for the effectiveness of feedback, but in his experiment it was given only after every 50 trials, and the nature of its effect was obscured.

The first study to be reported here is concerned with the two ideas presented by Holt (1958). The first is what Holt calls "job analysis" by which he means that the clinician should acquaint himself thoroughly with the job to be done, that is, the nature of the prediction he is to make. Holt believes that clinicians too often try to make predictions concerning criteria of which the predictor has only the vaguest understanding. In Experiment I below, some naïve clinicians were given definitional information concerning the criterion, others were not.

The second proposal to be investigated is what is referred to as "feedback." Holt indicates that the predictor must have the opportunity to discover what kinds of data afford indications of the trait to be predicted. In the investigations below, *J* was told whether each prediction he made was correct or incorrect immediately following that prediction and was given a moment to reflect on the information to determine whether such information might enable him to adjust his implicit hypotheses when making subsequent predictions. Experiments II and III are directed toward elucidating the specific ways in which feedback operates in the improvement of performances. Two alternative, but not mutually exclusive hypotheses are (*a*) that feedback operates by providing information by means of which the subject can adjust his implicit hypotheses or (*b*) that feedback serves a motivational function by convincing and reminding the subject that the task is one on which improvement is expected and possible.

EXPERIMENT I

METHOD

The prediction task.—It was necessary to devise a prediction task which was simple and which did not require excessive time. As an initial step, the dimensions of anxiety and pleasantness of personality were chosen to be predicted. Preliminary work indicated that these dimensions were meaningful to our subjects and potentially predictable. Target objects (*O*s) were selected from a class of 60 nursing students for whom a variety of measures were available. Twelve *O*s were chosen for each of the two variables, six representing the extreme high and six the extreme low value on each characteristic. Anxiety was defined in terms of the six highest and six lowest scoring girls on the *Pt* + *K* score of the MMPI. The mean score for the six anxious *O*s was 36.8 and for the nonanxious *O*s, 19.8. Pleasantness was determined by a peer-nomination technique for the opposite traits of "most pleasant" and "least pleasant." The six girls receiving the most nominations for "most pleasant" were designated as "pleasant" and the six receiving the most nominations for "least pleasant" were designated "unpleasant." For the pleasant *O*s the mean number of "most pleasant" nominations was 23.0 and the mean number of "least pleasant" votes was 1. The corresponding figures for the unpleasant *O*s were 1 and 26.6.

The materials given to *J*s from which they were to make their predictions were incomplete-sentence protocols taken from the Rotter Incomplete Sentences Blank (ISB) —College Form (Rotter, 1950). It was necessary to have test data which would have some meaning for *J*s and which would not require excessive time for study. Obviously, it was also hoped that the criterion groups would be potentially differentiable by means of their sentence completions. Again preliminary study supported the use of the procedures chosen, for in a pilot study a small group of subjects did predict at a better than chance level for the anxiety and pleasantness variables.

The investigations to be reported all assume at least a modest validity for the sentence-completion measure. While we have no specific evidence for the validity of these brief protocols against the criteria chosen, a review of the literature justifies some confidence in validity of sentence-completion measures for traits such as anxiety and sociability (Sechrest, in press).

For each *O*, four 5 × 8 inch data cards were prepared. Ten of *O*'s ISB completions were typed on each card with Card 1 consisting of every fourth completion beginning with the first; Card 2 of every fourth completion beginning with the second, etc. Since there were 4 data cards for each of the 24 *O*s, there were 96 data cards which were divided into four groups of 24 each. The four groups of cards were formed first by dividing the cards on the basis of the characteristic of O to be predicted. The resulting two groups were further divided into two more groups by putting Data Cards 1 and 2 together to form one group and Data Cards 3 and 4 together to form another group. Half of the Js made their predictions from Data Cards 1 and 2; the other half from Cards 3 and 4. Each J, although making 24 predictions, actually made 2 separate predictions for each of 12 different Os. It should be pointed out that Js were not told that Os would be repeated during the prediction series. They were led to believe that they would be making predictions about 24 different Os.

Procedure.—The experimental characteristics of the groups were established on the basis of the two types of predictions to be made and the two independent variables, *information* and *feedback*. The main experimental groups consisted of Js predicting either anxiety or pleasantness. Each group was subdivided into groups of Js receiving (a) information plus feedback, (b) information but not feedback, (c) no information but feedback, and (d) no information and no feedback. This resulted in eight groups of Js.

The *information* given to the appropriate groups of Js consisted of: (a) a definition of anxiety accompanied by six examples from the Pt scale of statements which anxious persons might make, and six statements which would be endorsed by nonanxious persons, or (b) a brief description of social pleasantness and an explanation of the voting procedure employed to get the criterion data. The information was given to J before he made any of his predictions. *Feedback* consisted of telling J whether he was right or wrong following each prediction.

Upon entering the experimental room, each J was seated at a small table, opposite and facing the experimenter (E), but separated by a screen preventing visual observation so the J could see neither E nor the materials. The following instructions were then read, as appropriate, to J:

This is a study to test the ability of college students to predict whether a person is (anxious or nonanxious; pleasant or unpleasant) from the results of a sentence completion test taken by the person.

You will be given a card on which appear ten sentences. The underlined words are those originally given to the person, and the remainder of each sentence indicates the way in which the person completed the sentence. You will be given 45 seconds in which to read and study the sentences, and at the end of this time I will ask for your prediction. Please do not give your prediction until I ask for it. (After you have made your prediction, I will tell you whether you are "right" or "wrong." You will then be given an additional 15 seconds in which to study the sentences in the light of this information. You are to use this information to help you make more accurate predictions in the future.) (You will then be given an additional 15 seconds in which to study the card.) You will then be given another card, from which you will make another similar prediction. This process will be repeated until you have made 24 predictions from 24 different sets of sentences. All of the individuals are female and are in their first year of nurses' training at a large hospital.

Following these instructions, *J*s in the information groups were given the appropriate definitions and information about the criterion variables. The appropriate set of cards was then shuffled, by *J*, and placed face down behind the screen. Then each card was, in turn, handed to *J*. The *J* was given 45 seconds to study the sentences and then was asked for his prediction. Then, whether given feedback or not, all *J*s were given an additional 15 seconds to study the card, so that each *J* spent a total of 60 seconds on each card. Preliminary study indicated that the period was sufficient and near the maximum that *J*s could be kept at the task.

The *J*s' responses were recorded as either correct or incorrect. The score was simply the total number of correct predictions.

Judges.—The *J*s were 96 male undergraduates enrolled in introductory psychology. One random order of experimental conditions was preestablished, and as each *J* appeared he was placed in the appropriate group. A total of 12 *J*s was run in each of the eight experimental groups.

RESULTS

The means and standard deviations for all groups are given in Table 1. The means for these three groups indicate a trend in the expected direction. Each group receiving feedback has a higher mean score than its

TABLE 1
THE MEAN AND STANDARD DEVIATION OF PREDICTIVE ACCURACY SCORES FOR
EACH GROUP

	Variable Predicted	
Condition	Anxiety	Pleasantness
Feedback		
Information		
M	14.25	13.83
SD	1.88	1.70
No information		
M	13.42	13.17
SD	2.71	1.75
No feedback		
Information		
M	13.92	13.00
SD	2.46	2.45
No information		
M	12.75	12.00
SD	1.88	1.35

corresponding no-feedback group, and each information group has a higher mean than its corresponding no-information group. Two approaches were taken to the statistical analysis of the data. An analysis of variance yielded a significant effect ($F = 4.72$, *df* 1, 88) only for the triple interaction of Feedback $\times$ Information $\times$ Traits predicted. Inspection of the means in Table 1 reveals that information seems to be the more important factor in predicting anxiety while for pleasantness feedback is relatively more important. It will also be noted that for both variables feedback plus information yields the highest mean performance, and no feedback plus no information yields the poorest scores.

A second analysis was performed by testing the effects of feedback—no feedback and information—no information against the expectation of a chance performance, that is, 12 correct predictions out of 24. Table 2 presents the results of the four chi-square tests which ensued from the analysis. The results clearly indicate that the .5 accuracy level (i.e., chance) is untenable as a hypothesis for subjects serving under either feedback or information conditions, but it is quite tenable for subjects who had either no feedback or no information.

There are several limitations in the investigation which might have attenuated the magnitude of the effects observed. It is obvious that the prediction task was quite a demanding one, for across all conditions the accuracy scores were generally low. There are three reasons the scores might have been so low. First, Js may not have been particularly well motivated to improve their predictions and, thus, may not have made use of information or feedback given to them (see Experiment II). Second, the 10-sentence ISB protocols may not have provided a sufficient basis for the prediction of the criterion variables. Third, the measurement operations involved in the criterion variables may have been inadequate, resulting in an unnecessarily difficult prediction task. At the present time we tend somewhat to discount the latter two difficulties. Four reasonably well-trained graduate students who have performed the task have done quite well ($X = 18$ correct for anxiety) and have not found the problem to be a particularly unusual or difficult one.

TABLE 2

CHI-SQUARE ANALYSIS FOR EFFECTS OF EXPERIMENTAL VARIABLES ON PREDICTIVE ACCURACY ACROSS TWO TRAITS

Group	Greater than Chance Accuracy	Less than Chance Accuracy	X^2
Feedback	36 (24)	12 (24)	12.00*
No feedback	26 (24)	22 (24)	.33
Information	36 (24)	12 (24)	12.00*
No information	26 (24)	22 (24)	.33

* $p < .001$.

EXPERIMENT II

One deficiency of Experiment I was that while it did demonstrate that feedback resulted in a more accurate performance, it did not demonstrate that feedback *improved* performance from trial to trial. The possibility existed that the feedback groups started off better, perhaps by reason of having greater interest in the task. In view of the relatively small number of judges employed in the experiment and the anticipated fluctuations of trial by trial scores, it was decided to do an additional experiment. However, during the course of Experiment I a question also arose concerning the motivation of all the judges, for it was supposed that if the motivation were not sufficiently high the judges might not care enough about the experiment to want to take advantage of the feedback in order to improve their accuracy. Therefore, it was decided in Experiment II to incorporate an external incentive in order to determine whether motivational level and feedback might interact to produce a better performance.

Another aspect of prediction as a clinical task was called to the attention of the investigators by consideration of the total clinical situation. For the most part, the predictions that clinical psychologists try to make involve estimates about the absolute level in a given subject of the trait or characteristic they are trying to predict. That is, they try to say just how high, on some hypothetical scale with an implied zero point, the subject stands on some such trait as anxiety or a characteristic such as favorability of response to treatment. Such judgments are comparable to a psychophysical method, the method of single stimuli, used for scaling such things as brightness of lights.

In actuality clinical psychologists may often be setting themselves an unnecessarily difficult task, for if one examines the uses to which many of their judgments are put, it may be found that comparative or, as they are called here, *differential* judgments are more appropriate. For example, take the judgment of a clinician about the risk of suicide for a given patient and his subsequent recommendation that the patient either be put on suicidal precautions or not be put on suicidal precautions. In some degree all disturbed persons must be regarded as constituting a suicidal risk, but to keep all such persons under close surveillance is impossible. It is likely that the number of persons on suicidal precautions typically approximates a constant, and that for any patient, the question of his being on the list depends upon the risk he constitutes relative to the total patient group. It is altogether likely that the above argument holds also for the assignment of inpatients to treatment by psychotherapy. Whether or not a patient receives psychotherapy depends very little on the absolute probability of his response to it; the relevant issue is whether there are more worthy candidates.

While it is quite difficult to get reliable judgments of many characteristics on an absolute scale, very subtle distinctions may be quite regularly made when patients are compared with each other. Many, probably most, patients can be accurately described as "very anxious" or as "having conflicts in authority relations," and it is important to distinguish among them. What we wish to do, in a psychophysical sense, is to provide anchor points which will facilitate the judgments which need to be made.

Therefore, Experiment II provided for two judging tasks or "types" of predictions. One is the standard, absolute kind of judgment in which *J* has to say "pleasant" or "unpleasant." The second is a differential prediction in which *J* has to say, in this instance, which of *two* protocols (representing two individuals) most probably was given by a pleasant person.

The design of Experiment II can be seen clearly in Table 3. Half of the *J*s made differential and half absolute predictions; half of each of those groups received a monetary incentive, and half did not, and half of the *J*s received feedback, and half did not. Each *J* made 24 predictions in the manner described previously except that the differential group looked at 24 *pairs* of protocols rather than 24 single ones. Again the protocols were 10-item incomplete sentence protocols. In this case, following on the interaction in Experiment I, which suggested that prediction of social pleasantness was relatively more improved by feedback, that was the criterion to be judged. The incentive offered was 10 cents for every

TABLE 3

MEAN NUMBER OF CORRECT PREDICTIONS IN BLOCKS OF EIGHT TRIALS FOR EXPERIMENT II (16 SUBJECTS/CELL)

	Block of Trials		
	1–8	*9–16*	*17–24*
Differential prediction			
Feedback	5.25	5.38	4.88
Incentive			
No feedback	4.00	3.94	3.81
Feedback	3.50	4.25	4.88
No incentive			
No feedback	4.38	3.94	4.00
Absolute prediction			
Feedback	4.25	4.50	3.75
Incentive			
No feedback	3.94	4.19	4.38
Feedback	4.75	4.44	3.94
No incentive			
No feedback	4.44	3.88	3.81

prediction correct over 12 and an additional 10-cent bonus for every correct prediction over 18.

The dependent measure was the number of correct predictions by each *J*, accumulated over blocks of eight trials. Thus, there were three scores for each *J*, and, if improvement in accuracy took place, the scores should increase from Block 1–8 to Block 17–24.

JUDGES FOR EXPERIMENT II

Once again *J*s were volunteers from introductory psychology classes, in this case from two large universities. The three independent variables at two levels each produced eight separate conditions. There were 16 *J*s serving each condition, a total of 128 in all.

RESULTS

The mean scores for the various experimental groups in blocks of eight trials are given in Table 3. For the independent variables, an analysis of variance showed that only feedback produces a significant effect ($F = 9.33$, df 1, 120; $p < .01$). Reference to Table 3 shows that those subjects serving under feedback conditions performed in a manner superior to those who did not receive feedback. Neither type of prediction nor the occurrence of an incentive, however, produced a significant effect on the accuracy of the judgments. There was a significant triple interaction ($F = 7.17$, df 1, 120; $p = .01$) between type of prediction, feedback, and in-

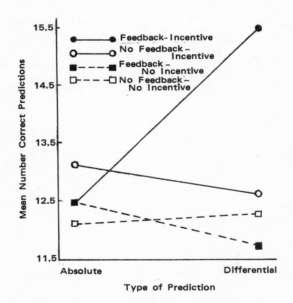

FIGURE 1. Interaction between type of prediction, feedback, and incentive conditions.

centive. Inspection of Figure 1 reveals that the subjects serving in the feedback-incentive-differential condition performed very much better than subjects in any other condition.

Taking into account the blocks of trials, there is no main effect for trials; that is, across all groups there was apparently no overall improvement from the first block of eight trials to the last block of eight trials. There are three triple interactions involving blocks of trials, all significant beyond the .01 level. Figure 2 shows the interaction between feed-

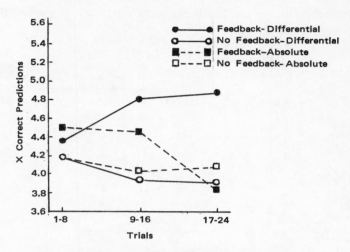

FIGURE 2. Interaction type of prediction and feedback condition across trials.

back, type of prediction, and trials $(F = 4.94, df\ 2, 240;\ p < .01)$. The most outstanding feature of the graph is the fact that the results for the feedback differential group are in the opposite direction from the trend for the feedback absolute group. Those subjects making differential predictions who received feedback improved their performance over the three blocks of trials. Those subjects making absolute predictions, in spite of the fact they were receiving feedback, became worse over the three blocks of trials. The general trend for the other groups not receiving feedback was also to become worse.

The interaction between incentive, type of prediction, and trials $(F = 6.12, df\ 2, 240;\ p < .01)$ is presented in Figure 3. Here, once again, there are rather sharp and opposite trends involving two of the groups. The group making differential predictions tended to improve over the three blocks of trials when they were not receiving an incentive. The group making absolute predictions got worse over the three blocks of trials when they were not receiving an incentive. The trend for the other two groups is somewhat similar, showing a fairly substantial decline from a high level performance on the second block of eight trials to the third block of eight trials. Both these groups, it will be noted, were receiving an incentive.

Finally the interaction of feedback, incentive, and trials $(F = 5.03, df\ 2,240;\ p < .01)$ is diagramed in Figure 4. This very complex interaction is quite difficult to interpret, the largest arithmetic discrepancy appearing on the second block of eight trials between the feedback incentive group and the no feedback, no incentive group. The feedback incentive group shows an early improvement in its performance and then a very substantial drop on the last block of eight trials, whereas the no feedback, no

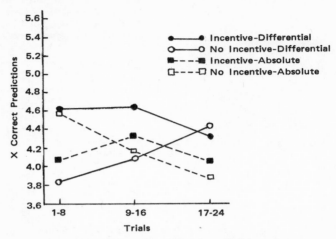

FIGURE 3. Interaction of type of prediction and incentive condition across trials.

incentive group shows a general decline in ability to make the kind of prediction required.

In the above experiment, the importance of feedback in facilitating accuracy of clinical predictions is clearly demonstrated. The effect produced by feedback is large, and its importance seems to be about equal in combination with any one of the other two independent variables. However, the best performance occurs in a group which has the advantage of all three of the independent variables which were thought, on an *a priori* basis, to facilitate prediction. When a group is not only receiving feedback, but is operating with an incentive and is making differential as opposed to absolute predictions, its performance is superior to that of any other group.

An admittedly surprising and somewhat disappointing outcome of Experiment II was the failure to find a significant interaction between feedback and blocks of trials which would suggest that subjects receiving feedback improved over trials. The fact that feedback was significant only as a main effect and in complex interactions suggests the possibility that feedback might operate in some manner other than as a source of information leading to an improving level of performance. One possibility is that feedback may operate as a cognito-motivational variable. That is, when a subject is receiving feedback in a prediction situation, he is led to believe that the task is an important one and that improvement in his performance is possible. On the other hand, for a subject not receiving feedback it may be easy to conclude that the task is so simple that it requires no particular expenditure of energy on his part. Thus,

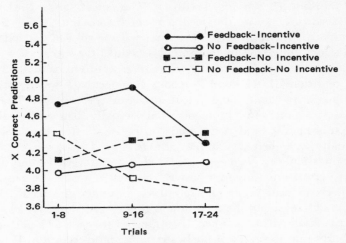

FIGURE 4. Interaction of feedback and incentive
conditions across trials.

the subject not receiving feedback may perform the tasks with the investiture of considerably less attention and energy than the subject receiving feedback, who knows that the task is not an easy one but that it is presumably possible to do. It will be noted that in both of the experiments reported all subjects were required to spend an equal amount of time in the accomplishment of the task although it cannot be determined that they used their time equally well.

If, however, feedback does not serve an informative function but serves only a motivational or attitudinal purpose in the experiment, then it should not matter how feedback is actually given. In Experiment III to be reported below, the relationship between the response of the subject and the occurrence of feedback was systematically manipulated in an attempt to determine whether the effect of the feedback is reduced when its informational function is minimized or eliminated.

EXPERIMENT III

METHOD

The same materials as were used for Experiments I and II were employed in Experiment III. However, since the results for differential prediction in Experiment II were not clear-cut, the procedure was simplified by requiring only absolute predictions in Experiment III. Experiment III consisted of four conditions of feedback:

Condition I. Feedback. The Js were given feedback concerning the accuracy of their predictions in the manner previously described.

Condition II. Random Feedback. The Js were given the same amount of "feedback" as in the feedback condition, but it was administered randomly with respect to the accuracy of the subject's actual predictions. Thus, on a random, predetermined schedule, the subject was told that his prediction was right or wrong without respect to his actual performance.

Condition III. Reversed Feedback. The feedback was given in the same manner as in Condition I, but its direction was reversed. That is, Js were told "pleasant" for protocols that actually had been elicited from unpleasant Os, and were told "unpleasant" for protocols that had actually been elicited from pleasant Os.

Condition IV. No Feedback. Under the Reversed condition, if feedback served only an informative function, it would be possible for the subjects to achieve as high accuracy as under the feedback condition simply by reversing the direction of their predictions. However, feedback that is reversed could prove disrupting to the subject's performance if it requires him to reverse a fairly strong initial disposition. If feedback has no informational value and only a motivational value, then performance under reversed feedback should be equally as high as under feedback since implicit in the notion of the noninformational value of feedback is the idea that the subject will ignore it for purposes of decision making. In condition IV, subjects responded under the standard no feedback conditions.

Judges.—Subjects in Experiment III were run by two different Es, both female. One E ran 11 subjects in each of the four conditions in the spring quarter of the academic year. The other E ran 10 subjects in each of the four conditions in the winter quarter of the following academic year. Thus there were 21 subjects in each of the four conditions, a total of 84 Js in all. Once again, all Js were volunteers from introductory psychology classes.

RESULTS

In Table 4 are presented the means for the four experimental conditions given in blocks of eight trials.

An analysis of variance showed a highly significant ($F = 7.83$, df 3, 76; $p < .01$) main effect for the experimental conditions. Reference to Table 4 shows that the feedback condition produced the highest level of accuracy, followed fairly closely by the random-feedback condition. Reverse feedback and no feedback are inferior to the other two conditions. There was no significant difference between results for the two Es, but there was a significant Conditions $\times$ Experimenters interaction $(F = 4.15, df\ 3, 76; p < .05)$. However, the interaction will be ignored here, since the E variable is completely confounded with the particular experimental population from which Js were drawn and the time of the year at which the experimental data were collected. It cannot be determined which differences between the two Es produced the significant interaction.

Once again, there was no main effect significant for the variable of blocks of trials, thus again suggesting that there is no overall improvement in performance across trials for the four experimental groups.

TABLE 4

MEANS FOR FOUR EXPERIMENTAL CONDITIONS BY BLOCKS OF EIGHT TRIALS

	Trials		
Condition	1–8	9–16	17–24
Feedback	4.52	4.95	5.67
Random feedback	5.14	4.71	4.43
Reversed feedback	4.48	4.00	4.10
No feedback	4.29	3.76	4.38

Moreover, on this occasion there were no significant interactions involving the blocks of trials variable.

DISCUSSION

Perhaps the most general and important conclusion to be drawn from the experiments reported is that feedback is an important variable determining accuracy of clinical prediction but that the information contained in the feedback may be of less importance than the mere occurrence of feedback. The failure to obtain clear-cut evidence for improvement in performance across trials in Experiments II and III taken with the similarity in performance of the feedback and random feedback groups in Experiment III suggests strongly that a paramount effect of feedback is on the level of motivation or interest of the subject in the experimental task. Feedback may facilitate performance by indicating to the J that the task is an important one about which he should be concerned and by suggesting that improvement in his performance is possible if he will only pay attention to the material with which he is given to work.

It must be noted that the prediction task we have used is quite a difficult one and, for college sophomores at least, the asymptote for accuracy is at a fairly low level. Perhaps in subsequent investigations if a prediction task is used which is easier, in the sense of permitting a higher level of accuracy, it will be demonstrable that the effects of feedback accrue for a reasonably long time in a training series. Certainly what has been suggested concerning the necessity for feedback in clinical prediction situations supposes that improvement in clinical prediction will take place over a long period of time, perhaps even among very expert clinicians. Even though previous investigations have often led to such a conclusion, it would be disappointing to discover that all the improvement in predictive accuracy that is possible occurs during the first two or three psychology courses that students take.

On the other hand, even if the effect of feedback is only motivational, its importance in actual clinical situations is not to be disparaged. It might very well be that if, in clinical situations, there were more systematic feedback available to clinicians about the outcomes and accuracy of their predictions, a greater intellectual interest in clinical prediction problems could be elicited along with a generally higher level of accuracy. If clinical psychologists are not firm in their belief that their predictive efforts are important, or are to be utilized and evaluated, disinterest in and neglect of these skills becomes quite understandable. No matter what the level of the psychologist, the systematic feedback of information about the people who utilize and evaluate his predictions cannot help but be of interest and importance to him.

The slight but apparent superiority in Experiment III of the feedback to the random-feedback group as well as the distinct inferiority of the reverse-feedback group suggests that feedback does have *some* informative function. If feedback served only to develop the interest of J in his task, then reversing the feedback should not be detrimental to his level of performance. However, in this experiment, it was shown that reversing feedback involves a definite disruption. It seems quite likely that for the kind of prediction involved in this particular task Js have some initial bias concerning the relationship between sentence completions and social pleasantness, but, as is indicated by the performance of the no feedback group, that bias does not permit any substantial level of accuracy in prediction. However, the requirement in the reverse feedback group that the bias be ignored, in fact its contradiction by the experimental feedback, involves a disruption which prevents J from using whatever information he obtains from the feedback simply to reverse his predictions and achieve a higher level of accuracy. Within the limits of this experimental situation and the number of trials employed, feedback is of value only when it does not contradict the initial assumptions of J about what it is he is trying to predict and how he is to go about it.

It is of interest that neither the incentive manipulation nor type of prediction produced a significant main effect on the accuracy with which the predictions were made. Apparently, within the limits of the small incentive used in Experiment II, an incentive to do well or to improve the accuracy of one's predictions is not of greater importance than whatever inherent incentives are operating in the experimental situation, for example, desire to please E, desire to enhance self-esteem, etc. Moreover, differential predictions do not automatically lead to greater level of accuracy than absolute predictions. Each of these variables seems to have its effect only in conjunction with the other and with the occurrence of feedback. Then their influence seems marked.

The interpretation of triple interactions is always risky, but there are a few points about the interactions reported in Experiment II that seem reasonable. First, the combination of feedback and a differential prediction task does lead to increased accuracy across trials, and the differential prediction task may result in improvement across trials when there is no incentive. But what is clearer is that absolute prediction tasks yielded either no improvement or decrement in accuracy across trials whether there is feedback or incentive or not. Further work on the differences between absolute and differential prediction tasks is clearly demanded.

The interaction portrayed in Figure 4 between feedback, incentive, and trials is, as has always been noted, quite complex, but the clearest and most understandable trend is for the no feedback, no incentive group to decline rather sharply across the three blocks of eight trials. Just why the feedback incentive group should have shown an initial improvement and then a sharp decline is not easy to understand.

The effect of an external incentive in a complex performance situation may not always be what would seem to be anticipated on an *a priori* basis. One possibility is that the imposition of an external incentive establishes a set in the J to expect a substantial degree of accuracy and improvement in his performance. If, as was the case in this very difficult prediction task, the achievement of a very substantially high level of accuracy is difficult, it is even possible having established an initial set on the part of J that he will be able to perform well and acquire a worthwhile amount of money may lead to discouragement and even hostility when the task proves to be too difficult for him. Thus, at least in some of the conditions, the drop on the last series of trials in accuracy of prediction by groups receiving an incentive may have resulted from disappointment and even "giving up."

Although it was ignored in the latter two experiments, the variable of preinstruction or job analysis as suggested by Holt (1958) is an important one for consideration by clinical psychologists and is deserving of more extensive experimental study. Results of Experiment I, albeit with naïve clinicians, suggest that instruction about and consideration of the nature of the criterion to be predicted facilitates the making of accurate predictions. Clinical psychologists are generally not as well informed as they should be about the indicators and signs of many of the variables or traits about which they attempt to make predictions. For example, one suspects that very few clinical psychologists are particularly well informed about the functions of the central nervous system and the effects that disruptions can be expected to produce on tests.

Another equally good example, although for somewhat different reasons, is the prediction concerning the response of a patient to psychotherapy. The prediction, in the abstract, that a patient will or will not respond to psychotherapy is very nearly a meaningless one and cannot be expected to be made with any high level of accuracy. Before such a prediction can be made it would be necessary for the predicting clinician to have a complete understanding of the kinds of psychotherapy to be applied to the patient, the length of the psychotherapy he is to receive, and perhaps even a great deal about the personality of the individual who is to give the therapy.

Obviously there may be objections that the present studies of clinical predictions have grossly oversimplified the predictive task, the prediction situation, and have used judges who are scarcely comparable to clinical psychologists. But the vast samples of expert clinicians which should be available for research simply are not, and in any case it would be wasteful of their time and effort. An attempt to check major findings on smaller samples of clinical psychologists and graduate students is being made. In one pilot investigation involving eight graduate students in clinical psychology, there was a clear-cut effect which could be attributable to feedback. Unfortunately, because of an experimental confounding with order of materials used, this effect will have to be checked with an additional sample. Nonetheless, even with very difficult kinds of materials and more sophisticated clinical *J*s, important effects of the feedback variable are evident. Thus it is hoped that findings presented here will have a fairly substantial generality to different kinds of prediction tasks and to different samples of *J*s.

REFERENCES

AMMONS, R. B. Effects of knowledge of performance: A survey and tentative theoretical formulation. *Journal of General Psychology*, 1956, 54, 279–99.

HOLT, R. R. Clinical and statistical prediction: A reformulation and some new data. *Journal of Abnormal and Social Psychology*, 1958, 56, 1–12.

JACKSON, M. The effects of frequency, extremeness, consistency, and order of the stimulus on clinical judgment. Unpublished doctoral dissertation, Northwestern University, 1962.

LUFT, J. Implicit hypotheses and clinical predictions. *Journal of Abnormal and Social Psychology*, 1950, 45, 115–19.

MEEHL, P. E. *Clinical versus statistical prediction.* Minneapolis: University of Minnesota Press, 1954.

MURRAY, D. C., & DEABLER, H. L. Drawings, diagnoses, and the clinician's learning curve. *Journal of Projective Techniques*, 1958, 22, 415–20.

OSKAMP, S. The relationship of clinical experience and training methods to several criteria of clinical prediction. *Psychological Monographs,* 1962, **76** (28, Whole No. 547).

ROTTER, J. B. *Incomplete sentences blank—college form.* New York: Psychological Corporation, 1950.

SECHREST, L. Testing, measuring, and assessing people. In E. Borgatt & W. Lambert (eds.), *Handbook of personality research.* Chicago: Rand McNally & Co., in press.

Selected References

BRAMEL, DANA, "Selection of a Target for Defensive Projection," *Journal of Abnormal and Social Psychology* (April, 1963).

BRIAR, SCOTT, "Clinical Judgment in Foster Care Placement," *Child Welfare* (April, 1963).

———, "Use of Theory in Studying Effects of Client Social Class on Students' Judgments," *Social Work* (July, 1961).

CRAIG, MANDE M.; FURST, PHILLIP W., "What Happens After Treatment? A Study of Potentially Delinquent Boys," *Social Service Review* (June, 1965).

CROSS, HENRY A.; HARLOW, HARRY F., "Prolonged and Progressive Effects of Partial Isolation on the Behavior of Macaque Monkeys," *Journal of Experimental Research in Personality* (March, 1965).

DRIEBLATT, IRWIN; WEATHERLY, DONALD, "An Evaluation of the Efficacy of Brief-Contact Therapy with Hospitalized Psychiatric Patients," *Journal of Consulting Psychology* (December, 1965).

EVAN, WILLIAM, "A Laboratory Experiment on Bureaucratic Authority," *American Sociological Review* (December, 1961).

GAMSON, WILLIAM, "An Experimental Test of a Theory of Coalition Formation," *American Sociological Review* (August, 1961).

LANG, PETER; LAZOVIK, A. DAVID; REYNOLDS, DAVID, "Desensitization, Suggestibility, and Pseudotherapy," *Journal of Abnormal Psychology* (December, 1965).

LORR, MAURICE; McNAIR, DOUGLAS M.; MICHAUX, WILLIAM M.; RASKIN, ALLEN, "Frequency of Treatment and Change in Psychotherapy," *Journal of Abnormal and Social Psychology* (April, 1962).

MALLICK, SHEHBAZ K.; McCANDLESS, BOYD R., "A Study of Catharsis of Aggression," *Journal of Personality and Social Psychology* (December, 1966).

MYERS, JEROME L.; MYERS, NANCY A., "Secondary Reinforcement in Children as a Function of Conditioning Associations, Extinction, Percentages and Stimulus Types," *Journal of Experimental Psychology* (May, 1963).

ORCUTT, BEN, "A Study of Anchoring Effects in Clinical Judgment," *Social Service Review* (December, 1964).

POSER, ERNEST, "The Effect of Therapists' Training on Group Therapeutic Outcome," *Journal of Consulting Psychology* (August, 1966).

REID, WILLIAM, "Client and Practitioner Variables Affecting Treatment," *Social Casework* (December, 1964).

ROBINS, LEE; GYMAN, HARRY; O'NEAL, PATRICIA, "The Interaction of Social Class and Deviant Behavior," *American Sociological Review* (August, 1962).

SCHULMAN, ROBERT E.; SHOEMAKER, DONALD J.; MOCLIS, IRVIN, "Laboratory Measurement of Parental Behavior," *Journal of Consulting Psychology* (April, 1962).

WALLACH, MICHAEL A.; KOGAN, NATHAN; BEM, DARYL, "Diffusion of Responsibility and Level of Risk Taking in Groups," *Journal of Abnormal and Social Psychology* (March, 1964).

WYER, ROBERT, "Effect of Child-rearing Attitudes and Behavior on Children's Responses to Hypothetical Social Situations," *Journal of Personality and Social Psychology* (October, 1965).

ZANDER, ALVIN; WULFF, DAVID, "Members' Test Anxiety and Competence: Determinants of a Group's Aspiration," *Journal of Personality* (March, 1966).

THREE | # Quantitative-Descriptive Studies

Definitions

In our classification system, a research study must meet several requirements before it can be classified as quantitative-descriptive.

1. The first requisite is that *the study must not be classifiable as an experimental study.*
2. The second requisite is that *the study must include variables which are amenable to measurement and, hence, can provide quantitative descriptions.* There must be provisions for the systematic collection of data for the purpose of accurately describing relations among variables.
3. Thirdly, *the study must have one of the following purposes pertaining to the seeking of knowledge: the testing of hypotheses, or the accurate description of quantitative relations among variables selected for inclusion in the research.*

Quantitative-descriptive studies may be defined in the following way:

Quantitative-descriptive studies are empirical research investigations which have as their major purpose the delineation or assessment of characteristics of phenomena, evaluation of programs, or the isolation of key variables. These studies may use formal methods as approximations to experimental design with features of statistical reliability and control to provide evidence for the testing of hypotheses. All of these studies use quantitative devices for systematically collecting data from populations, programs, or samples of populations or programs. They employ personal interviews, mailed questionnaires, survey sampling procedures, and/or other rigorous data gathering devices.

Four subtypes of quantitative-descriptive studies are identified according to the primary purpose of the investigation. These subtypes are hypothesis testing studies, program evaluation studies, population description studies, and studies searching for variable relationships. All of these subtypes must satisfy the requirements for the definition of quantitative-descriptive studies. *Hypothesis testing studies* include explicit hypotheses which guide the research inquiry. Typically, the hypotheses are derived from theory. In the testing of cause-effect relationships, formal methods such as the use of contrast groups and matching procedures may be used to approximate experimental design. Investigators may

139

use purposive sampling procedures in seeking to "test" hypotheses concerned only with the association between independent and dependent variables. For example, one community may be selected purposively due to its reported high incidence of crime. The investigator may wish to demonstrate in that community that his hypothesis pertaining to different types of gangs for different types of criminal activity is plausible.

Studies which seek to *evaluate programs* are similar to studies which seek to test hypotheses. However, in program evaluation studies, the hypotheses may be implicit rather than explicit, and the hypotheses are typically not derived from theory. Program evaluation studies frequently originate from practical interests, and they are all concerned with some aspect of the effects of a program or a technique. On the contrary, hypothesis testing studies, as defined here, do not include such evaluative purposes. Program evaluation studies and field experiments may have the same objectives with respect to program evaluation; their chief distinction is in regard to the research procedures employed to achieve the purposes of the study. Hence, those program evaluation studies that contain the requisites for experimental studies would be classified as field experiments. The reader is referred to Suchman (1967) who discusses a variety of research designs which have been used in evaluation studies.

Studies which seek *accurate descriptions* of the characteristics of populations are typically geared to answering specific questions posed by the investigator. These studies usually follow survey procedures, and they have the purpose of describing simple facts about selected populations, organizations, or other collectivities. These studies often employ the same procedures as do research studies which seek to discover quantitative relations among specified variables. The primary distinction is that of the researcher's purpose. In a study which seeks *quantitative relations between variables,* the investigator attempts to discover correlations among the variables he includes in the survey. These correlations are then used to form the basis of hypotheses for future research investigations. Population description studies often try to answer specific questions of fact, such as what the family composition is of an immigrant population; in studies of variable relationships, the questions of interest often arise from the analysis of the findings themselves.

Definitions for each of the four subtypes of quantitative-descriptive studies are presented below.

1. *Hypothesis testing studies* are those quantitative-descriptive studies which contain in their design of research explicit hypotheses to be tested. The hypotheses are typically derived from theory, and they may be either statements of cause-effect relationships or statements of association between two or more variables without reference to causal relationship.
2. *Program evaluation studies* are those quantitative-descriptive studies which

are concerned with seeking the effects of a specific program or method of helping. Such programs may contain a variety of objectives pertaining to health, education, and welfare. Hypotheses may not be explicitly stated, and they frequently are derived from the objectives of the program being evaluated rather than from theory. Such studies may employ a variety of procedures to approximate experimental design.

3. *Population description studies* are those quantitative-descriptive studies which have as their primary function the accurate description of quantitative characteristics of selected populations, organizations, or other collectivities. These studies frequently use survey procedures. They usually employ sampling methods to claim representativeness, and they contain a large number of variables. Some of these studies are descriptive of characteristics of designated populations such as roles, functions, needs, attitudes, and opinions.

4. *Studies that search for variable relationship* are those quantitative-descriptive studies which are concerned with the finding of variables pertinent to an issue or situation and/or of the relevant relations among variables. Usually neither *a priori* hypotheses nor specific questions are formulated to guide the research. Survey procedures may be used, and a large number of potentially relevant variables are included in such studies. Sometimes there is an interest in seeking variables with predictive value; sometimes the interest is in establishing "types" by showing different constellations of variables.

Guideline Questions

The guideline questions for quantitative-descriptive studies are grouped into three major categories: classification, evaluation, and utilization. As we indicated in regard to guidelines for experimental studies, these questions are not exhaustive and are not to be applied mechanically. The quantitative-descriptive studies reproduced represent some of the subtypes of quantitative-descriptive studies and provide a source for the reader to apply the guideline questions which follow. They allow the reader the opportunity of developing his own version of the guidelines for further assessment of social research.

CLASSIFICATION:

1. What is (are) the specific purpose(s) of the study?
2. What research methods do the authors use to accomplish their purposes?

3. Why is the study classified as quantitative-descriptive? How does it differ from experimental and exploratory studies?
4. How should the study be sub-typed: hypothesis testing, program evaluation, population description, searching for variable relationships?

EVALUATION:

I. PROBLEM FORMULATION

1. How does the author utilize the literature in conceptualizing the problem for study?
2. What major concepts are formulated for the study and how well are they defined conceptually and operationally?
3. If the study has as its purpose the testing of hypotheses, what are the hypotheses, and what independent and dependent variables are proposed by the author?
4. What assumptions are made by the author in regard to the selection of variables for study?
5. What contingent variables are recognized by the author, and how are they handled, i.e., through assumptions or controls?
6. To what extent is the quantitative-descriptive approach appropriate for investigating the problem for study?

II. RESEARCH DESIGN AND DATA COLLECTION

1. Could other alternative designs have been used more appropriately to carry out the purposes of the study?
2. If the study sought to test hypotheses, what efforts were made to approximate experimentation, and to maximize internal and external validity?
3. What sampling procedures were employed in the study?
4. How were the data specifically collected, and how were potential sources of bias taken into account?
5. To what extent did the author attempt to increase the reliability and validity of the measurements in the study?

III. DATA ANALYSIS AND CONCLUSIONS

1. Does the author use descriptive statistics or statistics for inference in his analysis of the data, and is the choice of statistics appropriate to the data and the assumptions of the study?
2. If hypotheses are tested in the study, are they supported by the data?
3. Are the author's claims for the findings consistent with the data?
4. Were cross tabulations introduced in analyzing the data in order to take into account potentially contingent variables?

5. What are the author's principal conclusions? Are they consistent with the data?
6. What are the implications of the findings as defined by the author? Are they logically related to the data and conclusions stated by the author?
7. To what extent did the researcher accomplish his purposes set forth for the study?

UTILIZATION:

1. What objects of social work interest are addressed by the research (recipients, the process of serving, purveyance of services) ?
2. To what extent is the research relevant to the social work purposes of treatment, enhancement, or prevention?
3. On what levels does the research view the objects of social work interest? Is it concerned with individuals, groups, organizations, communities, or society?
4. Is the level of knowledge achieved by the research useful to social work primarily as empirical findings ("facts" or empirical generalizations), conceptual contributions (concepts, hypotheses, theories), or methods (for diagnostic or treatment procedures) potentially applicable to practice?
5. After evaluation, how valid is the research judged to be?
6. How engineerable are the variables identified in the research?
   a. How available (accessible and manipulable) are the variables for possible control by practitioners?
   b. How much difference in the practice situation will it make if the variables are manipulated?
   c. How feasible is it to manipulate variables of the research in the practice situation (economic feasibility, ethical suitability, organizational constraints) ?
7. What types of use can be made of the research (direct application, indirect or complementary application, general stimulation of ideas) ?

Exemplars

Seven examples of quantitative-descriptive studies are reproduced in this section. Not all of the sub-types are included in the selections but the problems of assessing research typical of this broad class of studies are well represented. Quantitative-descriptive studies often make use of available data and this introduces additional considerations of assessment. Examples of such studies are included. The straightforward report of survey results is not represented by a separate selection since the problems of assessing such studies are present within most of the other types of quantitative-descriptive studies. Research to test tentative hypotheses and research to establish empirical relationships among variables appear increasingly in the social work literature. The selections presented here include a number of such studies.

MARGARET K. BACON, IRVIN L. CHILD,
HERBERT BARRY, III

8

*A Cross-Cultural Study of
Correlates of Crime* [*][1]

A number of researchers have analyzed the sociological and psychological background of delinquents and criminals and compared them with a noncriminal control population, in order to discover what conditions give rise to criminal behavior; for a recent review, see Robison (1960). The present paper reports on variations among a sample of preliterate societies in the frequency of crime, in order to determine what other known features of these societies are associated with the occurrence of crime. The cross-cultural technique (Whiting, 1954), in which each society is taken as a single case, is a unique method for studying crime and has certain advantages: the index of frequency of crime in a society represents the average among its many individuals and over a span of many years, so that the measure is likely to be more stable and reliable than a measure of criminal tendency in a single individual. Some of the cultural features which may be related to crime show wider variations among societies than within a single society, permitting a more comprehensive test of their significance. Results which are consistent in a number of diverse societies may be applied to a great variety of cultural conditions instead of being limited to a single cultural setting.

If certain cultural features foster the development of criminal behavior, they should be found preponderantly in societies with a high frequency of crime; factors which inhibit crime should be found largely in societies which are low in crime. Thus the cross-cultural method may help us discover psychological and sociological variables which have a causal relationship to the development of crime; the importance of these variables may then also be tested intraculturally. On the other hand, variables identified as possible causes of crime within our society may be tested for broader significance by the cross-cultural method.

[*] From: Margaret K. Bacon, Irvin L. Child, Herbert Barry, III, "A Cross-Cultural Study of Correlates of Crime," *Journal of Abnormal and Social Psychology*, Vol. 66, No. 4 (April, 1963), pp. 291–300. Copyright 1963 by the American Psychological Association, and reproduced by permission.

[1] This research was supported by grants from the Social Science Research Council; the Ford Foundation; and the National Institute of Mental Health, United States Public Service (M-2681).

We wish to express appreciation to Selden D. Bacon for many helpful suggestions in the preparation of this manuscript, and to James Sakoda for generously providing us with a program permitting rapid calculation of our results on the IBM 709. We also wish to thank Pearl Davenport, Hatsumi Maretzki, and Abraham Rosman, who made many of the ratings employed in our calculations.

145

The possible causal factors which we have explored are principally concerned with child training practices, economy, and social structure. Hypotheses concerning these factors, as they have been presented by other writers or as they have occurred to us, will be described in connection with the presentation of our results.

METHOD

Sample.—The sample used in this study consists of 48 societies, mostly preliterate, scattered over the world. They were taken from a larger group of 110 societies which were selected on the basis of geographical diversity and adequacy of information on aboriginal child training practices. The present sample of 48 consists of those societies whose ethnographies were searched and found to provide sufficient information to permit comparative ratings on criminal behavior by three independent research workers.[2]

Ratings.—We have included two types of crime in our study: *theft* and *personal crime.* These two were chosen because they are relatively easy to identify and almost universal in occurrence. Also, they represent two quite different types of behavior. Thus we are able to clarify antecedents common to both types of crime and those characteristic of only one. Judgments were always made in relation to the norms of the culture under consideration. Theft was defined as stealing the personal property of others. Property included anything on which the society placed value, whether it was a whale's tooth or a song. Personal crime was defined by intent to injure or kill a person; assault, rape, suicide, sorcery intended to make another ill, murder, making false accusations, etc., were all included.

The method of comparative ratings was used to obtain measures of frequency. Three raters independently analyzed the ethnographic material on each society and made ratings on a seven-point scale as to the

---

2 The 48 societies included in the study are as follows: Africa—Ashanti, Azande, Bena, Chagga, Dahomeans, Lovedu, Mbundu, Thonga; Asia—Andamanese, Baiga, Chenchu, Chukchee, Lepcha, Muria, Tanala, Yakut; North America—Cheyenne, Comanche, Flatheads, Hopi, Jamaicans (Rocky Roaders), Kaska, Kwakiutl, Navaho, Papago, Tepoztlan, Western Apache; South America—Aymara, Cuna, Jivaro, Siriono, Yagua; Oceania—Arapesh, Balinese, Buka (Kurtachi), Ifaluk, Kwoma, Lau Fijians (Kambara), Lesu, Manus, Maori, Pukapukans, Samoans, Tikopia, Trobrianders, Trukese, Ulithians, Vanua Levu (Nakoroka). All information was obtained from ethnographic studies available in the literature or in the Human Relations Area Files. Ratings were, so far as possible, of the aboriginal practices of the group in order to reduce the influence of acculturation. All ratings used in this study have been filed with the American Documentation Institute. Order Document No. 7450 from the ADI Auxiliary Publications Project, Photoduplication Service, Library of Congress; Washington 25, D. C., remitting in advance $1.75 for microfilm or $2.50 for photocopies. Make checks payable to: Chief, Photoduplication Service, Library of Congress. All intercorrelations among variables for our sample of societies appear in the same document.

relative frequency of the type of crime under consideration. Thus a rating of 4 on theft would mean that the frequency of theft in a given society appeared to be about average for the sample of societies. Ratings of 5, 6, and 7 represented high frequencies and those of 3, 2, and 1 were low. Societies in which the behavior did not occur were rated as 0. Each rating was classified as confident or doubtful at the time that it was made. No rating was made if the analyst judged the information to be insufficient. We have included all societies on which all three analysts made a rating, whether it was confident or doubtful, and we have used the pooled ratings of all three analysts. The reliability of these pooled ratings is estimated as +.67 for Theft and +.57 for Personal Crime. These estimates were obtained by averaging (using a z transformation) the separate interrater reliabilities, and entering this average into the Spearman-Brown correction formula.

Most writers in this field make a distinction between delinquency and crime largely on the basis of the age of the offender. The nature of our evidence does not permit us to make such a clear distinction. Ratings were made in terms of the relative frequency of specific types of criminal behavior in the adult population. Since the age at which adulthood is considered to have begun varies from one society to another, ratings may in some cases have included individuals young enough to be considered adolescent in our society and therefore delinquent rather than criminal. The distinction does not appear to be crucial in this study.

The measures of possible causal variables consist of ratings which have been derived from several sources. Each will be described in the following section. Except where noted (for certain variables in Tables 3 and 4), none of the three people who made the crime ratings participated in any of the other ratings.

HYPOTHESES, RESULTS, AND DISCUSSION

Our results will be presented under three main headings: Correlates of Crime in General, Correlates Specific to Theft, and Correlates Specific to Personal Crime. As this classification suggests, we have found it useful to consider the antecedents of crime as either general or specific, i.e., leading to a general increase in criminal behavior, or associated with only one major category of crime. A correlation of +.46 was found between frequency of Theft and frequency of Personal Crime. This indicates that the two variables show a significant degree of communality ($p < .01$) and also some independence.

CORRELATES OF CRIME IN GENERAL

Our principal findings concerning common correlates of both Theft and Personal Crime are relevant to a hypothesis that crime arises partly as a defense against strong feminine identification. We will begin with an account of this hypothesis.

In our society crime occurs mostly in men, and we have no reason to doubt that this sex difference characterizes most societies. Several writers have called attention to the sex role identification of males as especially pertinent to the development of delinquency in our society. It is assumed that the very young boy tends to identify with his mother rather than his father because of his almost exclusive contact with his mother. Later in his development he becomes aware of expectations that he behave in a masculine way and as a result his behavior tends to be marked by a compulsive masculinity which is really a defense against feminine identification. Parsons (1954, pp. 304-305) notes further that the mother is the principal agent of socialization as well as an object of love and identification. Therefore, when the boy revolts he unconsciously identifies "goodness" with femininity and hence accepts the role of "bad boy" as a positive goal.

Miller (1958) has made a study of lower-class culture and delinquency which is also pertinent in this connection. He points out that some delinquent behavior may result from an attempt to live up to attitudes and values characteristic of lower-class culture. He also notes that many lower-class males are reared in predominantly female households lacking a consistently present male with whom to identify. He feels that what he calls an almost obsessive lower-class concern with masculinity results from the feminine identification in preadolescent years.

Whiting, Kluckhohn, and Anthony (1958), in a cross-cultural study of male initiation rites at puberty, found these rites tended to occur in societies with prolonged, exclusive mother-son sleeping arrangements. Their interpretation of this relationship is that the early mother-infant sleeping arrangement produces an initial feminine identification, and later control by men leads to a secondary masculine identification. The function of the initiation ceremony is to resolve this conflict of sexual identification in favor of the masculine identification. The authors further predict that insofar as there has been an increase in juvenile delinquency in our society, "it probably has been accompanied by an increase in the exclusiveness of mother-child relationships and/or a decrease in the authority of the father."

The hypothesis that crime is in part a defense against initial feminine identification would lead to the expectation that all factors which tend to produce strong identification with the mother and failure of early identification with the father would be positively correlated with the frequency of crime in the adult population. The factor that is easiest to study is the presence of the father. It seems reasonable to suppose that successful identification with the father is dependent on his presence.

Therefore, societies which differ in the degree to which the father is present during the child's first few years should differ correspondingly in the degree to which the boy typically forms a masculine identification.[3]

Whiting (1959) has made use of Murdock's (1957) classification of household structure and family composition to distinguish among four types of households which provide a range from maximal to minimal degree of presence of the father. They are as follows:

Monogamous Nuclear.—This household is the usual one in our society. The father, mother, and children eat, sleep, and entertain under one roof. Grandparents, siblings of the parents, and other relatives live elsewhere. The effective presence of the father in the child's environment is thus at a maximum.

Monogamous Extended.—Here two or more nuclear families live together under one roof. A typical extended family consists of an aged couple together with their married sons and daughters and their respective families. In such a household, the child's interaction with his father is likely to be somewhat less than in the single nuclear household.

Polygynous Polygynous.—The polygynous household consists of a man living with his wives and their various children. Here the child is likely to have even less opportunity to interact with his father.

Polygynous Mother-Child.—This type of household occurs in those

TABLE 1

FREQUENCY OF THEFT OR PERSONAL CRIME IN RELATION TO FAMILY STRUCTURE AND HOUSEHOLD

Family Structure and Household[a]	Frequency of Theft		Frequency of Personal Crime	
	Low	High	Low	High
Monogamous Nuclear	7	2	5	4
Monogamous Extended	7	3	6	3
Polygynous Polygynous	7	6	3	7
Polygynous Mother-Child	1	11	3	9

Note.—Each entry in the table gives the number of societies in our sample which have the particular combination of characteristics indicated for that row and column.
The total number of cases in the left-hand and right-hand parts of this table and in the various divisions of succeeding tables varies because lack of information prevented rating some societies on some variables. In testing each relationship we have of course been able to use only those societies for which the relevant ratings are available. The division into "low" and "high" was made as near the median as possible.
a See Murdock (1957).

polygynous societies where each wife has a separate establishment and lives in it with her children. In these societies the father either sleeps in a men's club, has a hut of his own, or divides his time among the houses of

---

[3] The whole problem of the mechanism whereby identification occurs has been omitted from this study. In all theories it would appear that identification with the father would be in some degree a function of the frequency of the presence of the father.

his various wives. The husband usually does not sleep in the house of any wife during the 2 to 3 years when she is nursing each infant. Thus the mother may become the almost exclusive object of identification for the first few years of life.

Table 1 shows the number of societies with low and high frequency of Theft and Personal Crime within each of the four categories of household type. As the opportunity for contact with the father decreases, the frequency of both Theft and Personal Crime increases. This result agrees with our hypothesis. If the family structure and household is treated as a four-point scale, it yields a correlation of +.58 with frequency of Theft and of +.44 with frequency of Personal Crime; both correlations are statistically significant ($p < .01$). If we compare the extremes of the distribution—contrasting Monogamous Nuclear households (which provide the maximum opportunity for identification with the father) with Polygynous Mother-Child households (which provide the minimum opportunity for identification with the father)—this relationship is clearly demonstrated; 18 of the 21 societies fall in the predicted quadrants for Theft, and 14 out of 21 for Personal Crime.

Several results of empirical studies in our society appear consistent with this finding. One is the frequently reported relationship between broken homes and delinquency, since in the majority of cases broken homes are probably mother-child households. Robins and O'Neal (1958), for example, in a follow-up study of problem children after 30 years, refer to the high incidence of fatherless families. Glueck and Glueck (1950) report that 41.2% of their delinquent group were not living with their own fathers, as compared with 24.8% of a matched nondelinquent group. These data suggest that a relatively high proportion of the delinquents came from what were essentially "mother-child" households.

A recent book by Rohrer and Edmonson (1960) is also relevant. Their study is a follow-up after 20 years of the individuals described in *Children of Bondage* by Davis and Dollard (1941). The importance of the matriarchal household typical in a Southern Negro lower-class group, and its effect on the emotional development of the young boy and his eventual attitudes as an adult, are stressed throughout. The following passage summarizes, in its application to their (Rohrer & Edmonson) particular data, an interpretation consistent with those we have cited in introducing this hypothesis.

Gang life begins early, more or less contemporaneously with the first years of schooling, and for many men lasts until death. . . . Although each gang is a somewhat distinct group, all of them appear to have a common structure expressing and reinforcing a gang ideology. Thus an organizational form that springs from the little boy's search for a masculinity he cannot find at home becomes first a protest against femininity and then an assertion of hypervirility.

On the way it acquires a structuring in which the aspirations and goals of the matriarchy or the middle class are seen as soft, effeminate, and despicable. The gang ideology of masculine independence is formed from these perceptions, and the gang then sees its common enemy not as a class, nor even perhaps as a sex, but as the "feminine principle" in society. The gang member rejects this femininity in every form, and he sees it in women and in effeminate men, in laws and morals and religion, in schools and occupational striving (pp. 162–63).

CORRELATES OF THEFT

Although we shall consider correlates of Theft in this section and correlates of Personal Crime in the next section, each table will show in parallel columns the relation of a set of variables both to Theft and to Personal Crime. This will facilitate comparison and avoid repetition. How each of these variables was measured will be described in the section to which it is most pertinent.

The first variables to be considered are concerned with child training practices. Most of the child training variables have been developed in our research and described in an earlier paper (Barry, Bacon, & Child, 1957). These variables may be briefly described as follows:

Overall childhood indulgence.—The period of childhood was defined roughly as covering the age period from 5 to 12 years, or to the beginning of any pubertal or prepubertal status change. In making ratings of childhood indulgence, factors relevant to indulgence in infancy—such as immediacy and degree of drive reduction, display of affection by parents, etc.—if operative at this later age, were taken into account. In addition, the raters also considered the degree of socialization expected in childhood and the severity of the methods used to obtain the expected behavior.

Anxiety associated with socialization during the same period of childhood.—This was rated separately for each of five systems of behavior: Responsibility or dutifulness training; Nurturance training, i.e., training the child to be nurturant or helpful toward younger siblings and other dependent people; Obedience training; Self-reliance training; Achievement training, i.e., training the child to orient his behavior toward standards of excellence in performance and to seek to achieve as excellent a performance as possible.

In rating the training in these areas, an attempt was first made to estimate the Total Pressure exerted by the adults in each society toward making the children behave in each of these specified ways (Responsible, Nurturant, Obedient, Self-Reliant, and Achieving). The *socialization anxiety* measures were based on an estimate of the amount of anxiety aroused in the child by failing to behave in a responsible, self-reliant, etc. way, and they reflect primarily the extent of punishment for failure to show each particular form of behavior. The measures of Total Pressure reflect both this and the extent of reward and encouragement.

Wherever boys and girls were rated differently on any of the above variables of socialization, we used the ratings for boys.

The relation of the crime ratings to these and other variables of child training is presented in Table 2. It is clear that Theft is significantly related to several variables of child training.

First, theft is negatively correlated with Childhood Indulgence, i.e., societies with a high rating of Childhood Indulgence tend to have a low frequency of theft in the adult population; and, conversely, societies with a low rating of Childhood Indulgence show a high frequency of Theft.

TABLE 2

CHILD TRAINING FACTORS ASSOCIATED WITH THEFT OR PERSONAL CRIME

Factor	Theft		Personal Crime	
	N	r	N	r
1. Childhood Indulgence[a]	45	−.41[e]	42	−.10
2. Responsibility Socialization Anxiety[a]....	43	+.48[e]	41	+.20
3. Self-Reliance Socialization Anxiety[a].....	43	+.35[d]	41	+.24
4. Achievement Socialization Anxiety[a]......	36	+.41[d]	35	+.20
5. Obedience Socialization Anxiety[a]........	40	+.32[d]	39	+.06
6. Dependence Socialization Anxiety[b]......	31	+.14	28	+.56[e]
7. Mother-Child Sleeping[c]	20	+.40	19	+.46[d]
8. Infant Indulgence[a]	—	—	—	—
9. Age of Weaning[a]	—	—	—	—
10. Oral Socialization Anxiety[b]	—	—	—	—
11. Anal Socialization Anxiety[b]	—	—	—	—
12. Sex Socialization Anxiety[b]	—	—	—	—
13. Aggression Socialization Anxiety[b]........	—	—	—	—
14. Nurturance Socialization Anxiety[a].......	—	—	—	—
15. Total Pressures toward Responsibility, Nurturance, Self-Reliance, Achievement, and Obedience[a]................	—	—	—	—

Note.—In this and the following tables the correlations are Pearsonian coefficients, thus reflecting all available degrees of gradation in score rather than simply classifying societies as high and low. Factors 8–15 showed no significant relationship with either Theft or Personal Crime.
a See Barry, Bacon, and Child (1957).
b See Whiting and Child (1953).
c See Whiting, Kluckhohn, and Anthony (1958).
d $p \leq .05$.
e $p \leq .01$.

Frequency of Theft is also positively correlated with socialization anxiety during the period of childhood with respect to the following areas of training: Responsibility, Self-Reliance, Achievement, and Obedience. It should be emphasized that Total Pressures toward those four areas of socialization are not significantly correlated with Theft. Therefore it is apparently not the area or level of socialization required which is significant, but rather the punitive and anxiety provoking methods of socialization employed.

These findings on child training in relation to Theft may be summarized and interpreted by the hypothesis that theft is in part motivated by feelings of deprivation of love. Our data indicate that one source of such feelings is punitive and anxiety provoking treatment during childhood. Such treatment during infancy may tend to have a similar effect, as suggested by a correlation of −.25 between frequency of Theft and

TABLE 3

SOCIOECONOMIC FACTORS ASSOCIATED WITH THEFT OR PERSONAL CRIME

Factor	Theft		Personal Crime	
	N	r	N	r
1. Social Stratification[a]	44	+.36[d]	40	+.16
2. Level of Political Integration[a]	43	+.34[d]	39	+.02
3. Degree of Elaboration of Social Control[b]	43	+.46[e]	40	+.04
4. Accumulation of Food[c]	—	—	—	—
5. Settlement Pattern[a]	—	—	—	—
6. Division of Labor by Sex[a]	—	—	—	—
7. Rule of Residence (Patrilocal, Matrilocal, etc.)[a]	—	—	—	—
8. Extent of Storing[b]	—	—	—	—
9. Irrationality of Storing[b]	—	—	—	—
10. Severity of Punishment for Property Crime[b]	—	—	—	—
11. Severity of Punishment for Personal Crime[b]	—	—	—	—

Note.—Ratings of Factors 3, 10, and 11 were made in connection with the analysis of crime by two of the three raters (H. Maretzki and A. Rosman). Ratings of Factors 8 and 9 were made by one of the raters (H. Maretzki) but in connection with an analysis of food and economy. Factors 4–11 showed no significant relationship with either Theft or Personal Crime.
[a] See Murdock (1957).
[b] Bacon, Child, and Barry (unpublished).
[c] See Barry, Child and Bacon (1959).
[d] $p < .05$.
[e] $p < .01$.

Infant Indulgence. This correlation falls slightly short of significance at the 5% level. It is of special interest that substantial correlations with socialization anxiety in childhood tended to occur in the areas of training in Responsibility, Achievement, and Self-Reliance. These all involve demands for behavior far removed from the dependent behavior of infancy and early childhood and close to the independent behavior expected of adults. If we assume that lack of adequate indulgence in childhood leads to a desire to return to earlier means of gratification and behavior symbolic of this need, then we would expect that pressures toward more adult behavior might intensify this need and the frequency of the symbolic behavior. Theft, from this point of view, would be seen as rewarded partly by its value as symbolic gratification of an infantile demand for unconditional indulgence irrespective of other people's rights or interests.

The results of the early study by Healy and Bronner (1936) seem directly pertinent to our findings and interpretation. They found that a group of delinquents differed from their nondelinquent siblings primarily in their relationships with their parents; the delinquent child was much more likely to give evidence of feeling thwarted and rejected. It seems reasonable to assume that such feelings would often, though not always, indicate a real deprivation of parental love. Glueck and Glueck (1950) also found that their delinquents, compared with matched non-delinquents, had received less affection from their parents and siblings and had a greater tendency to feel that their parents were not concerned with their welfare. It was also noted that fathers of the delinquents had a much greater tendency to resort to physical punishment as a means of discipline than fathers of the nondelinquents. This agrees with our observation that more punitive methods of socialization are associated with an increased frequency of theft.

Compulsive stealing (kleptomania) has been interpreted by psychoanalysts (see Fenichel, 1945, pp. 370-71) as an attempt to seize symbols of security and affection. Thus this form of mental illness, in common with more rational forms of stealing, may be regarded as being motivated by feelings of deprivation of love.

Table 3 summarizes the relationship between our two measures of crime and a number of aspects of economy and social organization on which we were able to obtain ratings. Theft shows a significant relationship with only three of these measures: Social Stratification, Level of Political Integration, and Degree of Elaboration of Social Control. Social Stratification was treated as a five-point scale ranging from complex stratification, i.e., three or more definite social classes or castes exclusive of slaves, to egalitarian, i.e., absence of significant status differentiation other than recognition of political statuses and of individual skill, prowess, piety, etc. Level of Political Integration was also treated as a five-point scale ranging from complex state, e.g., confederation of tribes or conquest state with a king, differentiated officials, and a hierarchical administrative organization to no political integration, even at the community level.[4] Elaboration of Social Control is concerned with the degree to which a society has law making, law enforcing, and punishing agencies.

Our findings indicate that theft is positively correlated with each of these three measures. In other words, with an increased Level of Political Integration, Social Stratification, and Elaboration of Social Control there is an increase in the frequency of Theft. These variables show no significant relationship with frequency of Personal Crime. Each of these institutional conditions seems capable of arousing feelings of insecurity and resentment, and hence may be similar in this respect to parental deprivation. Therefore the correlation of these institutional conditions with Theft might be tentatively interpreted as consistent with our hypothesis

---

[4] Both variables are taken from Murdock (1957). Our manner of treating his data is described in Barry, Child, and Bacon (1959).

about motivational influences on Theft. It is obvious that other interpretations might be made from the same data. For example, a high frequency of crime may give rise to increased elaboration of social control.

Table 4 presents the relation of both Theft and Personal Crime to certain adult attitudes on which we were able to obtain ratings. Frequency of Theft is positively related to Sense of Property and negatively related to Trust about Property. This may indicate merely that the

TABLE 4
ADULT ATTITUDES ASSOCIATED WITH THEFT OR PERSONAL CRIME

Attitude	Theft		Personal Crime	
	N	r	N	r
1. Sense of Property	43	+.45c	40	+.25
2. Trust about Property	43	−.31b	40	−.27
3. General Trustfulness	42	−.28	40	−.40c
4. Environmental Kindness in Folk Tales	23	−.47b	21	−.30
5. Environmental Hostility in Folk Tales	23	+.36	21	+.56c
6. Communality of Property	—	—	—	—
7. Competition in the Acquisition of Wealth	—	—	—	—
8. Generosity	—	—	—	—
9. n Achievement in Folk Tales[a]	—	—	—	—

Note.—Attitude 3 was rated by one of the three raters (A. Rosman) in connection with the analysis of crime. Attitudes 1, 2, 6, 7, and 8 were rated by another of the three raters (H. Maretzki) in connection with the analysis of food and economy.
Attitudes 6–9 showed no significant relationship with either Theft or Personal Crime.
a See Child, Veroff, and Storm (1958).
b $p \leq .05$.
c $p \leq .01$.

greater the importance of property, the greater the variety of acts which will be classified as Theft, or that a high frequency of Theft gives rise to an emphasis on property. But it may also mean that the greater the importance of property, the more effectively does Theft serve the personal needs to which it seems to be related.

Frequency of Theft is also negatively correlated with Environmental Kindness in Folk Tales. This folk tale measure requires some explanation. It was taken from an analysis of folk tales made by one of the authors (MKB) without knowledge of the societies from which the sample of folk tales was taken. In making the analysis, each folk tale was divided into units of action or events as they related to the principal character or the character with whom the listener would be expected to identify. Each unit was then classified in one of a number of different categories including that of environmental kindness. Classification in this category means that the particular unit involved action or state of affairs definitely friendly or nurturant to the principal character. Thus our results show that societies high in frequency of Theft tend to have folk tales which do not represent the environment as kind. Thinking of the environment as lacking in friendly nurturance seems entirely consistent with the relative absence of parental nurturance which we have already found to be correlated with frequency of theft.

CORRELATES OF PERSONAL CRIME

Inspection of Tables 2, 3, and 4 reveals that the significant correlates of Personal Crime are different from those for theft. In no instance does a variable in these tables show a significant correlation with both Theft and Personal Crime.

Frequency of Personal Crime shows a significant positive correlation with Dependence Socialization Anxiety, a rating taken from Whiting and Child (1953). In making this rating, an estimate was made of the amount of anxiety aroused in the children of a given society by the methods of independence training typically employed. This estimate was based on the following factors: abruptness of the transition required, severity and frequency of punishment, and evidence of emotional disturbance in the child.

Ratings on mother-child sleeping are taken from Whiting et al. (1958). In this study societies were placed into two categories: those in which the mother and baby shared the same bed for at least a year to the exclusion of the father, those in which the baby slept alone or with both the mother and father. According to our results there is a high positive relationship between prolonged, exclusive mother-child sleeping arrangements and frequency of Personal Crime.[5]

Inspection of the child training factors associated with frequency of Personal Crime suggests that the conditions in childhood leading to a high frequency of personal crime among adults are as follows: a mother-child household with inadequate opportunity in early life for identification with the father, mother-child sleeping arrangements which tend to foster a strong dependent relationship between the child and the mother, subsequent socialization with respect to independence training which tends to be abrupt, punitive, and productive of emotional disturbance in the child.

We would predict that this pattern of child training factors would tend to produce in the child persistent attitudes of rivalry, distrust, and hostility, which would probably continue into adult life. The results obtained with ratings of adult attitudes (Table 4) support this view. Frequency of Personal Crime is negatively correlated with General Trustfulness. Frequency of Personal Crime is also positively correlated with Environmental Hostility in Folk Tales. Classification of a folk tale

---

[5] The variable of mother-child sleeping might be considered to favor feminine identification. In that event, the fact that it shows correlations in the positive direction with both types of crime tends toward confirmation of the findings in our earlier section on Correlates of Crime in General.

unit in this category means that the particular unit involved definite deception, aggression, or rejection in relation to the principal character. This variable was not highly related to that of environmental kindness although the results obtained with the two are consistent with each other. The correlation between them was only −.34, most folk tale units not falling in either of these categories. Our results indicate that societies which are rated as relatively high in the frequency of Personal Crime have folk tales with a high proportion of events representing the environment as hostile. If we may infer that the content of folk tales reflects the underlying attitudes of the people who tell them, then this finding, as well as those with our other measures of adult attitudes, supports the view that personal crime is correlated with a suspicious or distrustful attitude toward the environment.

An analysis by Whiting (1959) of the socialization factors correlated with a belief in sorcery is relevant to this aspect of our results. He points out that a belief in sorcery is consistent with a paranoid attitude. According to Freudian interpretation, paranoia represents a defense against sexual anxiety. Whiting presents cross-cultural data in support of a hypothesis, based on Freud's theory of paranoia, that a belief in sorcery is related to a prolonged and intense contact with the mother in infancy followed by a severe sex socialization. The same hypothesis might be applied to frequency of Personal Crime, since we have evidence that Personal Crime is correlated with a suspicious, paranoid attitude in adult life, and sorcery is after all one form of Personal Crime. Our results for Personal Crime, in common with Whiting's sorcery, show a correlation with mother-child household and prolonged mother-child sleeping. However, we found no significant correlation with severe sex socialization but rather with severe dependence socialization. We do not feel that these findings negate the Freudian interpretation, because dependence socialization, bearing as it does on the child's intimate relation with his mother, necessarily is concerned with the child's sexual feelings in a broad sense.

GENERAL DISCUSSION

We would like to emphasize the value of the cross-cultural method for exploring the possible determinants of crime. When each society is used as a single case, and is classified according to crime and other variables for the entire society over a period of years, the measures are likely to be reliable; comparison among societies provides great diversity in frequency of crime and in the other variables to be related with it.

The cross-cultural method may help us to identify variables with a causal relationship to crime. For example, our cross-cultural data suggest that high differentiation of status within a society is a favorable condition for a high frequency of Theft, and that a high frequency of Personal Crime is associated with a generalized attitude of distrust. These relationships should be subjected to more systematic and intensive tests within our own society than has hitherto been done.

Variables which have been suggested, whether in empirical studies or theoretical discussions, as possible causes of crime within our society may be tested for broader significance by the cross-cultural method. It has been argued, for example, that within our society delinquent or criminal behavior is likely to develop if the boy has been raised without adequate opportunity to identify with the father. These suggestions have often been made in connection with family patterns that are said to characterize certain classes or groups within our society; the cross-cultural findings indicate that a high frequency of both Theft and Personal Crime tends to occur in societies where the typical family for the society as a whole creates lack or limitation of opportunity for the young boy to form an identification with his father. Therefore the cross-cultural method supports the theory that lack of opportunity for the young boy to form a masculine identification is in itself an important antecedent of crime.

Another instance of such confirmation in a broader sense is the following: In our society delinquents have been reported to express feelings of alienation from their parents. It is unclear, however, whether this reflects their parents' actual treatment of them, or merely their own subjectively determined perceptions. Our cross-cultural data (in common with some of the findings within our own society) indicate that a high frequency of Theft is correlated with an actual low degree of indulgence during childhood.

Other theories about the antecedents of crime, when tested with the cross-cultural method, have not been confirmed in this broader framework. For example, pressures toward achievement were not significantly related to frequency of crime, although such a relationship is implied by theories of delinquency which emphasize the discrepancy between culturally induced aspirations and the possibility of achieving them. This negative result in our sample of societies does not deny the existence of such a relationship within our society, but it does indicate a limitation on its generality.

REFERENCES

BARRY, H., III, BACON, MARGARET K., & CHILD, I. L. A cross-cultural survey of some sex differences in socialization. *J. abnorm. soc. Psychol.*, 1957, 55, 327–32.

———, CHILD, I. L., & BACON, MARGARET K. Relation of child training to subsistence economy. *Amer. Anthropologist*, 1959, 61, 51–63.

CHILD, I. L., VEROFF, J., & STORM, T. Achievement themes in folk tales related to socialization practice. In J. W. Atkinson (ed.), *Motives in fantasy, action, and society*. Princeton: D. Van Nostrand Co., Inc., 1958, pp. 479–92.

DAVIS A., & DOLLARD, J. *Children of bondage*. Washington: American Council on Education, 1941.

FENICHEL, O. *The psychoanalytic theory of neurosis*. New York: W. W. Norton & Company, Inc., 1945.

GLUECK, S., & GLUECK, ELEANOR. *Unraveling juvenile delinquency*. New York: Commonwealth Fund, 1950.

HEALY, W., & BRONNER, A. F. *New light on delinquency and its treatment*. New Haven: Yale Univer. Press, 1936. (Republished 1957)

MILLER, W. B. Lower class culture as a generating milieu of gang delinquency. *J. soc. Issues*, 1958, 14, 5–19.

MURDOCK, G. P. World ethnographic sample. *Amer. Anthropologist*, 1957, 59, 664–87.

PARSONS, T. *Essays in sociological theory*. (Rev. ed.) Glencoe, Ill.: Free Press, 1954.

ROBINS, L. N., & O'NEAL, PATRICIA. Mortality, mobility and crime: Problem children thirty years later. *Amer. sociol. Rev.*, 1958, 23, 162–71.

ROBISON, SOPHIA M. *Juvenile delinquency: Its nature and control*. New York: Holt, Rinehart & Winston, Inc., 1960.

ROHRER, J. H., & EDMONSON, M. S. (eds.). *Eighth generation: Cultures and personalities of New Orleans Negroes*. New York: Harper & Row, Publishers, 1960.

WHITING, J. W. M. The cross-cultural method. In G. Lindzey (ed.), *Handbook of social psychology*. Vol. 1. *Theory and method*. Cambridge, Mass.: Addison-Wesley Publishing Co., Inc., 1964, pp. 523–31.

———. Sorcery, sin and the superego: A cross-cultural study of some mechanisms of social control. In M. R. Jones (ed.), *Nebraska symposium on motivation: 1959*. Lincoln: Univer. Nebraska Press, 1959, pp. 174–95.

———, & CHILD, I. L. *Child training and personality*. New Haven: Yale Univer. Press, 1953.

———, KLUCKHOHN, R., & ANTHONY, A. The function of male initiation ceremonies at puberty. In Eleanor E. Maccoby, T. Newcomb, & E. L. Hartley (eds.), *Readings in social psychology*. (3rd ed.) New York: Holt, Rinehart & Winston, Inc., 1958, pp. 359–70.

WILLIAM A. GAMSON

9   *Reputation and Resources in
Community Politics**

In the post mortem which accompanies any political defeat, the losing group will typically take itself to task for various failures. There is, in such analyses, a tendency to assume that the exercise of influence alone determines the outcome of a decision. The other side is seen as having been more effective—as having spent more resources or as having used its resources more efficiently. While this may be true, it is also possible in such cases that the losing side was quite effective while the winning side did little or nothing to further their cause. The exercise of influence is only one element in the outcome of political issues.

It is helpful, in speaking of influence, to start with the notion of a decision to be made. Influence can then be handled very well, as Dahl has suggested,[1] using the notion of conditional probability. The amount of influence a social unit has had on a decision is represented by the difference between the probability of the desired outcome before and after the influence attempt. To say that one has influenced a decision means simply that he has changed the probability of the desired outcome in the intended direction.[2] By such a definition, the presence or absence of influence cannot be clearly inferred from whether or not the would-be influencer is on the winning side of a decision. A partisan group in a community may start with little chance of an alternative being accepted. By waging a vigorous fight they may reach a point where acceptance or rejection is touch and go. Ultimately, of course, the measure will either pass or fail, but we should not judge this group to have had influence only if it passes. The move from an almost certain failure to a near-miss is a mark of their influence. Similarly, a victory cannot be taken as *prima facie* evidence of influence since a narrow victory by a partisan group in a situation in which they would have won doing nothing is no indication of influence.

This paper is concerned with understanding the outcome of community issues and, in particular, with the role that those with a general

* Reprinted from *The American Journal of Sociology, Vol. 72*, No. 2 (September, 1966), pp. 121–31. Reproduced by permission of the University of Chicago Press, and the author.
1 Robert Dahl, "The Concept of Power," *Behavioral Science,* II (July, 1957), 201–15. Herbert A. Simon and James G. March have suggested similar formulations.

2 One might wish to talk of changes in an unintended direction as "negative influence," but this issue is not relevant for the discussion here.

reputation for influence play in such outcomes. Factors other than influence may, in some cases, put severe limits on the possible effects which partisan groups or individuals may have. Accordingly, it seems useful to take as a working assumption the asymmetry of the influence task for different partisan groups. Those on one side of an issue are likely to have a natural advantage over those on the other side, an advantage which will enable them to win if they simply hold their own in an influence contest.

What is the nature of this "natural advantage"? Most broadly, it is the advantage that falls to those who do not carry the burden of proof. In relatively stable situations, this advantage is held by those who would maintain a present arrangement against those who would alter it. Many community issues arise from the presentation of a proposal to alter some existing facility or service or to add some new facility. The burden of proof in such cases generally rests with the side proposing the change. For example, if a new school is proposed, those who oppose it may raise any number of questions about need, cost, design, site, and so forth. It is not necessary to resolve such questions in order to block action on this proposal; if they remain unanswered, this is generally sufficient.

The communities studied here are not undergoing acute crises. They are, then, a special case in which the natural advantage falls to those who would maintain existing conditions. To admit the existence of such an advantage is not to argue that those who desire change will fail but only that they will fail in the absence of influence no greater than that exercised by the other side. In the discussion which follows, special attention is given to the role of "reputational leaders" in such an influence process.

REPUTATION AND RESOURCES

A number of investigators interested in the operation of power in the community have elicited lists of names of community "leaders." Typically, a panel composed of heads of civic associations or some other group actively involved in public affairs is asked to nominate individuals and the nominees are in turn interviewed.[3] This "reputational method" of studying community power has been sharply attacked both for the interpretations that are made of the list of names obtained and, in more basic ways, for the use of such questions at all. To quote Polsby, "asking about reputations is asking, at a remove, about behavior. It can be

---

[3] It is not my intention to review or even cite such studies here. Nelson Polsby's *Community Power and Political Theory* (New Haven, Conn.: Yale University Press, 1963) has a reasonably complete list of citations and a highly critical review of these studies. See esp. pp. 45–68.

argued that the researcher should make it his business to study behavior directly rather than depend on the opinions of second hand sources."[4]

What does it mean, we may ask, when an individual or group of individuals is frequently named as "influential" by those involved in community political affairs? Are such reputations meaningless in themselves, telling us no more at best than we might more efficiently learn from studying actual influence over decisions? Reputation, I will argue, is a resource; as such, it refers to potential influence rather than influence in use. Reputation is not simply the manifestation of the possession of large amounts of resources but is, itself, a resource in the same sense that money, wealth, or authority might be. This argument requires some discussion of the concept of resources.

What is it that an influencer uses to exercise influence? In any decision, there exists some "thing" or "weight" such that if enough of this weight is applied to the decision-makers the probability of an alternative being accepted or rejected will be changed. This thing must satisfy two important conditions to be considered a resource. First, it must be possessed by or, more accurately, *controlled* by the influencer. He must be able to determine its use. Second, he must be able to bring it to bear on decision-makers in interaction with them.

Since in any society certain things are widely valued, certain resources are both of high applicability across a variety of decision-makers and of high stability of value over time within a particular set of decision-makers. It is the possession of such general resources rather than of more idiosyncratic ones that is of significance for understanding the stable potential to influence the outcome of decisions.

Many authors have distinguished among the ways that resources are used to produce influence.[5] The most relevant distinction for the present argument is implicit in a number of these discussions, but it is made most explicitly by Parsons. In the terms which will be used here, *sanctioning* influence is the addition of new advantages or disadvantages (conditional or not) to the situation of the decision-maker. *Persuasion* influence

---

4 *Ibid.,* p. 51.

5 These include John R. P. French, Jr., and Bertram Raven, "The Bases of Social Power," in Dorwin Cartwright (ed.), *Studies in Social Power* (Ann Arbor, Mich.: Institute for Social Research, 1959), pp. 150–67; Herbert Kelman, "Processes of Opinion Change," *Public Opinion Quarterly,* XXV (Spring, 1961), 57–78; Amitai Etzioni, *A Comparative Analysis of Complex Organizations* (Glencoe, Ill.: Free Press, 1961); Franz L. Neumann, "Approaches to the Study of Political Power," *Political Science Quarterly,* LXV (1950), 161–80; Morris Janowitz, *The Professional Soldier* (Glencoe, Ill.: Free Press, 1960); Herbert Goldhamer and Edward A. Shils, "Types of Power and Status," *American Journal of Sociology,* XLV (September, 1939), 171–82; John Harsanyi, "Measurement of Social Power, Opportunity Costs, and the Theory of Two-Person Bargaining Games," *Behavioral Science,* VII (January, 1962), 67–80; and Talcott Parsons, "On the Concept of Influence," *Public Opinion Quarterly,* XXVII (Spring, 1963), 37–62.

operates on the orientation of the decision-maker, changing the connection he sees between a decision outcome and his goals without the addition of any new advantages or disadvantages to the situation.

It is not difficult to conceive of sanctioning resources of high stability and generality. A person who holds a position of great potential influence in an elaborate network of institutional and interpersonal relationships possesses a powerful set of inducements. It is virtually certain that there will be some present or future alternative that he can influence that present decision-makers care about. Furthermore, it is a valuable political asset to have such a potentially influential person obligated to oneself.

Is it possible to talk about a similarly general basis of persuasion? Clearly, we can conceive of persuasion resources which are highly limited in scope. Expertness, for example, is only a resource for those areas in which the influencer is considered knowledgeable. Are there more generalized and stable persuasion resources?

A generalized reputation for "wisdom" or "good sense" is just such a stable persuasion resource. There are individuals who are respected by particular groups in a community not because of any *specific* expertness they may have on the issue at hand but because they are believed to be generally "knowledgeable," "sound," "reliable," "unselfish," "intelligent," and so forth. In other words, they are believed to possess certain stable personal qualities that transcend any given issue and make their opinion more convincing. A highly successful lawyer, for example, who actively participates in community affairs may find that his success is regarded by public officials as a sign of grace. While his persuasion resources on issues involving legal matters may be particularly great, he will carry with him a generalized reputation which acts as a resource— even on issues for which he has no special qualifications.

He has no persuasion resources, of course, among those who do not accept his reputation. Resources are categorized here in terms of their applicability to decision-makers. A spokesman who enjoyed the complete confidence of members of some solidary group would have a persuasion resource with respect to decisions made by his followers. However, his influence over this group might in turn be used as an inducement for public officials who wish the group's votes in an election.

A theoretical justification for identifying reputational leaders is being offered here. One asks about reputation simply to identify those who have reputation; such reputation is significant because it is a stable and generalized persuasion resource. Of course, we may quarrel with the method used to identify such people. One technique is to ask community decision-makers a question such as: "In many communities, there are people who are generally listened to when they take a position on community issues because they are believed to have good judgment. Are there any such people in ——?" Those who are frequently named form an operational definition of "people with stable persuasion resources." The validity of such a question concerns how well it measures reputation, not its connection with influence behavior.

Those who are named as "reputational leaders" simply comprise a pool of individuals with resources. No claim is made that they form a ruling elite or even a cohesive group of any sort; such claims must rest on demonstration of a number of additional characteristics. Those with resources may or may not be friendly with each other socially. If they all belong to the same clubs and organizations, this is an important additional fact about the organization of resources in the community. The list by itself tells us nothing about this fact.

Similarly, agreement on policy among reputational leaders is an empirical question. The list might contain, for example, political rivals who are never found on the same side. Or, it might contain individuals with different spheres of interest who tacitly or explicitly agree to remain neutral on issues outside of their major province. The only thing we wish to maintain about the list of reputational leaders is that, because they possess significant amounts of resources, their social organization is significant for the understanding of stable power relations in the community. The relations among members and their actions is a variable which will be related to the outcome of decisions in a variety of important ways.[6]

THE STUDY

The data to be presented here are drawn from a study of 54 issues in 18 New England communities. The towns were generally small, ranging in population from 2,000 to 100,000 with the median size about 10,000. Seven of the communities were essentially suburbs of Boston, three were resort towns, and the remaining eight were more or less independent cities with some industrial base of their own. All but two of the communities were in Maine or Massachusetts.

---

[6] The argument above focuses on persuasion resources. Most studies using the reputational method have not had such purposes in mind, and a variety of wordings have been used. What of asking for the names of people "who run the town," "who would be needed to get a new project across," or "who have a lot of influence on the outcome of decisions"? The responses to such questions may frequently include those who possess persuasion resources, but some individuals might be included for other reasons. It seems likely, although one would have to demonstrate this, that those frequently named individuals who do *not* possess persuasion resources do possess sanctioning resources. If this is true, then those who are named would still comprise a pool of individuals with resources and all of the above arguments for studying reputational leaders would apply.

Material on these communities was gathered through interviews with 426 informants, an average of 24 per town, supplemented by information from a variety of documents. Interviewing was done by teams of three or four individuals who stayed in each community for several days. Three issues were studied in each town, one of which—fluoridation—was common to all 18. The presence of a decision on fluoridation was, in fact, the basis of selection of these communities, and the 18 include all those New England communities which made a fluoridation decision during an 18-month period of data collection.

Respondents were asked to name the most important issues that had arisen in their town in the previous five years. Of the 54 issues studied, 26 were mentioned by a majority of the respondents in the town.[7] In 11 of the 18 towns, a majority mentioned a particular issue first or as most important and in all but one of these the issue was included in the 54 studied. Besides the 18 fluoridation issues 11 concerned schools, 11 were issues over the development of some new community facility or service, eight were zoning issues, and the final six were a miscellaneous assortment which included changes in the form of government and urban renewal.

The interviews themselves were with two categories of respondents— with active partisans on both sides of each of the three issues and with reputational leaders. The active partisans on the three issues studied were asked to name people in response to the following question: "In many communities, relatively few people are able to affect the outcome of issues sometimes because they are in a position to make key decisions or because they have the ability to persuade others to follow their leadership. Would you tell me the names of the most important and influential leaders in this community even if they do not hold public office?"[8] Those dozen individuals most frequently named were also interviewed and, in the course of the interview, asked this same question.

The criteria for inclusion on the list of reputational leaders should control for certain irrelevant variables between towns. Interviewers differed in the amount of probing they did for names, the total number of respondents interviewed in a town varied from 19 to 31, and the average number of people mentioned by respondents varied from town to town

---

[7] Issues were selected for study through examination of community newspapers and some informal checking with newspaper editors and city clerks. It was possible to miss issues on whose importance there was considerable consensus since this could not be discovered until the interviews were completed. Thus, five issues named by a majority of respondents were not studied.

[8] Unfortunately, this question is not the one called for by the theoretical argument above nor is it directed, as it should be, to a sample of decision-makers. Thus, to treat our reputational leaders as a pool of resource holders we must assume that those named have some kind of stable and general resources, though not necessarily persuasion resources.

depending on the degree of consensus that existed and the volubility of respondents. By using as a base the total number of mentions,[9] we can control for all of the above variables. In communities where (1) the interviewers probed vigorously, (2) a large number of interviews were taken, and (3) the respondents were prolific in their naming, a large number of total mentions will emerge. Requiring a fixed proportion of the total for eligibility means that an individual must be named more frequently in such a town than in one where few names are mentioned over all.[10]

Before we can assess the influence of reputational leaders on the outcome of the 54 issues, we must examine other aspects of these issues. Each is characterized by campaigns by one or both sides, but the intensity of these campaigns varies considerably. Furthermore, some of these efforts have as their object the adoption of some new proposal while others have the maintenance of existing arrangements as their goal. It is only against this backdrop that we can meaningfully connect winning efforts with influence. We must show that the active participation of reputational leaders on a side has some effect over and above the sheer amount of campaign activity and the natural advantage of defending the status quo.

Campaign Activity

All of those who were active on either side of an issue were asked a series of questions about the nature of campaign activities. These questions varied from such open-ended ones as "What did those in favor (opposed) actually do to promote their side, that is, what kinds of activities?" to a specific check list of 16 activities. On several items respondents were asked to compare the campaigns of the two sides. From these descriptions of activities, we characterized each side's campaign on two dimensions—the magnitude of total activity and the degree of organization.

For the first of these dimensions, each respondent's description was culled for statements characterizing the extent of particular activities or characterizations of the campaign as a whole (e.g., "they spent a tre-

---

[9] That is, $\sum mi$, where mi is the number of times the ith individual is mentioned.

[10] To be included, an individual must be mentioned more than some fixed proportion of the total mentions. The setting of such a fixed proportion is rather arbitrary, and I have set it here at 3 percent of the total because such a figure yields an average of about 10 people per community. The number per town ranges from 6 people at the low end to 13 at the other extreme. The number of mentions required for inclusion ranges from 3 to 8, with an average of about 4½. Since the average number of respondents per town is about 24, this means that a reputational leader is named by a minimum of about ⅕ of the respondents in his town, a figure obtained by dividing the average number of mentions required for inclusion (4.6) by the average number of respondents (24). This figure of ⅕ of the respondents provides some interpretation for the, by itself, meaningless criterion of 3 percent of the total mentions.

mendous amount of money on advertising and literature," "we spent a whole year trying to convince people with a tremendous campaign in the last four weeks"). Independent coders were asked to classify the amount of activity for each partisan group as either "great," "some," or "little."[11]

For the degree of organization, heavier reliance was placed on the check list of activities. Many of the activities, such as holding meetings to decide and plan what to do, distribution of literature to the general public, circulating petitions, and raising money to support activities, require some degree of formal organization. They are typically carried on by groups that establish an *ad hoc* organization for the purpose with publicly identifiable leaders or else are carried on by some existing organization in the community. Other kinds of activities require less formal organization but do require interaction among those implementing them. These include telephone campaigns, selective distribution of literature, and participating at meetings or discussions. Finally, there are activities that require neither formal organization nor interaction—for example, writing and answering letters to newspapers, attending or testifying at council meetings or other official proceedings, or simply talking informally to people one encounters. Each campaign was characterized by the highest degree of organizational activity carried on. If the first category of activities occurred, then the campaign organization was characterized as formal regardless of what semiformal and informal activities occurred as well. Thus, an informal campaign was one in which *only* informal activities occurred. Each of the 108 campaigns was coded as either formal, semiformal, or informal.

With each partisan group's campaign characterized in this way, it is possible to compare the two sides on each issue. Interestingly enough, the winning side has only a modest advantage in amount of activity and organization; it had either more activity or more organization on only 48 percent of the issues while the losing side had more on 33 percent.[12] For the remainder, the two sides were equal in activity and organization or, in one case, the winning side was higher on one criterion while the losing side had the advantage on the other.

On 48 of the issues it was possible to identify one side with an effort to change the status quo in some fashion while the other side favored postponement of action, further study of need, a counter alternative requiring less change, or simply the maintenance of existing arrange-

---

11 Initial coding plans were more ambitious, but difficulties in achieving satisfactory reliability forced resort to this crude classification. Intercoder agreement for these three categories was above 80 percent for the 108 campaigns being coded.

12 The base for these figures and for the subsequent analysis is actually 52 rather than 54 issues. Two of the issues are excluded because of ambiguity over the outcome, which made it impossible to designate a winner.

ments. The side identified with change was victorious in 42 percent of these cases against 58 percent for those who opposed the immediate action proposed.

It was hypothesized above that it takes more effort[13] to change the status quo than to maintain it, and Table 1 supports this. In almost two-thirds of the cases in which the side supporting change won, they made a greater campaign effort than the other side. However, when the side supporting no change won, they made a greater effort only a third of the time; two-thirds of the time they were able to win with no more effort than the losing side.

REPUTATION AND SUCCESS

There are two prior questions which we must ask about reputational leaders before we can examine their impact on issue outcome. First, to what extent are they actively involved as partisans on the issues studied? Second, to what extent do they act in unison when they are active; that is, how often are they predominantly on the same side? Having answered those questions, we can examine their impact when they are both active and relatively united.

Activity.—Activity is measured in two ways. Respondents were asked, for each issue studied, if they were at all active. If they answered affirmatively, they were asked to describe such activity; only efforts to affect the outcome are included here or, in other words, non-partisan activities are excluded. Respondents were also asked for the names of the people "who

TABLE 1
CAMPAIGN EFFORT AND SUCCESS IN CHANGING THE STATUS QUO

Winning Side	Supported Change		Supported Status Quo		Change Issue Irrelevant
	Percent	(N)	Percent	(N)	(N)
Made greater campaign effort.........	65	(13)	32	(9)	(3)
Made same campaign effort*.........	10	(2)	29	(8)	(0)
Made smaller campaign effort.........	25	(5)	39	(11)	(1)
Total (N = 52)	100	(20)	100	(28)	(4)

* Includes one case in which the winning side was higher on amount of activity but lower on amount of organization.

have done most of the work in favor (against)." There were some individuals who, out of circumspection or modesty, did not rate themselves as active but were named as active by others. An individual will be considered active on an issue either if he rates himself as active and can describe

---

[13] The phrase "campaign effort" refers to the measure of amount of activity and degree of organization taken in combination. A side will be characterized as having greater effort if it is at least equal on one of these measures and greater on the other.

some confirming partisan activity or if two or more other people rate him as active in favor or against.

A total of 161 reputational leaders were interviewed, 92 percent of those identified as such. How frequently are they active? First, it is worth asking what a finding of inactivity might mean. Only three issues were studied in each town. These were salient and controversial issues, but many decisions which affect large numbers of individuals never become controversial or attract widespread interest. Thus, the absence of signs of activity by reputational leaders does not preclude their activity on many other issues which were not studied. As it turns out, however, these cautions are largely unnecessary because 82 percent of the reputational leaders were active on at least one of the issues studied! Enlarging the number of issues studied per town could only have the effect of further cutting the already small pool of non-active reputational leaders. Furthermore, 41 percent of the reputational leaders were active on a majority of the issues studied. All in all, there can be little doubt that reputation for influence is highly associated with activity on issues in these communities.

Unity.—Do those reputational leaders who engage in partisan activities act as a cohesive force or do they compete to determine the outcome of the issue? There were 34 issues on which at least three reputational leaders were active; with less than three, it makes little sense to ask about the extent of agreement. The active reputational leaders are unanimous on only nine of the 34 issues. If we use a less stringent criterion than unanimity, we still find that there is two-thirds or less agreement on 11 of the 34 issues.

Caution is necessary in interpreting this evidence of disagreement among reputational leaders. Among the many decisions that arise in a community, it is those few which produce serious competition that are likely to become salient. A proposal on which reputational leaders were united in opposition might have difficulty reaching a stage where it would become salient enough to be cited as an "important" community issue. Similarly, a proposal on which reputational leaders were united in favor with no significant amounts of competing resources arrayed on the other side is also unlikely to have high salience or high ratings of community concern. Thus, our method of selecting issues may contain a heavy bias toward those issues in which there is a substantial amount of disagreement among major resource-holders.

Nevertheless, the amount of disagreement revealed here tends to discourage any view of the reputational leaders as a cohesive group united behind common objectives. While there may be unstudied issues on which unanimous agreement existed, there are also likely to be others on which significant disagreement existed. There were only two among the 18 communities studied in which active reputational leaders were undivided on all three issues; in only five of the 18 towns was there as much as 80 percent agreement on all three issues.

There is other evidence that the reputational leaders fail to comprise any sort of cohesive political force. In 12 of the 18 towns, the list of reputational leaders contains individuals who are known to be political rivals or even political enemies. In some cases, there are individuals with a long history of political combat; in others, there are spokesmen for rival solidary groups. In the remaining six communities where the pool of reputational leaders did not contain clear protagonists, there were many instances of no more than casual acquaintance among members of the list. All in all, with the exception of three towns with both issue agreement and no evidence of sustained political rivalry among members of the pool, reputational leaders fail to form anything resembling a cohesive united political clique.

Success.—When the reputational leaders are active and united, do they end up on the winning side? They do about 75 percent of the time on the issues studied here (17 of 23 issues). But perhaps they are simply fellow travelers, joining with the more active and organized side. It turns out, in fact, that they support the more active side only 56 percent of the time but are on the winning side about three-fourths of the time. Furthermore, as Table 2 shows, when the side with the smaller effort is victorious, it is just as likely to have reputational leader support as is the side with greater effort when it wins (35 percent versus 36 percent).

TABLE 2
REPUTATIONAL LEADER SUPPORT AND CAMPAIGN EFFORT

Winning Side	Made Greater Campaign Effort		Made Same Campaign Effort		Made Smaller Campaign Effort	
	Percent (N)		Percent (N)		Percent (N)	
Had reputational leader support......	36	(9)	20	(2)	35	(6)
Had divided or inactive reputational leaders	56	(14)	80	(8)	41	(7)
Had reputational leader opposition...	8	(2)	—	—	24	(4)
Total (N = 52)	100	(25)	100	(10)	100	(17)

It might be argued that reputational leaders are associated with successful outcomes mainly because they support the status quo and thus gain the natural advantage of such support. This is decidedly not the case; reputational leaders, when united and active, support the side favoring change more than twice as often as they support the side favoring the status quo (15 versus 6 times). This means that, to achieve victories, they must typically overcome the natural advantage of the other side. As Table 3 indicates, they are able to do this with some success. In fact, the side proposing change has considerable difficulty without the active support of the reputational leaders and their opposition amounts to a virtual veto. In half the cases where the winning side supported change, they had the support of the reputational leaders and only one success occurred against reputational leader opposition. When the winning side supported the status quo, they had the support of the reputational leaders only 18 percent of the time.

TABLE 3

REPUTATIONAL LEADER SUPPORT AND SUCCESS IN CHANGING THE STATUS QUO

Winning Side	Supported Change		Supported Status Quo		Change Issue Irrelevant
	Percent	(N)	Percent	(N)	(N)
Had reputational leader support......	50	(10)	18	(5)	(2)
Had divided or inactive reputational leaders	45	(9)	64	(18)	(2)
Had reputational leader opposition...	5	(1)	18	(5)	—
Total (N = 52)	100	(20)	100	(28)	(4)

Is the support of reputational leaders or a stronger campaign effort more likely to produce a victory for the side favoring change? With so few cases, it is not easy to disentangle variables. However, Table 4 has some suggestive evidence that reputational leader support may be most critical. With such support, the side favoring change is successful two-thirds of the time *regardless* of relative campaign effort. However, such campaign efforts clearly make an important difference when reputational leaders are divided or inactive. The side favoring change wins almost half the time with a greater campaign effort but only one-sixth of the time when it fails to make a greater effort.

TABLE 4

REPUTATIONAL LEADER SUPPORT AND CAMPAIGN EFFORT BY SUCCESS IN CHANGING THE STATUS QUO

Side Favoring Change	Had Reputational Leader Support				Had No Reputational Leader Support*			
	Had Greater Effort		Had No Greater Effort[a]		Had Greater Effort		Had No Greater Effort	
	Percent	(N)	Percent	(N)	Percent	(N)	Percent	(N)
Won	67	(6)	67	(4)	47	(7)	17	(3)
Lost	33	(3)	33	(2)	53	(8)	83	(15)
Total (N=48[b])...	100	(9)	100	(6)	100	(15)	100	(18)

* Cases where reputational leaders were opposed and where they were divided or inactive are combined here.
a Cases of equal effort and of smaller effort are combined here.
b Four cases in which change was not an issue are omitted here.

It is instructive to look at the six cases in which the reputational leaders were united and active on the losing side. Two of these were efforts to have comprehensive zoning plans adopted, one involved the approval of a new high school, one a major change of land use in the central business district, and one an ambitious and expensive harbor-development project. In four of these five cases, the leaders of the defeated forces felt that they had lost a round but that the fight was not over. However, they spoke of modifying the alternative in important ways—of asking the town for half a loaf or of toning down the proposal in various ways.

None of the variables discussed here illuminate the sixth defeat. It involved the rezoning of a considerable area of land from residential use to business use. Reputational leaders were active and united against the proposal, participated in a campaign which was apparently *more* extensive in both organization and activity than the other side, and were beneficiaries of the natural advantage of defending the status quo. I can do no more with this case than present it as evidence that the arguments above are not tautological.

CONCLUSION

Reputational leaders are not presented here as a ruling elite. They are presented as an aggregate of individuals with resources. In particular, I have argued that their reputation is itself a resource and not simply an indicator of resources. If this argument is correct, then we ought to find that they have some success in influencing the outcome of issues when they are active and united. Unfortunately, we cannot simply look at whether they are on the winning or losing side because other factors besides their influence are affecting the outcome. The factors focused on here were the amount of campaign effort and whether the campaign aimed at changing or preserving the status quo. The data indicated that a more active or more organized campaign was necessary to change the status quo than to maintain it.

Reputational leaders are, with few exceptions, active on at least one of the three issues studied in their respective communities. However, they are frequently active on opposite sides, although this may merely reflect a method of issue selection which emphasized controversy. When they are both active and united, they are on the winning side about three-fourths of the time. This is not merely a function of their participation on the more active side, for they have as high a proportion of victories when they support the less active side. Furthermore, they may be making a contribution to the campaign effort and thus exercising additional influence through their contribution to this variable. Nor is their success an artifact of the natural advantage gained from supporting the status quo. On the contrary, they achieve their success *against* this advantage. They are united and successful in support of change two-thirds of the time.

In short there seems to be some reality to reputation. This reality is consistent with a theoretical interpretation of reputation as a resource. I have no desire to defend the past uses and abuses of the reputational method, but neither am I inclined to heed Wolfinger's "plea for a decent burial."[14] A decent convalescence seems more in order.

---

[14] Raymond E. Wolfinger, "A Plea for a Decent Burial," *American Sociological Review*, XXVII (December, 1962), 841–47.

JANE R. MERCER

10 | *Social System Perspective and*
Clinical Perspective[*][1]

A growing body of sociological literature is diverging from the traditional treatment of deviance. This new approach, which we are calling
the "social system perspective," views deviance as a label emerging from
an interpersonal process in which one individual or group of individuals
defines the behavior or physical attributes of another individual or group
as "different," "strange," or beyond tolerable limits.[2,3,4] The social
system perspective contrasts sharply with the more conventional view of
deviance as an attribute of the deviant, a perspective we will call the
"clinical perspective." Both perspectives are useful in certain contexts;
however, it is essential that an investigator be aware of the perspective
which he is adopting in any given analysis. After defining more specifically what is meant by each of these concepts, we will attempt to illustrate
how the use of the social system perspective can assist in understanding
processes in the career patterns of persons who have been labelled mentally retarded.[5]

The clinical perspective is the frame of reference most commonly
adopted in studies of mental deficiency, mental illness, drug addiction,
and other areas which the students of deviance choose to investigate.[6,7]

[*] Reprinted from "Social System Perspective and Clinical Perspective: Frames of Refer-
ence for Understanding Career Patterns of Persons Labelled as Mentally Retarded,"
Social Problems, 13 (Summer, 1965), pp. 18–34, by the permission of the Society for the
Study of Social Problems, the journal and the author.

[1] Supported in part by the National Institute of Mental Health, Grant No. 3M-9130:
Population Movement of Mental Defectives and Related Physical, Behavioral, Social,
and Cultural Factors; and Grant No. MH-5687: Mental Retardation in a Community,
Pacific State Hospital, Pomona, California. Appreciation for assistance is expressed
to the Western Data Processing Center, Division of the Graduate School of Business
Administration, University of California, Los Angeles.

[2] Howard S. Becker, *Outsiders: Studies in the Sociology of Deviance,* Glencoe, Ill.:
The Free Press, 1963.

[3] Howard S. Becker, Editor, *The Other Side: Perspectives on Deviance,* Glencoe, Ill.:
The Free Press, 1964.

[4] John I. Kitsuse, "Society Reaction to Deviant Behavior: Problems of Theory and
Method," *Social Problems,* 9 (Winter, 1962), pp. 247–57.

[5] The author wishes to express appreciation to Harvey F. Dingman, Ph.D. and
Lindsey C. Churchill, Ph.D. for helpful suggestions and observations made in the
preparation of this manuscript.

[6] August B. Hollingshead and Fredrick C. Redlich, *Social Class and Mental Illness,*
New York: John Wiley and Sons, 1958, Chapter 11.

[7] H. E. Freeman and O. G. Simmons, "Social Class and Posthospital Performance
Levels," *American Sociological Review,* 2 (June, 1959), p. 348.

This viewpoint is readily identified by several distinguishing characteristics.

First, the investigator accepts as the focus for study those individuals who have been labelled deviant. In so doing, he adopts the values of whatever social system has defined the person as deviant and assumes that its judgments are the valid measure of deviance. The evaluations which have produced the definition "mental retardate," "drug addict," or "alcoholic" are taken as given, and the individual is perceived within the frame of reference of the evaluating group. Groups in the social structure sharing the values of the core culture tend to accept the labels attached as a consequence of the application of these values without serious questioning. For example, it seems obvious to a member of a middle class American family that there is something seriously wrong with any adult who cannot read or write. This opinion would be widely shared by other persons in the core groups, but not nearly so widely shared by persons in more peripheral social systems.

This acceptance of the core group definition of deviance as a starting point for investigation results in a second distinguishing characteristic of the clinical perspective: a tendency to perceive deviance as an attribute of the person, as a meaning inherent in his behavior, appearance, or performance. Mental retardation, for example, is viewed as a characteristic of the person, a lack to be explained. This viewpoint results in a quest for etiology. Thus, the clinical perspective is essentially a medical frame of reference, for it sees deviance as individual pathology requiring diagnostic classification and etiological analysis for the purpose of determining proper treatment procedures and probable prognosis.

The perceived necessity for accurate diagnosis leads to three additional characteristics of the clinical perspective: the development of a diagnostic nomenclature, the creation of diagnostic instruments, and the professionalization of the diagnostic function. In areas of deviance with a long social history, extensive effort has been expended in elaborating diagnostic nomenclatures, and a corps of professional diagnosticians has evolved with official sanction to label deviants by using complex instruments which require special training and skill to administer. This professional group acquires a position as the legitimate "labellers." The development of special labelling devices and measurements results in the formal codification of what is officially considered "normal," and written norms are created, on the basis of which individuals are labelled as deviant or non-deviant and assigned to sub-categories within the larger area of deviance.

The more formal the norms and the more elaborate the measuring devices, the stronger the tendency to professionalize the diagnostic function and to adopt a clinical perspective. This is very evident in the highly formalized and professionalized processes which operate in the labelling of the mental retardate. Low performance on carefully normed intelligence measures administered by duly trained and licensed professionals is the recognized criterion for placing persons in special education classes, hospitals for the retarded, or on categorical aid programs for the totally disabled. In areas where norms are still fluid and the diagnostic function less highly professionalized, as in definitions of juvenile delinquency, the tendency to see deviance as a trait of the individual is somewhat less pronounced.

When the investigator begins his research with the diagnostic designations assigned by official defining agents, he tends to assume that all individuals placed in a given category are essentially equivalent in respect to their deviance. If there are significant differences in the life careers of persons in the same category, such as difference in rates for admission or release from social institutions, the explanation for these differences is sought in some other attribute of the individual, i.e., his age, sex, body structure, or degree of physical handicap. Research design frequently follows a typical pattern. Individuals assigned to different categories of deviance are compared with each other or with a "normal" population consisting of persons who, for whatever reason, have escaped being labelled. The focus is on the individual.

Another characteristic of the clinical perspective is its assumption that the official definition is somehow the "right" definition. If persons in other social systems, especially the family, do not concur with official findings and refuse to define a member as "retarded," "delinquent," or "mentally ill," the clinical perspective assumes that they are either unenlightened or are evidencing psychological denial. It follows, then, that they need to be educated to understand the "real" situation or, if resistance is intense, need therapy to help them gain insight into the psychological roots of their denial.

Finally, when deviance is perceived as individual pathology, social action tends to center upon changing the individual or, that failing, removing him from participation in society. Prevention and cure become the primary social goals. Seldom considered are the alternative possibilities of redefining his behavior by modifying the norms of the social system or of attempting to locate the individual in the structure of social systems which will not perceive his behavior as pathological.

Uncritical acceptance of the frame of reference of the official defining group, whether it be psychiatrists labelling persons as mentally ill, criminal courts labelling persons as criminal, or psychometrists labelling persons as "gifted," "average," or "retarded," obviates the possibility of investigating the labelling process itself. It also rules out exploration of the possibility that different definitions of the individual's behavior may have been made by other social systems—for example, his family or friendship group—and that these alternative definitions may be even more significant in influencing his future career than the official definition. By ignoring the values of social systems other than the recognized defining agencies, we exclude from review many facets of the nature of deviance.

The social system perspective, on the other hand, attempts to see the definition of an individual's behavior as a function of the values of the social system within which he is being evaluated. The professional definers are studied as one of the most important of the evaluating social systems but within the context of other social systems which may or may not concur with official definitions.

Defining an individual as mentally ill, delinquent, or mentally retarded is viewed as an interpersonal process in which the definer makes a value judgment about the behavior of the persons being defined. Depending upon the role expectations current in the social system for the roles which the defined is playing, his behavior will be judged normal, subnormal, or superior. Role expectations vary from system to system according to the performance of persons playing roles. For example, if a sizeable percentage of the persons playing adult roles in a defining social system has little or no formal education and is unemployed and living on welfare, these persons are unlikely to regard such behavior as deviant, regardless of what labels may be attached to it by official agencies. Thus, the extent of deviation depends not only on the behavior of the individual, but also on the framework of norms within which the definer operates in making his judgments. Deviation is not seen as a characteristic of the individual or as a meaning inherent in his behavior, but as a socially derived label which may be attached to his behavior by some social systems and not by others.[8]

In order to understand what is meant by the label "mentally retarded," from this viewpoint, it then becomes essential to know who is defined by whom as retarded, and what impact the labelling has upon the career of the individual.

Customarily, research in mental retardation has proceeded under the assumptions of the clinical perspective. However, the second approach, which sees mental retardation as bound to a particular social system, has considerable value. If it is postulated that the label "mentally subnormal" is an evaluation of an individual made within a particular social system and based on the norms of that system, then it becomes clear that the label may not be applied to the person when he is evaluated by the norms of a different social system. Thus, it follows that a person may be mentally retarded in one system and not mentally retarded in

---

[8] Howard S. Becker, 1964, *op. cit.*

another. He may change his label by changing his social group. This viewpoint frees us from the necessity of seeing the person as permanently stigmatized by a deviant label and makes it possible to understand otherwise obscure patterns in the life careers of individuals. It turns attention from questions directed at determining whether the individual is "really" retarded and from discussions of "proper" diagnosis to such questions as: "Who sees whom as retarded?" "What are the characteristics of the social systems which attach different labels to the same individual?" and "What impact does differential labelling have on the life career of the person?"

The research reported in this paper attempts to answer these questions about a group of persons who shared the common experience of having been labelled retarded by official defining agencies and placed in a public institution for the retarded. The sample was selected to include two groups whose life careers took different courses at a critical juncture. One group was released to their families after a period of institutionalization, while the other group, after an equivalent period of institutionalization, remained residents of the institution.

The specific question which this study seeks to investigate within the above framework is: "Why do the families of some individuals take them back home after a period of institutionalization in a hospital for the retarded while other families do not, when, according to official evaluations, these individuals show similar degrees of deviance, that is, have comparable intelligence test scores, and are of equivalent age, sex, ethnic status, and length of hospitalization?"

In trying to answer this question we used a social system perspective. We anticipated that those patients who were released would tend to come from family social systems which were most distant, structurally, from societal core groups and which evidenced a style of life contrary to many middle class values. In such a social system the non-achieving, dependent person with a low intelligence score would be closer to group norms than in a high achieving, independent, upper status milieu.

The literature on the value systems of different classes in American society supports this as a plausible hypothesis. For example, Hyman, in a secondary analysis of several studies using national samples and spaced over a period of years, concluded that lower class persons place a lower evaluation on education achievement than middle class persons. In addition, they more frequently show a preference for a low paying job, if it is secure, than a high paying job involving risk, and consistently show a pattern of limited expectation and striving.[9] Hollingshead and Redlich,

---

[9] Herbert H. Hyman, "The Value Systems of Different Classes: A Social Psychological Contribution to the Analysis of Stratification," *Class, Status, and Power,* edited by Reinhard Bendix and Seymour M. Lipset, Glencoe, Ill.: The Free Press, 1953.

in their study of mental illness, found that lower status families are less likely to define the behavioral manifestations associated with emotional disturbance as a symptom of mental illness.[10] This finding for mental patients has been confirmed by other investigators.[11,12] Freeman and Simmons found that middle class families were less tolerant of the ex-mental patient's behavior and were more likely to exclude him, following release, than lower class families[13] Downey reports that more educated families demonstrate less interest in their children after placing them in a hospital for the retarded because they tend to view them in terms of their ability to be educated and anticipate they will be unable to conform to the family's career expectations.[14]

These differences in group norms should be evident not only in a different style of life but should be apparent in divergent definitions of the patient. If our reasoning is correct, the higher status family, because it is closer to core cultural values and thus closer to the values of the official defining agencies, should more frequently concur in the definition of the patient as "retarded," more frequently see the patient's condition as unchangeable, and have fewer expectations that he will ever be able to fill adult roles, since adult roles carry more demanding role expectations in higher status levels than lower status levels. This would also lead us to believe that there should be significant differences in the processes by which the patient was first labelled "retarded," differences that would somehow be congruent with the divergent definitions held by the families.

METHOD

Two groups of labelled retardates were studied. One group consisted of patients who had been released to their families from a state hospital for the retarded and the other group consisted of a matched group of patients still resident in the hospital at the time of the study.[15]

Specifically, the released group was made up of all patients released to their families during a three year period (1957-59), who had not been readmitted to another institution for the retarded at the time of the

---

[10] August B. Hollingshead and Fredrick C. Redlich, 1958, *op. cit.,* Chapter 11.

[11] E. H. Hare, "Mental Illness and Social Class in Bristol," *British Journal of Preventative and Social Medicine,* 9 (October, 1955), pp. 191–95.

[12] Bertram Mandelbrote and Steven Folkard, "The Outcome of Schizophrenia in Relation to a Developing Community Psychiatric Service," *Mental Hygiene,* 47 (January, 1964), pp. 43–56.

[13] H. E. Freeman and O. G. Simmons, *op. cit.,* p. 348.

[14] Kenneth J. Downey, "Parental Interest in the Institutionalized Severely Mentally Retarded Child," *Social Problems,* 11 (Fall, 1963), pp. 186–93.

[15] Pacific State Hospital, Pomona, California is a state supported hospital for the mentally retarded with a population of approximately 3,000 patients.

study, and who were reported to be living within a 100-mile radius of the hospital. Only those cases in which the family had assumed responsibility for the patient were included. Of the 76 patients who met these qualifications, it was possible to complete interviews with 63 of the families. Six families refused to be interviewed and seven could not be located.

Since we wished to focus this study on variables in the social systems from which these persons came, it was essential to match individual characteristics known to influence rate of release; consequently, the resident group was selected to match the released group in intelligence quotient, age, sex, ethnic status, and year of admission, other studies having demonstrated that these factors are related to the probability of release.[16]

The matched group of resident patients was selected in the following manner: all patients on the hospital rolls were sorted into two groups by sex, two groups by age, three groups by ethnic status, three groups by intelligence quotient, and two groups by year of admission. All released patients were likewise assigned to the proper category. Resident patients were then chosen at random from within each cell in sufficient numbers to correspond to the number of discharged patients also falling in that cell. Each resident case was required to have a family living within a one hundred mile radius of the hospital. If a case did not meet this requirement, another case was drawn randomly from the appropriate cell until there were an equal number of discharged and resident cases in each cell. Sex distribution in each group was 53 males and 23 females; ethnic distribution, 47 Caucasians, 20 Mexicans, and 9 Negroes.

Statistical tests comparing age, intelligence quotient, and year of admission for the patients in the two groups were made to determine if the matching process had indeed controlled for these factors. Table 1 presents the distribution of intelligence quotients, birth years, and years of admission for the interviewed cases. Of the 76 resident cases selected to match the released cases, interviews were completed with 70 families. Two refused to be interviewed and four families could not be located. Using a Kolmogornov-Smirnov Test of two independent samples, we found that all differences between the interviewed groups could be accounted for by chance.

When the 19 non-interviewed cases were compared with the 133 interviewed cases, no significant differences were found in the sex, age, I.Q., or ethnic status of the patients, or the socioeconomic level of the families. We concluded that no significant bias was introduced by inability to contact 19 of the families originally selected for study.

The hospital file for each patient selected for study was searched for

---

16 G. Tarjan, S. W. Wright, M. Kramer, P. H. Person, Jr., and R. Morgan, "The Natural History of Mental Deficiency in a State Hospital. I: Probabilities of Release and Death by Age, Intelligence Quotients, and Diagnosis," *AMA J. dis. Childr.*, 96 (1958), pp. 64–70.

relevant data and an interview was held with a family member. In 75 percent of the cases the mother was interviewed; in 8 percent the father was interviewed; and in the remaining cases some other relative served as informant. All but two of the interviews were held in the home of the respondent. Four graduate students in the behavioral sciences and the author served as interviewers. A letter from the hospital first explained that the research department was interested in learning more about its patients and their families, and an appointment for an interview was then made by telephone. In those cases in which the family had no phone, initial contacts were made without appointment.

TABLE 1

COMPARISON OF INTERVIEWED CASES BY BIRTH YEAR, INTELLIGENCE QUOTIENT, AND YEAR OF ADMISSION

Matched Variable	Released (63)	Resident (70)	Significance Level
Birth Year			
Before 1920	4	5	
1921–1930	13	12	
1931–1940	33	34	> .05[1]
1941–1950	12	17	
1951–1960	1	2	
Intelligence Quotient			
0–9	2	4	
10–19	2	1	
20–29	4	3	
30–39	6	4	> .05[1]
40–49	13	15	
50–59	14	18	
60–69	19	19	
70 +	3	6	
Year of Admission			
Before 1945	5	9	
1945–1950	20	14	
1951–1956	33	31	> .05[1]
1957 and later	5	16	

[1] The Kolmogornov-Smirnov Test of two independent samples was used.

Since this study focuses on factors in release, it is useful at this point to examine briefly the process by which a patient may be discharged to his family. In the hospital studied, a patient's release to his family may be initiated either by the family or as the result of a suggestion from a hospital staff member. In the latter case, release is contingent upon the family's willingness to reaccept the patient. Families offered the choice frequently reject the hospital's promptings.

To clarify the circumstances under which the released group returned to their families, the respondent was asked two questions: "Who was the most important person in getting you to take ——— out of the hospital?" and "What were the main reasons you decided to have ——— discharged from the hospital?"

In 12 cases the parents reported that someone in the hospital, i.e., a social worker, family care mother, or a ward technician, had first suggested that the patient could be released to the family. In the 51 remaining cases the families were the active agents in release. Reasons given by the families for seeking a discharge are described in Table 2.

It is clear from this table that most of the patients who returned to their families returned because the family made an effort to secure their

TABLE 2

THE RELEASE PROCESS AS REPORTED BY THE FAMILIES OF RELEASED PATIENTS

	f	%
Hospital Initiated Releases...	12	19
Family Initiated Releases		
Family opposed to placement from beginning......................	9	14
Parents lonely without patient or need him for some practical reason, e.g., to help with younger children, earn money, etc.	8	13
Patient was unhappy in the hospital. Hospital Failure: Mistreated patient, made him work too hard, etc.	6	9
Hospital Success: Patient improved enough to come home............	9	14
Home conditions changed to permit return, e.g., found patient a job, mother's health better, etc.	10	16
Total Released Cases	63	

release. Some families had been opposed to placement from the beginning while others, initially favorable to placement, had become disillusioned with hospital care because the patient was unhappy or because they felt he was mistreated. Others, expressing a more positive note, sought the patient's return because they missed him, because home conditions had changed to permit his return, or because his behavior had improved sufficiently to make them willing to reaccept him. Whatever their stated reason, however, the critical point for the present discussion is that most of these families actively wanted the patient at home.

FINDINGS

SOCIAL STATUS OF RELEASED PATIENTS

Several indices were used to measure the socioeconomic level of the family of each retardate. A socioeconomic index score based on the occupation and education of the head of the household, weighted according to Hollingshead's system, was used as the basic measure. In addition, the interviewer rated the economic status of the street on which the patient's home was located, rated the physical condition of the housing unit, and completed a checklist of equipment present in the household. As can be seen in Table 3, the families of the released patients rated significantly lower than the families of the resident patients on every measure. The heads of the households in the families of released patients had less education and lower level jobs, the family residence was located among less affluent dwellings, the housing unit was in a poorer state of repair, and the dwelling was less elaborately furnished and equipped. Contrary to the pattern found in studies of those placed as mentally ill,[17] it is the "retardate" from lower socioeconomic background who is most likely to be released to his family while higher status "retardates" are more likely to remain in the hospital.

TABLE 3

SOCIOECONOMIC DIFFERENCES BETWEEN PATIENTS RELEASED TO THEIR FAMILIES AND THOSE STILL RESIDENT IN THE STATE HOSPITAL

Socioeconomic Measure		Released Living at Home (63%)	Resident In State Hospital (70%)	Significance Level
Socioeconomic Index	Above Median.......	36.5	61.4	
Score of Head of	Below Median.......	61.9	38.6	< .01[3]
Household	Unknown	1.6	0.0	
Economic Status of Street [1]	Housing Value $10,000 and Above	29.0	55.1	< .05[3]
	Housing Value Less Than $10,000	71.0	44.9	
Condition of Housing	Run Down	48.4	23.2	
Unit [1]	Average	46.8	57.2	< .05[3]
	Above Average......	4.8	18.8	
Household Equipment	0–2	19.0	11.9	
Scale [1]	3–5	27.6	20.9	< .05[2]
	6–8	43.1	41.8	
	9–11	10.3	25.4	

[1] Some cases are not included because data were not available.
[2] Test of significance of difference between unrelated means was used.
[3] Chi Square test was used.

From the clinical perspective, several explanations may be proposed for these differences. It has been found in hospital populations that patients with an I.Q. below 50 are more likely to come from families which represent a cross-section of social levels, while those with an I.Q. between 50 and 70 are more likely to come from low status families.[18] Since persons with higher I.Q.'s have a higher probability of release, this could account for higher rates of release for low status persons. However, in the present study, the tested level of intelligence was equal for both groups, and this hypothesis cannot be used as an explanation.

---

[17] August B. Hollingshead and Fredrick C. Redlich, 1958, *op. cit.*, Chapter 11.

[18] Georges Sabagh, Harvey F. Dingman, George Tarjan, and Stanley W. Wright, "Social Class and Ethnic Status of Patients Admitted to a State Hospital for the Retarded," *Pacific Sociological Review,* 2 (Fall, 1959), pp. 76–80.

A second possible explanation from a clinical perspective might be based on the fact that persons who have more physical handicaps tend to be institutionalized for longer periods of time than persons with few handicaps.[19] Should it be found that high status patients have more physical handicaps than low status patients, then this could account for the latter's shorter hospitalization. Data from the present sample were analyzed to determine whether there was a significant relationship between physical handicap and social status. Although released patients tended to have fewer physical handicaps than resident patients, this was irrespective of social status. When high status patients were compared with low status patients, 50% of the high status and 56% of the low status patients had no physical handicaps. A chi square of 1.9 indicates these differences could be accounted for by chance variation.

A third explanation from the clinical perspective may hinge on differences in the diagnostic categories to which retardates of different social status were assigned. In addition to categorizing persons according to intelligence level as measured by tests, professional evaluators also assign them to categories according to the physical symptomotology and supposed etiology of their retardation.[20] Without going into an extensive discussion of this professional nomenclature, we can say that diagnostic labels give a rough measure of the extent of physical deformity which accompanies low intellectual performance. A diagnostic label of "familial" or "undifferentiated" ordinarily indicates that the individual has few or no physical stigmata and is essentially normal in body structure. All other categories ordinarily indicate that he has some type of physical symptomotology. Although released patients were more likely to be diagnosed as familial or undifferentiated than resident patients ($X^2 = 7.08$, $p < .01$), this, like physical handicap, was irrespective of social status. Fifty-seven percent of the high status retardates, and 69% of the low status retardates were classified as either undifferentiated or familial, a difference which could be accounted for by chance.

Since differences in the release rates of different status level patients to their families cannot be explained within the clinical perspective as due to differences in the individual characteristics of patients from high and low status families, we turn to an exploration of differences in the social systems from which the patients came for a possible explanation of the dissimilarity of their life careers.

DIVERGENT DEFINITIONS

In analyzing social status, four types of situations were identified. The

---

[19] G. Tarjan, S. W. Wight, M. Kramer, R. H. Person, Jr., and R. Morgan, 96 (1958), *op. cit.*, pp. 64–70.

[20] National Committee for Mental Hygiene, *Statistical Manual for the Use of Institutions for Mental Defectives*, New York: NCMH, 1946.

modal category for resident patients was high social status with a smaller number of resident patients coming from low status families. The modal category for released patients was low status with a smaller number of released patients coming from higher status families. If we are correct in our hypothesis (that higher release rates for low status patients are related to the fact that the family social system is structurally more distant from the core culture and that its style of life, values, and definitions of the patient are more divergent from official definitions than that of high status families), we would expect the largest differences to occur when high status resident families are compared to low status released families. The two non-modal categories would be expected to fall at some intermediate point. For this reason, the analysis of all subsequent variables has retained these four basic classifications.

Table 4 presents the responses made to three questions asked to determine the extent to which the family concurred in the official label of "retardation," the extent to which they believed the patient's condition amenable to change, and the extent to which they anticipated that the individual could live outside the hospital and, perhaps, fill adult roles. The patterns of the divergent definitions of the situation which emerged for each group are illuminating.

When asked whether *he* believed the patient to be retarded, the high status parent more frequently concurred with the definitions of the official defining agencies while the low status parent was more prone to disagree outright or to be uncertain. This tendency is especially marked when the two modal categories are compared. While 33.3% of the parents of the low status released patients stated that they did not think the patient was retarded and 25.6% were uncertain whether he was retarded, only 4.6% of the parents of high status resident patients felt he was not retarded and 20.9% were uncertain.

When parents were asked whether they believed anything could change the patient's condition, the differences between all groups were significant at the .02 level or beyond. The high status parent was most likely to believe that nothing could change his child's condition, and this was significantly more characteristic of parents whose children were still in the hospital than those who had taken their child from the hospital on both status levels.

When asked what they saw in the future for their child, all groups again differed significantly in the expected direction. The modal, high status group was least optimistic and the modal, low status group, most optimistic about the future. Fully 46% of the parents of the latter group expressed the expectation that their child would get a job, marry, and fulfill the usual adult roles while only 6.9% of the modal high status group responded in this fashion. High status parents, as a group, more frequently see their child playing dependent roles. It is interesting to

TABLE 4
PATTERNS OF DIVERGENT DEFINITIONS

Question	Response Categories	High Status Resident (43) %	High Status Released (23) %	Low Status Resident (27) %	Low Status Released (39) %	High Status Low Status	High Status Resident Low Status Released	High Status Resident High Status Released	Low Status Resident Low Status Released
1. We know that many people have told you ___ is retarded but we want to know what you think. Do you think he/she is retarded?	Yes	74.4	47.8	66.6	41.0				
	Uncertain	20.9	39.1	14.8	25.6	$< .02^1$	$< .02^1$	NS1	NS1
	No	4.6	13.0	18.5	33.3				
2. Do you believe anything can change ___'s condition?	Nothing	74.3	39.0	66.6	33.3				
	Uncertain	2.3	17.3	11.1	38.4	$< .02^2$	$< .001^2$	$< .01^2$	$< .01^2$
3. What do you see in the future for ___?	Training, Medical Care, etc.	23.2	43.4	22.2	28.2				
	Dependent in Institution	83.7	13.0	74.0	2.5				
	Dependent at Home	9.3	60.8	22.2	48.7	$< .02^2$	$< .001^2$	$< .001^2$	$< .001^2$
	Normal Adult Roles	6.9	26.0	3.7	46.1				

[1] The Kolmogorov-Smirnov Test of two independent samples was used.
[2] The Log-Likelihood Ratio Test was used. (Barnett, Wolf, "The Log-Likelihood Ratio Test [The G-Test]: Methods and Tables for a Test of Heterogeneity in Contingency Tables," *Annals of Human Genetics*, Vol. 21, Part 4, June 1957, pp. 397–409.)

note that, although a large percentage of parents of released patients believe the patient will be dependent, they demonstrate their willingness to accept responsibility for the retarded child themselves by their responding that they foresee him having a future in which he is dependent at home. Only 9.3% of the high status and 22.2% of the low status parents of the resident patients see this as a future prospect. Release to the family clearly appears to be contingent upon the willingness of the family to accept the patient's dependency, if they do not foresee him assuming independent adult roles.

FACTORS IN THE LABELLING PROCESS

From the social system perspective, retardation is viewed as a label placed upon an individual after someone has evaluated his behavior within a specific set of norms. Retardation is not a meaning necessarily inherent in the behavior of the individual. We have seen that the parents of low status, released patients tend to reject the label of retardation and to be optimistic about the future. We surmised that this divergent definition could well be related to factors in the process by which the child was first categorized as subnormal, such as his age at the time, the type of behavior which was used as a basis for making the evaluation, and the persons doing the labelling. Consequently, parents were asked specifically about these factors. Table 5 records their responses.

Children from lower status families were labelled as mentally subnormal at a significantly later age than children from high status families. Seventy-nine percent of the patients in the high status, modal group were classified as retarded by the age of six while only 36.1 percent of those in the low status, modal group were identified at such an early age. The largest percentage of low status retardates were first classified after they reached public school age. This indicates that relatives and friends, who are the individuals most likely to observe and evaluate the behavior of young children, seldom saw anything deviant in the early development of lower status children later labelled retarded, but that the primary groups of higher status children did perceive early deviation.

This is related to the responses made when parents were asked what first prompted someone to believe the patient retarded. The modal, high status group reported slow development in 48.8% of the cases and various types of physical symptoms in an additional 20.9%, while only 14.7% and 11.8% of the modal, low status parents gave these responses. On the other hand, 55.9% of the modal, low status group were first labelled because they had problems learning in school, while this was true of only 9.3% of the modal high status group.

When parents were asked who was the most important person influencing them in placing the child in the hospital, a parallel pattern emerged.

TABLE 5
FACTORS IN THE LABELLING PROCESS

Question	Response Categories	High Status		Low Status		Significance Levels			
		Resident (43) %	Released (23) %	Resident (27) %	Released (39) %	High Status Low Status	Resident High Released Low	Resident High Released High	Resident Low Released Low
1. How old was ____ when someone first said he was retarded?	1-2 years	44.1	18.1	23.2	16.7	$< .001$[1]	$< .02$[1]	NS[1]	NS[1]
	3-6 years	34.8	50.0	30.2	19.4				
	7-10 years	9.3	22.7	11.5	30.5				
	11-14 years	4.6	0.0	11.5	16.7				
	15 or over	6.9	9.1	23.2	16.7				
2. What was there about ____ that made you/them think he/she might be retarded?	Slow Development	48.8	30.4	19.2	14.7	$< .005$[2]	$< .001$[2]	NS[2]	NS[2]
	Physical Symptoms	20.9	17.3	26.9	11.8				
	Behavioral Problems	20.9	21.7	15.4	17.6				
	Couldn't Learn in School	9.3	30.4	38.5	55.9				
3. Who was the most important person in getting you to place ____ in the ____ hospital?	Family	27.9	43.4	48.1	25.6	$< .01$[2]	$< .001$[2]	NS[2]	$< .01$[2]
	Medical or Psychological Person	37.2	30.4	11.1	2.5				
	Police or Welfare	13.9	17.3	18.5	64.1				
	Schools or Other	20.9	8.6	22.2	7.6				

[1] The Kolmogornov-Smirnov Test of two independent samples was used.
[2] The Log-Likelihood Ratio Test was used. (Barnett, Wolf, The Log-Likelihood Ratio Test [The G-Test]: Methods and Tables for a Test of Heterogeneity in Contingency Tables," *Annals of Human Genetics*, Vol. 21, Part 4, June 1957, pp. 397–409.)

Medical persons are the most important single group for the modal high status persons while the police and welfare agencies loom as very significant in 64.1% of the cases in the modal, low status group. These findings are similar to those of Hollingshead and Redlich in their study of paths to the hospital for the mentally ill.[21] Of additional interest is the fact that the person important in placement differentiates the low status released from the low status resident patient at the .01 level. The resident low status patient's path to the hospital is similar to that of the high status patient and markedly different from released low status persons. When authoritative figures such as police and welfare are primary forces in placement, the patient is more likely to return home.

We interpret these findings to mean that when the family—or persons whose advice is solicited by the family, i.e., medical persons—is "most important" in placing a person in a hospital for the retarded, the primary groups have themselves first defined the individual as a deviant and sought professional counsel. When their own suspicions are supported by official definitions, they are more likely to leave the patient in an institution.

Conversely, when a person is labelled retarded by an authoritative governmental agency whose advice is not solicited and who, in the case of the police, may be perceived as a punishing agent, the family frequently rejects the official definition of the child as retarded and withdraws him from the institution at the first opportunity. This attitude was clearly exemplified by one mother who, when asked why the family had taken the child from the hospital, replied, "Why not? He had served his time."

The influence of the police as a factor in labelling the low status person as retarded may actually be greater than that shown in Table 5. Fifty percent of the low status retardates had some type of police record while only 23 percent of the high status subnormals were known to the police, a difference significant beyond the .01 level.

CHARACTERISTICS OF PRIMARY SOCIAL SYSTEMS

We have seen that there is a significant difference between the images which high status parents and low status parents have of their children. Although the children in both groups are equivalent, from a clinical perspective, in the amount of retardation, the high status parent is more convinced that his child is retarded, has classified him as retarded at a younger age, is more likely to believe that nothing will change his condition, and sees him as likely to have a future in which he will be dependent either in an institution or at home. On the other hand, the low status parent lived with his child for a longer time before anyone

---

[21] August B. Hollingshead and Fredrick C. Redlich, 1958, *op. cit.*, Chapter 11.

labelled him as retarded and is less willing to say, unequivocally, that the child is retarded. He is more likely to believe the condition is amenable to change and is more prone to believe the patient will be able to assume adult occupational and marital roles. These differences were revealed in their most striking form when the two modal categories were compared.

From the social system perspective, it is our interpretation that these differences exist mainly because the style of life and normative expectations of the low status family are widely discrepant from those of the high status family. In ascertaining whether or not the differences in the style of life of various social levels which were found in other studies apply to this sample, we compiled Table 6 showing some of the characteristics of the primary social systems from which these patients came.

Persons with low intelligence scores are noticeably limited in their ability to acquire basic educational skills even in the most elementary academic disciplines. Inspection of the educational level of the mothers of low status retardates reveals that many of them are not significantly more proficient than the patient. Over 75% of the mothers of low status patients had completed junior high school or less and none of the low status, modal mothers had gone to college. It should be noted that even within the high status group, the mothers of released patients have significantly less education than the mothers of resident patients.

Although parents may be limited in the amount of education they themselves achieve, they may still have high expectations for their children. The education of the oldest sibling who had completed his education was used as an index of the education which a "normal" child in the family is expected to achieve. Over half of such siblings of low status patients had dropped out of school before completing high school and less than 10% had any college training. In contrast, only about a fourth of the high status siblings had dropped out of school and approximately half had had some college training. Clearly, the minimal educational attainment of the patient would not appear so deviant to a low status family in which other family members also had limited educations as it would to a high status family in which many family members of the retardate's generation have had college training.

Looking at the other end of the scale, 33.3% of the modal, low status retardates had one or more siblings who had also been labelled retarded. Only 2.3% of the resident high status patients had such siblings.

The adult with low mental ability tends to be a person who must be dependent on other people for support. He is often able to function in the community only if he can establish a dependency relationship with some other adult, usually a parent or normal spouse, or if he is able to lean on a public or private agency for support. When the records of the

TABLE 6

CHARACTERISTICS OF PRIMARY SOCIAL SYSTEMS

Characteristic	Response Categories	High Status Resident (43) %	High Status Released (23) %	Low Status Resident (27) %	Low Status Released (39) %	Significance Levels High Status / Low Status	Significance Levels High Resident / Low Released	Significance Levels High Resident / High Released	Significance Levels Low Resident / Low Released
1. Education of the Mother	Some College	26.8	14.2	3.8	0.0	< .001[1]	< .001[1]	< .01[1]	NS[1]
	High School Graduate	39.0	19.0	7.6	10.5				
	Partial High School	17.0	23.8	7.6	13.1				
	Junior High or less	17.0	42.8	80.7	76.3				
2. Education of Oldest Siblings Who Have Completed Schooling	Some College	46.0	57.8	10.5	5.5	< .005[1]	< .01[1]	NS[1]	NS[1]
	High School Graduate	23.0	21.0	36.8	41.6				
	Less than High School	30.6	21.0	52.6	52.7				
3. Number of Siblings Labelled Retarded	None	97.6	91.3	85.1	66.6	< .02[2]	< .001[2]	NS[2]	NS[2]
	One or more	2.3	9.5	14.8	33.3				
4. Dependency Status of Family at Admission	Financially Independent	95.2	86.9	54.2	65.8	< .001[2]	< .001[2]	NS[2]	NS[2]
	Supported by Relatives or Agencies	4.7	13.1	45.8	34.2				
5. Ethnic Status	Caucasian	79.0	74.0	37.0	46.1	< .001[3]	< .01[3]	NS[3]	NS[3]
	Mexican or Negro	20.9	26.0	62.9	53.8				

[1] The Kolmogorov-Smirnov Test of two independent samples was used.
[2] The Log-Likelihood Ratio Test was used. (Barnett, Wolf, "The Log-Likelihood Ratio Test [The G-Test]: Methods and Tables for a Test of Heterogeneity in Contingency Tables," Annals of Human Genetics, Vol. 21, Part 4, June 1957, pp. 397–409.)
[3] The Chi Square Test was used.

families were studied to determine family dependency at the time of admission to the hospital, 37% of the low status families was found to have been dependent upon public agencies or relatives while only 8% of the high status families had depended upon outside assistance. With such a high rate of dependency in low status families, an adult who depends upon Aid to the Totally Disabled or other sources of support would not be greatly different from others in his group. In fact, he is frequently regarded as an asset, since his welfare payments provide additional family income.

There was further evidence that the low status families occupied a more peripheral relationship to the core social structure than the high status families. Although ethnic group was controlled in the original matching of resident and released groups, when the sample was subdivided by social status, the Mexican and Negro groups, not surprisingly, were concentrated in the lower social levels. These ethnic minorities have been marginal to the main stream of American life and are least likely to share the achievement orientations of the core groups.

When a retardate lives in an environment in which dependency is a common way of life, minimal education the rule rather than exception, and occupational achievement limited, his own dependent, educationally deficient, occupationally restricted mode of life does not deviate markedly from that of his family and associates. Under these circumstances, his intellectual deficit is less obvious and his role performance more acceptable to his group than in an environment in which his parents and siblings are highly educated, adult persons are self-supporting, and upward mobility is commonplace.

DISCUSSION AND CONCLUSIONS

The life space of the individual may be viewed as a vast network of interlocking social systems through which the person moves during the course of his lifetime. Those systems which exist close to one another in the social structure tend, because of overlapping memberships and frequent communication, to evolve similar patterns of norms. Most individuals are born and live out their lives in a relatively limited segment of this social network and tend to contact mainly social systems which share common norms. When an individual's contacts are restricted to a circumscribed segment of the structure, this gives some stability to the evaluations which are made of his behavior and to the labels which are attached to him.

However, when the person's life career takes him into segments of the social network which are located at a distance from his point of origin, as when a Mexican-American child enters the public school or a Negro child gets picked up by the police, he is then judged by a new and different set of norms. Behavior which was perfectly acceptable in his primary social systems may now be judged as evidence of "mental retardation." At this point, he is caught up in the web of official definitions. However, because he has primary social systems which may not agree with these official labels, he may be able to return to that segment of the social structure which does not label him as deviant after he has fulfilled the minimal requirements of the official system. That is, he can drop out of school or he can "serve his time" in the state hospital and then go home. By changing his location in social space, he can change his label from "retarded" to "not much different from the rest of us." For example, the mother of a Mexican-American, male, adult patient who had been released from the hospital after being committed following an incident in which he allegedly made sexual advances to a young girl, told the author, "There is nothing wrong with Benny. He just can't read or write." Since the mother spoke only broken English, had no formal schooling, and could not read or write, Benny did not appear deviant to her. From her perspective, he didn't have anything wrong with him.

The child from a high status family has no such recourse. His primary social systems lie structurally close to the official social systems and tend to concur on what is acceptable. Definitions of his subnormality appear early in his life and are more universal in all his social groups. He cannot escape the retarded label because all his associates agree that he is a deviant.[22]

It is interesting to consider the role which a public institution for the retarded may play in making it possible for high status persons to find a new location in social space. Observation of release histories of some persons discharged following work placement programs seems to reveal that an institution for the retarded may serve as a social leveler, an escalator which carries the high status person away from high status primary social systems and downward in the social structure. After a period of institutionalization, he may be released to occupy a position as a domestic servant, common laborer, or other of the less demanding roles found at the bottom of the social structure. Downward social mobility may well be a latent function of the public institution for the retarded which is seldom recognized. To a lesser extent this same process seems to operate when higher status patients are placed in foster homes following a period of institutionalization. These homes are frequently found in less affluent neighborhoods and are run by persons of lower social status, often members of ethnic minorities.

---

22 Lewis Anthony Dexter, "On the Politics and Sociology of Stupidity in our Society," in *The Other Side: Perspectives in Deviance,* edited by Howard S. Becker, Glencoe, Ill., The Free Press, 1964, pp. 37–49.

In conclusion, tentative answers may be given to the three questions raised earlier in this discussion. "Who sees whom as retarded?" Within the social system perspective, it becomes clear that persons who are clinically similar may be defined quite differently by their primary social systems. The person from lower status social systems is less likely to be perceived as mentally subnormal.

"What impact does this differential definition have on the life career of the person?" Apparently, these differential definitions do make a difference because the group which diverges most widely from official definitions is the group in which the most individuals are released from the institution to their families.

Finally, "What are the characteristics of the social systems which diverge most widely from official definitions?" These social systems seem to be characterized by low educational achievement, high levels of dependency, and high concentrations of ethnic minorities.

A social system perspective adds a useful dimension to the label "mental retardation" by its focus on the varied definitions which may be applied to behavior by different groups in society. For those interested in the care and treatment of persons officially labelled as mentally subnormal, it may be beneficial in some cases to seek systematically to relocate such individuals in the social structure in groups which will not define them as deviant. Rather than insisting that a family adopt official definitions of abnormality, we may frequently find it advisable to permit them to continue to view the patient within their own frame of reference and thus make it easier for them to accept him.

HENRY J. MEYER, WYATT JONES,
EDGAR F. BORGATTA

II

The Decision by Unmarried Mothers to Keep or Surrender Their Babies*

Although research in the social work area has been growing in volume, the amount of rigorous description and hypothesis testing thus far reported is limited. Casework, like other counseling and therapeutic endeavors, has been forced to operate largely on the basis of clinical generalizations. Only recently have there begun to appear systematic studies in which the procedures of the behavioral sciences have been brought to bear on the problems with which social workers deal, on the procedures they follow, and on the effectiveness of these procedures. Such studies reflect, to be sure, the relatively primitive level of scientific achievement that characterizes the behavioral, as contrasted with the more developed sciences. They provide evidence, however, that the methods of science, incapable as they are of replacing the "wisdom" and "art" of the practitioner, can correct and supplement that wisdom and art, and in some instances provide new insights and new tools for carrying out the social worker's task.

A long-range objective in any area of social practice is to evaluate the effectiveness of specified treatment procedures for known types of persons and problems. In casework and other kinds of therapy, the objectification of goals, the specification of treatment, and the measurement of effectiveness in achieving goals are of great complexity. Before strictly evaluative research can be incorporated into an agency program, considerable exploration in a descriptive and analytical sense is necessary. Indeed, it is imperative.

Social agencies assume responsibilities for facilitating difficult decisions and for assisting in the achievement of optimum solutions to difficult problems. One function of the type of research reported here is to make more precise some of the knowledge upon which such responsibilities can be fulfilled.[1] This paper deals with a narrow segment of this vast field of practice, in particular with some of the variables, especially background characteristics, believed to be associated with the decision

* Reprinted with permission of the National Association of Social Workers, from *Social Work, Vol. 1,* No. 2 (April, 1956), pp. 103–09. Reproduced by permission of the authors and the journal.

[1] For the past two years a research program at Youth Consultation Service of the Diocese of New York, Inc., has focused on exploring the effects of casework and group therapy on young unmarried mothers and other adolescent girls. This research was made possible by a grant from the Vincent Astor Foundation.

which unmarried mothers served by a casework agency make with respect to the disposition of their babies.[2]

The value of this study may lie as much in the manner of analysis as in the results. It is an example of how information already available to social agencies may be turned into more useful knowledge. It will be recognized that the variables used in the study have been precisely those which are now recorded in fairly standardized form in the case records. As additional information is thus recorded the results of research of this type can be made more definitive.

Our exploration has been from two points of view, reported in two sections. The first analyzes the relationships of selected background characteristics of unmarried mothers to the decision to surrender or to keep the baby. It is therefore concerned with the empirical prediction of that decision from information generally available on first contact with the clients. The second section uses a factor analysis to isolate distinctive clusters of interrelated background characteristics along with some additional variables associated with casework treatment and evaluation. Factor analysis may be viewed as a way of developing an economical description of the major syndromes or combinations of characteristics that appear among the unmarried mothers in the caseload of this agency. Because the data with which the investigators had to work were largely sociological in character, the syndromes identified represent essentially a description of social background factors. As standardized descriptions and measures of psychological variables become available, syndromes can be identified which describe personality and interpersonal as well as social background factors. The field of casework has identified, of course, through the case study method and the experience of practice, major syndromes associated with various social and personal problems which bring people to social agencies. The factor analytic method used here is suggested as a way of sharpening up these generalizations and of adding new ones which may not emerge out of clinical experience, unaided by the tools of quantitative analysis.

For the unmarried mother the decision she must make about her baby is usually fraught with anxiety, discomfort, and conflict. Caseworkers recognize that the decision itself is only a part of the total problem for the mother. That a decision will be made is inevitable, since not making

---

2 In the relevant literature on the unmarried mother, only the following two items appear to be directly pertinent to this research:

J. S. Hasmer, "Traits Predictive of the Successful Outcome of Unmarried Mothers' Plans to Keep Their Children," *Smith College Studies in Social Work*, Vol. 12 (1942), pp. 263–301.

Ruth Rome, "A Method of Predicting the Probable Disposition of Their Children by Unmarried Mothers," *Smith College Studies in Social Work*, Vol. 10 (1940), pp. 167–201.

a decision to surrender the baby is, by default, a decision to keep it. Caseworkers are concerned with the way the decision is made as well as with the content of the decision itself. A comprehensive study would include such aspects of the total problem as: (a) the factors related to the outcome of the decision; (b) the process by which the decision is reached; (c) examination of what constitutes an appropriate decision; (d) the effect of casework treatment in improving the decision. This report is concerned primarily with the first of these. Other aspects of the problem are being studied in the on-going research project at Youth Consultation Service of the Diocese of New York.

BACKGROUND CHARACTERISTICS AND THE DECISION

All unmarried-mother cases active at Youth Consultation Service for the period January 1 through June 30, 1954, were selected as the sample for this analysis. From the records of these 128 cases, background data for each was obtained, including such items as age, race, religion, education, employment history, financial status, family composition, residential history, and relation to the putative father. There were 28 girls who had not made final disposition decisions at the time of the initial analysis and, since these were not used, the sample for this part of the research is reduced to 100 cases.

In this sample, 40 of the girls surrendered their babies for adoption and 60 retained custody of them. When distinguished by race, 32 of the 52 white girls surrendered and 20 kept; whereas among the 48 Negro girls, 8 surrendered and 40 kept. The difference between white and Negro girls in this respect is sufficiently large so that it cannot be attributed to chance.[3]

The tendency of Negro girls to keep their babies in higher proportions than do white girls could reflect a cultural factor that makes for more tolerance and acceptance of out-of-wedlock children among Negroes. It is likely, however, that this is at least in part a social class rather than a cultural difference. Only 40 percent of the sample is Negro, but 68 percent of the 63 girls whose socioeconomic status is designated "working class" are Negro. It is possible, too, that Negro girls believe it is difficult to have their babies adopted and that this would affect their decisions.

The group of 8 Negro girls who surrendered their babies was too small to permit identification of statistically significant background factors which differentiate them from the 40 Negro girls who kept their babies. The remainder of the analysis in this section is therefore confined to the white girls in the sample.

---

[3] The level of statistical significance used in this paper is .05.

Analysis of the background characteristics of the 52 white girls reveals seven dichotomized items that have significant positive correlations (r_{phi}) with the decision to surrender:

Religion: non-Catholic	.45
Education: attended college	.39
Marital status of putative father, single	.41
Age: under 18	.35
Employment status: in school	.37
Financial status: family-supported	.27
Socioeconomic status: white collar, proprietary, or professional class	.34

By trying out combinations of these variables, it was found that the first four (religion, education, marital status of putative father, and age) permitted the most accurate classification of the cases on the basis of whether they kept or surrendered their babies. The white girl with two or more of these positive items present in her background is likely to surrender her baby ($r_{phi} = .63$). If one or none of these positive items is present, the girl is likely to keep her baby. This short "test" for the disposition decision classifies 83 percent of the cases accurately. The same level of accuracy is obtained for Negro girls simply by predicting that all of them will keep their babies (83 percent). Thus the general prediction for Negro and white girls combined, on the assumption that the observed relationships will be maintained, is that 83 percent of the cases will be accurately classified from the knowledge of these four variables and the identification of the girl as Negro or white.

To find out whether this "test" would hold for a different sample of cases, it was applied to 175 closed cases for which final decisions were known for the years 1952 and 1953 and for new cases that had entered the agency between July and October 1954. For the white girls in this new sample, 77 percent were accurately classified and for Negro girls the percentage previously observed was maintained (84 percent). For the combined sample, the decisions were thus properly predicted for 80 percent of the cases.

Presentation of these findings does not imply that an empirical prediction such as this one can be substituted for the clinical judgment of the caseworker. It is the worker who still must decide, for each case, what the likelihood is that a girl will surrender or keep her baby, how appropriate the decision would be under all the circumstances, how to handle the client's feelings and attitudes about the decision, and what service and treatment plans should be carried out. It does, however, challenge the worker to formulate more deliberately the basis for diagnosis and for planning, particularly in cases where the judgment and plan are at odds with the statistical probabilities of the case.

DESCRIPTION OF FACTORS

For a further analysis of background and other variables, it is desirable to discover how these then are interrelated. Factor analysis is an appropriate statistical operation for this purpose. It permits one to identify which variables cluster together, on the one hand, and which clusters of variables, on the other hand, are independent of one another.

The sample used for the factor analysis overlaps that used for the more simple correlation analysis reported in the preceding section. It includes the 223 cases available from the 1953 and 1954 caseloads. In addition to background information certain facts about the treatment periods were recorded, such as duration of contact with the agency and attendance at group therapy sessions. For 157 of the cases, ratings by caseworkers were obtained[4] as to the client's degree of involvement in treatment, her decisiveness and realism with regard to the decision about her baby; and her satisfaction with the final decision.

From a total of 28 different variables whose interrelationships were examined, 19 were retained for the factor analysis.[5] These variables, treated as dichotomized items of information in each case, are identified as follows:

VARIABLES OF THE FACTOR ANALYSIS

1. Disposition of baby: surrender—keep
2. Age: under 21—21 or over
3. Race: white—nonwhite
4. Religion: non-catholic—Catholic
5. Education: not high school graduate—high school graduate or more
6. Employment: white-collar job—other or none
7. Financial status: self-supporting—family-supported or other
8. Birthplace: out-of-state—New York State or foreign
9. Nativity of parents: native-born—foreign-born
10. Prepregnancy residence: live at home—live elsewhere

---

[4] The rating forms were developed after extensive discussion with the casework staff and were intentionally general in character, i.e., they used large, broad categories rather than a large number of small, selected ones. The ratings must be accepted with caution because some of them were necessarily made after the mother's decision was known. In such rating procedures, there is great danger that the rating made of one variable will influence that of the others. There is further danger that the caseworkers will understandably use the final decision itself as a criterion when rating variables believed to be associated with that decision.

[5] Cross-tabulations for Negro and white cases separately as well as for the total sample were made but no meaningful distinction by race was apparent. For the correlation matrix, r_{phi} was used. The technical decisions made in developing the factor analysis, the intercorrelation matrix, and the orthogonal rotated factor matrix were reported in the original paper.

11. Socioeconomic status of family: middle or upper class—working class
12. Marital status of parents: living together—broken home
13. Marital status of putative father: single—married
14. Residence during pregnancy: maternity shelter—other
15. Duration of agency contact: less than 6 months—6 or more months
16. Group therapy: some—none
17. Attitude toward disposition: decisive—indecisive
18. Quality of the decision: realistic—unrealistic
19. Client's psychological functioning: good—poor

Five substantial factors were extracted in the analysis. A factor is a construct, such as social class, that takes a number of interrelated variables and summarizes them in a single new variable. Its great virtue is the virtue of all statistical measures—it permits reduction of what would be an unmanageable number of separate bits of information into a summary statement with which the human mind can work. It brings together what is already known in such a way that we can see relationships that were formerly obscured by a mass of detail. The reduction of 19 of the variables listed above to 5, without a significant loss of the predictive values of the information provided by the 19 variables, is evidence of the utility of factor analysis. It is difficult enough to juggle five variables in arriving at diagnostic and treatment decisions; only a genius or Univac is able to give simultaneous consideration to 19!

In this study, Factor 1 appears to be a *social class* factor. Cases with a high loading in this factor, i.e., cases which are effectively described by the variables which make up this factor, are characterized by coming from white, nonbroken, middle- or upper-class families, having held a white-collar or professional job, living in a shelter during pregnancy, having group therapy experience while in the shelter, and surrendering the baby. Described negatively, this factor is characterized as non-white, working class, without shelter experience and therefore without group therapy, keeping the baby, coming from a broken home, and having had domestic, factory, or no work experience.

Factor 1	Loading
14. Shelter residence during pregnancy	.79
16. Group therapy experience	.72
11. Socioeconomic status (middle or upper)	.63
3. Race (white)	.60
1. Disposition of baby (surrender)	.58
6. White-collar employment	.32
12. Parents living together	.32

Girls whose decisions about the disposition of the baby are characterized by caseworker rating as *appropriate handling* of the situation constitute the type of person indicated by a high loading in Factor 2. Rated as decisive, realistic about the decision, and as functioning well psychologically, this type also lives at home in an unbroken family, has short contact with the agency, and decides to surrender the baby. The opposite characterization—unrealistic, indecisive, poor psychological functioning, from a broken home and living alone, with six or more months' contact with the agency, and deciding to keep the baby—seems to describe what may be the caseworker's view of inappropriate handling of the difficult social situation involved in unmarried motherhood. In general, it would appear that the definition of appropriateness is surrendering the baby while remaining with the family of orientation. Presumably, the implication is that of a realistic facing of the problem by the girl and her family.

Factor 2	Loading
18. Realistic decision	.56
17. Decisive attitude in decision	.52
19. Good psychological functioning	.48
1. Disposition of baby (surrender)	.45
10. Home residence before pregnancy	.45
15. Less than 6 months' contact with agency	.30

Factor 3 seems, in its positive and negative aspects, to describe a *rural-urban* continuum. The rural pole is characterized as native born but not in New York State, non-Catholic, having both parents native born, and being nonwhite. The urban pole is New York State or foreign born, Catholic, of foreign-born parentage, and white. The southern Negro of comparatively recent residence in New York appears to be indicated on the one side and the second-generation, Catholic, white girl of New York on the other.

Factor 3	Loading
8. Birthplace out of New York State	.59
9. Parents native born	.53
4. Religion (non-Catholic)	.50
3. Race (nonwhite)	.47

The fourth factor appears to describe the *emancipated* woman. On the one side, the type is characterized by the self-supporting, white woman, 21 years of age or over, well educated, holding a white-collar or professional position, and living away from home. Viewed conversely, the cluster primarily describes the young, economically dependent, vocationally inexperienced girl of limited education who is living at home.

Factor 4	Loading
7. Self-supporting financial status	.82
2. 21 years of age or over	.77
5. Education (high school graduate or more)	.57

Factor 4 (Cont'd)   *Loading (Cont'd)*
   6. White-collar employment   .51
 10. Prepregnancy residence not at home   .36
   3. Race (white)   .32

Factor 5 is least clear among the factors. Coming from a working-class family but having a good education, or conversely, coming from a middle- or upper-class family and having little education define this type. The variables seem to suggest upward or downward *social mobility.*

Factor 5   *Loading*
   5. Education (high school graduate or more)   .63
 11. Socioeconomic status (working class)   .56

The five types that emerge from the factor analysis constitute meaningful distinctions within the caseload of the agency. With respect to the decision to keep or surrender the baby, only the first two factors are involved. The decision is strongly associated with social class (Factor 1). It is somewhat less strongly associated with the second factor—appropriate handling of the social situation from the viewpoint of the caseworker. Thus, the analysis suggests that the higher the social class, the more likely the girl is to surrender the baby. In addition, it appears that the more realistically the situation is faced without disturbing the normal pattern of the girl's family life, the more likely she is to surrender the baby.

SOME IMPLICATIONS OF THE RESEARCH

In our first analysis, we found that the disposition decision for unmarried mothers coming to this particular agency could be predicted on an actuarial basis for about 80 percent of the cases. If this level of accuracy were found to prevail generally,[6] the test based on these variables would provide a means, hitherto unavailable, whereby social agencies might anticipate at the beginning of contact the disposition decisions of their clients and use this information in the planning of their services and treatment for unmarried mothers. Administratively, an indication of the girl's ultimate decision would enable the agency to make appropriate contacts with adoption agency, foster home, boarding home, or to make whatever arrangements might be required. Thus a considerable saving in agency time and energy might be effected and smoother interagency cooperation achieved.

In addition to administrative advantages, the possibility of anticipating the unmarried mother's decision might serve to alert the caseworker to special problems in cases in which the predicted decision differs from

---

[6] Application of the "test" variables to 33 cases constituting the unmarried-mother caseload of a social agency in Brooklyn properly classified 76 percent of the cases with respect to surrendering or keeping the baby.

that which the caseworker believes to be most appropriate in the light of casework objectives. Furthermore, with knowledge of the modal behavior of major segments of the caseload, it is possible to hypothesize that persons who conform to the characteristic decisions of their peers will make the most satisfactory decisions. With this in mind, a meaningful theory might be devised that could facilitate the interpretation of exceptional cases in terms of social psychological factors.

In the second section of the paper we have presented types which may be said to arise empirically from the interrelationships among the variables observed. These types will be familiar in the experience of workers in agencies of this kind. But an analysis of this sort sharpens the distinctions observed and may correct impressions. For example, the impression that the distinction between Nego and white girls is a cultural distinction of importance in the decision about the baby may be more plausible than actual. Our data suggest that what appears to be a distinction of color or race may more appropriately be a distinction associated with social and economic conditions. The rural-urban difference, on the other hand, which might be expected to reflect the greatest actual divergence in culture, does not in this analysis have any important bearing on the decision the mother makes about her baby.

The range of variables included in this research is limited to those readily available in comparable form from the case records of all the cases in our sample. Research in progress seeks to extend these limits to include not only greater detail of social background, but personality, behavioral, and treatment variables as well. Our identification through factor analysis of clusters of background characteristics encourages us to investigate the relationship of such factors to psychological syndromes and diagnostic types which are more familiar in the practice of casework.

If standardized information with respect to psychological and other so-called dynamic variables were comparable to information about background which has been used in this study, an analysis such as here presented would lead to greater understanding of the client's behavior. Our study indicates the predictability of the unmarried mother's decision to keep or surrender her baby. It may be anticipated that further analysis of social and psychological variables recorded in standardized form will increase both the predictability of the decision and the understanding of factors related to it. The challenge for the social worker in this respect is to objectify and record those professional insights which he utilizes in his daily practice.

LILIAN RIPPLE, ERNESTINA ALEXANDER

12 | *Motivation, Capacity, and Opportunity as Related to the Use of Casework Service: Nature of Client's Problem**

Casework service has as its function helping people who are experiencing difficulty in their social adjustment. Assessment of the client's ability to use help and determination of appropriate treatment must be meaningfully related to the client's current problem situation. In each case situation the problem can, of course, be identified and described in all of its individuality. The difficulty arises when it is necessary, as in the current study of motivation, capacity, and opportunity, to find some classification scheme which permits grouping together those clients with similar problems. Initially we did not attempt to develop a classification scheme. Instead, we followed the practice common in casework of having narrative statements prepared by the study judges. Three statements were required to describe the problem as defined by the client, by the caseworker, and by the judge herself. A classification scheme was subsequently developed and applied to these narrative statements. This article describes the scheme and our experience in applying it. Some of the implications of "problem" in analyzing and evaluating motivation, capacity, and opportunity are illustrated by use of preliminary findings.

PROBLEM = PERSON-IN-SITUATION

Dissatisfaction with problem-classification schemes in social work has been chronic and universal. We have no intent of presenting a historical review of this dissatisfaction and its causes. A few of the well-recognized anomalies in most classification schemes merit mention, however, for it was an attempt to avoid these that led to the scheme that we developed. We may or may not have succeeded; we may, and probably have, introduced anomalies of our own. Because the present study is concerned wholly with clients of voluntary family casework agencies, our comments are confined to problem-classification schemes used by such agencies, although we incline to the view that the comments are more generally applicable.

Problem-classification schemes usually have been established to serve a particular purpose but with the hope, even the expectation, that they

* Reprinted from the *Social Service Review*, Vol. XXX, No. 1 (March, 1956), pp. 38–54, by permission of The University of Chicago Press, the journal and the authors.

could serve one or more secondary purposes.[1] Over the years, categories tend to be modified and a system's basic structure may be reorganized to take account of changes in agency objectives, practices, and clientele. Concurrently, what were originally seen as secondary uses of a scheme may become primary and competing. As a consequence, problem-classification schemes have evolved into check lists whose categories not only are not mutually exclusive but, further, may describe problems, solutions, requests, services, causes, consequences, conditions, or mere statements of status (e.g., "unmarried mother"). For most cases it becomes necessary to check a number of different classifications which often, somehow, fail to convey much notion of what the problem is all about. The difficulty may be illustrated by the hypothetical situations of Mr. Smith and Mr. Jones. Mr. Smith requests assistance in adjustment of debts which have resulted from chronic mismanagement; the economic strains and stresses, plus other factors, have led to postponement of needed medical care; there is also some marital conflict. Mr. Jones, on the other hand seeks help in relation to long-standing marital conflict; he also has problems of income-management and his wife has a mild chronic dysfunctioning for which she resists needed medical attention. In both cases the same problem classifications are applicable: "economic," "marital conflict," "physical illness." Yet, one immediately senses that these two situations differ considerably. Even if the particular system used differentiates "major" problems, the situation is not greatly improved, for one immediately faces the question: major in what sense—of greatest concern (to the client or to the caseworker?), of greatest urgency in a time-sequence sense, of greatest importance to future well-being of the family? It appeared to us that the primary obstacle to using, or adapting, any existing problem-

---

[1] The committee that recommended the original uniform statistical system for family welfare agencies, for example, noted that "figures for problems presented are of value for publicity and for the information of the staff and directors," seemingly envisaging a definite major purpose and a somewhat less clear secondary purpose; see "Report of the Committee on Statistics of the American Association of Societies for Organizing Charity," *Charity Organization Bulletin*, VI (new series), Nos. 10 and 11 (September, October, 1915), 134. Subsequently, emphasis was given, at least by individual agencies, to use of the data for evaluation; for an interesting discussion of this use, see Elinor Blackman, "Some Tests for Evaluation of Case Work Methods," *Proceedings of the National Conference of Social Work, 1925*, pp. 246–50. More recent recommendations focus on use of problem data for publicity but not the statistics *per se*. In 1940, for example, the Family Welfare Association of America stated, "It is expected that the list [of problems and services] will highlight the case load by offering ready access to specific kinds of situations which may be suggestive to the case worker in describing the work of the agency . . . to the public" but also should "be a useful guide in making special studies . . . [and] in so far as the use of the [statistical] card requires analysis of individual case work problems and their treatment, it may assist the worker to clarify and evaluate the service of the agency to the particular client": see, *F.W.A.A. Statistical Card No. 1A: Explanation of Use and Definition of Terms* (New York: Family Welfare Association of America, 1940), pp. 2–3.

classification schemes with which we were familiar is their inability to convey what might be termed the problem-at-issue in a way which permits grouping cases that have some central feature in common.

We turned, then, to a simple definition of problem, "a question proposed for solution"[2] and to our conception, by no means unique, of casework as a problem-solving process. The implication of taking these two concepts as the foundation on which to build a classification scheme is twofold: (1) we are concerned not with aggregating problems but with that question which currently is identified—whether by client, by caseworker, or by both—as requiring solution; (2) we are not concerned with describing a problem *per se* but with describing, though broadly and crudely, the person-in-situation as this has relevance to common elements of problem-solving.[3] In other words, we sought to develop a system that would contain a relatively small number of mutually exclusive categories which would describe both the problem situation and the client's relationship to it.

Viewed in this light it seemed that two classes of problems could be identified: (1) that in which the "question for solution" involves external, that is, environmental, maladjustments or deficiencies and, concomitantly, the problem-solving process contains at least some elements of acting upon that environment; and (2) that in which environmental circumstances *per se* have minor, if any, place in defining the "question for solution" and, consequently, the problem-solving process to be set in operation does not involve acting upon that environment. One additional distinction is needed to transform this dichotomy into a classification that more fully delineates the person-in-situation, namely, some way of indicating the part the client has played in creating the problem.[4]

A structure for developing a classification system along these lines already existed in the criteria developed by the casework faculty of the School of Social Service Administration of the University of Chicago for selection of cases for teaching. With the objective of providing progression in the learning experiences of students, the faculty had evolved a three-stage sequence moving from "simplicity" to "complexity." The criteria for these three stages essentially defined the groups that we wished to isolate.[5] First, there are the "victims of circumstance" for whom there

---

2 *Webster's New International Dictionary*, 2d ed., unabridged, p. 1971.

3 In this connection see, especially, Gordon Hamilton's discussion of the nature of problem in relation to diagnosis which particularly stresses the concepts of "present need" and "person-in-situation" in *Theory and Practice of Social Case Work* (2d ed. rev.; New York: Columbia University Press, 1951), pp. 213 ff.

4 While theoretically this distinction could apply to both of the two main classes of problems, in fact we have found the distinction necessary only for the first group—that in which the problem involves external factors.

5 Charlotte Towle, *The Learner in Education for the Professions* (Chicago: University of Chicago Press, 1954), pp. 288 ff., 293–94, 307.

is an "obvious connection between their social problems, their disturbed feelings about their problems, and their external circumstances. Furthermore, their feelings are commensurate with the extent of the stress." Second, there are the "people who have had some part in creating their problems or whose problems have activated underlying personality conflicts," but they also reach the agency "because they need specific services rather than help with troubled relationships or their own personality disturbance *per se* . . . for, despite their own part in creating the social problems, they now have realistic adversity" with which to deal. Finally, there are those clients whose "range in personality difficulties is from mild to gross pathology" and who may be experiencing difficulties in social adjustment but whose "own emotional disturbance or personality problem is in the foreground."

Using these three basic differentiations, the classification scheme divides all situations into (1) those in which the problem to be solved is defined at least in part by external (as opposed to psychological) factors: (*a*) the client is the "victim of circumstance" or (*b*) the client has contributed substantially to the creation of these circumstances, and (2) those in which the problem is one of interpersonal relationships or personality disturbance. The final eight-category system merely provides for closer identification of the focal aspect of the problem:

1. Economic dislocation.
2. Social dislocation.
3. Economic maladjustment.
4. Social maladjustment.
5. Interpersonal conflict (overt conflict between two people) .
6. Intrafamilial conflict (overt conflict involving three or more persons but all within the family group) .
7. Maladaptive interpersonal relationship (between two people or involving three or more persons all within the family group—without overt conflict) .
8. Personality disturbance or behavior disorder not otherwise classified.

As is immediately apparent, the first four categories describe "external problem" and the last four, "psychological problem" situations.

EXTERNAL PROBLEMS

Situations characterized by external problems are classified on two bases: dislocation versus maladjustment and economic versus social. The distinction between dislocation and maladjustment is the one previously discussed, that is, the "victim of circumstance" has a problem defined as "dislocation"; the person whose behavior or attitudes have created or exacerbated his difficulties has a problem defined as "maladjustment."

The distinction between economic and social hinges upon whether or not the problem to be solved is limited to obtaining more income for ordinary maintenance; if so, the problem is classed as "economic," but if the problem arose because of a change in the family's or individual's situation which requires planning with the client or his family to effect an adjustment to the changed circumstances over and beyond financial assistance and/or the use of special resources not commonly available to or used by the ordinary family with a moderate income, the problem is classified as "social." For both of these groups illness is often the "circumstance" which created the problem and the illness may have psychogenic features. The family agency, however, is not a medical agency and the illness *per se* is not the "question for solution" in the family agency; consequently, as in the illustration below, if currently the client's response to his illness and its consequences is "normal," his problem would be classified as "dislocation" regardless of the underlying psychological implications of his illness.

The situations of Mr. P. and Mr. C. illustrate the differences between problems of "economic dislocation" and of "social dislocation":

Mr. P., a 61-year-old man, requested financial assistance until he was able to return to work, having recently been hospitalized for treatment of diabetes and rheumatoid arthritis. Return to his usual employment was medically contraindicated and a vocational retraining program was underway. Mr. P. had been deserted many years before by his emotionally disturbed wife and was living with his sister and her family. Despite serious illness which created severe financial pressures in the sister's home, relationships were positive and the family wished to have Mr. P. remain with them. They were willing to provide a home but beyond this could not contribute to his support. Mr. P. had always been self-supporting, was making good progress in his retraining program, and was eager to return to work; he was more than reluctant to be dependent upon his sister and her husband, feeling that his presence in the home deprived the family of necessities.

While it is true that Mr. P.'s problems include two chronic illnesses and vocational displacement, he is under medical supervision and is in a retraining program; "the question for solution" when he comes to the family agency is that of obtaining sufficient funds for his maintenance during the remainder of his vocational training program. For Mr. C., in contrast, the problem is not essentially lack of income although he, also, is seen as a "victim of circumstance":

Mr. C. requested homemaker service for care of two children, ages seven and four, because of Mrs. C.'s inability to care for them or to manage the household. She had recently been discharged from the hospital, where she had had the fourth operation within a year; her illness was now diagnosed as terminal cancer. Various relatives had helped with care of the children but all had their own family responsibilities and they had exhausted their financial reserves to help Mr. C. meet excessively high medical expenses. In addition to the financial pressure, Mr. C. was reacting to the trauma of the recent diagnosis of his wife's illness and the emotional strain on the entire family group was overpowering. Mrs. C., though unaware that her illness was terminal, felt discouraged and inadequate because she could not care for her home and children. The children were upset and "out of hand," reacting to the many separations from their mother, and the uncertainty about which relative would care for them next.

The classification of "social," rather than "economic," dislocation is based both upon the need for special resources and assistance (in the form of homemaker service) beyond the usual demands upon moderate-income families and upon the need for planning and help in adjusting to the changed family situation.

The category of "social maladjustment" is one of the best illustrations of classification requiring differentiation from two other categories. Many of the "social" problems had developed from external factors over which the client had little if any control; originally, that is, the client had been a "victim of circumstance." Is his problem one of "social disloca-tion" or of "social maladjustment"? We found it possible to make a distinction by carefully evaluating—and in many cases it was not easy—*what the problem for solution was as the client came to the agency:* at that point was he still the "victim of circumstance," or through his reaction to the original dislocation and/or his efforts to cope with it had he exacerbated the problem so that "maladjustment" was the end result? In addition to differentiating "maladjustment" from "dislocation," it was also necessary to differentiate "social maladjustment" from "personality disturbance." The difficulty here was not so much with definition as with the need to shift our own frame of reference. "Maladjustment" as a term carries with it a connotation that personality factors are of import; moreover the category "social maladjustment" had specifically been defined to mean that the client through his attitudes and behavior had created or exacerbated the problem. In the early stages of applying the classification scheme, we were tempted to place in "personality disturb-ance" those situations in which the pathology was severe. We had con-stantly to remind ourselves that the crux of the distinction lay in whether or not "the question for solution" involved resolving difficulties in the environmental situation. In so doing we were able to train ourselves out of any notion that "social maladjustment" implied less pathology than "personality disturbance."

The situation of the T. family points up the factors involved in classifying the problem as "social maladjustment" even though elements of "dislocation" and of "personality disturbance" were also present:

A neighbor telephoned the agency to request financial assistance for the T. family because Mr. T. had been unable to work steadily, having had to stay at home frequently to care for four children, ranging in ages from four to twelve, during

Mrs. T.'s illness with a complicated pregnancy. When Mr. T., a man in his early thirties, was seen, he was discouraged and described how he had struggled for six months with a steadily deteriorating situation. Before Mrs. T.'s current pregnancy, she had also been employed; the picture that emerged from his presentation was of a young wife who not only had shared much of the financial responsibility but had also been the emotional mainstay of the family. Mr. T. had a history of asthmatic attacks which subsided when he did not have full responsibility for support of the family. Since his wife's illness, he had had a recurrence of these attacks which had accounted in part for his irregular employment. During these periods, relatives gave some help. Excessive responsibility was placed upon the twelve-year-old for care of her mother and siblings as well as for household management. Even when Mr. T. was not needed in the home, he was reluctant to go to work, excusing himself on the basis of feared asthmatic attacks and a series of minor ailments, but he was equally reluctant to take medical care.

Although the difficulties in this family situation stemmed from Mrs. T.'s illness, a classification of "dislocation" is unsuitable in view of Mr. T.'s current response to the situation. On the other hand, "personality disturbance" fails to convey the adequacy of functioning of this family unit and of Mr. T. as long as Mrs. T. was able to occupy her role of supporter and stabilizer, or to show that, regardless of his basic personality difficulties, currently Mr. T.'s maladaptive functioning is responsive to the changed situation in his family.

PSYCHOLOGICAL PROBLEMS

Psychological problems are described by four categories which are differentiated on the basis of whether or not there is a relatively defined focal aspect of the problem and what that aspect is. The first two, "interpersonal conflict" and "intrafamilial conflict," differ only in the number of persons involved in the conflict. Use of either category necessitates that there be overt conflict; this, however, does not necessarily mean violent quarreling, but rather that there is recognized difference and disagreement—between two people, if classified as interpersonal conflict; among three or more, if classified as intrafamilial conflict. Frequently, as was true of Mrs. D., one conflicted relationship was originally presented as the problem but with further exploration almost total intrafamilial conflict was described:

Mrs. D. sought help because of school difficulties of her 15-year-old son, which she attributed solely to the father's poor relationship with John, resulting in the boy's fear of male teachers and frequent friction with them. Mr. D. refused to take any responsibility for interceding for John at school in a situation in which it appeared that he needed support from his parents. Mrs. D. wanted help in knowing how she could foster a better relationship between John and Mr. D. and seemed to be asking for service for Mr. D. Exploration revealed long-standing marital discord; Mrs. D. had been protective and possessive in her relationship with John; both John and his younger sister Mary had constantly been drawn into quarrels between the parents, John usually "siding with" the mother and Mary, with the father.

Instead of one conflicted relationship, there were four sets of such relationships or, in other terms, two opposed alignments: Mrs. D. and John versus Mr. D. and Mary. Actually, each of these alignments could separately be described as "maladaptive interpersonal relationship" but "intrafamilial conflict" seems better to describe this embattled situation.

While both interpersonal conflict and intrafamilial conflict could be included under the general heading of "maladaptive interpersonal relationship," this specific category was reserved for those situations in which the problem lay in the relationship between two or more persons but in which there was not *overt* conflict. A classic example of this type is the possessive overprotective mother and the passive fearful child. We early made an arbitrary decision that parent-child relationship problems involving a preadolescent would be placed in this category regardless of the child's behavior symptomatology unless there was definite evidence to support another classification. Our use of narrative descriptions prepared before the classification system had been devised proved to be a handicap; we could not always tell whether or not the situation was seen as one of *overt* conflict or, rather, as "acting-out" behavior of a child in his efforts (frequently unconsciously motivated) to find ways of adjusting to an environment which, to a greater or lesser degree, was depriving him of the emotional nourishment necessary for growth and development. Mrs. Y. and her young son illustrate a situation classified as "maladaptive interpersonal relationship" in spite of much stress and aggression:

Mrs. Y. sought the agency's help in handling the problem of behavior of six-year-old Peter, the "middle child" of three boys. In the past few years she had found Peter's behavior difficult and puzzling. She spoke first of his "slowness," resistance to carrying out developmental tasks—learning to dress, bathe, and feed himself—which annoyed her greatly. He demanded help, did not do as well as his four-year-old brother nor as well as his older brother had done at his age. More irritating was his yelling and shouting that he hated her whenever she refused any request. Peter teased and tormented his brothers, striking them physically at the slightest provocation. Of the three boys, Peter was the only one who was still enuretic at night. Mrs. Y. was also anxious about his school adjustment; she had frequently been called to school because of Peter's inability to sit still, his disobedience, and his difficulty in relationship with other children. Lying was prevalent both at home and in school.

Mrs. Y. placed responsibility for the problem on her inconsistent handling. She thought there was something "wrong" in the relationship between her and Peter which accounted for his behavior and wanted help in understanding this as well as help in handling him in other ways than spanking and threatening. Mrs. Y. revealed that she lost her temper, yelled back at him, and was more impatient with him than with the other two boys. She wondered whether he had been given too much affection—both parents were partial to him as a baby and Mr. Y. still favored him and was stricter with the other two boys. Peter was born after Mr. Y.'s discharge from the Army so was "really like a first child to him."

Although there was certainly "quarreling" between Mrs. Y. and Peter, it is difficult to see this as "overt conflict" between two antagonists each of whom acts toward the other in recognition of disagreement where the conflict and resolution of that conflict is the "question for solution." Peter's behavior appears much too unconsciously motivated, and the relative strength and responsibility of each person for his own behavior appears much too unequal to yield a classification of "overt interpersonal conflict"; rather, the problem as defined by the client herself, by the caseworker, and by the judge was classified as "maladaptive interpersonal relationship."

For the final category in the classification scheme—"personality disturbance or behavior problem not otherwise classified"—the key words are *not otherwise classified*. The three other categories in the "psychological problems" group and two of those in the "external problems" group also involved personality disturbance, ranging from mild to severe pathology. The distinction is made not on the basis of severity of disturbance but on the presence or absence of some focalized "question for solution." Mr. T. and both Mr. and Mrs. D., previously described, had more serious personality disturbances than did many clients whose problems were classified as "personality disturbance." This category thus describes the person with pervasive maladaptive behavior which, however, may be quite mild. Differentiation is made, of course, between whether it is the client or another person whose problem is "personality disturbance."

APPLICATION OF THE CLASSIFICATION SYSTEM

Definitions for the eight categories, criteria for distinguishing among them, and some additional sub-classifications[6] were refined and amplified in two "tests" of the system. When the major categories had been specified and at least partially defined, the system was tested on a 10 percent random sample (39 clients).[7] Each client included in the study

---

[6] These subclassifications provided for further specificity as to the focal aspects of the problem. In the current study they are of limited usefulness because of the small numbers involved in most subcategories, partly because one-third of the entire group are found in "interpersonal" or "intrafamilial" conflict, leaving relatively small groups when the remaining cases are distributed among even the other six major categories.

[7] Because different figures reported in the remainder of this article may prove confusing, we recapitulate the reason for these differences. The total number of clients for whom data were obtained numbered 394; this total group was included in classifying problems. Of these 394 clients, however, 43 were judged to be in "short-term completed service" cases; these cases are omitted from the main analysis comparing clients who continued beyond the exploratory phase of casework service and those who discontinued before having as many as five interviews. Consequently, the current "study group" includes 351 clients. The 43 clients omitted in this study will be picked up for analysis in the second study which follows the continuers through to case closing.

had originally been rated independently by three experienced case-workers (judges) who were required to write narrative statements of the problem as defined by the client, by the caseworker, and by the judge herself. These statements referred to the time of the first interview but, if the problem was defined differently by the end of the period for which material was available, additional statements were also required. Three coders[8] applied the classification scheme to these narrative statements. The coders were asked to evaluate carefully whether or not, despite different wording or minor variations in emphasis, the narrative statements on the three schedules for a given client could be considered essentially in agreement. On the other hand, they exercised care in maintaining differentiations which did exist so that if one classification would apply to the statements on two of the schedules, they did not become overinfluenced and give the same classification to the third schedule. This permitted use of amplifying but noncontradictory material on the three original schedules. The three coders agreed in their classification of 81 percent of the statements and for all but 4 of the 386 statements at least two of the coders gave the same classification.

In a second test using another 10 percent random sample each coder was given only one of the original schedules. The purpose of this test was to obtain some indication of whether or not the agreement was spuriously high because all three original sets of statements had been used. In this test, then, each problem classification was made by one coder from the narrative statements of one of the three judges who originally rated the case. There was complete agreement in 75 percent of the classifications and in all but two cases at least two of the coders using original statements by two different judges arrived at the same problem classification. After a considerable interval, each coder classified the schedules previously classified by the other two coders. In the great majority of instances the two reviewing coders gave the same classification as had the original coder; that is, the differences were not in coding but in the statements by the original judge.

It was found that most of these disagreements concerned one of two types of situations. In cases involving unmarried mothers the statement of the problem as defined by the caseworker and by the judge tended to be brief and it was often impossible on the basis of the material to know whether or not the appropriate classification was social "dislocation" or social "maladjustment."[9] This difficulty arose, of course, because we had

---

8 Ernestina Alexander, Rebecca Cohen, and Rose Wheeler.

9 For some unmarried mothers, of course, the appropriate classification was in one of the "psychological problems" categories; these were not the situations that presented difficulty. Most unmarried mothers, at least among those included in this study, did not present their disturbed selves or the "unmarried parenthood" *in toto* as the problem, nor was it initially so taken by the caseworker or judge; rather, the "question for solution" was maintenance, living arrangements, planning for a child, or a similar need.

not initially known the basis that we would use for problem classification; therefore, the judges did not know what narrative material would be most relevant. Faced with the dilemma, however, we decided that all we could do in such situations was arbitrarily to classify the problem as defined by the caseworker and by the judge (but not by the client) as "social maladjustment" unless there was evidence to support another classification. The second general difficulty was in differentiating between "interpersonal conflict" and either "maladaptive interpersonal relationship" or "personality disturbance" in the caseworker's and particularly the judge's definitions of problem. For the latter we had a better recourse through use of the rating schedule. While we did not wish to use actual ratings—of motivation, capacity, and opportunity—in arriving at the problem definition, there were two items which the judges were to use only if they defined the problem as mainly one of interpersonal conflict. In doubtful classifications, then, the coders were permitted to request information as to whether or not these two items had been used by the particular judge whose statement they were attempting to classify.

These two tests and the resulting clarification of definitions satisfied us that the classification system was usable although by no means perfect. The second test, also, had seemed to indicate that the coders were not contaminated in their classifications by having access to all three schedules simultaneously. In applying the classification system to the total study group, each set of three schedules for a given client was independently classified by two coders[10] who then conferred to reconcile any differences. Out of a total of 1,270 classifications,[11] conference to reconcile differences was required for slightly less than 20 percent. In only 21 instances was it not possible for the team of two coders to reconcile their differences; in these cases one or both of the authors reviewed the material and attempted to reconcile the classifications.

CLIENT VERSUS PROFESSIONAL DEFINITION OF PROBLEM

It is a common experience in comparing clients' views of their problems

---

[10] In addition to Rebecca Cohen and Rose Wheeler, who had worked on the tests, the other two coders were Selina Reed and Jennie Zetland.

[11] This represents "instances of classification." If the coder thought that all three judges' statements described the same problem and, consequently, used only one problem classification, this is one instance of classification; if she thought two statements described the same problem and used one classification for them but thought the third statement required a different problem classification, this is two "instances of classification." There are, thus, at least three "instances of classification" for every client—one each for the problem as defined by the client, by the caseworker, and by the judge at the time of the first interview—if all three judges' statements agreed throughout. More "instances of classification" arise if either the judges' statements were not in agreement throughout or if there was any redefinition of the problem by the end of the case material used for the study.

with those of professional social workers to find many reversals of "external" and "psychological" classifications. Three of the categories in the present system—economic dislocation, social dislocation, and personality disturbance of another person—essentially place the problem outside the client. These three categories were used for 45 percent of the clients' definitions of problem at the time of the first interview and for less than 10 percent of the study judges' definitions of problem.[12] It is precisely in relation to this phenomenon that the present classification system seems most useful. These reversals did not involve crossing over from "external" to "psychological" as here defined. They represent the difference between "dislocation" and "maladjustment," in the "external problems" group, and between "personality disturbance—other person"

TABLE 1

CLASSIFICATION OF THE PROBLEM AS DEFINED BY THE CLIENT AND BY THE
STUDY JUDGE AT TIME OF FIRST INTERVIEW
(Numerals indicating problem categories in column headings refer
to same categories, by number, as listed in stub.)

Category of Problem as Defined by Client	Total	Category of Problem as Defined by Judge							
		I	II	III	IV	V	VI	VII	VIII
Total	351	4	30	15	81	121	36	49	15
I. Economic dislocation..	34	4	24	—	5	—	—	1	—
II. Economic maladjustment	7	—	6	—	—	—	—	1	—
III. Social dislocation	85	—	—	15	55	3	2	9	1
IV. Social maladjustment..	24	—	—	—	19	—	—	5	—
V. Interpersonal or intra-familial conflict*	117	—	—	—	1	108	—	8	—
VI. Maladaptive interpersonal relationship.....	22	—	—	—	—	—	19	2	1
VII. Personality disturbance —client	23	—	—	—	—	1	1	21	—
VIII. Personality disturbance —other than this client	39	—	—	—	1	9	14	2	13

* Because of the very small number classified as "intrafamilial" conflict, and the high agreement in client's and judges' definitions for this and the "interpersonal" conflict group, these two categories are here combined. In the one instance when the judge defined problem as "social maladjustment," the client had defined it as "intrafamilial conflict"; all 8 involving switches to "personality disturbance-client" were ones in which the client had defined the problem as "interpersonal conflict."

and relationship difficulties, in the "psychological problems" group. Table 1 presents the cross-classification of clients' and judges' definitions of the problem. In almost six cases in ten, client and judge defined the problem identically; over half of these cases involved interpersonal or

___

12 Throughout, the judge's rather than the caseworker's definition is used because of the necessity of using the former in relation to the judge's ratings of motivation, capacity, and opportunity. The caseworker's and the judge's definitions were in agreement for 84 percent of the clients. Thirty-two of the 61 instances of nonagreement involved the "dislocation" versus "maladjustment" categories in the "external problems" group; 17, "personality disturbance" versus "interpersonal conflict" or "maladaptive interpersonal relationship"; 2, the last two named categories; and 10 involved crossovers from "external" to "psychological" problems categories.

intrafamilial conflict. For all but a small number of the remaining cases, the difference was the one already mentioned, with the largest group being those in which the client defined the problem as economic or social "dislocation" and the judge, as economic or social "maladjustment."

NATURE OF PROBLEM AND DIFFERENTIAL CONTINUANCE RATES

There is a definite association between the nature of the problem and continuance of client and agency beyond the exploratory phase of service—somewhat over one-half the "external problems" group and slightly less than one-third of the "psychological problems" group continued to at least a fifth in-person interview. Table 2 presents the number of continuers and discontinuers and the proportion of continuers for the major problem categories, using first the client's and then the judge's definition of the problem.

Although some of the frequencies are very small, the consistency in proportion of continuers for each category, taking either the client's or the judge's definition, is notable. The differences among the various categories in the proportion of continuers are likely to occur by chance less than one time in a thousand. Obviously, much of the difference reflects the greater tendency to continuance among clients with external problems. Within this group, the difference between the "dislocation" and the "maladjustment" categories is not significant. Among the "psychological problems" categories, there is a significant difference between "maladaptive interpersonal relationship" and the other categories taken either individually or all three together.[13]

With differences such as these in the proportion of continuers in the various categories, taking separately the client's and the judge's definition of the problem, one would expect differences between cases in which client and judge agree and those in which they define the problem differently.

---

[13] For both the client's and the judge's definition the differences between "maladaptive interpersonal relationship" and the three other categories combined are significant at the .01 level; the χ^2 values, respectively, are 8.08 and 8.00. Because the "interpersonal or intrafamilial conflict" categories make up such a large part of total, each category within the "psychological problems" group was also compared with each other category. Taking the problem as defined by the client, the χ^2 values and their probabilities for "maladaptive interpersonal relationship" compared with each other category are as follows: "interpersonal or intrafamilial conflict," $\chi^2 = 7.46$ (P < .01); "personality disturbance—other person," $\chi^2 = 6.70$ (P < .02); "personality disturbance—client," $\chi^2 = 2.67$ (.1066 > P > .1003). For the problem as defined by the judge the data for "maladaptive interpersonal relationship" compared with the other categories are, "interpersonal or intrafamilial conflict," $\chi^2 = 8.78$ (P < .01); "personality disturbance—other person," $\chi^2 = 2.91$ (P < .10); "personality disturbance—client," $\chi^2 = 2.78$ (P < .10).

The highest proportion of continuers, approximately 7 in 10, was found among the "external problems" cases in which client and judge defined the problem similarly; if the client defined the problem as "dislocation" and the judge as "maladustment," 5 in 10 continued; if the client defined the problem as "external" and the judge as "psychological," less

TABLE 2

CONTINUERS AND DISCONTINUERS CLASSIFIED ACCORDING TO PROBLEM AS DEFINED BY THE CLIENT AND AS DEFINED BY THE JUDGE

Problem	Client's Definition*				Judge's Definition a			
	Total	Con-tinuers	Discon-tinuers	Propor-tion of Con-tinuers	Total	Con-tinuers	Discon-tinuers	Propor-tion of Con-tinuers
Total	351	144	207	.41	351	144	207	.41
Economic or social dislocation	119	59	60	.50	19	12	7	.63
Economic or social maladjustment	31	20	11	.65	111	60	51	.54
Interpersonal or intra-familial conflict	117	34	83	.29	121	32	89	.26
Maladaptive interper-sonal relationship...	22	13	9	.59	36	19	17	.53
Personality disturbance —client	23	8	15	.35	49	17	32	.35
Personality disturbance —other person	39	10	29	.26	15	4	11	.27

* $\chi^2 = 24.746$; P < .001.
a $\chi^2 = 26.395$; P < .001.

than 4 in 10 clients were continuers.[14] In the "psychological problems" group, however, the differences relate more to whether or not the problem is defined as "maladaptive interpersonal relationship" than to agreement or non-agreement between the client's and the judge's definitions. When both client and judge defined the problem as "maladaptive interpersonal relationship," 6 in 10 clients continued; when they differed but one defined the problem as "maladaptive interpersonal relationship" and the other as "personality disturbance," either of the client or of another person, 5 in 10 continued; when client and judge defined the problem similarly but in some category other than "maladaptive interpersonal relationship," not quite 3 in 10 countinued; and, finally, when they differed but neither defined the problem as "maladaptive interpersonal relationship," slightly over 2 in 10 continued. The significant

---

[14] The difference between similar definition and both types of differing definitions is significant at the .05 level; the difference between the two types of differing definitions is not significant: (1) similar definition versus client defines as "dislocation" and judge as "maladjustment," $\chi^2 = 6.09$ (P < .02); (2) similar definition versus client defines as "external" and judge as "psychological," $\chi^2 = 7.05$ (P < .01).

differences, then, are associated with either or both defining the problem as "maladaptive interpersonal relationship" versus neither so defining it.[15]

RELATIONSHIP OF PROBLEM TO MOTIVATION, CAPACITY, AND OPPORTUNITY

Having established a problem classification system which seemed to provide meaningful groupings of clients and which could be applied with satisfactory consistency, and having confirmed our original expectation that the various problem categories were associated in different ways with continuance or discontinuance, our next step was to examine the ratings on motivation, capacity, and opportunity. This study is directed toward examining the proposition that the client's use of casework service is determined by his motivation, his capacity, and the opportunities afforded him both by his environment and by the social agency from which he seeks help. Two subpropositions were specified, namely, that:

1. The client with appropriate and adequate motivation and adequate capacity to whom the services offered are appropriate and supplied in an adequate manner makes use of casework help provided forces outside of agency, or client, influence are not too restrictive and unmodifiable.
2. The client who is poorly and inappropriately motivated, who lacks capacity, and to whom the services offered are inappropriate or poorly supplied does not make use of casework help.

In what specific terms, however, may we describe "adequate" capacity or "inappropriate" motivation or "appropriate" service? Further, are there not many case situations in which neither client nor service may be classified at either extreme?

The mass of data obtained from 53 ratings for 351 clients obviously requires some organization so that clients who "look alike" may be grouped together and descriptions then formulated for each of the groups. An obvious means of achieving this grouping is to develop some method of scoring the various ratings on motivation, capacity, and opportunity. The original 53 ratings were reduced to 24 items for which scoring was necessary.[16] This reduction came about in part through

---

15 When both define the problem as "maladaptive interpersonal relationship" compared with both agreeing on some other category or differing but neither defining the problem as "maladaptive interpersonal relationship," the χ^2 values and probabilities are, respectively, 6.84 (P < .01) and 5.30 (P < .05); when one defines the problem as "maladaptive interpersonal relationship" compared with both agreeing on some other category or differing but neither defining the problem as "maladaptive interpersonal relationship," the χ^2 values and probabilities are, respectively, 3.58 (P < .10) and 3.24 (P < .10).

16 See appendix to this article for a list of the 24 items used and the categories employed for each.

combining several original items to produce one item, e.g., three items rating the client's intellectual functioning were combined into one item, and in part through omitting items which seemed to measure some factor already covered by one or more other items. This was true, for example, of one comprehensive assessment item in relation to capacity and another relating to service. A similar kind of omission related to those situations in which pairs of items had originally been used, one to describe and another to evaluate the same material. In some instances the descriptive item was included; in others, the evaluative one. Among the items assessing motivation, for example, one which describes what the client sought from the agency was omitted both because theory does not postulate that any particular type of request is *ipso facto* more favorable than another and because there is no significant difference for this item between countinuers and discontinuers within each of the two major "problems" divisions. With respect to its paired item, however, namely, the appropriateness of what the client was seeking, theory does postulate a relationship between continuance and seeking an appropriate service, and for the present study group the difference between continuers and discontinuers is significant.[17] On the other hand, a reverse decision was made with respect to a pair of items describing and evaluating the appropriateness of the worker's activity in assuring the client that a solution could be found to his problem. In this instance there is not a significant difference between continuers and discontinuers associated with whether or not the worker was judged to have acted appropriately (in 93 percent of the cases the worker's activity was rated "appropriate") but there is a significant difference associated with the several categories describing the worker's activity.[18] For one or another of these reasons, 12 of the original items were omitted from the scoring system.

Scoring systems generally are of two types. In one system the possible responses to each item are dichotomized to presence or absence of some condition, attribute, etc.; values of zero and one are assigned to the two halves of the dichotomy; and the values are summed over all items. The second general type of scoring system provides for more than a dichotomized classification and/or assigns values other than zero and one to the possible responses.

In the present study a scoring system of the first type was used for preliminary analysis of first-interview data. For each of the major items, that category was selected which from theory would be expected to be a "negative pointer," that is, to be unfavorable to continuance. For each item a value of one was assigned to this unfavorable category; a value of zero, to all other categories in that item. Negative rather than positive

---

[17] $\chi^2 = 24.85$; d.f. $= 2$; P $< .001$.
[18] $\chi^2 = 31.77$; d.f. $= 2$; P $< .001$.

signs were used because for many items theory is more explicit regarding the unfavorable category than regarding one of several possible favorable categories. For example, with respect to the client's hope that his problem can be resolved, theory is explicit that low hope would not be favorably associated with continuance; it is not clear, however, whether high hope is substantially more favorable than moderate hope. The intent of this scoring system was to determine whether or not negative pointers are associated with discontinuance; their absence, with continuance. The range of theoretical scores runs from zero if there are no negative pointers to 23 if there are negative pointers in every item[19]; in fact, the highest obtained score was 16.

On the average the discontinuers have just about twice as many negative pointers as do the continuers: 4.62 compared with 2.24. Almost half the continuers have no negative pointers or only one, compared with one-fifth of the discontinuers, while two-fifths of the latter and one-tenth of the continuers have six or more negative pointers. Although the negative pointers scoring system showed significant differences between continuers and discontinuers,[20] it was of limited value and had minimal possibilities for improvement. In part its limitations arose from the fact that in each of the four major areas a high proportion of clients have no negative pointers. That is, while only about one-fifth of the clients have no negative pointers at all, two-fifths have no negative pointers in capacity; slightly over one-half have none in motivation and a like proportion in service; and for two-thirds there are no negative pointers in environment.

While the negative pointers scoring was abandoned as the basic analytical technique in this study, we shall return in later reports to discuss some of its features which may prove useful for early identification of clients whose motivation, capacity, and environmental situations are so unfavorable that continuance is extremely unlikely. In other words, presence of a substantial number of negative pointers is strongly indicative of discontinuance. We must look to factors other than the absence of negative pointers, however, to identify the characteristics of the continuers and of all but the most handicapped discontinuers. For this purpose we developed and applied our main scoring system and here the crucial importance of the nature of the problem began to be more fully revealed.

In this scoring system three or more categories are used for most items. Primarily the problem to be solved in such scoring is what value to attach to each of the categories within an item. In a three-category item, for example, does one give a weight of three to the "best," i.e., most favor-

---

[19] One of the 24 items—planning with respect to the next interview—was omitted since theory does not postulate a specific unfavorable category.

[20] The difference between means was significant at the .001 level: "t" $= 7.79$; the difference in three groups of scores (0–1, 2–5, 6 and over) was also significant at the .001 level; $\chi^2 = 51.02$.

able category; two, to the next; and one to the least favorable—thus assuming that the middle category is twice as good as the lowest and the top is half again as good as the middle? Or does one assign weights of four, two, and one, assuming each category is twice as good as the one below it?—but then, of course, the top category is four times better than the low category. The complexities of logic involved in such arbitrary assignment of scores could be multiplied by endless examples. For many types of work it makes relatively little difference. For the present analysis, we thought it might make a difference. To use again an earlier illustration, is moderate hope a halfway house between high hope and low hope, or is it closer to one or the other? Since we were trying to find that combination of factors most favorable to continuance, we decided to approach this objective directly and to develop scores for each category in each item by taking the ratio of continuers to discontinuers in that category. That is, if in one category there were 50 continuers and 25 discontinuers, the ratio (score) would be 2.0 while if in another category there were 25 continuers and 50 discontinuers the ratio (score) would be .50.

These ratios were computed and scores were developed separately for the "external problems" and the "psychological problems" groups. The preliminary analysis had seemed to suggest not that the nature of the problem was an additional and important variable but that it was of paramount importance. Negative pointers were more discriminating for the "psychological problems" than for the "external problems" group; further, some factors highly associated with continuance (or discontinuance) among cases involving external problems seemed to have little if any discriminating power among cases where the problem was mainly psychological, and vice versa.

The item calling for a rating of the client's hope that his problem may be resolved illustrates the way in which particular factors differ for the two groups of cases. In the "external problems" group there were 52 continuers and 25 discontinuers judged to have high hope, giving a ratio of 2.08 (52/25) while the ratios for moderate and low hope were, respectively, .62 and .61. For the clients in the "psychological problems" group the comparable ratios were .47, .42, and .28. These differences in ratios reflect three factors: (1) difference in the relative importance of the categories within this item; (2) difference in the relative importance of this item compared with other items; and (3) difference in the ratio of continuers to discontinuers in the total group of "external problems" versus "psychological problems" cases. With respect to this last difference, that is, even if the ratings on hope bore no relationship to continuance or discontinuance, there would still be a difference between the two groups because in the "external problems" group the ratio of continuers to discontinuers was 1.24 while in the "psychological problems" group (excluding the "maladaptive interpersonal relationship" category) the ratio was .4. Hope does make a difference, however, and has a different effect in the two groups. Among the "external problems" cases it is almost three and one-half times as favorable to have high hope as to have either moderate or low hope but among the "psychological problems" cases it is not quite twice as favorable to have high hope as to have low hope and there is almost no difference between high and moderate hope. In addition, high hope contributes a heavier share to the total score for "external problems" cases. It is, for example, "tied" for first place in importance among the five items measuring motivation while for the "psychological problems" cases it is in fourth place with the client's goal regarding psychological equilibrium, appropriateness of what he is seeking from the agency, and strength of drive in a positive direction all exceeding hope as indicators of continuance.

In summary, for the purpose of examining patterns of motivation, capacity, and opportunity associated with continuance of agency and client beyond the exploratory phase, we developed a problem-classification scheme believed to permit operationally useful groupings of clients. It was ascertained that there are differences in the proportion of continuers associated with the various problem categories and, further, that the several facets of motivation, capacity, and opportunity appear to have different implications depending upon whether the problem for solution as the client comes to the agency does or does not have significant external features. The specific findings regarding major patterns will be presented in subsequent articles. We do not claim to have a perfect scheme or one with general applicability. It has proved useful in the present study but we must caution that our attention is still focused on the exploratory period of service in these cases. The system may prove more useful in characterizing the major presenting problem than in describing more complex constellations of problems that emerge during on-going service.

APPENDIX

Basic Items Used in Scoring Motivation, Capacity and Opportunity
(Numbers refer to the item numbers on the original schedule.) [1]

Motivation

8. Appropriateness of service sought by client (appropriate; potentially appropriate; inappropriate).
10. Client's discomfort in his life situation (high; moderate; low).

---

[1] *Social Service Review*, XXIX (June, 1955), 187–92.

11. Client's hope that his problem may be resolved (high; moderate; low).
12. Client's goal with respect to equilibrium (modify current basis; retain good basis; retain indeterminate basis; retain poor basis).
13. Client's drive with respect to resolution of the problem (strong drive in a positive direction; moderate drive in a positive direction; weak drive in a positive direction; drive in a negative direction).

CAPACITY

14 and 15. Client's affect toward worker (strongly positive; moderately or low positive or ambivalent; neutral; negative).
16. Client's engagement in shared participation with worker (does; does not).
17–18–19. Client's level of intellectual functioning (high; moderate; low).
22. Client's use of defenses in relation to resolution of the problem (constructive; both constructive and destructive; destructive).
23. Adequacy of client's past functioning (high, moderate or indeterminate; low).
5 and 6. Client's acceptance of responsibility for existence of the problem (appropriate; some; none).

ENVIRONMENT

25 and 26. Social and economic conditions (restrictive but modifiable; not restrictive; restrictive and unmodifiable).
27. Role played by other persons not involved in an interpersonal conflict with the client (supportive; neutral; indeterminate; impeding).
28. Motivation of other persons involved in an interpersonal conflict with the client to work toward resolution of the conflict (high; moderate; indeterminate; low; inapplicable).
29. Capacity of other persons involved in an interpersonal conflict with the client to work toward resolution of the conflict (high; moderate; indeterminate; low; inapplicable).

SERVICE

30 and 31. Worker's affect toward client (strongly positive; moderately positive; neutral; ambivalent or negative).
32. Worker's engagement in shared participation with client (does; does not).
33. Worker's perceptiveness and sensitivity to client's presentation of himself and his problem (high; moderate; low).
34. Worker's efforts in relation to clarifying the problem (no effort necessary or predominantly relevant and worker attempts to make relevancy clear to client; predominantly relevant but worker does not attempt to make relevancy clear to client; irrelevant or little or no effort made).

224 | QUANTITATIVE-DESCRIPTIVE STUDIES

35. Worker's explanation of agency function or service (specific to this client's problem or to problems of type presented by client; general in terms of agency processes or no explanation apparently given).

37—II. Plans with respect to next interview (to explore problem further; to "work" on problem; general discussion).

39. Understanding between client and worker regarding problem to be worked on (shared understanding of problem; divergent or opposed views of problem).

41. Appropriateness of worker's activity in relation to client's recognized discomfort (appropriate as to direction; inappropriate as to direction).

43. Worker's activity in relation to assuring a resolution of the problem (assures that situation can at least be improved; gives no assurance that situation can be improved but implies that worker and client will try to do so; indicates doubt that situation can be improved or gives no indication).

W. RICHARD SCOTT

13 | *Reactions to Supervision in a Heteronomous Professional Organization**

Professional organizations are organizations in which members of one or more professional groups play the central role in the achievement of the primary organizational objectives.[1] Professionals are employed by many types of organizations in varying capacities but only in a relatively few of these are they expected to perform the primary operations. Thus, engineers serve as inspectors and quality control officers in many industrial firms; scientists are often employed by research and development departments of industrial concerns, but they generally are viewed as serving goals which are secondary or auxiliary to the major objectives of the enterprises. However, clinics employing physicians, law firms hiring lawyers, schools and colleges staffed by teachers and professors, and welfare agencies employing social workers—these and similar organizations depend on professional employees to carry on their central activities and achieve their primary purposes and hence may be included in the category of professional organizations.

AUTONOMOUS OR HETERONOMOUS

Two types of professional organizations may be distinguished. The first, following Weber, may be called "autonomous" in that organizational officials delegate to the group of professional employees considerable responsibility for defining and implementing the goals, for setting performance standards, and for seeing to it that standards are maintained.[2] The professional employees often organize themselves—as a "staff" in hospitals, as an "academic council" or "senate" in universities—to assume these responsibilities. Individual professionals are expected to be highly skilled and motivated and to have internalized professional norms

* Reprinted from *Administrative Science Quarterly*, Vol. 10, No. 1 (June, 1965), pp. 65–81, by permission of the author and the journal.

1 For another definition of the professional organization, see Amitai Etzioni, *A Comparative Analysis of Complex Organizations* (New York: Free Press, 1961), p. 51.

2 In his discussion of the corporate group (an organization is a specific type of corporate group), Weber defines as "autonomous" the group whose legitimate order "has been established by its own members on their own authority. . . ." See Max Weber, *The Theory of Social and Economic Organization*, trans. by A. M. Henderson and T. Parsons (Glencoe, Ill.: Free Press, 1947), p. 148.

so that little external surveillance is required. If necessary, however, formal or informal sanctions may be applied by the colleague group.[3]

In an autonomous professional organization, a more or less well-demarcated boundary is set up between those tasks over which the professional group assumes responsibility and those over which the administrative officials have jurisdiction. Even when a professionally trained person occupies an administrative position the boundaries tend to remain intact so that the professional official exercises authority over subordinates on administrative procedure but is permitted only to proffer advice to them on professional tasks.[4] Specific kinds of professional organizations which are likely to conform to the autonomous pattern include general hospitals, therapeutic psychiatric hospitals, medical clinics, the better colleges and universities, and scientific institutes and research organizations devoted to basic research.[5]

In the second type of professional organization, called "heteronomous"[6] professional employees are clearly subordinated to an administrative framework, and the amount of autonomy granted professional employees is relatively small. An elaborate set of rules and a system of routine supervision controls many if not most aspects of the tasks performed by professional employees, so that it is often difficult if not impossible to locate or define an arena of activity for which the professional group is responsible individually or collectively.[7] Examples

---

[3] This description should not be interpreted as implying that professionals are in fact able to exercise effective control over one another or that their members are equal in ability to control. On the ability of professionals to exercise effective control, see Eliot Freidson and Buford Rhea, "Processes of Control in a Company of Equals," *Social Problems*, 11 (1963), 119–31; and on differential control among professionals, see Etzioni, *op. cit.*, p. 256.

[4] See Mary E. W. Goss, "Influence and Authority among Physicians in an Outpatient Clinic," *American Sociological Review*, 26 (1961), 39–50. Goss reports that the physician-in-charge exercised authority over other physicians with respect to the scheduling of student assistants, rooms, and patients, but, although he routinely reviewed patients' charts, he was expected to offer only suggestions on patient care to his fellow physicians.

[5] The following studies provide some documentation for a relatively autonomous legitimate order established and operated by professionals in each of the settings: Harvey L. Smith, "Two Lines of Authority: The Hospital's Dilemma," in E. G. Jaco, ed., *Patients, Physicians, and Illness* (Glencoe, Ill.: Free Press, 1958), pp. 468–77; Alfred H. Stanton and Morris S. Schwartz, *The Mental Hospital* (New York: Basic Books, 1954), pp. 69–80; Talcott Parsons, "The Mental Hospital as a Type of Organization," in M. Greenblatt, D. J. Levinson, and R. H. Williams, eds., *The Patient and the Mental Hospital* (Glencoe, Ill.: Free Press, 1957), pp. 118, 125–28; Goss, *op. cit.*; Burton R. Clark, "Faculty Authority," *Bulletin of the American Association of University Professors*, 47 (1961), 293–302; and Barney G. Glaser, "Attraction, Autonomy, and Reciprocity in the Scientist-Supervisor Relationship," *Administrative Science Quarterly*, 8 (1963), 379–98.

[6] In the heteronomous corporate group, the legitimate order "has been imposed by an outside agency." Weber, *op. cit.*, p. 148.

[7] While it is not the purpose of this paper to account for the emergence of these two types of professional organizations, it may be noted that the stronger professions

of professional organizations often corresponding to this type include many public agencies—libraries, secondary schools, social welfare agencies —as well as some private organizations such as small religious colleges and firms engaged in applied research.[8]

The basis of the proposed typology is the amount of autonomy granted to professionals by the administrative control structure. Previous research on professionals suggests that they place a high value on their autonomy. A number of studies have been conducted within autonomous structures on the reactions of professional workers to the administrative hierarchy and on the manner in which professional and administrative problems are reconciled and accommodated. However, with one notable exception,[9] there have been relatively few attempts to examine in detail the reactions of professional workers to the more severe control structures encountered in heteronomous organizations.

This article will examine some data on professionals in a heteronomous organization obtained from a case study of a public welfare agency. The focus here will be on the reactions of workers to the agency's system of routine supervision, since this is one of the critical points at which the administrative structure of the agency impinges on the individual professional worker. Since all data were obtained from a single agency, one cannot generalize to other welfare organizations, and certainly not to other kinds of heteronomous organizations.

REACTIONS TO SUPERVISION

CHARACTERISTICS OF AGENCY

All data were collected in a public social work agency located in a city of approximately 100,000. The agency served the city and its surrounding county and will be referred to as "County Agency." The two largest agency divisions were responsible for administering the Federal cate-

---

do appear to enjoy a mandate which allows them "to define what is proper conduct of others toward the matters concerned with their work," which is largely denied to the weaker professions. See Everett C. Hughes, *Men and Their Work* (Glencoe, Ill.: Free Press, 1958), p. 78. Etzioni also points out that a majority of the professions found in the heteronomous type of structure are composed of women, which undoubtedly has considerable bearing on their inability to acquire a fully legitimate professional status. See Amitai Etzioni, *Modern Organizations* (Englewood Cliffs, N. J.: Prentice-Hall, 1964), p. 89.

[8] For representative studies of such structures, see Robert D. Leigh, *The Public Library in the United States* (New York: Columbia University, 1950); Howard S. Becker, "The Teacher in the Authority System of the Public School," *Journal of Educational Sociology*, 27 (1953), 128–41; Harold L. Wilensky and Charles N. Lebeaux, *Industrial Society and Social Welfare* (New York: Russell Sage Foundation, 1958); and William Kornhauser, *Scientists in Industry: Conflict and Accommodation* (Berkeley: University of California, 1962).

[9] Kornhauser, *op. cit.*

gorical assistance program and such child welfare functions as foster home placement and adoptions. The study focused on the professional staff of the agency. Ninety-two case workers were organized into 12 work groups, each under a supervisor. The average work group consisted of one supervisor and seven case workers. Lengthy questionnaires were returned by 90 of the 92 case workers, and interviews were conducted with 11 of the 12 first-line supervisors.

A good case can be made for regarding County Agency as an example of a heteronomous organization. Many of the restrictions on the agency program originated outside of the agency itself, as explained in this excerpt from a booklet distributed by County Agency describing its operations to the public:

Unlike the private agency, the policies and procedures of the public welfare department as well as the amount and the kind of assistance that the department may grant, are legally prescribed. The County Council, County Commissioners, General Assembly (State Legislature) and the Congress of the United States, all have a voice in what the department may do and how it shall do it.

When asked to react to some of the specific Federal and State provisions importantly affecting agency programs,[10] case workers were found to be overwhelmingly opposed to them. For example, 84 percent of the workers felt that residence requirements governing client eligibility for assistance should be removed or reduced, and 99 percent of the workers felt that budgetary ceilings set by the State to govern the amount of assistance should be either removed entirely or raised. More generally, 88 percent of the workers expressed agreement with the statement that "the professional progress of this agency and others like it in this State is held back by the conservatism of the [State's] public and legislature."

Workers were likewise upset by certain requirements imposed by the local agency administration. In particular, 72 percent of the workers believed that their case loads were too large to allow them to perform adequate case work with their clients, and 85 percent felt that they were required to spend too much time filling out the various forms required by agency procedures. In short, workers in County Agency believed that the kind of services they could perform for clients—their professional function—was rather severely constrained by the administrative and legal framework within which they were required to operate.

County Agency did not differ greatly from other public welfare agencies in the extent to which worker autonomy in dealing with clients was limited by administrative considerations. It did appear to differ from

---

[10] For a summary of these provisions, see Helen I. Clarke, *Social Legislation* (2nd ed. rev.; New York: Appleton-Century-Crofts, 1957), pp. 562–63; and *Characteristics of State Public Assistance Plans under the Social Security Act* (U.S. Department of Health, Education and Welfare, Social Security Administration, Washington, D.C.: U.S. Government Printing Office, 1956).

them, however, in the extent to which its staff was professionalized. The director held graduate degrees in both social work and social work administration, and all division heads held graduate degrees in social work. All of the first-line supervisors and 42 percent of the case workers had taken at least some courses in graduate schools of social work. These figures compare favorably with those for a national sample of social workers employed in public agencies.[11]

SUPERVISION IN SOCIAL WORK

Social workers, unlike many professionals, do not view supervision as superfluous if not insufferable, but as a professional necessity. The following quotation illustrates their view:

In the eyes of the social work profession, supervision by personnel skilled in imparting knowledge and techniques and in helping workers to recognize and profit by their errors without ego destructiveness is mandatory for client welfare and professional growth.[12]

It is apparent, however, that the term "supervision" is used in a special sense by the profession; the role is defined as being that of an educator rather than an administrative superior.[13] This definition may be partly the result of the relatively short formal training period—a two-year graduate program is the basic educational requirement—and partly the result of the lack of any formal professional preparation for the majority of social workers.[14] Here then, we have a profession which regards tutorial supervision as a necessity for both trained and untrained workers and to this extent helps to legitimate the agency's control structure by providing a professional rationale for it.[15]

---

11 For additional information on the characteristics of the agency and the composition of its staff, see Peter M. Blau and W. Richard Scott, *Formal Organizations* (San Francisco: Chandler Publishing Co., 1962), pp. 254–57.

12 Lloyd E. Ohlin, Herman Pivan, and Donnell M. Pappenfort, "Major Dilemmas of the Social Worker in Probation and Parole," *National Probation and Parole Association Journal*, 2 (1956), p. 219.

13 See Wilensky and Lebeaux, *op. cit.*, p. 237, where they point out that "in courses in supervision in schools of social work, leadership is more often conceived in terms of education than of command. . . ."

14 According to the national survey conducted in 1950 by the Department of Labor, although two-thirds of the social workers in this country were college graduates, only two in every five had any graduate study in a school of social work and only one in five had earned a graduate degree in social work (U.S. Department of Labor, Bureau of Labor Statistics), *Social Workers in 1950* (New York: American Association of Social Workers, 1952), p. 8.

15 This view has recently begun to come under attack within the profession. "Another source of stress is the often discussed problem of the social worker's independent and responsible functioning, held as a value but often impeded by agency hierarchical structure and tradition. The most prominent feature of this area of stress is the system of prolonged supervision." See Lydia Rapaport, "In Defense of Social Work," *Social Service Review*, 34 (1960), p. 71.

Type of Supervision Preferred

When workers in County Agency were asked the following question:

Social work is one of the few professions that provides for the persistent routine supervision of both the new and the experienced worker. Do you think, all things considered, that this is a good arrangement?

exactly half (44) stated that it was "a good arrangement," the other half admitted that it had both "advantages and disadvantages," but none felt that it was "not a good arrangement." In order to determine what *kind* of supervision workers preferred, they were asked to choose between the following pairs of qualities in a supervisor:

a. A supervisor well-versed in social and psychological theory.
b. A supervisor with several years of on-the-job experience.
a. A supervisor who will require the worker to make most of the decisions.
b. A supervisor who will make most of the decisions himself.
a. A supervisor who will stick very closely to procedure.
b. A supervisor who is quite flexible with regard to procedure.
a. A supervisor who checks quite closely on your work.
b. A supervisor who lets you work pretty much on your own.
a. A supervisor who is skilled in teaching casework techniques.
b. A supervisor who is skilled in agency policy and is a good administrator.

It was recognized that a worker might have difficulty choosing between some of these pairs of qualities, but the intent was to force workers to choose between characteristics associated with a professional (*a, a, b, b, a*) as opposed to a bureaucratic approach to supervision. As might be expected, agency workers in large measure preferred professional qualities in a supervisor with the exception that as many wished their supervisor to have had on-the-job experience as desired him to be well-versed in theory. Thus of about 85 workers responding, 49 percent preferred a supervisor well-versed in theory; 95 percent, a supervisor who would let workers make their own decisions; 78 percent, a supervisor who was flexible with regard to procedure; 69 percent, a supervisor who would let them work on their own; and 70 percent, a supervisor who was skilled in teaching case-work techniques.

Worker Orientations

It is particularly important when dealing with "weaker" professions like social work to differentiate between types of workers because of the wide variations in worker training and degree of contact with the profession. Advanced training in a school of social work was selected as the basis for distinguishing between types of workers, and while this may appear to be a rather weak index of professional orientation, it may be argued that in a profession where only the minority of workers have had any exposure to professional training centers, it is not without significance.[16]

One-third (10 of 30) of the workers with some graduate training in social work stated a preference for all five of the professional character- istics as compared to one-sixth (8 of 47) of the workers lacking graduate training. This finding holds for each of the five paired choices considered separately, although in some cases the differences between the two groups of workers is small. Also, to the question:

In general, do you feel that supervisory positions in this agency should be filled only by workers with a master's degree in social work, or by any good worker with sufficient experience?

sixty-one percent of the (33) workers with some graduate work preferred supervisory positions to be held by a person with an advanced degree as compared to 40 percent of the (53) workers lacking graduate training.

SUPERVISOR ORIENTATIONS

Supervisors, like workers, differ in the degree to which they are pro- fessionally oriented, and the same dimension—exposure to professional training centers—was employed to differentiate between types of super- visors. Since all supervisors had some graduate training in social work, however, it was decided to utilize number of hours of graduate training as the criterion measure, with the median taken as the point of division. Supervisors having 18 hours of graduate work or less were assigned to the "low-exposure" group ($N = 7$); those having more than 18 hours were assigned to the "high-exposure" category ($N = 4$). All supervisors assigned by this procedure to the high-exposure group had taken at least a full year of graduate work (30 hours or more), whereas those assigned to the low-exposure group had taken only a half year's work (18 hours) or less, there being a broad gap in the distribution at the point of division.[17]

In order to describe the supervisor's behavior as viewed by his subord- inates, workers were asked to check a series of statements if they felt that they were applicable to their present supervisor. These data, differen-

---

[16] Exposure to professional training centers was found to be positively correlated, although not strongly, with orientation to professional reference groups external to the agency (e.g., teachers, professional books and journals, etc.). See Blau and Scott, op. cit., pp. 66–67.

[17] As was the case with workers, there again appeared to be a positive correlation between amount of graduate work and orientation to outside reference groups. All four supervisors in the high-exposure category reported their main source of pro- fessional stimulation to come from some person or group external to the agency, whereas only two of the seven supervisors in the low-exposure category located their main source of professional stimulation outside the agency.

tiated by supervisor's exposure to professional training centers, are presented in Table 1. It is clear that on the three descriptions of professional qualities, workers under supervisors having high exposure to training centers were more likely to see their supervisor as exhibiting these qualities than workers under supervisors with low exposure to training centers. As to bureaucratic orientation of supervisors, the data indicate that the low-exposure supervisors were more likely to be viewed as exhibiting bureaucratic qualities than the high-exposure supervisors.

TABLE 1

PROFESSIONAL TRAINING OF SUPERVISORS AS RELATED TO DESCRIPTIONS BY THEIR WORKERS.

Professional and Bureaucratic Qualities of Supervisor	Exposure of Supervisors to Graduate Study	
	High (N = 28)	Low (N = 49)
Professional statements*	%	%
Tries to teach and help me when I make a mistake............	82	63
Has a good background in social work theory..................	89	45
Is a good teacher of case-work methods and techniques.........	64	45
Bureaucratic statements*		
Sticks very closely to rules and procedure.....................	43	63
Is pretty strict with workers..................................	14	31
Checks my work very closely.................................	36	53
Is quite expert on the laws and policies pertaining to the agency.	64	69
Sometimes forces his decisions on me........................	14	27

* All statements preceded by "My supervisor."

These data suggest that supervisors vary in their approach to subordinates, as perceived by the subordinates themselves, and that an important determinant of their approach is their degree of exposure to professional training centers. The data also may be viewed as providing some validation for the use of degree of exposure to training centers as an indicator of professional orientation among supervisors.

There is also evidence that professionally oriented supervisors were evaluated more highly than those less professionally oriented. It was noted earlier that exactly half of the workers in the agency regarded routine supervision as "a good arrangement." However, when workers were differentiated by type of supervisor, 77 percent of the (22) workers under professionally oriented supervisors in contrast to 45 percent of the (42) workers under less professional supervisors felt that the arrangement was a good one. Also, workers were asked:

Would you favor the agency's hiring more specialists (for example, medical social workers, psychiatric social workers) with whom you could consult with regard to some of your case problems?

Thirty-six percent of the (25) workers under professional supervisors strongly favored the hiring of more specialists, while 60 percent of the (45) workers under less professional supervisors strongly favored such a policy, indicating that workers under professional supervisors were more likely than those under less professional supervisors to feel that they were obtaining the technical assistance needed to deal with the problems of their clients.[18] When asked:

Would you prefer to be given a freer hand in working with your case load than you are given by your supervisor?

89 percent of the (28) workers under professionally oriented supervisors felt that they were given the right amount of freedom rather than stating that they preferred more freedom or that they had too much freedom, as compared to 72 percent of the (46) workers under less professional supervisors.

Finally, workers were asked to check a series of statements relating in general to the perceived effectiveness of their supervisor. These statements together with worker responses to them appear in Table 2. Professionally oriented supervisors were viewed as more effective in being

TABLE 2

PROFESSIONAL TRAINING OF SUPERVISOR AS RELATED TO WORKER'S
EVALUATION OF EFFECTIVENESS.

Effectiveness of Supervisor	Exposure of Supervisors to Graduate Study	
	High (N = 28)	Low (N = 49)
Effective statements*	%	%
Is quite sure of himself and self-confident.....................	68	45
Backs me up in conflicts with clients........................	68	43
Ineffective statements*		
Has very little control over his workers......................	0	8
Sometimes is impatient and loses his temper..................	7	20
Sometimes is reluctant to make decisions that he should make..	7	25

* All statements preceded by "My supervisor."

more self-confident and more likely to come to the aid of workers in their conflicts with clients. By contrast, the less professional supervisors were seen as less effective in being somewhat more likely to lack control over workers, to lose their tempers, and to resist making decisions within their jurisdiction.

While no one of these findings taken separately is particularly convinc-

[18] Since the number of professionally oriented workers under professionally oriented supervisors was slightly higher than that under less professional supervisors, these results might be due to worker rather than supervisor orientation. This, however, is not the case. Thirty-six percent of both the (11) professionally oriented workers and the (14) nonprofessionally oriented workers under professional supervisors strongly favored hiring more specialists.

ing, the over-all pattern exhibited by the several findings supports the view that a majority of workers tended to evaluate more highly the performances of professionally oriented as compared to less professionally oriented supervisors.

LOCATION OF REFERENCE GROUPS

WORKER'S FIRST REFERENCE

To determine the type and location of professional reference groups for workers, they were asked:

From which of the following sources do you obtain the greater part of your intellectual and professional stimulation in connection with your work?

Workers were asked to select and order three sources from the following list: (1) my colleagues here in the agency; (2) my immediate supervisor; (3) my division head; (4) the director of the agency; (5) professional people outside the agency (teachers, conference speakers, etc.) ; (6) professional books or journals; and (7) others (to be specified). If attention is limited to the first choice, it was found that 77 percent of the (22) workers under professionally oriented supervisors selected their own supervisor as their primary source of professional stimulation as compared to 45 percent of the (42) workers serving under nonprofessionally oriented supervisors. Professionally oriented supervisors appear to serve at least in some measure as the voice of the profession for their subordinates and are in the happy position by helping to determine the criteria by which they are evaluated by workers. This may help to account for their being more highly evaluated by their subordinates.

Supervisors, however, are not the only source of professional stimulation within the agency. It appears to be the case in this agency that workers are not only subject to a legitimate order fashioned by federal and state law-making agencies as interpreted and implemented by the administration, but much of whatever professional influence exists is filtered through the administrative apparatus. If those workers who selected either their division head or the director of the agency as their primary source of professional stimulation are added to those selecting their immediate supervisor, nearly three-fourths (72 percent) of the workers in this agency reported their main source of professional stimulation to be a member of the administrative hierarchy of the organization.

PROFESSIONAL STANDARDS

Whether the professional standards set by administrative superiors are as high and as "pure" as those set by the profession itself can be explored to some extent by comparing the evaluations of the supervisors made by professionally oriented workers and by nonprofessionally oriented workers, holding orientation of supervisor constant. It will be recalled that the indicator of professional orientation for workers is whether they have had some exposure to professional training centers *outside the agency*. If the standards obtained from the worker's exposure to professional sources external to the agency are in fact higher than those obtained by workers from their experiences within the agency, then the trained workers should be more critical of their supervisors than the untrained workers. Since workers generally tended to be more critical of the less professional than of the professional supervisor, one would expect trained workers to be highly critical of the less professional supervisor and only moderately critical of the professional supervisor, whereas the untrained worker would be only moderately critical of the less professional supervisor and only slightly critical of the professional supervisor. And indeed, 54 percent of the (13) trained workers as compared to 66 percent of the (15) untrained workers under professional supervisors felt that routine supervision was a good thing; and 25 percent of the (16) trained workers as compared to 53 percent of the (30) untrained workers under less professional supervisors upheld the value of routine supervision. And although there were no differences between groups of workers under professionally oriented supervisors concerning the desirability of hiring specialists, 36 percent of each group strongly favoring such a policy, workers under less professional supervisors conformed to the predicted pattern: 73 percent of the (15) trained workers but only 53 percent of the (30) untrained workers favored hiring specialists. This suggested that exposure to professional training centers made the trained group more critical of the professional advice received from their own supervisor.

Most of the relevant data, however, again come from the statements to which workers were asked to respond in describing their present supervisor. These data appear in Table 3. Since the present focus is on evaluations based on professional criteria, the proportion of workers who fail to ascribe professional characteristics, or who ascribe bureaucratic characteristics to their supervisor, or who consider their supervisor ineffective will be taken as an indicator of the level of criticism directed toward the supervisor.[19]

The over-all pattern of the worker responses appears to be consistent with the predicted reactions, suggesting that professionally trained workers tend to be more critical of the professionalism of their super-

[19] Note that although these are the same questions utilized in Tables 1 and 2, wording of some of the entries has been changed for this presentation so that all percentages within the table represent negative evaluations in terms of professional criteria—that is, larger percentages indicate that a higher proportion of the workers involved were critical of their supervisor. The changes were made only to facilitate comparisons among the percentages.

visors. As can be seen from the professional statements, on five of the six comparisons trained workers were more critical of their supervisors than untrained workers, holding constant supervisor's exposure to professional training centers. For the bureaucratic statements, the predicted reactions held for workers under high-exposure supervisors for four of the five comparisons, but were reversed on all comparisons involving workers under low-exposure supervisors. A possible explanation for this discrepancy is that the less professionally oriented supervisors may have been less strict, less apt to check closely, and less likely to attempt to force their decisions on their better trained workers because many of these workers had at least as much training as they. There is some evidence to support the hypothesis that the less well-trained supervisors gave differ-

TABLE 3

PROFESSIONAL TRAINING OF SUPERVISORS AND SOCIAL WORKERS AS RELATED TO CRITICAL ATTITUDES OF WORKERS.

Critical Attitudes of Workers	Exposure of Supervisors to Graduate Study			
	High Exposure		Low Exposure	
	Worker Exposed (N = 13)	Worker Not Exposed (N = 15)	Worker Exposed (N = 17)	Worker Not Exposed (N = 32)
Professional statements*	%	%	%	%
Does *not* try to teach and help me when I make a mistake....................	23	13	53	28
Does *not* have a good background in social work theory....................	8	13	71	47
Is *not* a good teacher of case-work methods and techniques.......................	46	27	59	53
Bureaucratic statements*				
Sticks very closely to rules and procedures..	54	33	59	62
Is pretty strict with workers..............	23	7	23	34
Checks my work very closely..............	38	33	47	57
Is quite expert on the laws and policies pertaining to the agency...............	62	67	53	78
Sometimes forces his decisions on me.......	23	7	23	28
Ineffective statements*				
Is *not* sure of himself or self-confident.....	38	27	59	53
Does *not* back me up in conflicts with clients	38	27	59	56
Has very little control over his workers....	0	0	12	6
Sometimes is impatient and loses his temper	15	0	29	16
Sometimes is reluctant to make decisions that he should make...................	8	7	35	19

* All statements preceded by "My supervisor."

ential treatment to their trained and untrained workers. When workers were asked if they would prefer to have a freer hand in working with their case load than they were given by their supervisor, responses permitted were: (a) yes, would prefer more freedom; (b) have about the right amount of freedom; and (c) have too much freedom; would prefer more guidance and control from supervisor. As indicated by Table 4, none of the workers under professionally trained supervisors stated that they had "too much freedom," but 19 percent of the (16) trained workers as compared to 7 percent of the (30) untrained workers stated that they would prefer more supervision than they were getting at present. Obviously, the differences are so small that these findings are merely suggestive, but it appears that there is some tendency for the less professional supervisors to undersupervise their trained workers so that they desire more control. And such a tendency would account for the unexpected reversal.

TABLE 4

PROFESSIONAL TRAINING OF SOCIAL WORKERS AND SUPERVISORS AS RELATED TO DEGREE OF FREEDOM PERMITTED BY SUPERVISOR.

Degree of Freedom Preferred	Exposure of Supervisors to Graduate Study			
	High Exposure		Low Exposure	
	Worker Exposed (N = 13)	Worker Not Exposed (N = 15)	Worker Exposed (N = 16)	Worker Not Exposed (N = 30)
	%	%	%	%
Have right amount of freedom............	92	87	69	73
Would prefer more freedom...............	8	13	12	20
Have too much freedom..................	0	0	19	7

The pattern of responses for the effectiveness statements (Table 3) appears to be generally consistent with the original predictions. On five of the ten comparisons, trained workers were more critical of their present supervisor than the untrained workers, holding supervisory orientation constant, and did not differ from the untrained workers in their responses to the remaining statements.

SUMMARY

Data obtained from a case study of a public welfare agency have been utilized to illuminate further the attitudes toward supervision where professional workers operate within a heteronomous structure, allowing them relatively little autonomy in the conduct of their work. In this study on the reactions of workers to the agency's routine system of supervision, workers in general were found to accept the system, although the degree of acceptance was found to vary with the professional orientation of both workers and supervisors. Professionally oriented workers were more critical of the system than nonprofessionally oriented workers and workers supervised by professionally oriented supervisors were less critical of the system than workers serving under less professionally oriented supervisors. Nearly three-quarters of the workers reported some member of the agency hierarchy to be the major source of professional stimulation, indicating that most workers looked chiefly to the agency officials for their professional norms and standards rather than to a source external to the agency. That standards transmitted through the agency hierarchy were not as high as those transmitted through external sources was indicated by the finding that workers exposed to professional training centers tended to hold higher standards for supervisors—hence were more critical of their supervisor—than workers who had not had such exposure.

ALVIN ZANDER, THEODORE NEWCOMB, JR.

14 | *Group Levels of Aspiration in United Fund Campaigns**

It often happens that a subgroup in an organization periodically must set a goal for the larger unit. The objective chosen in such a situation serves several functions: it defines a particular need of the inclusive body and it places a demand upon persons outside the goal-setting group. In performing its role, the subgroup is likely to receive influence attempts from parts of the larger body and to originate pressures itself on other parts. How does its unique position affect the goals the subgroup chooses? How do others react to these goals?

The official goals established for United Fund community campaigns, usually by a committee responsible for that decision, and the amount of money raised in the subsequent solicitations, provide data relevant to the phenomena of interest here. The present study is restricted to an examination of events in such financial canvasses during several years, yet its findings may be typical of organizations in which there are repeated demands on people to furnish other resources.

Level of aspiration theory offers a convenient model for approaching answers to the above questions in United Funds, since it considers the origins of repeated goals and their relationship to repeated performances (Atkinson & Feather, 1966; Lewin, Dembo, Festinger & Sears, 1944). In studies of group-aspiration setting in the laboratory, moreover, it has been observed that the assumptions employed by members when selecting an aspiration level for their group are similar to the assumptions used by an individual when setting an aspiration for himself. A group aspiration, to illustrate, is chosen on the basis of the perceived probability of attaining the goal and the attractiveness of doing so; a more difficult goal is more attractive than an easier one; members raise the group's goal after the group has been successful and lower it after the group has failed; and group goals on the average tend to be slightly higher than past levels of performance (Zander & Medow, 1963). A stronger tendency to approach a given goal is aroused when members have a greater desire for achievement of group success (Zander & Medow, 1965; Zander & Wulff, 1966).

The official goals established by United Funds, and the changes in these goals, however, are not always what level of aspiration theory would

* From: Alvin Zander and Theodore Newcomb, Jr., "Group Levels of Aspiration in United Fund Campaigns," *Journal of Personality and Social Psychology*, Vol. 6, No. 2 (June, 1967), pp. 156–62. Copyright 1967 by the American Psychological Association, and reproduced by permission.

lead one to expect. The apparent attractiveness of particular goals and the probabilities seemingly attributed to certain levels of performance, as we shall see, often are such that the chosen goals cannot be attained, yet they are seldom lowered—a desire for group success then does not appear to be the dominating motive in goal selection. Several conditions typically exist in a United Fund organization which can affect the probability and attractiveness that members of a goal-setting committee attribute to potential goals.

First, the official goal is a joint decision which interests many persons, inside and outside the goal-setting group. In selecting its goal the committee is exposed to pressures from citizens in the community, including those associated with the agencies supported by the fund, those responsible for conducting major phases of the campaign, as well as those whose support is essential to the success of the effort. External agents, it is known, can influence a group's choice of a goal and can do this even when the proposed goal deviates widely from the group's past level of performance (Zander & Medow, 1963; Zander, Medow, & Efron, 1965) .

Second, those who are interested in the size of the fund, and who may seek to influence the official goal, place greater value on larger budgets. There is virtually no upper limit to the amount they may see as desirable, but there is some amount below which the budget should not be allowed to fall. An important consequence is that strong restraints exist against lowering the goal below what it has been in a prior year.

Third, goal setters assume that a community campaign can induce givers to provide what is asked. The purpose of a campaign goal is to arouse inclinations among potential contributors to give, and announcement of the goal is accompanied by social pressures exerted through advertising and solicitation which urge citizens to give what is needed.

Fourth, goals that contributors perceive to be unreasonably high have less influence on the size of the givers' contributions than goals they perceive to be necessary and attainable; a state of affairs goal setters may not always recognize.

These conditions suggest two assumptions about the nature of goal-setting in United Funds: (a) In choosing a goal, the decision-making committee is inclined toward selecting a higher goal than is reasonably attainable in the light of previous performance in that community; (b) this tendency becomes stronger as the need for more social welfare funds in the community becomes greater. The need becomes greater, it can be assumed, whenever a community fund fails to achieve its official goal.

Derivations from these assumptions describe specific events one may expect in the campaigns.

1. In general, a goal-setting committee whose official goal is not fulfilled is more likely to propose a more difficult future goal (for that

community) than a committee whose goal is attained; it tries again to achieve at least the level of goal that was earlier failed. Thus, committees with more failing campaigns, compared to those with more successful campaigns (*a*) fix their future goals at a greater distance above past levels of performance, and (*b*) change the levels of their goals a smaller amount from one year to the next.

2. As the amount of money per capita solicited in a community is lower (in absolute terms) and the fund's need for more money is therefore greater, the discrepancy between the past level of performance and the level of the future goal is larger, not smaller.

3. The discrepancy between past performance and future goal generates less improvement of performance in failing funds than in successful ones.

METHOD

Each year United Fund organizations conduct financial campaigns in many communities for the support of social welfare programs. The campaigns are similar from town to town in their organizational structures and methods. The similarity in procedures is largely due to materials provided by the United Community Funds and Councils of America, a national association. A local fund typically announces a goal in advance and widely publicizes its progress toward that goal.

The national association publishes a *Directory* each year. This volume contains the name of each community holding a campaign, its population, the goal of the campaign, the amount obtained, and the amount raised in the immediately past canvass. The basic data for this study were taken from the directories for the 4 years from 1961 through 1964. Thus, we have goals for 4 years and levels of performance for 5 years. In addition, the same agency provides, for the last 3 of these years, a pamphlet entitled, "Determinants of Fund Raising Potential." This document reports the Effective Buying Income (EBI) in each of these towns and the "amount raised each year as percent of EBI." The EBI is a summary index of financial data from each community, reported by *Sales Management Magazine,* describing the total amount of money available in the community for consumer purchases. The UCFCA suggests that the EBI index be used by campaign goal setters to allow a comparison of their local goal and performance with those of similar towns. Step-by-step procedures are provided for making these comparisons. It is not known how many funds do this, but probably more than a few do so. For present purposes the EBI will be taken as an indication of the amount of wealth in the community.

Data from communities providing complete information on all annual variables, save for a few omissions, were used. The towns chosen for this study had populations between 55,000 and 140,000, since the greatest number of cities reasonably similar in size was available within that range. The total number of communities within these restrictions, and the size of the sample, were 149.

From these records the following variables were employed: level of annual campaign goal, level of annual goal per capita, size of community, rate of community growth in population during the period observed, level of annual performance, and level of annual performance per capita. Two other variables were used which control the wealth of the community. The *quality of performance* is the level of performance for a given year divided by the EBI for that year. This percentage, it should be noted, was available concerning every community in the country among the materials provided by the UCFCA. The *difficulty of the goal* is the level of the campaign goal for a given year divided by the EBI for that year. This percentage was not contained in materials provided by the UCFCA. The correlation between the level of campaign goal and its difficulty is .57 ($p < .001$) ; thus we may assume that a higher campaign goal for a given community is usually a more difficult one.

RESULTS

Average Goal-Setting Events

It is informative to consider briefly the average values for separate events in the setting of United Fund goals. These results are reported on a per-capita basis for all communities in the sample and are the means of all four trials.

A fund establishes a particular *goal,* the number of dollars to be collected in the ensuing campaign. This is, on the average, $3.49 per person. The campaign is run and the level of *performance* is $3.34 per capita. Thus, the average campaign income differs from the average goal by an attainment discrepancy of $—.15. A new goal is set and the average *shift in goal* level from the goal of the previous year is upward, $.07. Thus the discrepancy between prior level of performance and the new goal (the *D* score) is $.22. The primary tendency, then, is to raise the future goal even though the past performance failed to attain a lower goal. The average gift amounts to .165% of the citizen's personal EBI.

The relation of certain social characteristics in these communities to the goals and the levels of performance are of interest. These characteristics are: size of community, rate of population growth, and wealth (EBI) per capita.

Larger communities select higher goals per capita than do smaller towns ($r = .28$, $p < .01$), but the larger cities set less difficult goals, considering the EBI available to each person ($r = -.16$, $p < .05$). The size of the community bears no relationship to the quality of the performance (i.e., to the level of performance as percentage of EBI). The rate of community growth is not significantly related to difficulty of the goal or to the quality of performance, but faster growing towns more often raise their goals than do slowly growing ones ($p < .001$). Communities with greater wealth per person set higher per-capita goals ($r = .16$, $p < .05$) but these tend to be less difficult levels ($r = .31$, $p < .01$) and the quality of the performance is lower ($r = -.28$, $p < .01$) than in towns with less per-capita wealth. In summary, funds in smaller towns and in those with less wealth per person tend to have more difficult goals for citizens, and towns with less wealthy citizens show a better quality of performance per capita.

DERIVATIONS

In the first derivation it was proposed that committees for frequently failing funds, compared to those for more successful ones, tend to fix their future goals higher above levels of performance; that is, committees set larger D scores following failures than following successes.

In order to examine the relationship between D score and frequency of success or failure, it is most convenient to separate the 149 funds into sets, each having a different record of success during the years observed. This procedure provides five types of towns: those with four successes and no failures ($N = 27$), those with three successes and one failure ($N = 30$), those with two successes and two failures ($N = 28$), those with one success and three failures ($N = 37$), and those with no successes and four failures ($N = 29$).

The mean of the per-capita D score for four years for each of the community types was as follows: four successes—no failures, $.06$; three successes—one failure, $.12$; two successes—two failures, $.21$; one success—three failures, $.25$; and no successes—four failures, $.42$. The grand mean is $.22$. The distribution among these values is significantly different by median test ($X^2 = 46.35$, $p < .001$). The mean D score in the consistently failing towns is reliably larger than in the consistently successful ones ($t = 3.96$, $p < .001$). These results are in accord with the first derivation.

The towns with more frequent failures, it is worth noting, do not have higher goals per capita than those with more frequent successes; instead, as may be seen in Figure 1, they tend to have somewhat lower goals than the more successful funds. The difference in the level of the goals for the consistently failing and the consistently succeeding towns, however, is not a reliable one $(p < .20)$. One can assume, then, that towns with different records of success are fairly similar in their goals.

In laboratory groups there is close adherence to the rule, "succeed, raise; fail, lower;" the level of aspiration is increased after a successful trial and lowered after an unsuccessful one. Do United Fund committees adhere to this rule? In four annual campaigns only three shifts in level of the goal are possible. Thus, in order to examine the goal shifts in communities with different records of success, during the campaigns for which these goals were selected the 149 towns were divided into four types: those with no successes and three failures $(N = 44)$, those with one success and two failures $(N = 40)$, those with two successes and one failure $(N = 33)$, and those with three successes and no failures $(N = 32)$. The dominant tendency in direction of goal shift was determined by an index in which each fund received a larger score when a shift in goal was upward from one year to the next and a smaller score when the shift was downward. The median index in the consistently failing towns was at the point indicating that no change in goal up or down was the most typical response; in the consistently successful towns the index was just below the maximum possible, indicating a strong tendency to shift goals upward. The distribution among the different index values was significant by median test $(X^2 = 10.82, p < .02)$. These results again support the first derivation.

Also, the median amount that the goal was moved from the level of the previous year's goal increased as the frequency of success in the town increased. In communities with no successes and three failures the median amount of upward shift in the goal was $.04, but in those with three successes and no failures the median amount of upward shift was $.13. The trend between these two extremes was in regular order. The values in this distribution were significantly different by median test $(X^2 = 19.41, p < .001)$.

Putting together the results concerning D scores and those describing shifts in goals from one year to the next, it is evident that the D scores are larger as shifts in goals are smaller. The correlation between these two is $-.27$ $(p < .01)$. The larger D scores in failing towns, it appears, are not due to raising the goal levels but to persisting efforts to reach previously unattained objectives.

We earlier noted that the towns with different records of success do not have significantly different goals. Given the apparent restraints against moving the goals after a failing campaign, it appears that larger D scores more often occur when the amount of money raised is, in absolute terms, low. This is the content of the second derivation.

It can be seen in Figure 1 that towns with larger D scores (more frequent failures) solicit considerably less money than towns with smaller D scores (more frequent successes). This last difference is reliable ($t = 2.58$, $p < .02$). Larger D scores, then, are associated with lower levels of giving per person, and with the deprivation resulting from such giving. It is of incidental interest that the proportion of EBI provided per person in the failing towns is .136 and in the succeeding towns, .193. The direction of the difference suggests that frequently failing communities get a smaller proportion of each citizen's income, but the result is not statistically significant ($t = 1.27$, $p < .15$).

A quite different attempt was made to determine if a community with greater need for more social welfare funds sets a higher D score. In this instance a need for welfare funds was surmised from indirect measures. The relationship between the D score and the following demographic variables was computed within each of the five types of towns. The variables were: EBI per capita (assuming that a community with less wealth per citizen requires more social services), percentage loss of EBI during 4 years (same type of assumption), size of town (larger towns often have areas with greater needs for social welfare), and rate of growth in community population (rapidly growing towns have increasing demands). None of these variables was significantly related to the size of D score.

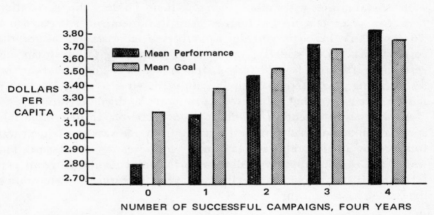

FIGURE 1. Mean level of goal and performance in communities differing in number of successful campaigns.

These results also indicate, one should note, that towns with separate records of success or failure do not differ in these social characteristics.

The final derivation was that the amount of discrepancy between past performance and future goal generates an improvement in performance less often in failing communities than in successful ones. The data relevant to this derivation were obtained by relating the size of the D score in a given year and town with the amount of subsequent change in performance. In this analysis the immediately past level of performance

QUANTITATIVE-DESCRIPTIVE STUDIES

serves as a common base for observing both changes in goal and changes in performance, while preserving the appropriate chronological sequence between them.

TABLE 1

D SCORE AND SUBSEQUENT PERFORMANCE PER CAPITA

D score (goal for year y + 1)	No. Campaigns	Change in Performance (year y to y + 1)		
		Decrease or None	Moderate Improvement	Much Improvement
Negative	129	58%	36%	7%
Moderately positive......	244	21%	53%	26%
Largely positive	220	27%	27%	46%

Note.—$\chi^2 = 478.15$, $p < .001$.

Ignoring the successfulness of the communities for a moment, it is evident in Table 1 that performance tends to improve as the D score increases. The value of X^2 for these distributions is unavoidably inflated since this analysis requires each community to be entered into the Table three times, once for each trial.

In communities with more successes than failures the correlation between a given D score and improvement in subsequent performance is .76 ($p < .001$), in towns with equal numbers of successes and failures the correlation is .73 ($p < .001$), and in towns with more failures than successes the correlation is $-.18$ (ns). It appears that a D score about the size set in failing towns (approximately $.40) is too large to serve as a stimulant to increased giving. These results support the third derivation.

An analysis of causation in the opposite direction, to determine if a specific amount of change in performance from one year to the next was followed by a comparable increase in D score, was not significant. The size of the D score appears to determine the subsequent change in performance, if any, rather than a given change in performance determining the change in subsequent D score.

DISCUSSION

The authors have examined the goals and the changes in these goals when a group must settle these matters for a larger social system. The approach to this study was based on assumptions implicit in the theory of aspiration setting and was concerned with the conditions in a United Fund goal-setting committee which affect the perceived probability and attractiveness of a given goal. The results indicate that unreasonably difficult goals are more often chosen when performance in the local fund is deficient.

It is striking that a number of the funds fail and fail again but do not lower their goals to a level that will make failure unlikely in the future. Such results suggest that failure was not as intolerable to the goal setters as lowering the goal would be. One might conceive of the goal-setting committee members in the failing funds as having a fear of the consequences of failure. Groups in which such a fear has been induced among members have been observed elsewhere to set very difficult goals, apparently in that case because failure at a different task was less dissatisfying than failure at an easier level (Zander & Medow, 1965; Zander & Wulff, 1966). Given, however, that many communities were willing to repeat their failures, that the failures were not caused by higher goals in the unsuccessful communities than in the successful ones, and given the greater value placed on higher income, it seems unlikely that fear of the consequences of failure had much impact upon the goal-selecting process. Rather, the main reasons behind the high and unattainable goals in the failing funds appear to be (a) a need to fulfill large budgets which have not been met in the past, and (b) a belief that high goals and strong social pressures will arouse contributors to increase the size of their gifts. The results suggest that acting in terms of such beliefs is not always beneficial to a financial campaign.

REFERENCES

ATKINSON, J. W., & FEATHER, N. *A theory of achievement motivation.* New York: John Wiley & Sons, Inc., 1966.

LEWIN, K., DEMBO, T., FESTINGER, L., & SEARS, P. Level of aspiration. In J. McV. Hunt (Ed.), *Personality and behavior disorders.* Vol. 1. New York: The Ronald Press Company, 1944. pp. 333–78.

ZANDER, A., & MEDOW, H. Individual and group levels of aspiration. *Human Relations,* 1963, 16, 89–105.

ZANDER, A., & MEDOW, H. Strength of group and desire for attainable group aspirations. *Journal of Personality,* 1965, 33, 122–39.

ZANDER, A., MEDOW, H., & EFRON, R. Observers' expectations as determinants of group aspirations. *Human Relations,* 1965, 18, 273–87.

ZANDER, A., & WULFF, D. Members' test anxiety and competence: Determinants of group's aspirations. *Journal of Personality,* 1966, 34, 55–70.

Selected References

AIKEN, MICHAEL; & FERMAN, LOUIS, "Job Mobility and Social Integration of Displaced Workers," *Social Problems* (Summer, 1966).

AIKEN, MICHAEL; & HAGE, JERALD, "Organizational Alienation: A Comparative Analysis," *American-Sociological Review* (August, 1966).

AKERS, RONALD L., "Socio-Economic Status and Delinquency Behavior," *The Journal of Research in Crime and Delinquency* (January, 1964).

BABCHUCK, NICHOLAS; & THOMPSON, R., "The Voluntary Association of Negroes," *American Sociological Review* (October, 1962).

BAILEY, MARGARET B., "Community Orientations Toward Social Casework," *Social Work* (July, 1959).

BAILEY, MARGARET B. & FUCHS, ESTELLE, "Alcoholism and the Social Worker," *Social Work* (October, 1960).

BERKOWITZ, NORMAN H.; & BENNIS, WARREN G., "Interaction Patterns in Formal Service Oriented Organizations," *Administrative Science Quarterly* (June, 1961).

BERNARD, JESSIE, "Marital Stability and Patterns of Status Variables," *Journal of Marriage and the Family* (November, 1966).

BLAU, PETER, "Orientation Toward Clients in a Public Welfare Agency," *Administrative Science Quarterly* (December, 1960).

BLUM, ARTHUR, "Peer Group Structure and a Child's Verbal Accessibility in a Treatment Institution," *Social Service Review* (December, 1962).

BLUM, ARTHUR; & POLANSKY, NORMAN A., "Effect of Staff Role in Children's Verbal Accessibility," *Social Work* (January, 1961).

BOEHM, BERNICE, "The Community and the Social Agency Define Neglect," *Child Welfare* (November, 1964).

BRUKIN, JOHN G., BRANDT, EDWARD, JR., & SHACKELFORD, MARGARET, "Incidence of Treated Mental Illness in Three Pennsylvania Communities," *American Journal of Public Health* (June, 1966).

BURCHINAL, LEE; & ROSSMAN, JACK E., "Relations Among Maternal Employment Indices and Developmental Characteristics of Children," *Marriage and Family Living* (November, 1961).

BURGESS, M. ELAINE, "Poverty and Dependency: Some Selected Characteristics," *Journal of Social Issues* (January, 1965).

CABEEN, CHARLES; & COLEMAN, JAMES, "Group Therapy with Sex Offenders: Description and Evaluation of Group Therapy Program in an Institutional Setting," *Journal of Clinical Psychology* (April, 1961).

COHEN, JACOB; & STRUENING, E. L., "Opinions about Mental Illness in the Personnel of Two Large Mental Hospitals," *Journal of Abnormal and Social Psychology* (May, 1962).

COLE, MINERVA G.; & PODELL, LAWRENCE, "Serving Handicapped Children in Group Programs," *Social Work* (January, 1961).

COLEMAN, JULES V.; JANOWICS, RUTH; FLOCK, STEPHEN; & NORTON, N., "A Comparative Study of a Psychiatric Clinic and a Family Agency," *Social Casework* (January and February, 1957).

DEASY, LEILA CALHOUN; & QUINN, OLIVE WESTBROOKE, "The Urban Negro and the Adoption of Children," *Child Welfare* (November, 1962).

DEFRIES, ZERA; JENKINS, SHIRLEY; & WILLIAMS, ETHELYN C., "Analysis of the Foster Care Case Load," *Child Welfare* (May, 1961).

DEWOLFE, ALAN; BARRELL, ROBERT; & CUMMINGS, JONATHAN W., "Patient Variables in Emotional Response to Hospitalization for Physical Illness," *Journal of Consulting Psychology* (February, 1966).

EATON, JOSEPH, "Symbolic and Substantive Evaluative Research," *Administrative Science Quarterly* (March, 1962).

EISENMAN, RUSSELL, "Birth Order, Anxiety, and Verbalizations in Group Psychotherapy," *Journal of Consulting Psychology* (December, 1966).

EYNON, THOMAS G.; SIMPSON, JOHN E., "The Boy's Perception of Himself in a State Training School for Delinquents," *Social Service Review* (March, 1965).

FANSHEL, DAVID, "A Study of Caseworkers' Perceptions of Their Clients," *Social Casework* (December, 1958).

FANSHEL, DAVID, "Studying the Role Performance of Foster Parents," *Social Work* (January, 1961).

FELLIN, PHILLIP; & LITWAK, EUGENE, "Neighborhood Cohesion Under Conditions of Mobility," *American Sociological Review* (June, 1963).

FREEMAN, HOWARD, "Attitudes Toward Mental Illness Among Relatives of Former Patients," *American Sociological Review* (February, 1961).

FREEMAN, HOWARD; & SIMMONS, OZZIE, "Feelings of Stigma Among Relatives of Former Mental Patients," *Social Problems* (Spring, 1961).

GEISER, PETER; & MCDONAGH, EDWARD C., "Decision Making Within a Professional Association," *Social Work* (July, 1962).

GREER, SCOTT; & ORLEANS, PETER, "The Mass Society and Parapolitical Structure," *American Sociological Review* (October, 1962).

GUNTER, GRACE; & POLANSKY, NORMAN A., "Predicting a Child's Accessibility to Individual Treatment from Diagnostic Groups," *Social Work* (July, 1964).

HALL, JAY; & WILLIAMS, MARTHA, "A Comparison of Decision-Making Performances in Established and *Ad Hoc* Groups," *Journal of Personality and Social Psychology* (February, 1966).

HARTLAGE, LAWRENCE, "Employer Receptivity to Former Mental Patients," *Social Casework* (December, 1958).

HAWLEY, AMOS, "Community Power and Urban Renewal Success," *American Journal of Sociology* (January, 1963).

JANOWITZ, MORRIS, "Public Perspectives on Social Security," *Social Work* (July, 1956).

JEFFERY, C. RAY, "Social Class and Adoption Petitioners," *Social Problems* (Spring, 1962).

KADUSHIN, CHARLES, "Social Distance Between Client and Professional," *American Journal of Sociology* (March, 1962).

KOGAN, LEONARD S., "The Short Term Case in a Family Agency, Part I, The Study Plan," *Social Casework* (May, 1957).

KOGAN, LEONARD S., "The Short Term Case in a Family Agency, Part II, Results of the Study," *Social Casework* (June, 1957).

KOGAN, LEONARD S., "The Short Term Case in a Family Agency, Part III, Further Results and Conclusions," *Social Casework* (July, 1957).

KOGAN, LEONARD; & BROWN, BENJAMIN, "Case Reapplications and Reopenings After First Closing," *Social Casework* (April, 1959).

KRAUSE, MERTON, "Predicting Client Discontinuance at Intake," *Social Casework* (June, 1962).

LAMBERT, CAMILLE, JR.; GUBERMAN, MILDRED; & MORRIS, ROBERT, "Reopening Doors to Community Participation for Older People. How Realistic?", *Social Service Review* (March, 1964).

LEVINE, SOL; & WHITE, PAUL, "Exchange as a Conceptual Framework for a Study of Interorganizational Relationships," *Administrative Science Quarterly* (March, 1961).

LUCHTERHAND, ELMER; & WELLER, LEONARD, "Social Class and the Desegregation Movement: A Study of Parents' Decisions in a Negro Ghetto," *Social Problems* (Summer, 1965).

MARDEN, PARKER, "A Demographic and Ecological Analysis of the Distribution of Physicians in Metropolitan America, 1960," *American Journal of Sociology* (November, 1966).

McCORD, JOAN; McCORD, WILLIAM; & THURBER, EMILY, "The Effects of Foster-Home Placement in the Prevention of Adult Antisocial Behavior," *Social Service Review* (December, 1960).

MERCER, JANE, "Social System Perspective and Clinical Perspectives: Frames of Reference for Understanding Career Patterns of Persons Labelled as Mentally Retarded," *Social Problems* (Spring, 1965).

MEYER, HENRY J.; BORGATTA, EDGAR F.; & FANSHEL, DAVID, "Unwed Mothers' Decisions About Their Babies: An Interim Replication Study," *Child Welfare* (February, 1959).

MOELLER, GERALD; & CHARTERS, W. W., "Relation of Bureaucratization to Sense of Power Among Teachers," *Administrative Science Quarterly* (March, 1966).

MURASE, KENNETH, "International Students in Education for Social Work: An Assessment by International Graduates of Schools of Social Work in North America 1948–57," *Social Service Review* (June, 1961).

PEARLIN, LEONARD, "Sources of Resistance to Change in a Mental Hospital," *American Journal of Sociology* (November, 1962).

PEARLIN, LEONARD; & ROSENBERG, MORRIS, "Nurse-Patient Social Distance and the Structural Context for a Mental Hospital," *American Sociological Review* (February, 1962).

PFOUTS, JANE, "The Influence of Interviewer Characteristics on the Initial Interview," *Social Casework* (December, 1962).

PILIAVIN, IRVING, "Conflict Between Cottage Parents and Caseworkers," *Social Service Review* (March, 1963).

PLATNICK, HAROLD L., "The Attitudinal Orientation of the Worker and Accuracy in Predicting Client Behavior," *Social Service Review* (March, 1965).

PUTNEY, SNELL; & MIDDLETON, RUSSELL, "Effect of Husband-Wife Interaction on Strictness of Attitudes Toward Child Rearing," *Marriage and Family Living* (May, 1960).

REISS, ALBERT J., JR.; & RHODES, A. LEWIS, "An Empirical Test of Differential Association Theory," *The Journal of Research in Crime and Delinquency* (January, 1964).

RICHARDS, CATHERINE V.; & POLANSKY, NORMAN A., "Reaching Working-Class Youth Leaders," *Social Work* (October, 1959).

RIPPLE, LILIAN, "Factors Associated with Continuance in Casework Service," *Social Work* (January, 1957).

ROSE, SHELDON D., "Students View Their Supervision: A Scale Analysis," *Social Work* (April, 1965).

ROSEN, BERNARD, "Family Structure and Achievement Motivation," *American Sociological Review* (August, 1961).

SCHUBERT, MARGARET, "Admissions Decisions," *Social Service Review* (June, 1963).

SCHUBERT, MARGARET, "Field Work Performance: Achievement Levels of First-Year Students in Selected Aspects of Casework Service," *Social Service Review* (June, 1958).

SCHUBERT, MARGARET, "Field Work Performance: Repetition of a Study of First-Year Casework Performance," *Social Service Review* (September, 1960).

SHYNE, ANN, "A Study of a Youth Bureau's Clientele and Services," *Social Service Review* (March, 1960).

SIEGEL, NATALIE, "A Follow-up Study of Former Clients: An Example of Practitioner Directed Research," *Social Casework* (June, 1965).

SKOLNICK, ARLENE, "Motivational Imagery and Behavior over Twenty Years," *Journal of Consulting Psychology* (December, 1966).

STRODTBECK, FRED; & SHORT, JAMES, "Aleatory Risks vs. Short-run Hedonism in Explanation of Gang Action," *Social Problems* (Fall, 1964).

TAEUBER, KARL, "Negro Residential Segregation: Trends and Measurements," *Social Problems* (Summer, 1964).

TERREBERRY, SHIRLEY, "A Volume of Service: A Study," *Social Service Review* (September, 1960).

TURNER, FRANCIS, "A Comparison of Procedures in the Treatment of Clients with Two Different Value Orientations," *Social Casework* (May, 1964).

ULLMANN, LEONARD P.; & BERKMAN, VIRGINIA CONNER, "Types of Outcome Found in the Family Care Placement of Mental Patients," *Social Work* (April, 1959).

VARLEY, BARBARA K., "Socialization in Social Work Education," *Social Work* (July, 1963).

VINCENT, CLARK, "Unwed Mothers and the Adoption Market: Psychological and Familial Factors," *Marriage and Family Living* (May, 1960).

VOSS, HARWIN, "Differential Association and Reported Delinquent Behavior: A Replication," *Social Problems* (Summer, 1964).

WILLIE, CHARLES V.; & WEINANDY, JANET, "The Structure and Composition of 'Problem' and 'Stable' Families in a Low-Income Population," *Marriage and Family Living* (November, 1963).

WOLINS, MARTIN, "The Problem of Choice in Foster Home Finding," *Social Work* (October, 1959).

YOUNG, RUTH; & LARSON, OLAF, "The Contribution of Voluntary Organizations to Community Structure," *American Journal of Sociology* (September, 1965).

ZIMMER, BASIL, "The Adjustment of Negroes in a Northern Industrial Community," *Social Problems* (Spring, 1962).

FOUR | # Exploratory Studies

Definitions

A research study that is classified as exploratory should meet several research criteria.

1. *It should not be classifiable as either an experimental or a quantitative-descriptive study.* However, there is one exception to this. Studies that search for variable relationships—a sub-type of quantitative-descriptive research—have the primary purpose of specifying hypotheses and finding associations by using quantitative procedures to describe the relationships among variables. Some studies, however, combine quantitative descriptions with qualitative descriptions in seeking to describe a phenomenon, and our sub-type of *combined exploratory-descriptive studies* was created to include those studies. The sub-type, therefore, includes aspects of both exploratory and quantitative-descriptive studies.

2. A second criterion for exploratory studies is that *relatively systematic procedures for obtaining empirical observations and/or for the analyses of data should be used.* However, the data may not be systematically analyzed in the form of quantitative descriptions. For example, Lewis' exploratory study of a poor family in Mexico City involved systematic taped recorded interviews of each member in a Mexican family (1961); the descriptions, however, were in narrative form.

3. A third criterion for exploratory studies is that *the investigator should go beyond the qualitative and/or quantitative description by attempting to conceptualize the interrelations among the phenomena observed.* This means that the investigator should attempt to construe his observations into some theoretical or hypothetical framework.

Exploratory studies may be defined as follows:

Exploratory studies are empirical research investigations which have as their purpose the formulation of a problem or a set of questions, developing hypotheses, or increasing an investigator's familiarity with a phenomenon or a setting to lay the basis for more precise future research. The intent to clarify or modify concepts may sometimes be predominant. Relatively systematic procedures for obtaining empirical observations and/or for the analyses of data may be used. Both quantitative and qualitative descriptions of the phenomenon are often provided, and the investigator typically conceptualizes the interrelations among properties of the phenomenon being observed. A variety of data collection procedures may be employed in the relatively intensive study of a small number of behavioral units. Methods which are employed include such procedures as interviewing, participant observation, and content analysis. Representative sampling procedures are typically not used. In some studies, there is a manipulation of an independent variable in order to locate its potential effects.

We have identified three sub-types of exploratory studies. These are combined exploratory-descriptive studies; studies which use specific data collection devices in searching for ideas; and studies which involve the manipulation of independent variables in demonstrating the feasibility of practical techniques or programs. *Combined exploratory-descriptive studies* employ both quantitative and qualitative descriptions of a particular phenomenon. Studies which use *specific data collection procedures* do not necessarily contain quantitative descriptions. They may attempt to summarize qualitative data in abstract, conceptualized categories in order to consider possible relationships that can be more accurately examined in further research. The distinguishing feature of the third sub-type of exploratory study is its *manipulation of independent variables* as if in an experiment. This type of study differs from experiments in that procedures to control for extraneous variables (such as random assignment of subjects) are usually not included. In addition, there may be only one unit for study as distinguished from experiments which must include many units for proper analyses.

Definitions for each of the three sub-types of exploratory studies are presented below.

1. *Combined exploratory-descriptive studies* are those exploratory studies which seek to thoroughly describe a particular phenomenon. The concern may be with one behavioral unit, as in a case study, for which both empirical and theoretical analyses are made. The purpose of these studies is to develop ideas and theoretical generalizations. Descriptions are in both quantitative and qualitative form, and the accumulation of detailed information by such means as participant observation may be found. Sampling procedures are flexible, and little concern is usually given to systematic representativeness.

2. *Studies which use specific data collection procedures* for developing ideas are those exploratory studies which exclusively use a single procedure to suggest generalizations. Such procedures may include content analysis and the critical incident technique. The purpose of these studies is to produce conceptual categories which can be operationalized for subsequent research; it is not to report accurate quantitative descriptions among variables.

3. *Experimental manipulation studies* are those exploratory studies which manipulate an independent variable in order to locate dependent variables which are potentially associated with the independent variable. Typically,

one behavioral unit is studied in its natural environment. Often the purpose of these studies is to demonstrate the feasibility of a particular technique or program as a potential solution to practical problems.

Guideline Questions

As with other major study types, guideline questions for the assessment of exploratory studies are grouped under three categories: classification, evaluation, and utilization. We emphasize again that the guideline questions are not exhaustive and are not meant to be applied mechanically. As the reader applies these guideline questions to the exploratory studies which follow, he can expect not only to gain skill in assessment of social research, but will also develop his own version of the guidelines as they pertain to each study.

CLASSIFICATION:

1. What is (are) the specific purpose(s) of the study?
2. What research methods do the authors use to accomplish their purposes?
3. Why is the study classified as exploratory? How does it differ from experimental and quantitative-descriptive studies?
4. How should the study be sub-typed: combined exploratory-descriptive, use of specific data collection procedures, use of experimental manipulations?

EVALUATION:

I. PROBLEM FORMULATION

1. What rationale is given by the authors for conducting the study? Is the study concerned with a theoretical and/or practical problem?
2. How does the author utilize the literature and his experience, in conceptualizing the problem for study?
3. What major concepts are formulated for the study and how well are they defined conceptually and operationally?

4. What assumptions are made by the author in regard to the selection of variables for study?
5. What sources of data are considered by the authors, and what types of data are sought for the study?

II. RESEARCH DESIGN AND DATA COLLECTION

1. Could other alternative designs have been used more appropriately to carry out the purposes of the study?
2. What sampling procedures were employed in the study? What alternative plans would have been appropriate?
3. What specific kinds of data were collected?
4. To what extent were potential biases minimized in the collection of data?
5. To what extent did the author attempt to increase the reliability and validity of the measurements in the study?

III. DATA ANALYSIS AND CONCLUSIONS

1. What are the findings of the study? Are they derived from qualitative, quantitative, or both kinds of data?
2. If statistics are employed in the study, are they appropriate to the data analyzed, and to the purposes of the study?
3. What concepts, hypotheses, ideas for future research are developed from the findings of the study?
4. Are concepts developed consistent with the findings? To what extent are new concepts developed, and old concepts modified or expanded?
5. Are the hypotheses developed researchable, i.e., stated in testable form?
6. In what ways could the authors have used their available data for further analyses and additional development of ideas consistent with their purposes?
7. Do the concepts and hypotheses developed in the study stem from the findings, from other literature, or from the initial biases of the authors?
8. To what extent have the authors achieved the purposes of the study?

UTILIZATION:

1. What objects of social work interest are addressed by the researchers (recipients, process of serving, purveyance of services) ?
2. What social work purpose does the research serve?
3. What is the level of knowledge of the findings of the research (concepts, hypotheses, empirical generalizations or facts) ?
4. How valid is the research?

5. How engineerable are the variables identified in the research?
   a. How available are the variables for possible control by practitioners?
   b. How much difference in the practice situation will it make if the variables are manipulated?
   c. How feasible is it to manipulate variables of the research in the practice situation (economic feasibility, ethical suitability, organizational constraints)?
6. What types of use can be made of the research (direct application, indirect or complementary application, general stimulation of ideas) ?

Exemplars

Seven exploratory studies are reproduced in this section. As with all of the studies printed in this book, they are intended to serve as sources for the research reader to increase his skills in assessment by actually assessing research studies.

T. AYLLON

15 *Intensive Treatment of Psychotic Behaviour by Stimulus Satiation and Food Reinforcement*[*]

INTRODUCTION

Until recently, the effective control of behaviour was limited to the animal laboratory. The extension of this control to human behaviour was made when Lindsley successfully adapted the methodology of operant conditioning to the study of psychotic behaviour (Lindsley, 1956). Following Lindsley's point of departure other investigators have shown that, in its essentials, the behaviour of mental defective individuals (Orlando and Bijou, 1960), stutterers (Flanagan, Goldiamond and Azrin, 1958), mental patients (Hutchinson and Azrin, 1961), autistic (Ferster and DeMyer, 1961), and normal children (Bijou, 1961; Azrin and Lindsley, 1956) is subject to the same controls.

Despite the obvious implications of this research for applied settings there has been a conspicuous lag between the research findings and their application. The greatest limitation to the direct application of laboratory principles has been the absence of control over the subjects' environment. Recently, however, a series of applications in a regulated pyschiatric setting has clearly demonstrated the possibilities of behavioural modification (Ayllon and Michael, 1959; Ayllon and Haughton, 1962). Some of the behaviour studied has included repetitive and highly stereotyped responses such as complaining, pacing, refusal to eat, hoarding and many others.

What follows is a demonstration of behaviour techniques for the intensive individual treatment of psychotic behaviour. Specific pathological behaviour patterns of a single patient were treated by manipulating the patient's environment.

The Experimental Ward and Control Over the Reinforcement

This investigation was conducted in a mental hospital ward, the characteristics of which have been described elsewhere (Ayllon and Haughton, 1962). Briefly, this was a female ward to which only authorized personnel were allowed access. The ward staff was made up of psychiatric nurses and untrained aides who carried out the environmental manipulations

* Reprinted from *Behaviour Research and Therapy*, Vol. 1 (May, 1963), pp. 53–61, by permission of the author and Pergamon Press.

under the direction of the experimenter. Using a time-sample technique, patients were observed daily every 30 minutes from 7:00 a.m. to 11:00 p.m.

The dining room was the only place where food was available and entrance to the dining room could be regulated. Water was freely available at a drinking fountain on the ward. None of the patients had ground passes or jobs outside the ward.

SUBJECT

The patient was a 47-year-old female patient diagnosed as a chronic schizophrenic. The patient had been hospitalized for nine years. Upon studying the patient's behaviour on the ward, it became apparent that the nursing staff* spent considerable time caring for her. In particular, there were three aspects of her behaviour which seemed to defy solution. The first was stealing food. The second was the hoarding of the ward's towels in her room. The third undesirable aspect of her behaviour consisted in her wearing excessive clothing, e.g., a half-dozen dresses, several pairs of stockings, sweaters, and so on.

In order to modify the patient's behaviour systematically, each of these three types of behaviour (stealing food, hoarding, and excessive dressing) was treated separately.

EXPERIMENT I

CONTROL OF STEALING FOOD BY FOOD WITHDRAWAL

The patient had weighed over 250 pounds for many years. She ate the usual tray of food served to all patients, but, in addition, she stole food from the food counter and from other patients. Because the medical staff regarded her excessive weight as detrimental to her health, a special diet had been prescribed for her. However, the patient refused to diet and continued stealing food. In an effort to discourage the patient from stealing, the ward nurses had spent considerable time trying to persuade her to stop stealing food. As a last resort, the nurses would force her to return the stolen food.

To determine the extent of food stealing, nurses were instructed to record all behaviour associated with eating in the dining room. This record, taken for nearly a month, showed that the patient stole food during two thirds of all meals.

PROCEDURE

The traditional methods previously used to stop the patient from stealing

---

* As used in this paper, "nurse" is a generic term including all those who actually work on the ward (attendants, aides, psychiatric and registered nurses).

food were discontinued. No longer were persuasion, coaxing, or coercion used.

The patient was assigned to a table in the dining room, and no other patients were allowed to sit with her. Nurses removed the patient from the dining room when she approached a table other than her own, or when she picked up unauthorized food from the dining room counter. In effect, this procedure resulted in the patient missing a meal whenever she attempted to steal food.

RESULTS

Figure 1 shows that when withdrawal of positive reinforcement (i.e., meal) was made dependent upon the patient's "stealing", this response was eliminated in two weeks. Because the patient no longer stole food, she ate only the diet prescribed for her. The effective control of the stealing response is also indicated by the gradual reduction in the patient's body weight. At no time during the patient's nine years of hospitalization had she weighed less than 230 pounds. Figure 2 shows that at the conclusion of this treatment her weight stabilized at 180

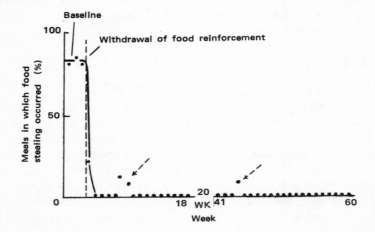

FIGURE 1. A response, food stealing, is eliminated when it results in the withdrawal of food reinforcement. The dotted arrows indicate the rare occasions when food stealing occurred. For purposes of presentation a segment comprising 20 weeks during which no stealing occurred is not included.

pounds or 17 percent loss from her original weight. At this time, the patient's physical condition was regarded as excellent.

DISCUSSION

A principle used in the laboratory shows that the strength of a response may be weakened by the removal of positive reinforcement following the response (Fester, 1958). In this case, the response was food stealing and the reinforcer was access to meals. When the patient stole food she was removed from the dining room and missed her meal.

After one year of this treatment, two occasions of food stealing occurred. The first occasion, occuring after one year of not stealing food, took the nurses by surprise and, therefore the patient "got away" with it.

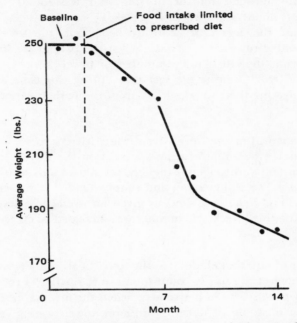

FIGURE 2. The effective control of food stealing results in a notable reduction in body weight. As the patient's food intake is limited to the prescribed diet her weight decreases gradually.

The second occasion occurred shortly thereafter. This time, however, the controlling consequences were in force. The patient missed that meal and did not steal again to the conclusion of this investigation.

Because the patient was not informed or warned of the consequences that followed stealing, the nurses regarded the procedure as unlikely to have much effect on the patient's behaviour. The implicit belief that verbal instructions are indispensable for learning is part of present day psychiatric lore. In keeping with this notion, prior to this behaviour treatment, the nurses had tried to persuade the patient to cooperate in dieting. Because there were strong medical reasons for her losing weight, the patient's refusal to follow a prescribed diet was regarded as further evidence of her mental illness.

EXPERIMENT II

CONTROL OF ONE FORM OF HOARDING BEHAVIOUR
THROUGH STIMULUS SATIATION

During the nine years of hospitalization, the patient collected large numbers of towels and stored them in her room. Although many efforts had been made to discourage hoarding, this behaviour continued unaltered. The only recourse for the nursing staff was to take away the patient's towels about twice a week.

To determine the degree of hoarding behaviour, the towels in her room were counted three times a week, when the patient was not in her room. This count showed that the number of towels kept in her room ranged from 19 to 29 despite the fact that during this time the nurses continued recovering their towel supply from the patient's room.

PROCEDURE

The routine removal of the towels from the patient's room was discontinued. Instead, a programme of stimulus satiation was carried out by the nurses. Intermittently, throughout the day, the nurses took a towel to the patient when she was in her room and simply handed it to her without any comment. The first week she was given an average of seven towels daily, and by the third week this number was increased to 60.

RESULTS

The technique of satiation eliminated the towel hoarding. Figure 3 shows the mean number of towels per count found in the patient's room. When the number of towels kept in her room reached the 625 mark, she started taking a few of them out. Thereafter, no more towels were given to her. During the next 12 months the mean number of towels found in her room was 1.5 per week.

DISCUSSION

The procedure used to reduce the amount of towel hoarding bears resemblance to satiation of a reinforcer. A reinforcer loses its effect when an excessive amount of that reinforcer is made available. Accordingly, the response maintained by that reinforcer is weakened. In this application, the towels constituted the reinforcing stimuli. When the number of towels in her room reached 625, continuing to give her towels seemed to make their collection aversive. The patient then proceeded to rid herself of the towels until she had virtually none.

During the first few weeks of satiation, the patient was observed patting her cheeks with a few towels, apparently enjoying them. Later, the patient was observed spending much of her time folding and stacking the approximately 600 towels in her room. A variety of remarks were made by the patient regarding receipt of towels. All verbal statements made by the patient were recorded by the nurse. The following represent typical remarks made during this experiment. First week: As the nurse entered

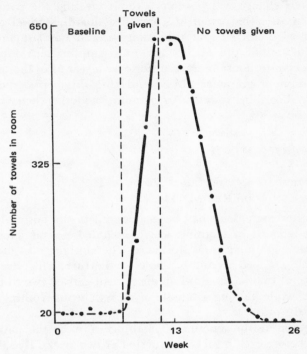

FIGURE 3. A response, towel hoarding, is eliminated when the patient is given towels in excess. When the number of towels reaches 625 the patient starts to discard them. She continues to do so until the number found in her room averages 1.5 compared to the previous 20 towels per week.

the patient's room carrying a towel, the patient would smile and say, "Oh, you found it for me, thank you." Second week: When the number of towels given to patient increased rapidly, she told the nurses, "Don't give me no more towels. I've got enough." Third week: "Take them towels away. . . . I can't sit here all night and fold towels." Fourth and fifth weeks: "Get these dirty towels out of here." Sixth week: After she had started taking the towels out of her room, she remarked to the nurse, "I can't drag any more of these towels, I just can't do it."

The quality of these remarks suggests that the initial effect of giving towels to the patient was reinforcing. However as the towels increased they ceased to be reinforcing, and presumably became aversive.

The ward nurses, who had undergone a three year training in psychiatric nursing, found it difficult to reconcile the procedure in this experiment with their psychiatric orientation. Most nurses subscribed to the popular psychiatric view which regards hoarding behaviour as a reflection of a deep "need" for love and security. Presumably, no "real" behavioural change was possible without meeting the patient's "needs" first. Even after the patient discontinued hoarding towels in her room, some nurses predicted that the change would not last and that worse behaviour would replace it. Using a time-sampling technique the patient was under continuous observation for over a year after the termination of the satiation programme. Not once during this period did the patient return to hoarding towels. Furthermore, no other behaviour problem replaced hoarding.

EXPERIMENT III

CONTROL OF AN ADDITIONAL FORM OF HOARDING THROUGH FOOD REINFORCEMENT

Shortly after the patient had been admitted to the hospital she wore an excessive amount of clothing which included several sweaters, shawls, dresses, undergarments and stockings. The clothing also included sheets and towels wrapped around her body, and a turban-like head-dress made up of several towels. In addition, the patient carried two to three cups on one hand while holding a bundle of miscellaneous clothing, and a large purse on the other.

To determine the amount of clothing worn by the patient, she was weighed before each meal over a period of two weeks. By subtracting her actual body weight from that recorded when she was dressed, the weight of her clothing was obtained.

PROCEDURE

The response required for reinforcement was stepping on a scale and meeting a predetermined weight. The requirement for reinforcement consisted of meeting a single weight (i.e., her body weight plus a specified number of pounds of clothing). Initially she was given an allowance of 23 pounds over her current body weight. This allowance represented a 2 pound reduction from her usual clothing weight. When the patient exceeded the weight requirement, the nurse stated in a matter-of-fact manner, "Sorry, you weigh too much, you'll have to weigh less." Failure to meet the required weight resulted in the patient missing the meal at which she was being weighed. Sometimes, in an effort to meet the requirement, the patient discarded more clothing than she was required.

When this occurred the requirement was adjusted at the next weighing time to correspond to the limit set by the patient on the preceding occasion.

RESULTS

When food reinforcement is made dependent upon the removal of superfluous clothing the response increases in frequency. Figure 6 shows that the patient gradually shed her clothing to meet the more demanding weight requirement until she dressed normally. At the conclusion of this experiment her clothes weighed 3 pounds compared to the 25 pounds she wore before this treatment.

Some verbal shaping was done in order to encourage the patient to leave the cups and bundles she carried with her. Nurses stopped her at the dining room and said, "Sorry, no things are allowed in the dining room." No mention of clothing or specific items was made to avoid focusing undue attention upon them. Within a week, the patient typically stepped on the scale without her bundle and assorted objects. When her weight was over the limit, the patient was informed that she weighed "too much." She then proceeded to take off a few clothes, stepped on the scale again, and upon meeting the weight requirement, gained access to the dining room.

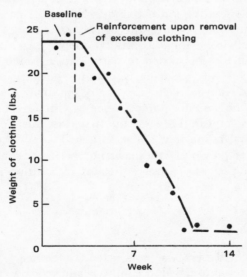

FIGURE 4. A response, excessive dressing, is eliminated when food reinforcement is made dependent upon removal of superfluous clothing. Once the weight of the clothing worn by the patient drops to three pounds it remains stable.

DISCUSSION

According to the principle of reinforcement a class of responses is strengthened when it is followed by reinforcement. A reinforcer is such when it results in a response increase. In this application the removal of excessive clothing constituted the response and the reinforcer was food (i.e., access to meals). When the patient met the weight requirement she was reinforced by being given access to meals.

At the start of this experiment, the patient missed a few meals because she failed to meet the weight requirement, but soon thereafter she gradually discarded her superfluous clothing. First, she left behind odd items she had carried in her arms, such as bundles, cups and handbags. Next she took off the elaborate headgear and assorted "capes" or shawls she had worn over her shoulders. Although she had worn 18 pairs of stockings at one time, she eventually shed these also.

During the initial part of this experiment, the patient showed some emotional behaviour, e.g., crying, shouting and throwing chairs around. Because nurses were instructed to "ignore" this emotional behaviour, the patient obtained no sympathy or attention from them. The withholding of social reinforcement for emotional behaviour quickly led to its elimination.

At the conclusion of this behaviour treatment, the patient typically stepped on the scale wearing a dress, undergarments, a pair of stockings and a pair of light shoes. One of the behavioral changes concomitant with the current environmental manipulation was that as the patient began dressing normally she started to participate in small social events in the hospital. This was particularly new to the patient as she had previously remained seclusive spending most of the time in her room.

About this time the patient's parents came to visit her and insisted on taking her home for a visit. This was the first time during the patient's nine years of hospitalization that her parents had asked to take her out. They remarked that previously they had not been interested in taking her out because the patient's excessive dressing in addition to her weight made her look like a "circus freak."

CONCLUSIONS

The research presented here was conducted under nearly ideal conditions. The variables manipulated (i.e., towels and food) were under full experimental control. Using a time-sample technique the patient was observed daily every 30 minutes from 7:00 a.m. to 11:00 p.m. Nurses and aides carried out these observations which were later analysed in terms of gross behaviour categories. These observations were in force for over a year during which time these three experiments were conducted. The results of these observations indicate that none of the three pathological behaviour patterns (i.e., food stealing, hoarding and excessive dressing) exhibited by the patient were replaced by any undesirable behaviour.

The patient displayed some emotional behaviour in each experiment, but each time it subsided when social reinforcement (i.e., attention) was not forthcoming. The patient did not become violent or seclusive as a consequence of these experiments. Instead, she became socially more accessible to patients and staff. She did not achieve a great deal of social success but she did begin to participate actively in social functions.

A frequent problem encountered in mental hospitals is overeating. In general this problem is solved by prescribing a reduction diet. Many patients, however, refuse to take a reduction diet and continue overeating. When confronted with this behaviour, psychiatric workers generally resort to two types of explanations.

One explanation of overeating points out that only with the active and sincere cooperation of the patient can weight reduction be accomplished. When the patient refuses to cooperate he is regarded as showing more signs of mental illness and all hopes of eliminating overeating come to an end.

Another type of explanation holds that overeating is not the behaviour to be concerned with. Instead, attention is focused on the psychological "needs" of the patient. These "needs" are said to be the cause of the observable behaviour, overeating. Therefore the emphasis is on the removal of the cause and not on the symptom or behaviour itself. Whatever theoretical merit these explanations may have, it is unfortunate that they fail to suggest practical ways of treating the behaviour itself. As a consequence, the patient continues to overeat often to the detriment of his health.

The current psychiatric emphasis on the resolution of the mental conflict that is presumably at the basis of the symptoms, is perhaps misplaced. What seems to have been forgotten is that behaviour problems such as those reported here, prevent the patient from being considered for discharge not only by the hospital personnel but also by the patient's relatives. Indeed, as far as the patient's relatives are concerned, the index of improvement or deterioration is the readily observable behaviour and not a detailed account of the mechanics of the mental apparatus.

Many individuals are admitted to mental hospitals because of one or more specific behaviour difficulties and not always because of a generalized "mental" disturbance. For example, an individual may go into a mental hospital because he has refused to eat for several days, or because he talks to himself incessantly. If the goal of therapy were behavioural rehabilitation, these problems would be treated and normal eating and normal talking reinstated. However, the current emphasis in psychotherapy is on "mental-conflict resolution" and little or no attention is given to dealing directly with the behavioural problems which prevent the patient from returning to the community.

REFERENCES

AYLLON, T. and MICHAEL, J. (1959) The psychiatric nurse as a behavioural engineer. *J. exp. anal. Behav.* 2, 323–34.

AYLLON, T. and HAUGHTON, E. (1962) Control of the behaviour of schizophrenic patients by food. *J. exp. anal. Behav.* 5, 343–52.

AZRIN, N. and LINDSLEY, O. (1956) The reinforcement of cooperation between children. *J. abnorm. (soc.) Psychol.* 52, 100–02.

BIJOU, S. (1961) Discrimination performance as a baseline for individual analysis of young children. *Child Develpm.* 32, 160–63.

FERSTER, C. B. (1958) Control of behaviour in chimpanzees and pigeons by time out from positive reinforcement. *Psychol. Monogr.* 72, 1–38.

FERSTER, C. and DeMYER, M. (1961) The development of performances in autistic children in an automatically controlled environment. *J. chron. Dis.* 13, 312–45.

FLANAGAN, B., GOLDIAMOND, I. and AZRIN, N. (1958) Operant stuttering: The control of stuttering behaviour through response-contingent consequences. *J. exp. anal. Behav.* 56, 49–56.

HUTCHINSON, R. R. and AZRIN, N. H. (1961) Conditioning of mental hospital patients to fixed-ratio schedules of reinforcement. *J. exp. anal. Behav.* 4, 87–95.

LINDSLEY, O. R. (1956) Operant conditioning methods applied to research in chronic schizophrenia. *Psychiat. Res. Rep.* 5, 118–39.

ORLANDO, R. and BIJOU, S. (1960) Single and multiple schedules of reinforcement in developmentally retarded children. *J. exp. anal. Behav.* 3, 339–48.

WILLIAM A. FAUNCE, DONALD A. CLELLAND

16 *Professionalization and Stratification Patterns in an Industrial Community**[1]

Various studies, notably the Lynds' *Middletown*[2] and Warner and Low's *The Social System of the Modern Factory*,[3] demonstrate that technologically induced changes in occupational structure have important consequences for community stratification patterns. These studies involved analysis of technological changes characteristic of a relatively early stage in the evolution of industrial production systems. Major changes in production technology have occurred since these studies were conducted. In this paper we will compare the results of earlier community studies with some data recently collected from a community in which the major employer is a highly automated, chemical-processing firm. Our primary concerns will be with the effects of technological change upon the occupational structure of the community and with the attendant effects of change in the distribution of occupations upon community class, status, and power arrangements.

Comparison of data from community studies requires some conceptual framework that relates the specific events occurring in each community to generalized community processes. Maurice Stein, in *The Eclipse of Community,* provides the elements of a framework of this kind.[4] He describes three processes that are largely responsible for shaping the character of contemporary industrial cities: (1) *industrialization* or the development of mass-production and mass-consumption techniques; (2) *urbanization,* which refers to the structural differentiation or segmentalization of the community; and (3) *bureaucratization* or the development of impersonal, legal-rational controls. It is our contention that a fourth process, *professionalization,* is becoming an increasingly important deter-

* Reprinted from the *American Journal of Sociology,* Vol. 72, No. 4 (January, 1967), pp. 341–50, by permission of the University of Chicago Press, and the authors.

[1] An earlier, abbreviated report of this study appeared in the British journal, *New Society* (November 7, 1963), with the title, "The Professional Society." The research was supported by a grant from the National Science Foundation and by the School of Labor and Industrial Relations at Michigan State University.

[2] Robert S. and Helen M. Lynd, *Middletown* (New York: Harcourt, Brace & World, Inc., 1929).

[3] W. Lloyd Warner and J. O. Low, *The Social System of the Modern Factory* (New Haven, Conn.: Yale University Press, 1947).

[4] Maurice Stein, *The Eclipse of Community* (Princeton, N.J.: Princeton University Press, 1960).

minant of the character of contemporary communities. This process involves an increase in the proportion of occupations requiring professional skills, that is, certified competence with respect to systematically ordered, abstract knowledge.

While industrialization, urbanization, bureaucratization, and professionalization may occur simultaneously, they do not ordinarily develop at the same rate. More typically, they form a sequence with a high level of development of one acting as a spur to development of the next. Increased professionalization is, in part, an outgrowth of the bureaucratic emphasis upon expertise and rationalism. Extensive use of bureaucratic organizational forms is partly a response to problems occasioned by increasing differentiation of community structure (urbanization as defined above). Increased structural differentiation is one of the consequences of industrialization. There is also a series of changes in production technology that parallels and is related to the sequence in which these processes develop.[5]

The initial stage in this sequence is the familiar shift from a handicraft to a mechanized form of production technology. Much has been written about the changes in division of labor and in stratification patterns typical of this early phase in the industrialization process. This period has been seen as characterized (1) by increasing occupational specialization with an increasing proportion of semiskilled machine operators in the labor force, (2) by a status-assignment system in which commodity display is the major status criterion and accumulation of wealth the dominant mobility pattern, (3) by a system of power in which the entrepreneur is dominant by virture of property ownership, and (4) by a class structure in which there is increasing class cleavage based upon differential access to property.[6]

With the shift from mechanized to automated production processes, the continuing bureaucratization of economic organizations, and the concomitant changes in form of division of labor, major changes in class, status, and power structures could be expected. The attributes of the community we studied are seen as typical of a developing period of professionalization characterized (1) by decreasing occupational specialization with an increasing proportion of professionals and technicians in the labor force, (2) by a status-assignment system in which contribution in one's field of work is a major status criterion and gaining professional

---

[5] Cf. William A. Faunce, "Automation and the Division of Labor," *Social Problems* (Fall, 1965), pp. 149–60.

[6] Lynd, *op. cit.;* Warner and Low, *op. cit.;* E. D. Smith, *Technology and Labor* (New Haven, Conn.: Yale University Press, 1939); and Constance M. Green, *Holyoke, Massachusetts: A Case History of the Industrial Revolution in America* (New Haven, Conn.: Yale University Press, 1939).

recognition an increasingly important mobility pattern, (3) by a system of power in which the professional is increasingly dominant, and (4) by a class structure in which there is decreasing class cleavage with class distinctions based upon access to education.[7]

From a general historical perspective, the period of professionalization has clearly not yet arrived, and the characteristics attributed to this period should be seen as projections of some current trends. Focusing upon contemporary communities, however, it is possible to find cities in which there is a sufficiently high level of professionalization to permit analysis of the effects of this process upon stratification patterns. The rest of this paper will be concerned primarily with data collected in one city of this kind.

COMMUNITY OCCUPATIONAL STRUCTURE

Establishing the nature and extent of relationship between technological change, community occupational structure, and stratification patterns is difficult in large, multi-industry cities. In cities of this kind there are likely to be a large number of alternative possibilities for employment at the same skill level. The effect of technological change upon the distribution of occupations is therefore less immediate and more difficult to establish. For this reason, most of the previous studies in this area have been of small or middle-sized cities in which there is one principal employer.

The research to be reported here was conducted in a community of this type. It is a city of about 25,000 inhabitants in which approximately half of the male labor force is employed by a large chemical-processing company. The chemical company has dominated the economy of the city and employed most of its labor force almost from its inception. Change in production technology has been fairly continuous during the history of this firm with the direction of change being toward increasingly automatic operation. The term "automation," as it is used in this paper, refers to the integration of production processes through the use of automatic materials-handling and automatic control devices. In this sense, chemical-processing is among the most highly automated American industries.

Table 1 indicates that there has been a high proportion of professionals in the labor force of this community for more than twenty years and that the proportion continues to increase more rapidly than in the typical small city. Certain other changes in the occupational composition

---

[7] These hypotheses grow out of a wide variety of previous studies of professionals. See, e.g., Howard M. Vollmer and Donald L. Mills (eds.), *Professionalization* (Englewood Cliffs, N. J.: Prentice-Hall, Inc., 1966).

of this city are also exaggerations of national and small city trends, such as, for example, the sharp decline in the proportion of operatives and laborers. The index of net redistribution indicates that changes in the occupational structure have been much greater than those occurring nationally or in the average small city over the 20 year period 1940–60 but that the more radical changes had taken place in the earlier decade. Comparison of Table 1 and Figure 1, however, suggests that some of these changes resulted from factors other than change in the composition of the chemical-plant work force. Thus, for example, the large change that occurred during the 1940's was not the result of the relatively slight change taking

TABLE 1

COMPARISON OF CHANGING OCCUPATIONAL DISTRIBUTION IN CITY STUDIED AND OTHER CITIES OF 10,000–50,000*

	1940	1950	1960
Professional and technical:			
City studied	19.2%	25.2%	28.7%
Mean, small cities	9.9	11.3	13.7
Managers, proprietors and officials:			
City studied	9.0	10.7	10.4
Mean, small cities	11.6	12.1	11.1
Clerical and sales:			
City studied	17.6	23.0	21.9
Mean, small cities	22.0	23.3	25.2
Craftsmen:			
City studied	14.4	14.6	13.8
Mean, small cities	12.9	14.9	14.0
Operatives:			
City studied	20.3	14.6	12.0
Mean, small cities	21.5	20.9	18.6
Private-household workers:			
City studied	5.9	2.3	4.0
Mean, small cities	6.5	3.4	3.7
Service workers:			
City studied	7.9	7.1	7.0
Mean, small cities	6.5	8.3	9.2
Laborers:			
City studied	5.7	2.5	2.2
Mean, small cities	7.2	5.8	4.5

	1940–50	1950–60	1940–60
Index of net redistribution: [a]			
City studied	13.3%	5.2%	15.2%
Mean, small cities	6.1	5.5	9.9

* Based on a 5 percent systematic sample of all urban places with populations ranging between 10,000 and 50,000 during the entire period 1940–60 (source: U.S. Census).

[a] Computed as the index of dissimilarity between the occupational distributions for any two dates. The index is one-half of the absolute values of the differences between the occupational differences for any two dates, taken occupation by occupation. This index is derived from Albert J. Reiss, Jr., "Change in the Occupational Structure of the United States, 1910 to 1950," in Paul K. Hatt and Albert J. Reiss, Jr. (eds.), *Cities and Society* (New York: Free Press, 1957), p. 425.

place in the occupational composition of the plant labor force. Rather, simple expansion of the plant labor force brought about major changes in the occupational structure of the community. Less than half of the plant employees live within the corporate limits of the city. As the work force doubled between 1940 and 1950, new hourly workers increasingly commuted from the surrounding area, but new salaried workers, especially the professionals, settled within the city. During the fifties, the two major changes in the occupational composition of the plant, an increase in the proportion of professionals and a decrease in the proportion of operatives, were not fully reflected in the community occupational distribution because an expansion of the city limits brought a disproportionate number of blue-collar workers into the city. Thus differential residence patterns exaggerated technologically induced changes in occupational composition during the forties, and annexation dampened the effect of such changes during the fifties.

The automated technology of the chemical-processing plant is, similarly, not the only factor producing changes in the composition of the plant work force. There have been organizational changes that increased efficiency of production, an expansion of research operations, and also growth in the corporate home office which is located in the same city.

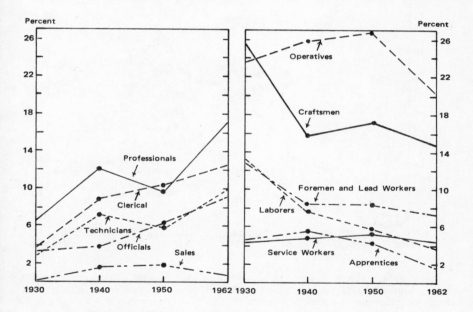

FIGURE 1. Percentage distribution by major occupational category for chemical-plant work force, 1930–62. *Left,* white-collar categories; *right,* blue-collar categories.

Automation has contributed, however, to the demand for professionals and has, more importantly, increased the *proportion* of professionals by decreasing the demand for semiskilled machine operators. Figure 2 presents a rough productivity measure and suggests the role that technological change has played in shaping the character of the work force in this firm. While sales have increased by 50 percent in the past ten years, the hourly work force has remained relatively constant. Interviews with industrial engineers, personnel officers, and other officials in the firm also support the assertion that automation has contributed to the professionalization of the work force.

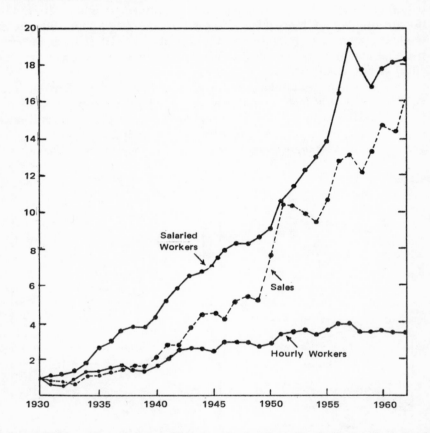

FIGURE 2. Sales and employment of hourly and salaried workers, indicating the ratio of yearly figures to 1930 figures. The *Sales* line is sales and transfers at market price from the community location, adjusted to 1939 dollars. Comparison of sales and hourly employment gives a rough indication of productivity. However, the picture of increased productivity is somewhat exaggerated, since increasing value added to products prior to shipment to this location has not been taken into account. The *Hourly* and *Salaried* employment lines are based on monthly means for the year.

Recent studies suggest that a decrease in functional specialization or in the *degree* of division of labor accompanies the integration of production processes resulting from automation.[8] While there has not been a decrease in the number of job titles in the particular plant we studied, there does appear to be a decrease in the degree of difference among the actual tasks performed under different job titles.

This pattern of change in division of labor—decreasing functional specialization and an increase in the proportion of professionals in the labor force—is in marked contrast with the findings of earlier community studies dealing with the impact of change in production technology. The dilution of skills and the emergence of an industrial proletariat is a well-documented aspect of the early stages of the industrialization process.[9] The development of special-purpose machinery, which produced the breakup of craft skills, also resulted in increased functional specialization and an increase in the *number* of semiskilled occupational specialties.

COMMUNITY STRATIFICATION PATTERNS

What are the implications of these differences in patterns of division of labor for community class, status, and power structures? Earlier community studies, like those conducted in Middletown and Yankee City, describe some distinct changes in stratification patterns that accompanied industrialization and its attendant changes in occupational structure.

In the period of craft production preceding industrialization, craft workers were highly respected, politically influential, and well paid. The age-skill hierarchy provided a clearly defined mobility channel and a status structure in which there were no large gaps between different status levels in the community. With the advent of mass-production technology, accumulation of wealth and commodity display supplanted craftsmanship as the basis for status assignment. Business-class mobility models were substituted for previous patterns. A distinct cleavage in the status structure developed between the increasingly wealthy entrepreneurial elite and the rest of the community. Community power, both in the sense of influence and in the sense of occupancy of important decision-making positions, was increasingly concentrated in the hands of the entrepreneur. These changes along with the growing impersonality of employer-employee relations, resulted in increased social-class cleavage and identification.

Our data suggest that the stratification patterns accompanying contemporary changes in the division of labor may be quite different from these. The data were collected through interviews with samples of people drawn from the occupational categories showing the greatest rate of change in the community. The samples were drawn in this way under the

---

[8] Faunce, *op. cit.*
[9] Lynd, *op. cit.*, pp. 39–89; Warner and Low, *op. cit.*, pp. 54–89.

assumption that the differences between the responses of people in occupations that are increasing and those that are decreasing as a proportion of the labor force would provide evidence regarding the direction of change in the community. Two samples were drawn from expanding occupations: a sample of 100 professionals, mostly chemists and engineers, and a sample of 100 laboratory and production technicians. A sample of 150 persons was drawn from occupations that are decreasing as a proportion of the work force, such as semiskilled machine operatives. The three samples were drawn randomly from lists of employees of the chemical-processing firm. Only persons living in the city were included in the original lists.

Interviews were eventually conducted with 95 of the professionals, 95 of the technicians, and 137 of the other hourly-rated workers.[10] The primary focus of the interview was upon information regarding attitudes toward the community; patterns of participation in community activities; and class, status, and power arrangements. Supplementary information was also collected through loosely structured interviews with 29 community leaders in major appointive and elective positions in the community.

Our data suggest that a stratification system with characteristics like those attributed above to a period of professionalization is emerging in this community. With respect to status criteria and mobility patterns, recognition in one's field appears in the process of becoming more important than either occupancy of important organizational positions or commodity display. Our respondents were asked what they would have to do to feel that they had gotten ahead or were a success. Of the professionals, who are already the largest occupational group in the community and are the most rapidly expanding, 42 percent gave responses like making a contribution to knowledge, gaining recognition in one's field, gaining the respect of colleagues, and other achievements related to intrinsic aspects of work. Twenty-one percent defined getting ahead in terms of promotion to a better job, while 24 percent mentioned increased income or more material possessions. The modal response for both the technicians and the hourly workers was security in the sense of having a steady income, being out of debt, or having money in the bank. The technicians, however, were approximately twice as likely as the workers to mention promotion as a definition of getting ahead and gave responses related to recognition in their field more than five times as often. These data are summarized in Table 2.

Additional support for our hypothesis is provided by the responses to the following question: "Different people regard different kinds of things

---

10 Of the twenty-three persons who were not interviewed, twelve were refusals, six had moved away, four were ill or deceased, and one could not be contacted.

as important in life. When you think about what really matters to you, what would you say are the central interests in your life?" Achievement-oriented responses to this question are interpreted here as the equivalent of statements regarding criteria for status assignment. Among the categories of response was one that included any reference to non-economic aspects of work and another made up of references to increased income or standard of living. Sixty-eight percent of the professionals listed aspects of work other than income as a central life interest, while only 26 percent mentioned higher income. Both the technicians and workers mentioned higher standard of living more often than intrinsically work-related goals, but the margin of difference was much smaller for the technicians.

Our data suggest, however, that bureaucratic-mobility patterns are also important. In response to the question, "What sort of goals have you set for yourself in your work or career?" 37 percent of the professionals referred to goals representing *intra*positional mobility, such as gaining recognition in one's field, but an equal proportion mentioned promotion or other goals related to *inter*positional mability. (Only six percent listed economic objectives.) Also, in response to a forced-choice question regarding preference for advancement by moving into a supervisory job or by gaining recognition for technical competence in their present jobs, 47 percent of the professionals indicated a preference for supervisory work, while 48 percent preferred recognition for technical competence. Taking all of our data into account, however, it appears that the professional-mobility model is becoming increasingly predominant and that, while the bureaucratic model may be a close second, the entrepreneurial model that characterized the early stages of industrialization is a distant third and is falling further behind.

Power arrangements also appear to approximate those we would expect in a community with a high proportion of professionals in its labor force. The professionals are more active in community affairs than either of the other groups, and the workers are least active by a considerable margin. Increasing influence in the community has apparently accompanied the high level of community involvement of professionals. Our respondents were asked whom they would go to see if they wanted to get some action started on any local problem. Fifty-eight percent of those who could answer the question listed persons with professional backgrounds. In response to a question dealing with occupational groups that have had most to do with bringing about change in the community, 37 percent of the combined samples mentioned salaried professionals; 27 percent, executives and managers; and 21 percent, merchants and businessmen. The remaining 15 percent of the responses were scattered among five other occupational categories. In response to another question, a slight majority of the respondents reported that they had observed *little or no change* in the amount of influence of any occupational group in the community. Among those who reported increased influence for any occupation, however, almost twice as many listed salaried professionals as any other group. Among those who reported *decreased* influence for any occupation, two groups, merchants and industrial managers, were mentioned much more frequently than any of the others. These are precisely the occupational groups who reportedly became more powerful as a result of earlier changes in production technology. Salaried professionals were mentioned as having decreasing influence by less than one percent of the respondents.

TABLE 2

"THE PHRASE 'GETTING AHEAD IN THE WORLD' MEANS DIFFERENT THINGS TO DIFFERENT PEOPLE. WHAT WOULD YOU HAVE TO DO TO FEEL THAT YOU HAD GOTTEN AHEAD OR WERE A SUCCESS?"

	Recognition in One's Field	Promotion to Better Job	More Income or Material Possessions	Security
Professionals (N = 95)	42%*	21%	24%	21%
Technicians (N = 95)	16	24	23	32
Workers (N = 137)	3	12	22	52

* Percentages do not total 100 because more than one answer was coded for each respondent and not all coding categories are included in the table. The percentages are of row rather than column frequencies.

Professionals appear to recognize their power in the community. In response to the question, "Do you think that people like yourself have much to say about how problems are handled or how the city is run generally?" 74 percent of the professionals answered "yes" without any qualification and another 14 percent gave a qualified but affirmative answer. Only 39 percent of the technicians and 42 percent of the workers gave an unqualified affirmative response.

The data presented so far suggest that professionals are perceived as having more influence than either the "bureaucrats" or the "entrepreneurs" in this community. There may be some bias in these responses since our samples were not drawn from the whole community but only from occupations that are increasing or decreasing as a proportion of the labor force. People in primarily bureaucratic or entrepreneurial positions are not represented among our respondents since they are a relatively stable segment of the labor force. The opinions expressed by our respondents, however, are consistent with the views of the community leaders who were interviewed, except that the latter attributed somewhat more influence to corporation executives. Fourteen of the 29 community leaders interviewed selected executives as the most influential group in the community, while 11 chose professionals.

The opinions of our respondents are also consistent with data regarding the occupational composition of those holding elective offices in the community. These data are summarized in Table 3. Professionals are the predominant occupational group in these positions currently, and, if the trend suggested by the data continues, they will be increasingly predominant in the future. Industrial executives or local merchants may still wield power behind the scenes, but at least at the level of "on-stage" power the professionals appear to have taken over.[11]

One of the most consistently reported findings from studies of communities undergoing industrialization is increased class cleavage. Our data suggest much less class cleavage than these earlier studies and indicate that class identification may be decreasing. Warner and Low cite the organizational strike in the shoe industry as evidence of increased social distance between classes in Yankee City. Various other studies use strikes as an index of class cleavage. There have been only two strikes since the union was organized in the community that we studied. One was a two-day wildcat strike in 1941. The other was a more prolonged strike in 1948 in which the strike vote carried, however, by only 54 percent of the workers who voted.

Earlier studies also suggest that the elimination of middle-status craft positions tended to increase the cleavage between people in working-class occupations and those in higher status positions. The growing number of technicians required by more advanced industrial technology would appear to fill this gap somewhat. The data in Figure 1 show that the increase in the proportion of technicians and clerical workers, who also fall in the margin between higher and lower status groups in the community, has more than made up for the decline in skilled craftsmen and that the technicians are increasing recently at a rate second only to the professionals.

To the extent that technological advances decrease demand for people in working-class positions, they have another important effect upon class structure. Young replacements for older workers are not hired, and the result is an aging working class. The average age of non-salaried workers in the chemical-processing firm that we studied increased from 37.2 to 41.2 in the five years preceding our study. Aging is generally regarded as

---

11 Schulze reports an instance of withdrawal of industrial executives from participation in community affairs. He interprets this finding as resulting from a policy of non-involvement of absentee-owned corporations in the affairs of the communities in which they are located. Cf. Robert O. Schulze, "Economic Dominants in Community Power Structure," *American Sociological Review* (February, 1958), pp. 3–9. Other studies have found economic leaders highly involved in the power structure of communities where there are locally owned industries. Cf. William H. Form and Delbert C. Miller, *Industry, Labor and Community* (New York: Harper & Row, Publishers, 1960), p. 310. In spite of the fact that the chemical firm in the city we studied is locally owned, professionals are much more active than executives in community affairs.

an important factor producing conservatism in political and economic views. A majority of the people in working-class positions in our sample indicated that they were either Republicans or politically independent. Most of them also labeled their political and economic views as conservative or middle of the road. Only 22 percent of the workers identified themselves as liberals. Of those in all three samples who reported any change in their views, a majority indicated that they were becoming increasingly conservative. Almost three-fourths of the combined samples reported that there was little difference between Republicans and Democrats on local issues. While there were a number of statistically significant differences between professionals and workers on specific political or economic issues, a majority of all three samples did not *perceive* any great difference between social classes in this community in their general political and economic attitudes.

TABLE 3

OCCUPATIONAL DISTRIBUTION OF ELECTED OFFICIALS,* 1930–62

	1930–34	1935–39	1940–44	1945–49	1950–54	1955–62
Executives and managers..........	28%	27%	13%	22%	23%	22%
Salaried professionals	17	27	38	53	55	64
Small business and independent professionals	25	19	23	17	13	14
Blue collar	29	28	26	8	8	0

* City council, school board, and, prior to 1945, the mayor.

Class identification does not appear to be strong in this community either. Only five percent of the three samples saw political parties as class based. Also, in answer to an open-ended question asking for a referent to the phrase "people like me," only 18 percent of the respondents used social class or class-related designations other than occupation. Of those who did, significantly fewer were professionals, suggesting even less class identification as the direction of change. The respondents were also asked to name their social class using the question developed originally by Richard Centers. Our data, in comparison with Centers', indicate a stronger tendency for both professionals and workers to call themselves middle class. Responses to various questions suggest that the basis on which these class distinctions are made is, increasingly, amount of formal education.

It is not our contention that automation has eliminated class differences. Social classes in the sense of political and economic interest groups having different styles of life are still very much in evidence in this community. It does appear, however, that the social distance between classes, the amount of class conflict, and the importance of class identification are not so great as in communities at earlier stages in the industrialization process.

SUMMARY

In this paper, data from a community in which the major employer is a highly automated chemical-processing firm have been compared with findings from community studies dealing with the effects of earlier stages in the evolution of industrial production technology. The occupational structure and the stratification patterns in the community we studied differ markedly from those reported in earlier studies. The direction of change suggested by this comparison can also be seen in the contrast between the attitudes and participation in community activities of professionals and technicians, who constitute an increasing proportion of the community labor force, and semiskilled workers, who are declining as a proportion of this labor force. Both the intercommunity comparisons and the pattern of change within the community we studied point to the development of a more cosmopolitan, occupationally based status-assignment system, increasing involvement of professionals in community power structure, and decreased social-class cleavage and identification.

Our concern is not limited to change within this particular community. We are suggesting that a shift toward the pattern of social stratification we have described is a general tendency in industrial communities. The findings of this study are, of course, insufficient to support such an assertion.

The community we studied does, however, contain a relatively unique set of attributes that are representative of the direction of change in industrial societies. Almost half of the male labor force in this community is employed by a company whose organizational structure typifies the direction of change in contemporary industrial firms. The predominant type of production technology in this industry, that is, a production system integrated through the use of automatic control devices and materials-handling, represents the direction of change in most major American industries. The pattern of change in labor-force composition in this community can be easily discerned as the dominant trend in national labor-force statistics.

We regard the research reported here as a case study of a community that in certain important respects has already arrived at the early stages of a period of professionalization toward which much of the rest of the society appears to be moving. The assertion that the contrast between our data and those of earlier studies represents a direction of change in industrial communities rests upon the following three assumptions: (1) that class, status, and power arrangements are in large part a function of the organizational structure, production technology, and form of division of labor in industrial communities; (2) that the evolution of these community attributes tends to occur as a particular sequence of developmental phases; and (3) that the community we studied and those studied earlier are typical of communities to be found at different phases in this sequence.

D. WELLS GOODRICH, DONALD S. BOOMER

17 *Some Concepts about Therapeutic Interventions with Hyperaggressive Children**

PART I

For the past three years the Child Research Branch of the National Institute of Mental Health has been studying residential treatment of hyperaggressive children.[1] During the first year of operation, several groups of children had been studied on the ward for periods of a few weeks or months; these groups served to facilitate an intensive in-service training program for the staff. The research described here was carried out during the second year of operation, coincident with the beginning of intensive long-term therapy with six chronically disturbed boys, nine to ten years of age. This stormy early phase of treatment was marked by daily explosions of anxious aggression by the patients. During this time the staff was inevitably faced with problems of setting limits to aggression.

The patients had been carefully selected according to a number of criteria, one of which was the presence of extreme acting-out behavior. All six had shown most of the following disturbances in chronic form: marked learning impairment, unmanageable impulsiveness in the school room, fire setting, stealing, and temper tantrums. All were organically sound, with at least average intellectual capacity. Before entering the hospital, most had been living with at least one parent. At the time of this study, about half of the 24 staff persons were child-care workers (nurses, group workers, recreation leaders, and attendants) who dealt with the children in the residence; other staff members included psychiatrists, teachers, social workers, and research workers.

The therapeutic program was built around four teams: (1) ward psychiatrist-nurse-attendant-group worker staff (that is, the "child-care staff"), (2) the teachers, (3) the psychotherapists, and (4) the psychiatric caseworkers who worked with the families and community agencies. The children usually attended play therapy sessions four times weekly. School sessions varied from one to three hours daily, in accordance with each child's capacity to sustain useful involvement. During the remainder of

* Reprinted from *Social Casework*, Vol. XXXIX, No. 4 (April, 1958) pp. 207–13. Reproduced by permission of the journal and the authors.
[1] This study was a part of the research program of the Child Research Branch, which is under the direction of Dr. Fritz Redl.

the time a diversified group program was maintained by the child-care staff. The project also supported two full-time research positions, those of the two authors. As clinicians without any treatment responsibilities, we were free to study the situation from a somewhat less involved position.

RESEARCH FOCUS

In limiting our research task to manageable proportions, we were guided by several specific interests and assumptions. We believed that over a certain reasonable span of time, treatment by skilled staff *does* produce real behavior changes in the patients. Furthermore, we assumed that, while many influences contribute to improvement in patients, one important class of "change agents" is the observable transactions between staff and children.

From our own experience as therapists we felt that therapeutically crucial events often take place in natural, unexpected ways. Thus, we felt that the creation of artificial laboratory observation situations would be undesirable. By the same reasoning, any research techniques employed within the residence should minimally interfere with clinical operations or with the lives of the children.

Until theoretical and technical issues are much clearer, it seems more profitable to explore the natural therapeutic situation systematically than to control arbitrary and perhaps naively-chosen variables. As Polansky[2] has reported, interpersonal events may be observed in a clinical setting without disruptive interference to staff or to patients, if appropriate staff policies and continuing reality orientation to staff and patients can be arranged.

For these reasons, then, we decided to study interactions between staff and patients. We quickly discovered that, even with four observers, it is physically impossible to gather and process data covering more than five percent of such transactions. Some theoretical guides must be employed to select situations. Pilot studies[3] employing the interpersonal system developed by Leary[4] and others convinced us that, while this method has useful applications, it is far too general for identifying the technical problems that may spell success or failure in the handling of hyperaggressive children. Indeed, at the present time no system of concepts exists which permits systematic testing of hypotheses that are germane to resi-

[2] Norman Polansky and others, "Problems of Interpersonal Relations in Research on Groups," *Human Relations,* Vol. II, No. 3 (1949), pp. 281–91.

[3] Unpublished studies carried out during 1954 and 1955, at the Child Research Branch, National Institute of Mental Health, by A. T. Dittmann, D. W. Goodrich, D. S. Boomer, and J. Handlon.

[4] T. Leary, *Multilevel Measurement of Interpersonal Behavior,* Psychological Consultation Service, Berkeley, Calif., 1956.

dential treatment. Investigators in this field must either seek patterns within the raw data of behavior on the basis of their own intuition and clinical experience or utilize a fairly abstract frame of reference based on global personality constructs. To be sure, within the private experience of therapists many specific hypotheses exist which relate directly to concrete therapeutic situations and which might be cast in a testable form. But upon which hypotheses should a large and expensive study be based? Increasingly we felt a need for concepts that would be less abstract than general theory and at a level near that of the working clinician. We felt that such concepts would provide us with some much-needed perspective before again embarking on a time-consuming program of direct observation.

Therefore, we set about to tap the clinical "know-how" of the staff, to organize their developing values about which transactions work under what conditions when dealing therapeutically with these patients. A system of such practical concepts, if related to one another in specific ways, we felt, would serve to define a range of problems for subsequent research. For this purpose we adopted a technique which was developed by Flanagan, the "critical incident" technique.[5]

CRITICAL INCIDENT TECHNIQUE

The critical incident technique has been widely employed as a means of defining the critical requirements of specific jobs in business and industry. The method, however, is applicable to a broad range of situations. Flanagan says, "The critical incident technique consists of a set of procedures for collecting direct observations of human behavior in such a way as to facilitate their potential usefulness in . . . developing broad psychological principles,"[6] a statement which reflected our precise need. Accordingly, we applied the method to the exploration of some relevant aspects of residential treatment.

The critical incident technique is an *inductive* method of building up generalizations by abstracting them from a large number of concrete events rather than by inferring them deductively from some superordinate concept or definition.

A typical industrial problem can serve to illustrate the logic of the technique. For the purposes of selection or training, for example, it becomes necessary to formulate a good working definition of an effective

---

[5] John C. Flanagan, "The Critical Incident Technique," *Psychological Bulletin,* Vol. LI, No. 4 (1954), pp. 327–28.

Critical is used here to mean relevant, salient, or significant; it does not necessarily connote "clinically critical" in the sense of an emergency or "therapeutically critical" in the sense of a *sine qua non* for therapeutic effectiveness.

[6] Flanagan, *op. cit.*

assembly line foreman. In order to construct tests or to derive performance criteria, it is necessary to learn what are the relevant attributes of a good foreman.

These attributes can best be stated as a set of interrelated abstractions. To be useful these abstractions must be, on the one hand, more specific than the vague global concept "good foreman" and, on the other hand, more general and more parsimonious than a catalog of the actual behaviors of good foremen in a variety of concrete on-the-job situations.

Schematically, the levels would look like this:

Global Concept	———	"Good Foreman"
System of Related Abstractions	—— —— ——	System of Related Attributes of Good Foremen
Range of Actual Behaviors	— — — — — —	Actual Behaviors of Good Foremen

There are several ways to set about the task of deriving concepts at a workable intermediate level of abstraction:

1. One can start from the top level with a sample of good foremen and by means of tests, interviews, and so forth, attempt to learn how they are like one another and unlike poor foremen. The difficulty here, of course, is that one must select tests or interview items in advance of the actual knowledge of what he is trying to measure. Thus, one is forced to make a large number of irrelevant determinations. Furthermore, unless there is a sufficiently wide variety of instruments employed, one runs the risk of leaving untapped some highly relevant aspects of foremanship.

2. One can also approach the intermediate level of abstraction directly by asking foremen and people associated with them, "What are the attributes of a good assembly line foreman?" The responses to such a question are likely to include *some* of the relevant attributes together with a number of irrelevant factors which, though admirable, do not have anything specific to do with the job in question. Furthermore the adequacy of these abstractions depends on the respondents' ability to formulate explicit generalizations from their own implicit experience. Many people are not accustomed to doing this, and the validity and clarity of their responses suffer thereby.

3. One can approach the desired conceptualization from below by gathering a large number of literal instances of foreman behavior, good and bad, and inductively building up the intermediate abstractions from this material. This last approach, in essence, is the critical incident technique.

At the top level of our conceptual pyramid was the idea, "Effective therapeutic intervention with hyperaggressive children"; at the bottom level were reports of literal behaviors of staff in transactions with the patients. Our belief was that, in this area of clinical pioneering, a philosophy of treatment is gradually being built up out of actual experience on the "battle lines," and that this philosophy must include a set of working concepts about when and how to intervene with the children. (These concepts would be at the intermediate level in the pyramid.) We expected that these concepts would differ in important ways from conventional formulations of psychotherapy because of the special orientation of this treatment program. It was within this context that we wished to consider research on the situation. By using the critical incident technique, we hoped to make explicit some of the implicit principles that our staff members were using, perhaps preconsciously, in their everyday contacts with these very difficult children.

Thus, the levels for our research study could be represented in this way:

Global Concept	———	"Effective Therapeutic Intervention"
System of Related Abstractions	—— —— ——	System of Related Concepts about Therapeutic Interventions
Range of Actual Behaviors	— — — — — —	Actual Staff Interventions

GATHERING AND CLASSIFYING THE INCIDENTS

We gathered our incidents by interviewing periodically all the people who had regular contact with the children: child-care workers, teachers, psychotherapists, administrators, and the director. Each of the 24 respondents was scheduled for a weekly 20-minute interview, held alternately by the two investigators from week to week. In practice we were not able to hold our respondents to this schedule. Some staff turnover occurred during the three months we were interviewing; illness, ward emergencies, and changes in work shift interfered, so that our interviewing was rather uneven. The number of interviews per respondent ranged from two to ten; the number of incidents reported per respondent ranged from three to twenty. Despite these irregularities we have no reason to feel that our information suffered from any systematic bias. In all, we conducted about 130 such brief interviews and collected about 240 of these anecdotal "critical incidents."

The structure of the interview was this: staff members were asked to relate in their own words an actual incident involving a child and an adult (himself or another) in which the adult *did* something which the respondent felt was either good or bad for the child, in terms of the over-all goals of residential treatment. Respondents were urged to be frank. To facilitate this, they were permitted to omit the names of the staff members involved if they preferred. We were not interested in which specific persons were involved. *In each incident we were interested in the description of the child's behavior and of the staff intervention to which a therapeutic value was attached.* At the end of each report we asked the respondent to verbalize the principle or generalization he felt that the incident illustrated.

After one or two such interviews, the respondents understood what was required and would automatically begin recounting incidents. The inter-viewer listened; took notes, asking clarifying questions where necessary; and dictated each incident with its related therapeutic principle as soon as possible. Code names were used for the adults and children involved.

Flanagan recommends that one continue to gather incidents until the point of diminishing returns is reached—where 50 to 100 new incidents do not add any new categories to the system. For reasons of expediency and time, we stopped interviewing with far fewer incidents than we would have liked; thus, our concepts must be regarded as suggestive rather than definitive.

The next step in the procedure was classifying the incidents. We had them typed one to a page and simply began to read and discuss them, building up groups of incidents that seemed to belong together. This is a subjective procedure, particularly at the beginning. One feels his way toward useful categories by searching for common themes underlying the respondents' choice of these incidents to illustrate "good" or "bad" clin-ical handling. After the initial set of concepts had been formulated so that substantially each incident could be assigned to a concept, our analysis took two directions: (1) reformulating the concepts so that they would begin to have some comprehensive relationship to one another, and (2) repeatedly sorting the incidents to provide continuous reference to reality for the emerging system of concepts.

Obviously, a single episode may illustrate more than one important principle of therapeutic handling. In some complex therapeutic incidents we could discern a dozen or more of our principles, plus therapeutic problems beyond the concern of this study. Throughout our work we preferred to assign parsimoniously each incident to the most dominant intervention principle that it illustrated. When concensus seemed impos-sible, the remedy we applied was to conceptualize the events at a still higher level of abstraction, establishing a new category which would express the totality of major issues illustrated by the incident.

In the course of a year our system of concepts passed through three distinct metamorphoses, each requiring a complete re-sorting of the incidents. The final outline is the basis for this report. After this final system of concepts had been developed, we carried out still another complete sorting in order to establish as clear a consensus as possible between us with regard to the category in which an incident was placed.

After these principles had been clearly formulated, it became necessary to exclude a number of incidents. The principal considerations that led us to discard incidents were:

1. The incident was ambiguous as to conditions or intent.
2. The stated value of the staff member ran counter to the generally-held values of the staff (for example, the efficacy of bribing a child) and was clearly an idiosyncratic practice of the respondent, based on some aspect of his personal difficulties in handling the children. We were extremely chary about discarding incidents on this basis, for obvious reasons, and invoked it only a few times.
3. The value, though treatment-relevant, did not actually concern an intervention (for example, communication among staff).

STUDY RESULTS

The final system of principles ordered *most* of the 240 episodes under 31 separate principles of therapeutic intervention with hyperaggressive children. These 31 principles can further be grouped meaningfully under four superordinate headings: (A) Promoting Personality Change; (B) Promoting Ego Growth; (C) Supporting Existing Ego Controls; and (D) A Staff Member's Management of Himself.

We do not consider these 31 principles or the four larger divisions to be in any sense complete. Indeed, we would be pleased if other investigators were motivated to extend both the breadth and depth of our formulations. We submit only that this system represents a careful description of some important aspects of residential treatment technique, with particular reference to problems encountered early in the treatment of hyperaggressive children. We believe secondarily that this system of principles illustrates the usefulness of the critical incident method for clinical research.

We now wish to describe the principles developed. Those grouped under three of the major headings—*promoting personality change, promoting ego growth, and a staff member's management of himself*—will be presented briefly. More detailed attention will be given to those under the heading, *supporting existing ego controls,* since in this area the experiences of our clinical staff were richest and, hence, our elaboration of principles is most extensive.

A. Promoting Personality Change by Helping Child to Learn to View His Own Behavior Evaluatively

1. Therapist[7] accepts temporary regressive modes of relatedness as a necessary step toward growth.
2. Therapist encourages child to talk about his view of symptomatic behavior in proximity to the actual behavior.
3. Therapist verbalizes child's preconscious feelings in order to promote awareness and discussion of them.
4. Therapist gently points out the self-defeating aspects of recent symptomatic behavior.
5. Therapist confronts child with a possible meaning of his immediate symptomatic behavior.
6. Therapist, without being punitive, confronts child with the unacceptability of symptomatic behavior.
7. Therapist limits child's acting out around a specific issue in order to clarify the conflictual basis of the behavior.

Under this heading we included episodes in which a staff person aimed at exposing the child's inner conflicts, at analysis of defensive behavior, or at fostering insight. Category 1 refers to instances in which a child was able to relinquish a pathological defense and direct more openly his infantile yearnings toward the staff member. Categories 2 and 3 describe different ways of helping the child to verbalize the feelings or associations that underlie symptomatic behavior. Three fairly active methods of trying to get the child to forego acting out long enough to take a fresh look at what he is doing are formulated under categories 4–6. The final grouping, 7, refers to limit-setting when this approach serves as a kind of confrontation.

If one chooses the psychotherapeutic process as a frame of reference for thinking about these concepts, category 1 describes an important way in which development of transference elements in the relationship may be fostered. Categories 2, 3, and 5 then may be seen as uncovering techniques aimed at latent content; 2 is based upon the principle of free association; and 3 and 5, upon interpretation. Within the psychotherapeutic context, categories 4, 6, and 7 describe confrontational tactics directed at defensive behavior or resistance.

As a single example of the incidents categorized as *promoting personality change,* the following incident was classified under (3) *Therapist verbalizes child's preconscious feelings in order to promote awareness and discussion of them:*

Ben, in this case a psychotherapist, had been told by one of the teachers that his patient, Sam, had drawn an unusual picture in school. It was all in black;

---

[7] As used in this report, for reasons of simplicity, "therapist" has a broad meaning, denoting any staff person who is in the position of dealing therapeutically with a child (that is, psychotherapist, teacher, group worker, nurse, ward administrator, and so on). Code names "Abe," "Ben," and "Connie" are used randomly to designate any staff member; and "Richard," "Sam," and "Tom" to designate any patient.

three-quarters of the picture was a large black blob, which represented a cliff. A human figure was jumping off this cliff. At the bottom of the cliff Sam had written his name. Several little circles at the bottom of the cliff he referred to as black feces. During the next interview, Ben said that he'd seen Sam's drawing. Sam replied that he meant the picture to be funny; he said he had intended to paint a banjo in the figure's hands. Ben replied that feelings like that probably aren't funny, and that Sam must have been very sad. Sam denied this, but during the next interview began talking about his feelings of sadness. This was the first time that he had been able to talk about his sadness without clowning and masking it with humor.

Clearly, the seven therapeutic tactics formulated under *promoting personality change* are a small beginning if one aspires to a comprehensive inventory of techniques for fostering analytic understanding and insight as part of residential treatment. For example, such an important concept as transference is conspicuously absent from this list. This omission does not imply that we minimize the role of insight or analysis in residential treatment. It may be a function of the fact that only three of the twenty-four respondents were psychotherapists and that the data were gathered during the early resistance phase of treatment.

B. Promoting Ego Growth

1. Therapist welcomes and encourages instances of positive or affectionate relatedness.
2. Therapist fosters rapport with the child by responding to his manifest interests.
3. Therapist assures child that adult support is available to him and encourages him to ask for it when he feels he needs it.
4. Therapist fosters child's self-esteem by helping him to value his own productions.
5. Therapist encourages new learning by responding to the manifest interests of the child.
6. Therapist stimulates child's motivation by judicious use of friendly supportive challenging, but never to the point where the child's control is seriously threatened.
7. Therapist helps child to anticipate the future consequences of a present action.
8. When a child's behavior necessitates forcible intervention, therapist explains clearly to the child why this is necessary.
9. Therapist chooses not to interfere with symptomatic behavior when he feels that the situation's outcome may help to clarify reality for the child.
10. Therapist, recognizing that children often need to "blow off steam," permits this in safe situations.
11. In dealing with disruptive symptomatic behavior, therapist periodically offers the child a chance to control himself before imposing outside management.

The staff procedures described above share the common theme that the therapist is working with the relatively conflict-free portion of the patient's ego. Included are tactics which aim at developing new skills, more satisfying relationships, greater self-esteem, more accurate reality testing, and so forth. Some of the traditional nursing and educational contributions are included here. By setting off this group of concepts, we do not mean to neglect the significance of insight-directed interventions as indirect ways of fostering ego growth, through resolving conflict and hence reducing the ego's involvement in defensive maneuvers. The concepts referred to here, however, are those in which a staff person *directly* fosters positive growth, temporarily bypassing the patient's interpersonal conflicts in order to do so.

Several of these concepts describe situations which are used by the staff member primarily to build rapport or to develop a feeling of genuine closeness with the child, for example, (2) *therapist fosters rapport with the child by responding to his manifest interests.* Throughout this study we have taken great care that the wording of each concept reflect as precisely as possible those incidents it subsumes. For example, (1) *therapist welcomes and encourages instances of positive or affectionate relatedness* was derived both from incidents in which the staff person accepted in a *welcoming* fashion an affectionate advance from the child and from incidents in which the staff person took special steps to *encourage* the child's emergent, more positive but not necessarily affectionate, relatedness.

Greater self-esteem may be stimulated in children who suffer defects in their attitudes toward themselves. The following episode illustrates concept (4) *helping children to value their own productions:*

For a long time Sam had been participating in school only by painting and he had been destroying all his paintings. Connie, in this case a teacher, had consistently encouraged him to save his paintings, adding that she thought it was a pity that he insisted on destroying everything he produced. She had persisted in trying to take the paintings away from Sam before he had a chance to destroy them, but he would always grab them out of her hands and destroy them. In this incident Connie failed to do this and he shouted at her angrily, "Aren't you going to take these f—— pictures out of my hands?" Then a few minutes later he said, in a menacing tone, "If you don't take these g–dd–m pictures, I *am* going to tear them up." Connie took the paintings and he did not take them away from her. Later she exhibited the pictures for all to see. Sam tolerated this for two days and then took them off the wall and destroyed them while accusing Connie of exhibiting them without his permission.

Connie said this was the beginning of a change over the course of many months in which Sam gradually learned to respect a few of his own productions and to save half a dozen of them.

Quite frequently in the early months of treatment with hyperaggressive children, staff members find themselves forced to impose outside controls to assist children to terminate a temper tantrum or an outburst of dangerous destructiveness. This kind of situation may provide opportunities to ask the child who is being held, or is about to be held, if he would like to attempt self-control rather than submit to imposed management. This periodic opportunity for self-control we have viewed as fostering the development of socially acceptable defenses in these primitive egos. Therefore, we have classed these incidents under the rubric *promoting ego growth* (category 11) rather than under *supporting existing ego controls*.

In quite a number of episodes reported to us, the staff member's "intervention" consisted of deliberate non-interference. For example, episodes were reported to us in which a child, motivated by paranoid misperceptions of a peer, leveled false accusations. When it seemed possible to establish this distortion, the child-care worker often chose to accept the obviously delusional accusation as a possibility and then to supervise the participants as they ascertained the facts for themselves. Here the pathological behavior was not interrupted when the staff person believed that the situation's outcome might help the child to clarify reality for himself (category 9).

In reviewing the 11 concepts that arose from those incidents presenting ego growth issues, one may group them into categories with regard to which of the patient's areas of ego function the staff seemed to be working with. For example, the first three categories principally have to do with helping the child to accept an adult relationship involving greater emotional closeness and adult support than the child had been able to permit earlier. The next three categories (4, 5, and 6) describe activity or craft situations in which the child's abilities and constructive motivations are encouraged and challenged. Categories 7, 8, and 9 have to do with certain cognitive defects in these impulsive children: their defective time sense (7); their tendencies toward distorted social perception (8); and their need to discover and test the real social consequences of their acts (9). In a similar frame of reference, categories 10 and 11 are concerned with ego functioning along a gradient of affect expression and impulse control.

PART II[*]

This report is based on a naturalistic but systematic exploration of the intervention concepts used by the staff of a residential center[8] for treating hyperaggressive boys. In Part I we presented the technique used, a modification of Flanagan's "critical incident" method. Part I also presented two groups of the derived concepts: those relating to (A) Promot-

* Reprinted from *Social Casework*, Vol. XXXIX, No. 5 (May, 1958), pp. 286–92. Reproduced by permission of the journal and the authors.

8 Under the direction of Dr. Fritz Redl, Chief, Child Research Branch, Clinical Investigations, National Institute of Mental Health.

ing Personality Change by Helping Child to Learn to View His Own Behavior Evaluatively, and to (B) Promoting Ego Growth, together with some illustrative clinical examples.

C. SUPPORTING EXISTING EGO CONTROLS

Preventive: (Avoid threatening existing ego controls)
1. Therapist recognizes that he is not obligated to interpret or limit symptomatic behavior that is not disruptive or currently operating as resistance.
2. Therapist deliberately avoids mobilizing currently uncontrollable core conflicts.
3. Therapist refrains from confronting child with his psychopathology when the intervention seems likely to generate a disruptive degree of anxiety.

Supportive: (Help child maintain ego controls under special stress)
1. Therapist is alert to situations that are likely to overload children's ego controls and he provides clear supportive structuring:
   a. During program transitions
   b. When props or activities contain high impulse-arousing potential
   c. In the calm periods immediately after blowups
   d. When the children are tired or physically uncomfortable
   e. When one child in a group becomes excited and threatens the controls of the others
   f. In an "open" situation without clear boundaries or sufficient adults to supply the usual constraint
2. Therapist helps child to maintain his ego control in a variety of situations by constantly evaluating the child's current frustration tolerance.
3. Therapist helps child to maintain or regain control by deliberate expression of positive interest.
4. Therapist firmly and clearly limits socially intolerable behavior.
5. When child's motor impulses become disorganized, disruptive, or destructive, therapist introduces an activity that permits a safer, more structured expression of the impulses.

Restitutive: (Help child regain control after temporary failure)
1. Therapist, when setting limits to disapproved behavior, relates the intervention to an established policy.
2. In dealing with a child who is temporarily flooded with anxiety, therapist promotes recovery by:
   a. Permitting the child to regain control in his own way
   b. Giving the child the undivided attention of a trusted adult
   c. Permitting the child as much interpersonal distance as he needs

The great variety of extremely uninhibited actions by these children provided us with a range of concepts about dealing with impulsive or panic behavior. As indicated above, we have formulated these episodes under the general heading of *supporting the patient's existing ego controls*. These interventions are further subclassified as *preventive*, before loss of control; *supportive*, under stress conditions; and *restitutive*, after loss of control. Many negative instances also are included, in which the reporting staff member, in recalling an episode, makes clear in what respect he failed to help the child manage anxiety. Also delineated here are the ego-supportive contributions of clear ward policies, of games, of constructive individual staff-patient and patient-patient relationships, and of the physical properties of the locale.

Preventive.—In the early phases of work with hyperaggressive children, much of the staff's effort must be aimed at avoiding provocation of anxiety in the patients; with very disturbed children this principle creates a difficult challenge for the staff. Certain nuclear conflicts may have to be avoided altogether for the first year or two of treatment, because whenever they are triggered, the child's ego is overwhelmed. In other, less central areas of symptomatic behavior, staff may wish to postpone confrontation or limit-setting until such a time as they feel that the child can integrate some improvement. Obviously, dependable interpersonal bonds must develop between staff and patients before really disturbing areas can be discussed openly or even expediently managed without disrupting effects. This means that, in the first year or two of residential treatment, the most successful strategy in many situations is to *avoid threatening existing ego controls*. A very simple episode of this type follows:

A tutoring session was going on in the room where the turtles were kept. This prevented Richard, who was outside the schoolroom, from feeding his turtle. He became very angry at this and had to be taken to his room. Actually, it would have been fairly simple for the teacher to hand the turtle out to the child and the accompanying child-care worker so that they could feed it in another room somewhere. The reporter felt that in this instance the rule not to interrupt tutoring should have been interpreted more flexibly.

Two of the incidents categorized here present the situation of a symptomatic fire-setter being observed by staff during an experience of pathological fascination with a safe fire. Other episodes where staff chose to follow the principle, *avoid threatening existing ego controls,* included instances in which a child violated a ward policy in a minor and non-disruptive way. Opportunities to intervene around such minor episodes of acting out, though frequent, were often deliberately avoided in this early phase of treatment in order to maintain ego integration.

In the same vein, with regard to certain episodes of major acting out, therapeutic abstinence was indicated simply because any intervention would have destroyed a patient's tenuous control over himself. For example, a hyperactive, highly excited child urinated aggressively on a counselor. Immediately after the episode the ward psychiatrist, following general policy, weighed the indications for an immediate interview with this child. When he observed, however, that the child was on the verge of panic, he decided that the interview itself would only have a disorganizing effect on the child. The procedure decided upon here was to postpone this interview several hours, and thus avoid generating a disruptive degree of anxiety.

Still another group of episodes is illustrated by the following:

Sam had had a bad cut in his leg which required several stitches. Today the Ward Administrator tells him that a doctor is soon coming to take the stitches out. This makes Sam anxious but, as usual, he handles his anxiety by pretending in a masochistic way that he enjoys his fears of bodily injury. He boasts that he is going to have his stitches out and how much fun it will be. Counselor Ben starts teasing Sam in a threatening manner, saying that the doctor is coming up with some big pliers with which he will take the stitches out. At first Sam becomes worried and says, "Oh, Ben, you don't mean that, do you?" and then he starts to punch Ben in a friendly, anxious manner. Ben responds by punching Sam back.

The reporter felt that was very poor handling because Sam's main psychological problem was his sado-masochistic manner of relating to other people. Ben, by encouraging and intensifying this, made Sam more anxious, perpetuating this pathological pattern of behavior.

The principle here is avoiding involvement with the child in patterns of interaction that had in previous instances mobilized his core conflicts and heightened his tension (category 2).

Supportive.—The child-care workers presented us with many episodes illustrating active counteraction of impulse arousal or preventive intervention in situations of rising tension. These we have grouped together under: *help child maintain ego controls under special stress.* The first sub-grouping contains six different types of situations in which the child-care workers were alert to the children's need for special direction: (1) *transitions between activities, places, or portions of the daily program;* (2) *impulse-arousing toys* (such as guns), *localities* (such as a dark, narrow passage), or *activities* (such as competitive racing); (3) *during the "calm" period immediately following a tantrum or group excitement;* (4) *on occasions* (such as toward the end of a rainy camping trip) *when children are physically tired or uncomfortable;* (5) *when the group itself is excitable and one child suddenly becomes contagiously aggressive;* (6) *in localities that have insufficiently secure geographical boundaries* (out in public, for example). Many of these episodes illustrated interesting specific techniques of prevention or early intervention, but we felt our respondents' main emphasis was on the alertness required in order to identify the developing situation in time for effective intervention.

In addition, the data here provided specific tactical suggestions. In some incidents the staff person's main activity was a careful evaluation of the child's current ability to tolerate frustration (category 2). This evaluation might, for instance, determine the vigor with which a counselor competed in a game against a child who hated to lose points, or it might modify the day's assignment of staff to particular children.

Quite often when a child was acting out only to a mild degree or showing preliminary signs of disturbance, this beginning ego disruption was reversed by deliberately responding to the child's immediate wishes (category 3). For example, Connie, a child-care worker, came upon Sam, who was depressed and sullen, having just been reprimanded by another counselor. She noted his dirty socks and offered to get him some clean ones. This simple show of helpful interest produced an immediate change in Sam's mood to one of jovial friendliness. Similarly, in another episode a child arrived at school from a psychotherapeutic interview still living out the fantasy that he was an Indian on the warpath. His face and arms were painted and he hopped excitedly from one desk to another, wanting the other children to pay attention to him. The teacher immediately began following him closely, talking calmly and steadily with him, seeking openings to involve him with her positively. She expressed admiring and curious interest in his exhibitionistic costume. He gradually quieted down and involved himself in the group project with the others.

Among the most common episodes were those in which the children expressed their sadistic or aggressive impulses toward adults or toward a peer scapegoat in a playful, partially controlled manner. Sam, for example, enjoyed shooting a popgun without warning directly in Connie's face. During another period, when a new Negro child had joined the group, several white boys began to taunt him regularly about his color. Or a child would dare another to play with matches or to try to touch a female counselor's breasts. In such situations of provocation, a commonly used staff technique for fostering new attitudes was a clear expression of spontaneous indignation at this behavior, coupled when necessary with firm limits to the disapproved behavior (category 4).

Another widely illustrated principle demonstrates the staff's familiarity with the impulse-channeling effectiveness of a variety of games (category 5). The interventions have in common the strategy of introducing a carefully chosen activity in order to prevent complete loss of control in an excited group. In a typical incident a child-care worker arrived in one of the bedrooms to discover a wild pillow fight in progress which was about to turn into a genuine fight. She quickly announced in an authoritative manner, "Look, if you're going to have a pillow fight, let's do it right! We'll go out in the hall and choose up sides. We'll also have some rules, like: You *throw* the pillows, you don't hang on to them and slug with them."

In a similar episode a counselor arrived on duty to discover that for several hours the boys had been continuously under high tension with frequent tantrums or fights. Therefore, he introduced the game "Pit," which is a noisy, very exciting, but clearly structured card game. The children took to this eagerly and played for an hour. This game permitted the children to express their feelings while maintaining a degree of self-control.

Restitutive.—A final large category of ego support concepts presents situations in which the child's behavior has already become quite impulsive, antisocial, or disorganized and in which the staff's primary task is to help the child recover himself. Obviously, the approach that is comfortable and effective to apply will depend upon a number of variables including the specific behavior, the social situation, the geographical setting, the quality of the relationship between staff member and patient, and the participants' personalities.

In the schoolroom, for example, Richard became furious with Sam, attacked him murderously, and was removed to another room alone with Connie. Still seething with anger, he requested something to eat. Milk and graham crackers were furnished. He then proceeded to crumble the crackers and spill the milk onto the desk, creating a gummy mass which he sloshed into his mouth, smearing himself liberally in the process. In her report to the investigators Connie characterized this behavior as "feeding his panic" and reported that this child was best able to recover ego control in his own individual way (category 2a) .

In another very similar situation, a boy began wildly to destroy objects in the classroom. Upon being removed to a separate room, he seized upon a cardboard box to break up. Responding to this shift from indiscriminate destructiveness to more focused hostility, the worker supplied him with boxes for several minutes until he stopped and smiled gratefully at her.

The data revealed that the staff believes, when dealing with such a disorganized ego state, it is useful (1) *to relate explicitly any active intervention to an established policy* so as to make as clear as possible to the child that the intervention is not arbitrary; (2) immediately *to assign one adult, who is trusted by the child, to remain with the child* until after full recovery; and (3) *during the recovery process to permit the child as much interpersonal distance as he needs.* In regard to the last point, the staff reported that in states of turmoil a too-close attendance on the child frequently remobilized anxiety and extended the difficulty.

D. Managing One's Own Conduct as a Staff Person

1. Therapist attempts to recognize, accept, and deal with his own anxieties as non-destructively as possible.
2. Therapist freely admits his human limitations in the face of children's uncompromising demands.
3. Therapist does not carry permissiveness to the point of tolerating extreme invasions of his personal integrity.

The concepts grouped under this rubric, while they do not strictly describe interventions or techniques, do describe principles that directly affect staff's interventions. In a number of the episodes, staff members experienced difficulty in managing their responses to the children because of mounting anxiety within themselves (category 1) . In two incidents, a staff member found himself in a situation where the children had been promised something which, at the last minute, could not be provided (category 2). Once on a Sunday morning the worker, forgetting about the proximity of the gymnasium to the hospital chapel, suggested a basketball game in the gymnasium. A few moments later, having arrived at the gym with the boys keyed up with anticipation, they discovered that a religious service was in progress which would be disturbed were they to play in the gymnasium. The adult noted within himself a temptation to invent an "alibi" rather than stating the truth about his forgetfulness and taking the inevitable barrage of abuse. In actuality, he admitted his error to the children and could then be more effective in helping them accept the frustration. The sources of stress upon the adult in such a situation are clearly multiple. Weeks of work may have gone into building trust and dispelling what is among hyperaggressive children a commonly held stereotype: "Adults never fulfill their promises." The worker's efforts to handle situations such as these may also be complicated by his sudden insight that his "error" may have expressed unconscious retaliation toward the patients.

During the gathering of data a number of rather dramatic episodes were reported in which a staff member, often a rather inexperienced one, responded with overpermissiveness or inappropriate passivity to a child's manipulations because of a desire to establish greater "trust" in the relationship (category 3). One child obtained the key to the locked ward months before this freedom was indicated, by persuading a new counselor that he would be more trusting and trustworthy if he were given the key. In another episode the only supervising adult submitted to a game in which he was effectively trussed up by the children until he could not move. A similar episode reported from the psychotherapy setting follows:

This incident occurred between Ben, a psychotherapist, and Richard. During the course of an hour, the child began throwing paint powder and water about the room. Ben did not intervene, but instead attempted to discuss this with him. Richard continued to throw water and paint about the room, with his excitement mounting all the time. In a very few moments the floor had become so slippery that Ben was unable to catch him and stop the behavior. At this point he had permitted the situation to become such that he was helpless to exert any outer control when Richard's inner controls were not functioning.

DISCUSSION

These intervention concepts may be applied (1) in developing residential treatment theory; (2) in contributing dimensions for differentiating staff roles; (3) in contributing criteria for staff selection or for evaluation of staff performance; (4) in providing material for use in staff training seminars; and (5) in providing hypotheses for future studies of the intervention techniques used in residential treatment. Before discussing these applications, we must mention again that our frame of reference is the first year of therapy with hyperaggressive children. As noted earlier, within this frame of reference we were able to map out only a portion of the intervention concepts being used by our staff. We hope that extension and modification of this system of principles will be carried out in other treatment settings.

1. Clinical practice often outstrips the development of theory. The basic psychoanalytic theory of therapy has been extended in practice to include modified treatment for kinds of patients who were not encompassed in the original formulations: psychophysiologic disorders, psychotic disorders, "borderline states," and neurotic disturbances in children. Time must pass before knowledge derived from this type of clinical pioneering can be formulated in terms removed from the actual cases. This time lag presents a problem in the extension of treatment theory, since theory can benefit from the refinement and elaboration that results from feedback from clinical practice.

The critical incident technique seems to be well suited to the task of ordering new and complex ideas and of deriving useful generalizations from a confusing mass of particulars. Such a tool assists in bridging the gap between valuable new clinical experiences and more refined or traditional concepts.

2. The 31 principles that emerge from this study describe 31 distinct classes of staff transactions with patients. A number of these concepts are tied to specific group situations, to specific ego states in patients, or to particular types of staff-patient relationship. A fascinating question which tempted us throughout the study is to what extent these tactics are appropriate *for all staff* who enter into a therapeutic relationship with these children. Or are some of these interventions quite role-specific? In either case, concepts such as these might be used as dimensions in research on the ever present problem of role-clarification and role-differentiation in the therapeutic team. And if a broader basis is sought for defining staff roles than that of intervention concepts alone, the critical incident method provides a means of tapping and integrating staff experiences. The generalizations that result from such a survey can point up both the similarities and differences in the contributions of ward administrator, psychotherapist, teacher, and child-care worker.

3. Related to role-definition are the problems of staff selection and staff evaluation. Investigators as well as clinicians encounter such questions as, "What kind of person makes a good child-care worker in this particular operation?" This, of course, is precisely the kind of question that the critical incident technique has been developed to answer for the armed services and industry. The dimensions that grow out of such a job

description study can be embodied in a selection instrument, the validity of which can be assessed in actual practice. Extremely relevant is the recent study by Wright[9] in which a Q-sort instrument based upon four critical concepts was able to predict success or failure in new child-care workers in a residential treatment school.

4. The classified episodes resulting from a critical incident study can also be useful in orienting and training new staff members. We are in the process of developing a training handbook incorporating our own study. The intervention categories are to be presented, each illustrated by a selection of the incidents that define the category. Such an arrangement can expose a new worker to a wide range of child-handling situations in a comparatively short time, as well as give him at least the outlines for a therapeutic point of view. Material organized in this way can provide the content for a series of training seminars and discussions. To avoid an oversimplified application of these concepts as a kind of "prescription," it is obviously important that this training material be used by competent supervisory clinicians who can present these tactical issues within the perspective of total residential treatment.

5. Finally, a critical incident study can be a very useful first step in developing a program of research based on a complex clinical operation. The system of concepts which results can help clarify the interrelationships within the staggeringly complex situations one commonly encounters in our field. A critical incident study can help investigators to develop a conceptual model of the operation and thus to plan a systematic research program at an appropriate level of complexity. For example, instead of focusing critical incident interviews as we did around the issue of therapeutic handling, one could focus such interviews with staff around other relevant issues: the patient behaviors that are conceived of as an expression of psychopathology, the group situations that are considered to have a therapeutic impact, criteria for judging improvement during residential treatment, and so forth. In some circumstances it might be possible to set up such interviews with patients themselves to elicit common themes in their own perceptions of the treatment experience.

One should bear in mind that the focus for the data-gathering interview limits the kinds of concepts which can be abstracted from the episodes. Our interest in hearing reports of interventions led the staff to report behavior within a context that highlighted intervention issues. Reports given within this specific context then contributed toward a conceptual framework designed to characterize and organize these iden-

---

9 Benjamin Wright, "Attitude Toward Emotional Involvement and Professional Development in Residential Child Care," unpublished manuscript, Orthogenic School, University of Chicago, 1957.

tical issues. Any attempt to use these same critical incidents to build a conceptual framework around different treatment issues not focused upon in the interview would seem unwarranted.

Second, none of these applications of the critical incident method can substitute for later rigorous investigations which test these concepts. In our own study, for example, we have no way of knowing to what extent the episodes reported to us *actually* were effective or ineffective. Further studies are necessary to determine whether our intervention concepts really are as useful as their wording would imply.

SUMMARY

Employing a modification of the critical incident technique, we collected 240 incidents of interventions with hyperaggressive children in residential treatment. From these data a system of intervention principles was evolved at an intermediate level of abstraction between the global concept, "effective therapeutic intervention," and the actual intervention incidents. These concepts characterize 31 intervention categories that seem to be particularly relevant to treatment problems posed to the staff by hyperaggressive children during their initial year in residential treatment.

Further development of such intervention concepts for other treatment settings and patients of differing ages or psychopathology would seem desirable. If further studies can be carried out using the critical incident technique, one might look forward eventually to having a relatively complete descriptive classification for therapeutic interventions. Such a classification would be a major contribution to research on residential treatment and the training of therapeutic personnel.

W. JOSEPH HEFFERNAN, JR.

18 *Political Activity and
Social Work Executives**

During the past two decades political and social action has become a
muted voice in social work circles. The kind of distinctly political activity
that was once so vitally a part of the social work operation is seldom seen
today. Certainly social workers of today are as vitally concerned with the
problems of those in need as were Jane Addams, Edith Abbott, and
Harry Hopkins. However, the means social workers have chosen to affect
those needs have become drastically altered. It is the purpose of this
paper to explore some of the reasons for and implications of this changed
pattern of social action activities.

EXPERT PROFESSIONAL DECORUM

Both historically and conceptually social work activities have been insep-
arably linked to governmental policy. There is a clear authoritative
statement on the social worker's obligation to concern himself with policy
questions in *Goals of Public Social Policy,* adopted by the Delegate
Assembly of the National Association of Social Workers in 1955 and
subsequently revised at the 1958 and 1962 Assemblies:

Social work is the profession which concerns itself with the facilitating and
strengthening of basic social relationships between individuals, groups, and
social institutions. It has, therefore, a social action responsibility which derives
directly from its social function and professional knowledge. This responsibility
lies in the following three areas: (a) the identification, analysis, and interpretation of specific unmet needs among individuals and groups of individuals,
(b) advancing the standard of recognized social obligations between society and
its individual members so that those needs will be met and a more satisfying
environment for all achieved, and (c) the application of specific knowledge,
experience, and inventiveness to those problems which can be solved through
social welfare programs.[1]

The method of effecting this influence is similarly prescribed:

In areas of social policy and program in which the profession of social work plays
a central or major facilitating role, its social action function involves the additional component of professional knowledge concerning organization and opera-

* Reprinted with permission of the author, and the National Association of Social
Workers, from *Social Work*, Vol. 9, No. 2 (April, 1964), pp. 18–23.
[1] New York: National Association of Social Workers, 1963, p. 10.

tion, policy implications, financing requirements, and personnel standards without which successful social policy can be neither made nor implemented. In the growing complexity of modern social organization, both governmental and voluntary, few policy-makers can be expected to have the technical knowledge implicit in all the fields of social responsibility with which they deal. Nor is it socially desirable that they should be exclusively dependent on those who administer such policies and programs for their guidance. The professional social work organization has, therefore, a positive responsibility to make the technical knowledge and experience of its membership available to those who make social welfare policies, whether in legislative, administrative, or community leadership capacities.[2]

The text writers emphasize this view that the social worker should involve himself as an expert and with proper professional decorum. This is especially true, the fledgling social worker is advised, when he is acting in his role as an agency representative. As a clear example of this, Kenneth L. M. Pray has stated *the* three principles applying to the participation of social welfare agencies in social action: the agency should (1) act only within the limits of the actual agreements of its lay and professional elements, (2) act only in areas appropriate to its function, and (3) not engage in partisan politics.[3]

These same views have been retained and are postulated in current textbooks on social welfare. Arthur Dunham, an acknowledged leader in the field of community organization, has written as follows:

The social worker may properly be an adherent of any cause on the basis of his convictions, but his acceptance of a role of leadership, or public advocacy on matters involving essentially technical issues should normally be within his area of professional or avocational competence.[4]

This prescription is, in Dunham's view, even more binding in questions of a "partisan nature." Referring to the impropriety of social workers involving themselves in political battles he had this to say:

... this principle would seem to apply rather strictly to partisan politics but not to nonpartisan social welfare issues. The Michigan Legislature passed what many social workers regarded as a superior social welfare reorganization act in 1937. The act came before the voters in 1938. Here the issue was nonpartisan (the act had been sponsored by both Republicans and Democrats) and there was no reason as far as partisan politics was concerned why a voluntary social agency should not support or oppose the act in this election on its merits.[5]

Further, this "expert professional decorum" approach to the formulation of welfare policy is given even more authoritative sanction in the

---

2 *Ibid.*, p. 11.

3 "Social Workers and Partisan Politics," *Compass*, Vol. 26, No. 5 (June, 1945), pp. 3–6.

4 *Community Welfare Organization* (New York: Thomas Y. Crowell Company, 1958), p. 63.

5 *Ibid.*, p. 59.

prescriptions of the ethical code of the former American Association of Social Workers:

In public statements or actions the social worker should make clear whether he is acting or speaking as an individual or as a delegated representative of a professional association or agency, and, at all times, be accurate, exercise proper restraint and show respect for the opinions of others.

This principle was retained in the new, and briefer, Code of Ethics of the existing professional organization, NASW: "I distinguish clearly, in public, between my statements and actions as an individual and as a representative of an organization."[6]

Current social work literature further explains, or justifies, this approach on a variety of grounds. Principal among these are: (1) the social worker's fear that political participation will do damage to the professional image, (2) the belief that the social worker's effectiveness depends on the confidence of policy-makers in his expertness and the value of his counsel, (3) the fact that since men of many political and ideological persuasions sit on private (and public) agency boards and strong action by the professionals on a peripheral issue may weaken their hand with the board on questions that are central to the agencies' operation, and (4) the fear of losing potential allies in future battles. Sanford Solender has indicated that these beliefs do not mean that social workers should not engage in public policy formulation; they do mean that social workers should follow newer and more effective forms of social action. He indicates that the new methods advocated are: (1) study and analysis of the issues leading to expert recommendations and remedial programs and (2) organized advocacy of particular courses of action through various professional and employment organizations.[7]

It should be pointed out that this pattern is not unique for social work. In fact, it seems to be almost the universal practice of professionals in all fields today. They seem to advocate nonpartisan expertness as the preferred role.[8]

LIMITED ROLE OF EXECUTIVE

Does the working executive agree with and follow these prescriptions of his profession in his own conception of his role in the formulation of welfare policy? From a pilot study, based on interviews with eight execu-

---

[6] *NASW News,* Vol. 6, No. 2 (February, 1961), p. 14.

[7] "Public Social Policy and Social Work Practice," *Social Work,* Vol. 3, No. 1 (January, 1958), pp. 3–11.

[8] *See* Herbert A. Simon, Donald W. Smithberg, and Victor A. Thompson, *Public Administration* (New York: Alfred A. Knopf, 1950); Harold Stein, *Public Administration and Policy Development* (New York: Harcourt, Brace & World, 1952); and Morris Janowitz, *Professional Soldier* (Glencoe, Ill.: Free Press, 1960), chap. 12.

members called, I could have told them to read the whole report, other social workers felt as I. But I couldn't do that. The aged weren't helped and my agency was hurt; the next time I will be for meals on wheels.

These comments indicate that the executives are placed in a position in which they feel they must follow the prescriptions of the profession. They seem to recognize that the expert-professional decorum approach, while necessary, lacks the central ingredients of really effective change. A community organization worker, commenting on the probe, "Some people say the Democratic party is more in accord with the goals that social workers hold for society and therefore social workers should be active as individuals in the Democratic party," demonstrated the bind that the social work executive feels he is in:

I agree with the statement in terms that I vote Democratic. I believe that it's true from a more logical point of view too. But I have to put over a fund drive so I refrain from playing an active role in the party. ——— County is solidly Republican and the people I work with in the community are prominent in that party. My own identification with the Democratic party might hurt the fund drive and I simply can't afford to do that.

PARTISAN NATURE OF WELFARE POLICY QUESTIONS

The clearest finding of this exploratory study is that social work executives feel it is necessary to avoid partisan identification. Some, at least, feel that the alternative approach of organized advocacy based on expert analysis can be equally, if not more, effective.

First, it is necessary to explore the partisan nature of social service and welfare policy questions. An examination of the voting records of the Michigan congressmen reveals that these questions are indeed highly partisan. A review of six selected issues in which NASW had indicated a preference of policy alternatives and for which a roll call was available in the *Congressional Quarterly Almanac* demonstrates that Democratic congressmen are far more likely to vote in a manner consistent with the recorded preferences of NASW than are Republicans. On the six issues the Democratic Index of Agreement was 1.00, while the Republican Index of Agreement was .375. If these issues are representative—and there is strong statistical evidence that they are (see Table 2)—then the choice between alternative patterns of dealing with welfare questions is partisan whether social workers like it or not.[9]

Further considerations have to be made but the central question is: Does the partisan nature of welfare questions imply that social work professionals, individually and collectively, ought to be partisan? Would

---

[9] Michigan politics are considerably bipolarized as a result of large city–small town out-state split. The liberal-conservative division is probably sharper here than in a "typical" state.

partisan identification inhibit the forward momentum of welfare goal achievement?

The social work literature seems to imply that the expression of social work's special knowledge will be sufficient to alter the patterns of voting. Without intending to question the intellectual capacity of our legislative

TABLE 2

VOTING RECORDS OF MICHIGAN CONGRESSMEN

	Issues						Index of Agreement with NASW
	1	2	3	4	5	6	
O'Hara (D.)	+	+	+	+	+	+	1.00
Ryan (D.)	+	+	+	+	+	+	1.00
Diggs (D.)	+	+	+	+	+	+	1.00
Lesinski (D.)	+	+	+	+	0	+	1.00
Nedzi (D.)	+	0	+	+	+	+	1.00
Griffiths (D.)	+	0	+	+	+	+	1.00
Dingell (D.)	+	0	+	+	+	+	1.00
Broomfield (R.) ...	+	+	+	—	0	—	.60
Bennett (R.)	0	0	+	+	—	—	.50
Knox (R.)	+	+	+	—	—	—	.50
Harvey (R.)	+	+	—	—	—	—	.33
Chamberlin (R.) ...	+	+	—	—	—	—	.33
Ford (R.)	+	+	—	—	+	—	.50
Meader (R.)	—	+	+	—	0	—	.40
Griffin (R.)	+	—	+	—	0	—	.40
Cederberg (R.)	+	—	0	—	—	—	.20
Hoffman (R.)	0	—	0	0	—	0	.00
Johansen (R.)	—	—	—	—	—	—	.00
Total +'s	14	10	12	8	7	7	

+ = Agreement with NASW
— = Disagreement with NASW
0 = No vote
Democratic Index of Agreement = 1.00
Republican Index of Agreement = 3.75

CR = 1-7/94 = .925
Coefficient of reproducibility = .925
(When CR = .900 the variable under consideration is said to be dominant.)

servants, to say that a congressman decides on a bill on the basis of the logical consistency of the pro and con arguments would do considerable damage to history. This notion also does violence to most of the theoretical concepts of political decision-making, at least as they have been defined in the last decade. The medicare bill, for example, has in one of its variant forms been before almost every session of Congress since 1934. In each of these sessions, committee hearings were held and the documents have poured forth. There is serious doubt that there is any argument pro or con that has not been placed before the House Ways and Means or Senate Finance Committees. To provide further expert analysis would be of little marginal value and it would be better to elect to Congress men who, from their record, indicate they will vote for medicare.

The central question, however, is: Would such a partisan position do damage to social workers' professional image or cost them allies in future battles? Political scientists sometimes speak of "co-optation," according to which a group takes into its midst those who are potential opponents, thus neutralizing them as a political force. Is it not possible that social workers are being co-opted by the men of conservative leanings on agency boards? It seems that the executive who lamented lost opportunity when asked to comment on the needs of the aged had the right idea, for if all social workers stood firm boards would soon learn that they are dealing with political liberals who cannot be co-opted from their stand. Such a position would require partisan identification, but political science research indicates that, although it is not the exclusive basis for measurement, the political party is the principal indicator for preferences of policy.[10] In treatment services social workers rely heavily on the findings of related academic disciplines. At a minimum it seems that before partisan positions are eschewed social work should explore seriously the empirical findings of political science. In view of the continuing vigor of the social work reform movement and the abundance of reform literature, it seems appropriate to subject the dogmas of reform to empirical and analytical tests. This has not been done. It is by no means clear that assuming the position of the expert implies that one has to abandon informed political and partisan activity.

---

[10] V. O. Key, *Public Opinion and American Democracy* (New York: Alfred A. Knopf, 1961), p. 432.

LEON R. JANSYN, JR.

19 | *Solidarity and Delinquency in a Street-Corner Group**

Questions have been raised as to whether gangs may be more usefully viewed as integrated groups, in the manner of Whyte's description of the Nortons[1] as mob-like assemblages under the leadership of disturbed persons,[2] or as loosely organized collectivities.[3,4] The data presented here from the study of one group over a long period of time help in determining the relative merits of these perspectives.

This study reveals (1) that severely delinquent gangs can have a relatively high degree of organization and (2) that such a gang can go. through phases of organization and disorganization and increases and decreases of solidarity. A realistic appreciation of the properties of the group can only be gained through extended, continuous observation.

The study is an attempt not to explain delinquency but to illuminate some of the ways in which variations in group activity are related to internal processes of the group and variations in group structure over time. Knowledge of such processes aids in the understanding of the episodic character of gang delinquency.[5]

Recent theories of gang delinquency are not explicit about the effects of the internal dynamics of the gang. There are many hypotheses about what goes on in gangs. Delinquency is learned; many personal needs are met; identities are formed; and techniques of neutralization, and rationalizations are developed and exercised. Perhaps most relevant to this study is the implication from Cohen's theory that the gang enhances the enthusiasm of the boys for delinquency, and Short's idea that participation in the gang affects aleatory elements, changing the probabilities of delinquency. For example, participation in the core group of a gang seems

---

* Reprinted with permission of the author, and the American Sociological Association, from *American Sociological Review,* Vol. 31, No. 5 (October, 1966), pp. 600–14.

1 William F. Whyte, *Street Corner Society,* Chicago: University of Chicago Press, 1943.
2 Lewis Yablonsky, "The Delinquent Gang as a Near Group," *Social Problems,* 7 (Fall, 1959), pp. 108–17.
3 Harold W. Pfautz, "Near Group Theory and Collective Behavior," *Social Problems,* 9 (Fall, 1961), pp. 167–74.
4 James F. Short, "Street Corner Groups and Patterns of Delinquency: A Progress Report," *American Catholic Sociological Review,* 24 (Spring, 1963), pp. 13–32.
5 James F. Short, and Fred L. Strodtbeck, "The Response of Gang Leaders to Status Threats: An Observation on Group Process and Delinquent Behavior," *American Journal of Sociology,* 68 (March 1963), pp. 571–79.

to have implications for the future illegitimate parenthood of the members. Status in the gang is as much a response to the changing structure of the group as it is an aspect of individual learning, needs or proclivities. The boys act with regard to the conditions within the gang. Here solidarity is evaluated as a dimension of the condition of the gang; knowledge of this dimension is necessary to understand the activity of the boys.[6]

The subjects were the Dons, an informal, autonomous, severely delinquent adolescent group.[7] This group was studied more or less systematically by direct observation over a period of five and one-half years. The author observed the group for slightly over two years. The data reported here cover fifteen months, during its fourth and fifth years. The data have been analyzed to show patterns of membership participation, changes in organization, and fluctuations in the frequency of the members' engagement in certain types of activity. The analysis leads to the recognition of an important relationship between organization and activity, and to a tentative general hypothesis: In corner groups deterioration of group solidarity is followed by an increase of group activity and a revival of solidarity.

METHOD AND SETTING OF STUDY

Two kinds of data are available for analysis, attendance records and daily narrative reports of group activities. The first are records of which boys participated with the group each day. These provide basic descriptions of the group. An index of solidarity is derived from the records of the daily number of man-hours which members of the group spent together during specified hours.

Social roles are revealed by the data. The attendance data are of

---

6 Examination of group factors in delinquency, especially those factors having to do with processes in the group, has been closely restricted to observation in an institutional setting; the observation of such a group process in the natural setting is quite uncommon. See Short and Strodtbeck, *op. cit.* p. 592.

7 Yablonsky, *op. cit.*, in his discussion of "near groups" points out that a gang may be the product of the attention of "detached workers": "Approaching the gang as a group, when it is not, tends to project onto it a structure which formerly did not exist." This is especially likely to happen in studies which do not make detailed observations over a long period of time. But even informal observation can establish the validity of a conception of a number of boys as a group. For example, in the case presented here, the group persisted for a number of years before and after the study was done and it was recognized as a group with a name by numerous adolescents, adults of the community, social workers, and the police and courts. The group, including a conception of who were members and some idea of a structure, existed several years before the author arrived. These conceptions were contained in written records of former observations of the group, and it was in terms of these conceptions that he was introduced to the group. The author's informal experiences with the group and all the above mentioned people confirmed the existence of this consensus as to the identity and reality of the group.

particular interest in this respect; they permit the distinction of two role patterns of participation, core members and fringe members. Concentration of attention on role-specific patterns of attendance is believed to be warranted: the relationship of attendance to activity suggests that these patterns may be as significant to the outcome of behavior as the more usual forms of role behavior such as planning, leading or directing.

Written daily accounts of the group's activity make up a second body of data. From these data we derive descriptions of the level of group organization and a chronology of group activity. The description of changing levels of organization is used to validate man-hours as an index of solidarity. In the last section of the paper changes in group organization are shown to parallel roughly the solidarity index. In this section we also investigate the relationship between the index of solidarity (viewed as the independent variable) and variations in group activity (viewed as the dependent variable).

The observer resided in the Don's neighborhood, and associated with the group as a "detached worker."[8] Systematic recording of the participation of the members was begun after three months of close association with the boys.

The activities of the group were observed by staying with the boys at their current gathering-place for the entire evening. Usually they assembled on a particular street corner. They also spent much time in either of two restaurants and in a recreational agency clubroom. They participated in the recreational agency as an agency club; a number of girls were members. Most of these girls were close friends of the boys and associated with them nightly outside of recreational agency club meetings. The girls formed a street-corner group in their own right, with a name. It resembled what has been referred to in the literature as an "auxiliary."

The observations were recorded in a diary. Participation was recorded by notation of the persons who were gathered in the group on each of 197 days over a period of one year.[9] Notations were also made of the persons

---

[8] The observer was employed by a civic group of local residents, whose sanction was invaluable to the research. This group had employed, over the years, a number of young men to associate with and, hopefully to influence some of the more troublesome boys in the area. Records of this work, including daily accounts of the activity of the Dons, the preceding and succeeding groups on their corner, and other similar groups, were valuable in understanding the boys' activity. The civic group has been working in varying degrees of intensity with groups and persons in this neighborhood for over twenty years in efforts to prevent delinquency. Much of the work has been conducted in cooperation with a state welfare agency. The detached worker program was coordinated with similar activities in a city-wide program. The wealth of information and experience represented by these efforts has been a source as well as a test for some of the ideas presented here.

[9] These days were scattered throughout the year. The author deliberately made his work week irregular, and varied days off from week to week. Occasionally other duties would keep him from meeting the group. Sundays are somewhat underrepresented in

who were present during each hour of the period from 7:30 to 10:30 p.m. on 149 of these days. The days were selected essentially by chance.

The study was conducted in a neighborhood where groups such as the Dons are commonplace. It is an inner-city workingclass neighborhood, one-half square mile in area, located two miles from the central business district. It ranks at the 85th percentile among the areas of the city according to the rates of official delinquency. For the past 25 years there has been extensive demolition of residential property in and adjacent to the neighborhood. This property has been replaced by a large public housing project and light industrial buildings. Further extensive slum clearance and redevelopment is planned for the area. It has been an area of first settlement of a series of immigrant groups, of which the Italians were the last major group; the ethnic composition is now mixed. From 1940 to 1957 the total population decreased from 27,145 to 24,074. However, there is a small but increasing number of Negro residents in the public housing projects.

A traditional, institutional form of association among male adolescents and young adults in the neighborhood is the social athletic club. Such clubs have been useful as mutual-aid societies and have assisted members in their aspirations toward occupational and social mobility. Though the use of this institutional form has declined, boys very often form autonomous groups with a view toward becoming such a club, hoping eventually to rent private premises for their gatherings.

The boys in the Dons were 14 to 16 years of age at the beginning of the study. Members of groups such as the Dons make up a large proportion of the very numerous official delinquents from this area. Of the 45 boys brought to the court from this area during the year of the study, nine were members of the Dons. Fifteen were members of the two groups which preceded and succeeded the Dons on their corner. Twenty-six of the 60 members of the Dons were adjudged delinquent by the county court at some time.

The possession of private premises is an ideal. There were ten or fifteen adolescent groups in the neighborhood who had such. Most are not long in the boys' possession; a group may have three or four stores during its career. The Dons succeeded, with the author's help, in renting a store several months after the study. They were unable to maintain this after the author left the area. After a period of having no store, they again rented one. This too, lasted only a few months.

The Dons also participated each year in the program of a recreational agency, and in this way obtained a clubroom. They were not all equally

the observations. When the author arrived after 7:30 p.m. or left before 10:30 p.m., it was not possible to observe the man-hours. Therefore a number of days had to be left out of the sample. There was no indication that the days observed differ in any systematic way from those not observed.

enthusiastic about this arrangement and there was constant division and contention, between those who were in favor of agency membership and those who were not. This contention divided the Dons into two overlapping and co-existing subgroups, the gang and the club. It was usual for the boys to assemble at a restaurant after the agency closed. The attendance at these two places reflected the division of the group.

ANALYSIS OF ATTENDANCE DATA

Membership, for the purpose of this study, is defined as the status of a boy who is observed to associate with the group with enough regularity to become familiar to the observer *and* who receives recognition as a member by at least two of the other boys.[10] Because attendance is often resumed after extended absences, all members were regarded as permanent during the year of observation.[11] Cumulative group membership increased during the year from 28 to 60 boys. Since the author associated with the boys for three months before this increase took place, he is fairly certain that almost all the additions were actually new members. Association with the group by some of these boys was infrequent and of short duration.

Attendance is defined as an observed appearance of a member with the group on any given evening during the hours of 7:30 to 10:30 p.m. The evening hours were chosen because this is the time most boys are present, and the time that external commitments to work, school, or family are least likely to intervene. Also, the attendance record is used to compare one day with another. It is more important then, that the criteria be permanent from day to day than that they result in a full representation of experience.

ATTENDANCE AND TIME SPENT TOGETHER

There are two problems in the analysis of the attendance data: first, to observe change in the descriptive categories, and second, to use these attendance data to assess variables related to solidarity and role. The

---

10 In no case was a boy's attendance as a member recorded until one week after his first observed appearance. Membership in a gang is a vague status and has not been precisely defined in the literature. For example, in Short's and Strodtbeck's researches in Chicago, the identification of members was largely a matter of the judgment of the "detached worker," it was not operationally defined, and the worker's criteria were not specified in detail. This is due both to the condition of field work and the diffuseness of gang membership itself. Objectivity was maintained by means of weekly interviews of the "detached workers" and by field observations by the research staff. See Short and Strodtbeck, "Street Corner Groups and Patterns of Delinquency," *op. cit.*, p. 17.

11 The purpose of this was to avoid the possibility of failing to record the attendance of any boy who, though absent for an extended period, for example by being in jail, was still important to the group. If such an absent member never returned, nothing would be lost, because the data refer only to boys whose presence with the group was actually observed.

final assessment of solidarity is made by use of daily man-hours spent together by the group.[12] In regard to the first problem, which is essentially one of description, the variables were selected with a view toward practicality and the ability of the variables to reflect changes in the dynamics and structure of the group. The data are presented in a summary fashion in Table 1. The semi-monthly means of all variables are reported. The first half of October and the first half of September are not reported. There were only two observations in the first instance and none in the latter.

COMPOSITIONAL STABILITY

Questions of solidarity obviously cannot be completely answered by means of daily man-hours. The attempt to use attendance data to assess solidarity, however, led to the assessment of compositional stability. Although this approach did not appear to result in a usable index of group solidarity, it provided interesting descriptive statistics concerning social roles in the group, and important corroboration for a number of the conclusions about roles, interpersonal relationships, and the structure of influence.

The assessment of compositional stability made it necessary to further limit the definition of the unit because a relatively constant interval between days to be compared is needed. Thus comparisons were made of all pairs of days in which the days were next to one another or separated by one day. For the entire study this procedure resulted in a reduction of the sample to one of 134 days, which is used in all presentations of attendance data.

The variable used to measure compositional stability is the duplication rate. The duplication rate for any pair of consecutive days is the ratio of the number of boys present on both days (counted twice) to the number of boys present on either day. The higher the rate, the more similar the composition of the group on those two days. The results of these calculations are presented in Table 2. The mean duplication rate for the group for the year was 0.63. This type of analysis is useful for questions of the extent to which the group is composed of the same persons from time to time.

An attempt was made to compare attendance at times more widely separated. Ten pairs of days were selected randomly, each pair having one day in October and one day in the following September. The mean was 0.68; accordingly, two-thirds of the group was likely to be the same at times separated by a year. The same method was applied to samples between October and each other month. January and February

---

12 Numerous indices of solidarity were attempted, some of which are described next. This one was chosen because of its concreteness, direct observability, objectivity and simplicity.

were very low and March the lowest, when paired with October. It is noteworthy that in March the group participated in an episode of mob violence and attracted the attention and constant surveillance of the police. The first half of March shows some of the lowest values for the measures in Tables 1 and 2, but the very low fringe duplication rates reveal that even this low level of attendance was achieved by a large number of different boys rather than by one group. The core group

TABLE 1

SEMI-MONTHLY MEANS OF DAILY ATTENDANCE VARIABLES AND NUMBER OF GROUP ACTIVITIES

	Attendance			Daily Man-Hours			Hours per Boy			No. of Days	Activities*		
	Core	Fringe	Total	Core	Fringe	Total	Core	Fringe	Total		A.G.	D.G.	I.D.
Oct.	—	—	—	—	—	—	—	—	—	—	2	2	4
	6.6	7.0	13.6	15.0	11.3	26.3	2.3	1.6	2.0	7	4	2	4
Nov.	8.0	12.3	20.3	22.7	24.3	47.0	2.8	2.0	2.3	3	2	0	0
	6.9	9.7	16.6	16.1	18.3	34.4	2.2	1.9	2.0	9	1	0	1
Dec.	6.9	10.5	17.4	15.8	19.9	35.6	2.3	1.9	2.1	8	0	0	2
	5.3	7.8	13.0	12.8	18.8	31.5	2.4	2.5	2.4	4	2	0	4
Jan.	6.9	6.1	13.0	15.3	11.0	26.0	2.2	1.8	2.0	8	2	0	0
	7.0	10.3	17.3	16.6	18.6	35.3	2.4	1.8	2.0	8	1	0	1
Feb.	5.7	7.5	13.2	12.7	12.6	24.8	2.1	1.5	1.9	11	1	0	1
	5.4	8.3	13.7	12.7	17.4	30.1	2.3	2.1	2.2	7	1	1	1
Mar.	5.5	5.3	10.8	14.3	11.2	25.5	2.6	2.0	2.4	6	3	2	4
	6.9	6.7	13.6	17.6	13.6	31.1	2.5	1.8	2.3	7	0	0	0
Apr.	7.8	11.0	18.8	20.4	24.6	45.0	2.6	2.3	2.4	5	1	1	0
	6.5	11.8	18.3	15.3	19.5	34.8	2.4	1.7	1.9	6	1	0	0
May	7.6	11.0	18.6	15.2	21.2	36.4	2.0	1.9	1.9	5	1	0	2
	6.2	9.0	15.2	13.2	16.0	29.2	2.2	1.8	1.9	5	1	0	3
June	6.7	9.7	16.3	16.0	16.7	32.7	2.4	1.7	2.0	3	1	1	0
	6.0	8.8	14.8	15.0	15.8	30.8	2.5	1.8	2.1	4	1	0	1
July	7.3	8.0	15.3	15.7	13.7	26.4	2.2	1.7	1.9	7	0	0	3
	8.7	8.0	16.7	18.3	14.0	32.3	2.1	1.7	1.9	3	1	0	2
Aug.	6.6	4.6	11.2	14.8	8.8	23.6	2.0	1.4	2.0	5	0	0	1
	6.7	8.1	14.9	14.9	14.9	29.7	2.3	1.8	2.0	7	1	1	4
Sept. ...	—	—	—	—	—	—	—	—	—	—	2	2	0
	8.0	7.8	15.8	19.0	15.3	34.3	2.4	2.0	2.2	6	1	1	1
Mean ...	6.7	8.5	15.2	15.6	15.8	31.4	2.3	1.8	2.1	—	—	—	—
Standard Deviation	0.9	2.0	2.4	2.4	4.0	5.7	0.2	0.2	0.2	—	—	—	—
Totals.	—	—	—	—	—	—	—	—	—	134	30	13	39

* A.G. = activity of the entire group
  D.G. = delinquencies of the entire group
  I.D. = delinquencies of individuals and cliques

showed different characteristics. Although it had an attendance and man-hours value in early March which were below the means for the year, its duplication rate was near the mean, indicating that the few boys who did participate early in March did so with greater regularity than did the fringe members. However, a word of caution needs to be added to this interpretation. The instability of the winter months as reflected in the duplication rate is partly due to low attendance because of cold weather.

CORE MEMBERS

Prior to analysis of the attendance data, and based on reported daily observations of group activity, nine boys were identified as core members. The criteria used were ability to influence the behavior of other boys,

TABLE 2

SEMI-MONTHLY MEANS OF DUPLICATION RATES

	Core	Fringe	Total	N*
Oct.	—	—	—	—
	.76	.30	.58	6
Nov.	.90	.55	.68	3
	.75	.55	.65	10
Dec.	.81	.63	.69	8
	.78	.55	.64	3
Jan.	.77	.45	.62	12
	.81	.59	.68	9
Feb.	.65	.46	.55	15
	.45	.47	.49	5
Mar.	.74	.27	.53	5
	.73	.30	.55	7
Apr.	.89	.55	.70	6
	.76	.65	.70	6
May	.79	.69	.73	7
	.83	.31	.52	4
June	.85	.48	.63	3
	.86	.67	.75	4
July	.81	.50	.65	6
	.70	.63	.67	3
Aug.	.71	.62	.67	4
	.82	.41	.62	6
Sep.	—	—	—	—
	.91	.47	.69	5
Mean	.76	.51	.63	—
Standard Deviation	.18	.21	.14	—

* N refers to the number of pairs of days in which days were next to one another or separated by one day.

and ability to attract a following.[13] The same nine boys were later identified by means of the quantitative attendance data.

---

[13] The identification of core members by any method which is demonstrably objective is difficult in this kind of field operation. Attendance records are useful; in this case they support the judgment of the author. There is, however, the need to assess characteristics like status and influence. For example, the boy who makes no suggestions or whose suggestions are often rejected is presumed to be of low status. Attracting a following is seen especially well in changes of meeting places, as described below.

This problem recurs in the literature; explicit definitions of status, and the criteria observed are not always stated operationally. See Whyte, op. cit., pp. 11–14, 326–27, and Short and Strodtbeck, "The Response of Gang Leaders to Status Threats" loc. cit. pp. 577–79. Short and Strodtbeck discuss the complexity of (often deliberately concealed) status in the gang. An operational definition is obviously difficult; Short and Strodtbeck offer no such definition in this article. In the present research it is extremely important that the author's judgment of status be supported, at least in the case of "core" status by the attendance data, and the companionship choice data discussed below.

In analyzing the attendance data, the record of each boy was examined. It was found that these same nine boys had the highest frequency of attendance, ranging from 79 to 121 days in the sample of 134. The identification of this group on the basis of independent qualitative data, and the finding that the same boys were highest in attendance, suggests that the concept of a core group in a street corner group is valid, precisely definable and significant to the behavior of the group.[14]

These considerations, added to the discussion of the duplication rate in the preceding section, provide evidence that the core group is much more than a statistical construct. Additionally, although the data are not discussed in detail here, records were made each evening of several instances of companionship choice. That is, notice was taken of subgroups of boys who were associating in some activity apart from the rest of the group, either talking together, engaged in some activity together, or just standing apart. Also, the changing composition of the group as boys came and went was recorded. The total instances of companionship choice for each month (75 to 100) were then arranged in a matrix, and by manipulation of rows and columns, three subgroups became apparent.[15] The core members distributed themselves among all of these subgroups in each month except March, in which they were all in one subgroup. This example of cohesiveness is believed to be a reaction to the crisis brought on by the riot, and further evidence of the greater solidarity of the core group in comparison to the fringe members. It is also a further indication of the ability of attendance data to reflect the operation of group dynamics.

DIFFERENTIAL ATTENDANCE OF CORE AND FRINGE MEMBERS

The hours per boy for the group, while related to total daily man-hours for the group, appears mainly to amplify the fluctuations determined by attendance. Attendance for the fringe group is closely related to group attendance and total daily man-hours, while attendance for the core group and hours per boy for both core and fringe are relatively stable. It appears then, that the behavior which causes greatest fluctuations in total daily man-hours for the group (the solidarity index) is the attendance of fringe members. This, incidentally, is consistent with the common conclusion that a corner group is made up of a nucleus of core members, and an extremely variable number of fringe members.

---

14 Such calculations do not preclude the possibility of change in the core group over a longer period of time, as well as the possibility of identifying a different core group if a different time period were observed. This consideration re-emphasizes the necessity, in any study of corner groups, of taking into account the extent and continuity of time of observations.

15 An illustration of the method is to be found in George C. Homans, *The Human Group*, New York: Harcourt, Brace & World, Inc., 1950, p. 83.

The specific hypothesis that the amount of time the group spends together is related to its activity is examined in the final section of this paper, in the discussion of solidarity and activity. However, if the proposition is tenable, these patterns of attendance become related to variations in activity and may be seen as part of the mechanism by which the group responds to its changing situation, and by which its activity is regulated.

ANALYSIS OF THE NARRATIVE DATA

LEADERSHIP AND INFLUENCE AS CHARACTERISTICS OF ORGANIZATION

The analysis of the activity reports is used in this section to describe the organization of the group. Organization, as used here implies a status structure of influence and the presence of implicit or explicit group goals. The readiness with which the observer can find evidence of the existence of these, in the boys' reported behavior, is a positive indicator of the level of organization. When little evidence appears in the reports, organization is presumed to be low. Influence is seen in such actions as expressing approval or disapproval, or instructing someone as to proper behavior. Status is judged by the amount of such behavior on the part of a member. Goals are defined as the apparent object of group activity at any given time.

In October there was ready evidence of both a group goal and a structure of influence. The observer reported on October 14, "The Dons have arranged to get a club room in the agency. . . . It appears that Paul has been the one who has pushed for this arrangement." The boys organized themselves around Paul, identified in this study as the club-segment leader, and directed their behavior toward the goal of becoming an agency club.

One of my earliest conversations with the boys occurred in July, two months before the agency club program started. In it, Paul expressed his persistent concern to involve the boys in this program. He continued to promote the idea among the boys, and apparently tried to recruit into the group boys who would be favorable.

Bobby, the gang-segment leader, was usually opposed to the idea; this gives an insight into the structure of leadership in the group. Another long-enduring interest on the part of many of the boys was to purchase uniform club jackets. Bobby was in favor of this idea but Paul was not. Nonetheless the group made the purchase.

The two leaders often supported each other's conflicting intentions. Each of them had his own following, but neither could consistently control the entire group. As observed below, the two leaders conferred on group problems, spoke for the group, and even acted as emissaries. Paul was more willing to act in the latter role.

The following excerpt, like the others, is included to illustrate the kinds of records that were kept, as well as to describe these particular situations. It relates an incident in which Paul exercised his influence by introducing, supporting, and encouraging a new boy into membership in the group:

Later, Paul and his group returned in John's car, John drove across the park without any lights on, and then drove around it again, this time with the lights on. When he stopped the riders came over and the boys talked about how they narrowly missed the trees. The other boys did not seem too impressed by this display, at least not as impressed as they were with an earlier fist fight. Some of them seemed somewhat critical, saying that the riders would have been sorry if they had hit an open sewer. . . .

We stayed around talking for a while when Bill, who had been refused admission to the club Wednesday night, said that he would like to break a window. He picked up a rock and after a few comments about where he should throw it he broke a window on the first floor of the project. The boys all ran, some got into John's car, and the others left on foot.

(*Daily Report,* October 10.)

The usual routine for introducing new members like Bill and John was to allow the candidate to "hang around" until the others either rejected him or became accustomed to him. In the latter case, explicit recognition followed, usually in the form of some kind of vote. The outcome of the vote was only rarely negative, and when it was the boys would usually vote again later on. The real issue was whether to have a vote and when it was to occur. Paul was trying to induct the new members without the preliminaries. In the case of John this was not contrary to the boys' desires, but Bill was not generally welcome. No one else, including Bobby, ever attempted this; Paul succeeded.[16] On November 18, Bill was elected into the club.

---

[16] Before the author came in contact with the group, Bobby had supported a friend of his in gaining membership. However, Bobby kept this boy in a personal friendship relationship. Paul wanted Bill brought into membership in his own right. This difference in approaches has to do with the instrumental-expressive difference between the two leaders. Paul as the task leader was not able to continue to lend personal support to an unpopular boy for a very long period of time because this might alienate the other boys from whom he wished to demand task performance. He needed the additional support of the new members but could not continue to be responsible for their actions. Bobby, in contrast, made no task demands and could stay aligned with his not-so-popular friend, and depend on his personal attraction to maintain the loyalty of his followers. It made no difference to him if he alienated someone this week; he would come back next week. Paul, however, when he needed task performance, needed it at a particular time; next week might be too late.

In contrast to this, a friend of Bobby's spent the whole summer in the process of induction.[17] It is significant, however, that he was much better socialized to the ways of the group when he finally was accepted. There follow a few excerpts about his career. At first the boys tended to be quite critical of Jim and ridicule everything he did. One time he was quite aggressive toward a smaller boy, completely in keeping with ordinarily acceptable and desirable behavior according to the norms of this group:

A young boy who appeared to be ten or eleven approached on the sidewalk and wanted to pass between the stand and the building. Jim was in his way, and the boy stood and waited and looked at Jim. Jim asked him what he wanted and he said to go through. Jim looked at him as if the boy was being impertinent and told the kid he could go around the stand in the street. Then Jim threatened to beat up the boy and approached him menacingly. The boy stood up to him and offered to fight. Meanwhile, the others were commenting and antagonizing the boy. Finally they let the boy past and everyone started commenting and criticizing Jim for picking on such a little kid. . . . The boys knew the kid's sister and informed Jim that the boy had six sisters and five bigger brothers. . . .

(Daily Report, July 17.)

This had occurred more than a month after Jim had begun to associate with the group. The following excerpts reveal how the other members acted toward him even after he was in association with the group for some time:

Earlier Jim said he was owed money by Jack and he intended to get it that night. Before he went to the shack Paul told Johnny that Jim wanted his money and that he hadn't better come around if he didn't have it. But he didn't seem to care. Apparently he was correct in not caring because Jim didn't say anything to him.

(Daily Report, July 25.)

The same day I discussed the organization of the Dons with another one of the "detached workers":

Andy and I spoke a little of the organization of the Dons. He feels that it is very loose at present and I agree; there are two leaders now, Bobby who is top man and Paul who is second. They are also divided into at least two cliques, and a group of unattached members. *There are a number of boys hanging around who are not considered members; Jim and Phil are such.* In Andy's view, Bobby is well respected and the boys turn to him for leadership because of his good sense, while Paul is feared for his strength and aggressiveness.

(Daily Report, July 25.)

Jim went on to gain more and more status and to become an important, well-accepted member. Bill became quite prominent during the critical

---

17 Neither of these inductees were strangers. They had known the members of the Dons for years, had attended school with them and probably had associated closely with them at times in the past. Neither however was a member of the group.

period of February, March and April, but soon after ceased his association with the group, never having gained much respect from the members.

Further discussion of the process of induction and the dynamics of status in the group is reported elsewhere.[18] We are concerned here with illustrating the kind of leadership and organization which existed. The ability to act successfully without general support of the group, and even to deviate, and still have the acceptance of the group is one mark of leadership. It is not the same kind of leadership as the kind wherein one influences and guides a consensus, but it is still leadership.

CHANGES IN ORGANIZATION AND LEVEL OF ORGANIZATION

As seen in well-attended meetings, parties, and socials, and in organization around various tasks and projects of the club, the group showed a continually increasing level of organization. Late in November, however, the boys began more frequently to raise questions about Paul's leadership. One report indicates that several higher-status members interfered with Paul's selection of a club room. Another states that, on November 25, the members elected one of the girls to the presidency of the club and made Paul the vice-president. Also, in November, Bobby, the leader of the gang, began to absent himself from the club, to attract a small group into association with him, and to demonstrate his influence in other ways. To understand the shifts of group organization, it is necessary to understand that the boys' interests alternated between club and gang goals. This duality is seen in the division of feeling toward the gang leaders and in a marked difference in the behavior of the leaders.

Under Bobby's leadership, the boys started having meetings of the Dons separate from those of the recreational agency club. These began late in November. Bobby, who was never enthusiastic about or active in club affairs, or Gene, one of the core members, presided over these meetings. Paul attended most, but never presided. He had always presided over the agency club meetings along with the president. Bobby was able to initiate these meetings and not care whether they were well conducted, or even, at first, well attended, partly because of the characteristics of his role as gang leader.

The gang goals include little that requires efficient performance of tasks. The gang leader can therefore be casual about developing his following, relate himself to the members in a more personal manner, and try to win loyalties of the more popular members. The club leader, however, is concerned about the performance of tasks and must choose followers from among those willing to work. These are not always the

---

[18] Leon R. Jansyn, "Group Structure and Ceremony in a Street Corner Group" (unpublished manuscript) 1962.

boys he likes, nor the most popular, nor the most solidly entrenched members. Also, unlike the gang leader, he must often relate himself to the members in a formal, instrumental way which is uncomfortable, at least for members of the Dons and apparently for many corner boys.

The fact that there is concern with both fighting and club activities at the same time is further evidence of duality of interest. This fact also enables the observer to make a useful distinction between "main interests" from time to time, by determining the degree to which members just talk about fighting as opposed to placing themselves in a position where fighting is imminent. Such a distinction is useful as an aid in assessing the level of organization. If lower-status members, for example, rather than leaders, place the group in a position of imminent conflict, it may be taken as evidence of disorganization in the group.[19]

Interest in club activities fell in December and many of the members began to gather in a nearby restaurant under Bobby's leadership. Some lower status members who had been recruited by Paul in October (Bill among them), participated in this change of loyalties, and a conflict between Paul and Bobby became apparent when some of the very-high-status boys also changed loyalties (after a Christmas party). One interesting expression of this change was the fact that Paul was the only member who said he was satisfied with the Christmas party. One other core member went so far as to say that the food was good. All others said nothing or were critical.

The fact that the boys left the club in the process of changing loyalties and that low-status members became influential in the group indicates that Bobby did not just usurp Paul's position but started a basic structural realignment. This implies a prior disorganization. The apparent disorganization of the preceding month was therefore real.

Interest in gang activities became more prominent. Apparently as an attempt to enhance their own position, several of the lower-status members actively participated in a growing conflict with another group. The boys again changed the location of their gatherings. The new gathering-place was three miles from the Dons' neighborhood and in the neighborhood of the group with which the conflict was developing. Paul had made unsuccessful attempts to arbitrate this conflict, even going on January 5 as emissary to discuss the dispute with members of the other

---

19 It is also difficult to determine whether this group is properly called a fighting gang. Though they conceived of themselves as such, and received considerable publicity as a warring gang from the metropolitan press, they were never observed in anything which might be called a "gang fight." There were legends of gang fights when they were younger, but their notoriety seems to be based on participation in a riot and numerous episodic assaults. This is not to minimize the harm done, but it may help to specify what is and is not a "gang war."

group. It appeared however that Bobby encouraged the boys in their conflict, as in the following report:

. . . On the way back, Tommy told how a couple of the Circles had come into the restaurant and were very nice to him. He said they talked to Bobby about stopping the Dons from fighting them but Bobby told them there was no stopping them now, as supposedly a number of other clubs from Thompson Street have joined the Dons. . . .

Earl repeated a theme that he has put forth in the past, namely that the reason people are getting smart with the Dons is because they have been inactive for so long. . . .

When Paul came into the place the boys told him about the fight they were going to have. They also told him that some of the Circles had phoned them this evening to try and get out of the fight. Paul seemed to think that this would be reason not to go but the boys told him they were not going to let the Circles cop a plea again. Paul then said, "Well, lots of luck to you," and told me that "If the guys think this is going to be a pushover, they've got another thought coming."

(Daily Report, February 13.)

A few days later many of the members were arrested while watching a fight between one of the Dons (a member of low status) and one of the boys from the other group. This incident is an example of placing the group in a position of imminent conflict, characteristic of the gang orientation. The fact that it was uncontrollable, and led by lower-status members, indicated the degree of disorganization. Early in March the boys participated in a riot originally intended as an attack on some Negro boys with whom another conflict had started. This conflict also was initiated by lower-status members. This riot, as mentioned above, received considerable attention from the police and newspapers. There were banner headlines, front page pictures and feature articles for several days. A number of the Dons and many strangers assembled and milled on the street near the corner. Suddenly someone threw a rock through a window and the mob dispersed, running in all directions and breaking windows in the process. Although considerable damage was done, the police prevented the activity from reaching serious proportions, as it might have done, had there been a re-assembly, by arresting several of the boys.

Several events in the two months following the riot suggest that the group was experiencing an increase in organization as well as continuation of interest in gang activities. They participated in formal meetings with representatives of the group of Negro boys who were objects of the hostility expressed in the riot. Bobby refused to participate in these meetings but encouraged Paul to do so. Paul reported to Bobby on the proceedings of each meeting. Bobby teased him one time, saying that

Paul would some day be famous as a great peacemaker, and then added that he, Bobby, would paint his face red, yellow and brown and be King of Brotherhood. The satire appeared to reflect the attitude of most of the boys and reflects Bobby's ascendance as leader during the period.

Second, there were more frequent expressions among the boys of the "proper" form of interpersonal relationships in the group. In contrast with the recruiting done by Paul in October, the group was "polled" before the introduction of a recruit at this time. Third, the conflict with the Circles continued, but no individual fights were held and an older group was called upon to help resolve the issues and suppress the conflict by a show of support for the Dons. The show of support was done in a way that made fighting appear to be out of the question, as each of the older boys was accompanied by his girl-friend. Other disputes were initiated with other groups, but this time by high-status members, and all the disputes were very highly controlled.

At least twice, early in April, it was noted that Tommy, one of the core members, severely criticized and insulted two of the lower-status members who were prominent in the Circles' conflict and threatened them with beatings if they caused any more trouble. Also, the group resisted attempts on the part of a Mexican clique to involve them in affairs and conflicts in the Mexican neighborhood. The Mexican clique then discontinued participation with the Dons. Paul also made overt demonstration of his subordination to Bobby.

The gang orientation continued and became firmly established in April. The boys in one instance adopted a uniform front of deception of the authorities in regard to the breaking of some school building windows. This deception was diffused even among non-members to the point where a non-member, on being arrested, tried to assume the blame for shooting at the windows. Open and obvious violative behavior, particularly vandalism, became quite common. This performance was by lower-status members. In May the two leaders withdrew from frequent participation with the group for approximately a month. From May through August, the group took on a segmented appearance. The leaders' return in July was followed by attempts to organize the group by getting the "segments" to gather in one place, and by re-entering the group in the recreational agency program. Neither of these attempts succeeded immediately. In August, with the group still quite segmented, the boys commenced a series of assaults and fights with Negro boys in the neighborhood. Outsiders frequently participated in these incidents. Also, at this time some of the members participated in several fights at a bathing beach.

The boys oriented themselves toward gang goals at times when the group was organized and at times when it was relatively disorganized. The same is true of club goals. The degree of organization in the group varies widely and does not appear to depend on the content, violative or not, of the boys' behavior. However, during disorganized times, the likelihood increases that more erratic persons, who are not highly regarded by the boys, will exert influence. It may be this aspect of group life which results in the gang appearing, as it does at times, to be a mob led by disturbed people who assume leadership for their own purposes. This kind of leadership does not imply much control over the group, since the group at these times appears to be very deficient in any kind of control. Leadership, in the sense of continuing influence over the members, appears to go to boys who are held in high regard by the members and who possess many of the qualities ordinarily associated with leadership.[20] Thus, the fact that disorganization occurs does not indicate that the gang is completely outside the scope of explanation by the usual theories of group dynamics, and does indicate that it is necessary to combine ideas of collective behavior and ideas of group dynamics to understand what many gangs do.

VARIABILITY IN MEANING OF MEMBERSHIP

Membership is defined as it is in this study so that attendance can be counted. Such a conception of membership might tend to give the group a more organized appearance than is warranted. However, the definition has a basic similarity to the boys' own conceptions, based on participation as evidence of membership.

Among the boys there was little agreement as to size of group or definition of membership at any given time. The reason for this disparity was not ignorance of who was and who was not a member. Consensus was high whenever the status of a particular person was at question. The fact of participation was at all times the final criterion. It was the abstract ideas of definition of membership and size of group which varied from boy to boy and in relation to varying purposes. Discrepancies in size and composition appeared when the boys were considering membership as related to different goals or to certain projects. Thus one must be clear, when considering membership, about the situation to which the use of the idea of membership is relevant. Also, the fact that the boys' conceptions vary while the researcher's remains the same emphasizes the need to be specific about the definition of membership when generalizing about gangs.

A CHRONOLOGY OF GROUP ACTIVITY

In order to examine the proposition that group activity is related to changes in unity as reflected in the index it is necessary to abstract

---

[20] A similar conclusion was drawn from data concerning later research by Short and Strodtbeck, discussed by Short in "Street Corner Groups and Patterns of Delinquency: A Progress Report," *American Catholic Sociological Review*, 24 (Spring, 1963), pp. 29–32.

categories of action from the daily narrative reports. These categories are intended to comprise a behavioristic index of changes in the frequency of group action in general and differences in the content of this action as well. The diary was examined in detail and all activity meeting the definitions of the following categories was noted.

The first, of most general significance, is "actions of the entire group," (A.G.). Then, because of a particular interest in delinquent activities as a special type of group activity, a subcategory of "delinquencies of the entire group," (D.G.) was defined. These are considered separately because delinquency was expected to show fluctuations similar to activity in general. The high frequency of delinquencies by the Dons adds to the interest and utility of delinquency as a class of activity. Since there is a similar interest in other delinquent acts of members, another category is defined as "delinquencies of individuals and cliques," (I.D.).

The following is a part of the chronology of group activities:

Feb. 15 The group decided to buy sweaters. (A.G.)
Feb. 17 A member had a fight with a member of Circles; those watching were arrested. (D.G.)
Feb. 28 A member was driving a stolen car. (I.D.)
Mar. 1 Two members tried to steal a car battery. (I.D.)
Mar. 2 A member fired a gun at a group of Negro boys and members chased the Negro boys. (D.G.)
Mar. 2 A member started a fight with some Negro boys. (I.D.)
          (The participation of the entire group was not apparent in this particular incident.)
Mar. 3 Many of the members participated in a riot. (D.G.)

Actions of the entire group are defined as those either involving the total membership at any given time, or planned, or supported, or anticipated and tolerated by the entire membership. Unless the participation of the entire group was obvious, the act was not so classified. A delinquent act is one which would be so judged by the police at the time and place it occurred if called to their attention.[21] Finally, all those delinquencies which are not actions of the entire group were considered to be delinquencies of individuals and cliques.

A list of the activities, both group and individual which are included in the Daily Reports, and which meet these definitions, amounts to 30 actions of the entire group (including 13 delinquent actions), and 39 delinquencies of individuals and cliques. The reliability of this procedure is obviously questionable. However, the list was made for analysis of another index of solidarity sometime before the present analysis was conceived. One reason the excerpts and part of the chronology are pro-

---

21 The problem of making a useful definition of delinquency is widely recognized, but not yet solved. For example, see the discussion by Herbert A. Bloch and Frank T. Flynn, *Delinquency*, New York: Random House, 1956.

vided, is so that the reader may know the nature of the qualitative data used. It is the rate of occurrence of these activities which is to be related to the variations in group solidarity.

LEVEL OF ORGANIZATION, MAN–HOURS, AND ACTIVITY

First, the relation between the rise and fall in degree of organization and the rise and fall of total daily man-hours is examined, and then the relation between daily man-hours and changes in frequency of group action.

The narrative material, related above, indicates that the group underwent a process of increasing organization in the fall. Late in December and throughout January and February the withdrawal from the club by the gang leader, and the restructuring of the group under his leadership, marked a period of disorganization. Leadership conflict and attempts by low-status members to increase their status became prominent as this disorganization progressed. After the riot, throughout March and April until another withdrawal by the leadership in May, signs of increasing organization were again observed. Stability of the gang orientation and segmentation of the group are aspects of a period of slow decline which ended in August, and was in turn followed by reinvolvement of active leadership. A rough parallel to this rise and decline exists in the curve of daily man-hours.[22] (See Figure 1.)

The periods where the high points occur are also periods of a high level of organization. The periods where the low points occur are the periods described above as relatively disorganized. The parallel is by no means exact. One interesting difference between man-hours and the division by analysis of the qualitative reports is that the decline in man-hours starts in both instances of disorganization long before the disorganization is apparent in the narrative. The rise in solidarity takes place briefly, during the early part of the organized periods. The rise is precipitous, while the decline is gradual. This is consistent with the theory underlying this paper. Solidarity, it appears, has a tendency to decline. It reaches a level

---

[22] In a previous report on these data, a different index was used. See Leon R. Jansyn, "Solidarity and Delinquency in a Street Corner Group: A Study of the Relationship Between Changes in Specified Aspects of Group Structure and Variations in the Frequency of Delinquent Activity," (unpublished M.A. thesis, University of Chicago, 1960). The former index, however, did not parallel any observed development of the group. On the contrary the social process of the group was divided according to divisions in the purely empirical trends of the index of solidarity. The present index has a different configuration of trends and, upon analysis of the activity reports from the point of view of "degree of organization," was found (as noted here) to conform to trends in organization. The present index was therefore considered more useful. Further relationships, such as role differentiation and identification of core members, confirmed the greater utility of the simple measure of daily man-hours.

where it becomes threatening to the boys. There is a spurt of group activity which generates interest and increases attendance and solidarity.

In order to test the relationship between the rate of occurrence of activities, and the trends in man-hours, it is necessary to divide the curve

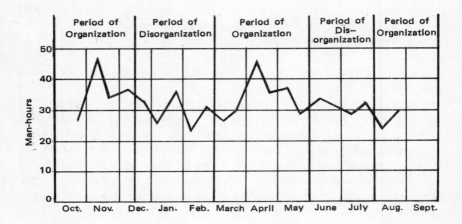

FIGURE 1. Semi-monthly means of the total daily man-hours spent together for the entire group, divided into periods of organization and disorganization as described in the analysis of the narrative reports.

into periods of rise and decline. It is difficult to determine valid division points by looking at the curve by itself. We will consider a period of rise to be marked by the beginning of the precipitous rise occurring early in the organized periods, and consider that they end when the rise reaches its highest point. The results of this analysis are presented in Table 3.

TABLE 3

TRENDS OF CHANGE IN THE NUMBER OF MAN-HOURS AND TRENDS IN FREQUENCY OF ACTIVITIES

Period	Direction of Change	Number of Semi-Monthly Periods	Number of Activities per Semi-Monthly Period	
			A.G.*	D.G.*
October to mid-November.........	Rising	3	2.67	1.33
Mid-November through February..	Declining	7	1.14	0.14
March through mid-April.........	Rising	3	1.33	1.00
Mid-April through July..........	Declining	7	0.86	0.14
August through September........	Rising	4	1.00	1.00
Totals		24	1.25	0.54

* A.G. = activities of the entire group; D.G. = delinquencies of the entire group.

From this analysis it appears that group activity in general, including group delinquencies, increases after low points in man-hours. The rate of activity then decreases after a high point is reached, only to increase again following the next low point.

There are many obvious problems in this analysis. The curve can be divided in many ways. It can be divided to dissipate the relationship. This is more true of activity in general than of the subset of delinquent activities (the relationship is stronger for group delinquencies). It appears that these boys found it easier to act as a group in a delinquent manner than in a conventional manner. The fact that the author helped the boys in carrying out conventional group activities and not with their delinquent ones adds to the importance of the relation between activity and group delinquency. In fact he worked against the hypothesis presented here by encouraging them in activities while solidarity was high.

Although the curve of solidarity can be divided in a way which eliminates the appearance of the relationship found here, no way has been found to divide it to show the opposite relationship. Because of these problems, sufficient data have been included that the reader may investigate alternative arrangements himself. It is also possible that other combinations of the data will produce better indices of solidarity. In spite of these difficulties, however, considerable leverage is gained on these problems by the use of the kind of data presented here. At least one can approach the problems in relatively objective terms.

INTERPRETATION OF FINDINGS

These findings are interpreted on the basis of the proposition that the solidarity of the group is important to the boys and its decline beyond a certain level is threatening to them. They respond to this threat by group action which arouses interest, and attracts and reinvolves members.[23] The content of their action is quite often delinquent. This is a result of the orientation the boys have developed, making delinquency easier for the group than conventional activity. This orientation arises from the tradition of the neighborhood, the response of the conventional community to their action, and the history of the group. Also the boys are quite delinquent individually. They have problems of being rejected at school and in other areas of contact with conventional society. They

---

[23] There are alternative interpretations, and the data are not conclusive. One might see increasing activity merely as a probable result of the influx of fringe members. The organizational change, however, would still be a phenomenon of interest as an intervening variable if this were the case. That the influx of fringe members is due solely to some extra-group cause is unlikely, however, in view of the precipitous increases in fringe and entire group attendance and man-hours, as opposed to the gradualness of decline which follows each of the increases.

often express considerable animosity toward teachers, police, certain ethnic groups (especially Negroes and Puerto Ricans), people from other neighborhoods and even some from their own neighborhood. In many ways the Dons were not well integrated into the life of the neighborhood. They "hung around" the public housing project and many lived in the project. This is not to say that they were not a part of the life of the neighborhood, but that they were a marginal group.

The boys saw many of the people whom they considered enemies to be a threat to them, to the group, to the neighborhood, and even to their way of life. It is partly in regard to these threats that the group is important to them. They see the group as a defense. There are many other threats, particularly from other adolescent groups. Altercations frequently arise between them and Negro and Puerto Rican groups, and groups from other locations or neighborhoods. Many of these arise out of interaction in school and other places where adolescents are brought together. Thus the group is important as a matter of self-defense. Finally, in the existing situation, there was a likelihood that a boy who did not belong to a group was always eligible for harassment by any of the numerous groups in the area.

It is also clear that these boys were comfortable in interaction with each other and desired such interaction. They are socialized to depend heavily on the response of their peers for the organization of their own life. Gans' discussion of peer-group society is especially relevant in this regard. Although he is not concerned with describing delinquent groups, his remarks seem to apply rather well to some aspects of the Dons' life when he discusses the West Ender's dependence on his group:

The West End adolescent, as noted before, is alive only with his peer group; outside it, he exists as a quiet and almost passive individual. With adults, he is likely to be lethargic and sullen, seeking always to minimize contact with them. In the peer group, however, the style of life is one of action-seeking. Much of the conflict between adolescent and adult therefore is that between the action-seeking and the routine-seeking patterns.

In the adolescent peer group, manifesting the episodic search for action in an almost pure, ideal-typical form, life alternates between killing time and searching for action. Some of it takes place right within the group, in a dialectic of conformity and competitiveness through which the individual realizes himself.[24]

The development of their own conception of their legitimate social roles may depend on experiences in an all-male peer group. Inability to participate successfully in such a group may be a threat to their own self conception. Miller found that the all-male adolescent group is a necessity in lower-class life:

[24] Herbert J. Gans, *The Urban Villagers*, Glencoe: The Free Press, 1962, p. 65, and generally pp. 64–83.

The "hanging" peer group is a unit of particular importance for the adolescent male. In many cases it is the most stable and solidary primary group he has ever belonged to; for boys reared in female-based households the corner group provides the first real opportunity to learn essential aspects of the male role in the context of peers facing similar problems of sex-role identification.[25]

Opportunities for occupation in the conventional world did not seem to be a great concern of these boys. They felt a heavy dependence on relatives, and on friends with "connections" to get jobs later on. As stated above in regard to integration, they were a marginal group. Perhaps this marginality accounts for the mixture of fighting and stealing in their activities. At any rate, they could not be seen as clearly participating in either a criminal or a conflict culture, but in a mixture.

Rather than the causes of delinquency, our main concern has been group solidarity and the influence of its changes on group activity. Though at times the group acts like a mob, these same boys make up a more or less well-organized group. In fact it appears that, unless the group is disorganized, mob-like behavior is unlikely.

The behavior of the boys may be understood as arising in part from experiences in activities which they pursue in response to concern aroused by instability in their peer group. The content of their behavior is to some extent culturally delimited; standards, definitions, and values are learned in association with their peers in the street corner group. But when they act, and how often, are controlled in part by variation in the solidarity of the group.

---

25 Walter B. Miller, "Lower Class Culture as a Generating Milieu of Gang Delinquency," *Journal of Social Issues,* 14 (1958), p. 14.

HENRY S. MAAS

20

*The Young Adult Adjustment of
Twenty Wartime Residential
Nursery Children**

This is a report, necessarily condensed, of a study of 20 young adults who, as preschool children in London during World War II, were placed for their physical safety by their parents in British wartime residential nurseries for at least one year. The purpose of the study was to clarify some questions about a working assumption in child welfare practice—that the preschool child who is separated from his parents and placed in any group care residence suffers irreversible psychological damage.

The literature on the problem of "maternal deprivation" and, more specifically, on the separation of the young child from his natural family has grown to almost overwhelming proportions since the 1930's.[1] A systematic review of this literature is obviously impossible here. Regarding the substantive complexities of the separation problem, Mary D. Ainsworth and John Bowlby wrote, in one of the latter's most cogent if least accessible contributions:

. . . it has become increasingly clear that "separation" is not a simple aetiological factor, and that the term refers to a wide range of events and an intricate complex of associated conditions, which in different constellations may have different effects on the course of development.[2]

Probably the clearest expression of child welfare's present working assumptions regarding separation and group care and their effects on the child is the review of research John Bowlby wrote for the World Health

* Reprinted by special permission of Child Welfare League of America, from *Child Welfare*, Volume XIII, No. 2 (February, 1963), pp. 57–72, and by permission of the author.

Author's Note—This study was done with the help of a small grant from the Institute of Social Sciences, University of California, Berkeley. During the data-gathering phase, 1960–61, the writer was studying on a Special Research Fellowship from the National Institute of Mental Health, U.S. Public Health Service, as a Visiting Member, The London School of Economics and Political Science, University of London. His indebtedness to his sponsor, Professor R. M. Titmuss, and the many others in England who helped to make this study possible obviously cannot find adequate expression in this note.

1 During 1961, two critical reviews of this extensive literature were published: Leon Yarrow, "Maternal Deprivation: Toward an Empirical and Conceptual Reevaluation," *Psychological Bulletin*, LVIII (1961), 459–90; reprinted in *Maternal Deprivation* (New York: CWLA, 1962), pp. 3–41; and Lawrence Casler, "Maternal Deprivation: A Critical Review of the Literature," *Monograph of the Society of Research in Child Development*, XXVI, No. 2 (1961), 1–64.

2 Mary D. Ainsworth and John Bowlby, "Research Strategy in the Study of Mother-Child Separation," *Courrier*, IV (1954), 105.

Organization over a decade ago.[3] While subsequent studies, including Bowlby's own investigations, have somewhat modified formulations found in the WHO publication, in essence the ideas of this report still echo through the halls of practice. It is here that we read:

". . . the infant and young child should experience a warm, intimate, and continuous relationship with his mother (or permanent mother-substitute). . . ." If not, we may expect to find "anxiety, excessive need for love, powerful feelings of revenge, and, arising from these last, guilt and depression." "In the second and third years of life, the emotional response to separation is . . . just as severe . . ."; ". . . vulnerability between three and five is still serious, though much less so than earlier." "Deprivation after the age of three or four . . . still results, however, in excessive desires for affection and excessive impulses for revenge, which cause acute internal conflict and unhappiness and very unfavorable social attitudes." ". . . sceptics may question whether the retardation is permanent and whether the symptoms of illness may not easily be overcome." "The long-term after-effects . . . can sometimes be calamitous . . .," with such results as "superficial relationships; no real feeling . . .; deceit and evasion, often pointless; stealing; lack of concentration at school." To the professional world of child care workers, the prescription is unequivocal: "To sum up, then, it may be said that group residential care is always to be avoided for those under about 6 years, that it is suitable for short-stay children between 6 and 12, and for both short-stay and some long-stay adolescents. It is also indispensable for many maladjusted children. . . ."[4]

Bowlby drew these conclusions from a review of his own research and that of Goldfarb, Spitz, and others. Effects were seen as permanent, though Bowlby noted in passing that " . . . the studies of Theis and of Beres & Obers show that many such children achieve a tolerable degree of social adaptation when adult."[5]

Also warranting observation are certain problems in study design. In regard to such problems, a recent Social Science Research Council report states:

Two animals—or children—exposed to the same stimulus probably will not respond in the same way because the sum of their experiences previous to the stimulus differ, as do experiences intervening between the observed stimulus and measurement of the desired response. This old dilemma in research is particularly troublesome in studies of the effects of deprivation, for the behavioral changes of greatest interest are those that are shown to be stable over time, and the greater the lapse of time, the greater the opportunity for different intervening experience. Mason [William A. Mason, conference participant] suggested that much parametric investigation is needed, on different ages at which separation occurs, the duration of the deprivation, and the reversibility of the apparent disorders developed.[6]

---

[3] John Bowlby, *Maternal Care and Mental Health* (Geneva: World Health Organization, 1951).

[4] *Ibid.*, pp. 11, 12, 23, 26, 57, 15, 25, 31, 137.

[5] *Ibid.*, p. 39.

[6] Francis H. Palmer, "Critical Periods of Development: Report on a Conference," *Items*, XV, No. 2 (1961), 16.

In the designs of the studies reviewed, some problems are common. First, while the question for investigation was the effects of separation, there was usually no control over the children's preseparation experiences. The children coming out of disintegrated family situations that necessitated their placement might have been damaged before they were separated from their parents. Could not one study children who were separated from intact families, free from gross pathology, so that preseparation experiences might be assumed to be noncontributory to whatever subsequent damage was found?

Second, the children studied had often been placed in what we would now agree were "bad" institutions, understaffed or staffed by persons influenced by the child care standards of their day and, consequently, more concerned with physical hygiene than with human feelings and responsiveness to the children. For others, as in the case of Bowlby's 60 former tuberculosis sanitorium children, the institutional experience involved much more than separation and residential group care, for these youngsters, under four years old, were "confined to cots for rest much of the time" and given gastric lavages, etc.[7] (Clearly, studies of ill children using medical facilities are not studies of simply childhood separation and group care.) But might not one control for institutional effect by studying children from different *kinds* of parent-substitute institutions, run according to different specifiable principles of child care, and compare the results?[8]

Third, children studied in followup investigations were sometimes selected from the caseloads of clinics and social agencies. For example, the 38 persons between the ages of 16 and 26 studied by Beres and Obers were "all taken from the Youth Service Department," set up for young people who, after early years in an infant home, later years in foster care, and then perhaps a cottage school, required "additional care." Obers and Beres note the "factor of selectivity" in their study and that "the degree of pathology in our series of cases is greater than might have been found if all cases . . . had been followed. . . . [but] it would have been altogether impossible to trace these."[9] Perhaps one could do just this—

---

[7] John Bowlby, Mary Ainsworth, Mary Boston, and Dina Rosenbluth, "The Effects of Mother-Child Separation: A Follow-up Study," *The British Journal of Medical Psychology*, XXIX, parts 3 and 4 (1956), 213, 215.

[8] Heinicke's comparative study of six residential nursery children and seven day nursery children is of this order. Christoph M. Heinicke, "Some Effects of Separating Two-Year-Old Children from Their Parents: A Comparative Study," *Human Relations*, IX, No. 2 (1956), 106–76.

[9] David Beres and Samuel J. Obers, "The Effects of Extreme Deprivation in Infancy on Psychic Structure in Adolescence: A Study in Ego Development," *The Psychoanalytic Study of the Child* (New York: International Universities Press, 1950), V, 214–15.

trace children in the community after they had left institutional care. Though they might well be found to be clients of mental health or welfare agencies, at least they would not have been located through a source that, by their presence in an active caseload, marks them as troubled people or people in trouble.

Fourth, the study of persons whose placements were in many different living groups encompasses the effects of considerably more than merely separation and early group residential care. A multitude of changes in living groups for children has been found to be associated with confusion about identity.[10] In trying to assess damage incurred by separation and group residential care alone, one should plan to study persons who have undergone just that—separation and placement in a single children's center. And, as a corollary criterion, early separation should not be equated with permanent severance from own parents. One should thus focus the study on children who have lived in a single group residence and who subsequently returned during childhood to their own families.

Fifth, it seems clear that the child's age at placement is a significant variable in separation research since the meaning of the experience to the child theoretically depends upon his stage of development at its inception. It is obviously possible to select persons age-grouped by separation age for comparison of the effects.

Finally, most of the research has been on the short-term effects on children. Irreversibility of damage is assumed, although there are a few conflicting reports concerning long-term effects on adults. Using a battery of interviews and tests, and drawing other observations from home visits and agency records, one could examine the present adjustment of criteria-meeting young adults. The separation literature indicates what to assess—certain aspects of their feeling life, inner controls, relationship patterns, role performance, and intellectual functioning—if theory on irreversibility of damage is to be tested.

BRITISH WARTIME RESIDENTIAL NURSERIES

Some of the problems cited seemed manageable if one chose to study young adults who had been separated from intact families, apparently free of gross pathology, and returned to their families during their childhood years after a stay of at least one year in a British wartime residential nursery. (The civilian evacuation scheme in wartime Britain involved about 400 residential nurseries before the war's end.) Richard Titmuss

---

10 See Factor II-a, p. 128, and Factor III-b, p. 134, in David Fanshel and Henry S. Maas, "Factorial Dimensions of the Characteristics of Children in Placement and Their Families," *Child Development*, XXXIII, No. 1 (1962); reprinted by CWLA, 1962.

and colleagues have described the problems in launching and operating this program.[11] A reading of their publications and others on the evacuation of British children suggested to me that, in 1960 or 1961, one might study young adults who, as preschool children, had been separated from their parents, not because of the disintegration of their families, but as part of a large-scale movement to send children to places that were, hopefully, remote from enemy bomb targets.

The Ministry of Health assumed from the start that " . . . separation might involve greater risks than did air-raids."[12] Psychiatric clinicians at a 1941 Tavistock Clinic meeting predicted:

There is in this situation a very real danger that the seeds of neurosis will be sown in an increasing number of children, and apart from the immediate distress and disability arising from this, there is the wider question of what these children will go through as adolescents and adults.[13]

But parents in London streets in 1939 were reading large black-and redlettered London County Council posters announcing registration and meeting places for the evacuation of children. When war broke out in September 1939, there were plans for children's flight. Earlier than this, there had been a brief trial-run evacuation of school children, including some from day nurseries. Of the wartime scheme for children, Susan Isaacs remarked in the *Cambridge Evacuation Survey*: "The parents who parted from their children, far from having failed them, were acting from a sense of duty, often at great sacrifice."[14] Here, then, was a "natural experiment" to study separation without the necessity of prior intrafamily trauma.

Young Children in Wartime and *Infants without Families,* by Anna Freud and Dorothy Burlingham,[15] made clear that within the British

11 R. M. Titmuss, *Problems of Social Policy* (London: His Majesty's Stationery Office and Longmans, Green and Co., 1950); also S. M. Ferguson and H. Fitzgerald, *Studies in the Social Services* (London: Her Majesty's Stationery Office and Longmans, Green and Co., 1954).

12 S. M. Ferguson and H. Fitzgerald, *op. cit.,* p. 234.

13 "War Strain in Evacuated Children," *British Medical Journal,* Issue No. 4177 (January 25, 1941), p. 129.

14 Susan Isaacs, ed., *Cambridge Evacuation Survey: A Wartime Study in Social Welfare and Education* (London: Methuen & Co., 1941), p. 14.

15 Anna Freud and Dorothy Burlingham, *Young Children in Wartime* (London: George Allen & Unwin, 1942), and *Infants without Families* (New York: International Universities Press, 1944).

Note, additionally, that in the mimeographed "after-care" newsletters from the Hampstead Nurseries, circulated through Foster Parents' Plan for War Children, Inc., New York, one finds the following observation as reported "by Mrs. Hansi Kennedy, a former worker in the Hampstead Nurseries." Bridget came to the Nursery in 1941, when she was 9 months old, and returned home shortly after her 5th birthday. . . . She . . . suffered acutely by Nursery life and the separation from her mother. . . . In Bridget's case, the absence of normal family-life in the first 5 years has so far shown no unfavorable after-effects; she has settled down well in her home surroundings and developed normally during the 6 years since her return home. It is, however, important wartime residential nursery program there was at least one child care center that differed radically from the literature's model of the understaffed and impersonal institution of prior separation research, and finally, advance correspondence assured me that some, if not many, of the former residents of at least two quite different wartime nurseries might be found in London in 1960 and 1961. But not until my early field work in London was completed could I be sure of what was feasible.

In fact, three quite different wartime residential nurseries provided alumni for the group of 20 adults in this study. The three nurseries will be called Nursery N, Nursery E, and Nursery S. To characterize and compare them, three dimensions will be used. (It must be remembered, however, that nurseries, like the children in them, change over time, and only a capsule presentation can be made here. Fuller documentation of the bases for my inferences, drawn from both contemporaneous reports and interviews with staff, will appear in a fuller report on this study.) The three dimensions are: (1) numbers of children and staff, (2) children's relationships with their parents, and (3) staff orientation to the children.

In brief, Nursery N is the middle-sized one in terms of numbers of children, with the most generous supply of staff members to children. Each staff person had at least one child assigned to her. A common pattern among the three- to five-year-olds was the assignment of living groups of about five children to one staff helper. Parents could visit at any time and there were "strong contacts with parents."[16] In a time of gasoline shortage, the fact that Nursery N was physically closer to London than either of the other two nurseries is important. With the older children in Nursery N, "we talked about parents, wrote to them. We had pictures of parents. Sunday nights were always exciting. There was a bus every Sunday. Some were very sad when Mummy had gone. Perhaps we can write a letter. We didn't put any child to bed who was upset. We took them in our rooms and talked to them. They could talk about it." This was a key to the Nursery N approach to children—the expression of feelings was encouraged, guided by a depth of psychological understanding of young children that was not present in either of the other two nurseries.

The second nursery, E, was the smallest, able to accommodate only about 20 children. Its staff consisted of a professionally untrained woman, Mrs. E, and her physiotherapist daughter, Miss E, with occasional part-time domestic help from the nearby Welsh village. Thus, the

---

to see whether this progress will be maintained during pre-adolescence and adolescence." *Hampstead Nurseries After-Care Ninth Half-Yearly Report,* April, 1951 (New York: Foster Parents Plan for War Children, 1951), pp. 1 and 6.

[16] All direct quotations regarding the nurseries are from interviews with the persons in charge.

ratio of staff to children was about ten to one. Deep in the Welsh countryside, Nursery E was the most inaccessible to the London parents whose children were routed to Mrs. E and her daughter through an East End settlement house. Interviews and the log book of Nursery E indicate that parents' visits were most infrequent. The alien nature of the East End culture to Mrs. E's stern Welsh world and her approach to the children are best suggested by her own words: "Those were very interesting days and I personally loved every one of them! Bedwetter, sleep walkers, lively heads, and sores. We got the better of the lot, and P was our only failure, and a doctor at the London hospital said he was incurable [as a bedwetter], poor lad. They were all fairly undisciplined —but very soon 'fell in' and we really were a very happy family—no friction anywhere." Nursery E was in marked contrast to the psychologically oriented Nursery N.

The third of the nurseries, S, was eventually the largest and had the highest ratio of children to staff. Nursery S had been a model day nursery school for the children of working mothers. Those who had been attending the school were evacuated as a unit like other school classes—starting out with 47 children who knew one another, their head teacher, and her three helpers. There was "no domestic help at first." Parents visited Nursery S at Christmas or Easter time, in a bus they arranged for themselves, and a festive spread was miraculously provided by Lady X, in whose home Nursery S was billeted. Many anecdotes suggest the teachers' possessiveness regarding the children in their charge during their country's time of crisis. The teachers were trained nursery school educators, not psychologists, as the head teacher remarked, "with their psychological jargon, their observations, and their graphs." These teachers told their children that they had left London because the King had wanted them to. Children's songs and games, spiritual values, God and country, and the wonders of nature were central themes. The time that the busload of parents was getting ready to leave and the geese were let loose to distract the children was described with delight. In Nursery S, I was told, weeping at parting occurred among the parents, but not among the children. (The statement, not the fact, is important.)

In brief contrast, then, substitute parenting at Nursery N was open and expressive; at Nursery E somewhat firm, if not stern, and suppressive; and at Nursery S, with its faith in God, King, and denial, rather inspirational and repressive, and quite possessive.

THE YOUNG ADULTS FOR STUDY

In addition to comparisons by type of residential nurseries, the plan for this study was to compare young adults grouped by age at separation. I wanted 20 persons, five from each of four different age-at-separation groups: the Ones, separated in the first year of life; the Twos, separated at about 2 to 2½; the Threes, separated at about 3 to 3½, and the Four-pluses, separated between 4 and 5. For obvious reasons, I wanted each age group to be composed of representatives of all three nurseries and, thus, each nursery group to span the age groups. Finally, relatively equal numbers of men and women seemed desirable.

WHERE THE SUBJECTS WERE FOUND

Procedures for selecting the young adults for study were quite different for the three nurseries. For 23 young adults who had been residents for at least one year, Nursery N provided a roster of names and addresses, together with age at placement. The addresses derived from their own 1958 letter survey of former residents. Six of the 23 were eliminated as ineligible because they were illegitimate children, over age (well past fifth birthday) at placement, or from gross-pathology family situations, involving death or institutionalization of parent. Of the 17 letters I mailed, six were returned "not known at this address," six did not reply, and five replied agreeing to see me, but one was a British soldier stationed in Germany. The final group of seven Nursery N young adults in the study comprised four of the responders (one of the four being a young woman whose sister had written for her as well as for herself) and three of the six nonresponders. Because the ages at separation of these three fitted my design needs, I chose to make repeated home visits until I found them in. (The unchosen three of the six nonresponders were a sibship of three sisters, and I already had three pairs of sibs in the study.)

Nursery E gave me a roster of 20 names and the ages at placement of all children who had spent a year or more in Wales. There were London (East End) addresses, as of World War II, for 15 of them, and for five there were only names. Using the Register of Electors (dated 10 October 1959) for the Metropolitan Borough of Bethnal Green, I found two of these families still at the same address. One of them proved to be a major source of leads—which new housing estates others had moved into, whose brother ran which pub, who had boxed recently at a settlement house that would know his address. By sole-wearing footwork, I discovered the addresses of nine persons on the list. Had I needed them, I probably could have located all but three of the others. Two of these, however, would have been eliminated from the study. The seven I approached, selected first according to my design needs for age at separation and second for a relatively balanced sex distribution, all agreed to participate in the study; no one I visited refused.

Nursery S, the former day nursery school located in a stable working-class neighborhood, had had as its head teacher a woman who lived where she taught and who was still in casual contact with the parents of some of her former charges. Having obtained their addresses from their parents because she herself was eager to see them grown-up, she invited eight of them, with their spouses, to a party at her house to meet me. Four came, and the other four telephoned or wrote apologies. Three of those who attended the party and two who did not constitute the Nursery S study group. The twentieth young adult had been a resident of a nursery, called Nursery O, directed by a woman now affiliated with the psychotherapeutic group that ran Nursery N. Since no other adults who had been separated and placed during their first year of life were available to me from Nurseries E and S, and I already had three in this age group from Nursery N, I included him.

DESCRIPTION OF THE YOUNG ADULTS

Since the findings of our study concern the adjustment of these 20 young adults, some data on their backgrounds should be reported. Of the eight women and 12 men, aged 19 to 26 years, just half were 21 years old or less when they were studied in 1960-61 (Table 1). They grew up primarily in working-class families, nine of them in London's East End. About a third were in families headed by unskilled workers—e.g., a stoker, a dustman (garbage collector)—another third were the children of bus or lorry drivers or tailors, and the final third were in families another notch or two up the occupational ladder—a grocer who owned his shop, a clerk-salesman, a teacher.

There were three pairs of siblings—two sisters, two brothers, and a brother and a sister. My tabulation of numbers of siblings in their families and the ordinal position of the persons studied indicates a range from two only children to the third of nine children. The 20 occupy 13 different sibling statuses.[17] When interviewed, all but one of the subjects

---

[17] As the sibling statuses and family size happen to be quite evenly represented among the four age-at-separation groups and the three nursery groups, so, I assume, are many other less readily describable family variables. Specifically, in reference to sibling status among the 20 persons, there are two only children (A,V); three who are the first of two (F,H,W); four who are the second of two (C,K,T,Z); two who are the fourth of six (G,J); and one each of the following: first of three (Q), second of three (B), third of four (M), fourth of four (Y), fifth of five (D), second of six (P), third of six (R), second of nine (L), and third of nine (X). Defining small families as one- or two-child units and large families as those having three or more children, we find that each age-at-separation group has two or three small and large families, except for the Threes, who split one and four. Nursery N splits three and four; Nursery E, three and four; Nursery S, two and three. Similarly, top, middle, and bottom statuses are quite evenly distributed among age and nursery groups.

There is, however, one aspect of family life not evenly distributed. All four parents who were widowed by 1960–61 were confined to the Ones. A's father died when he was 12, C's when she was 11, and B has no memory of her father, who died during the second year after her return home. B grew up with her mother and two siblings,

were living either with their parents or with their spouse and children. In 16 cases both parents were still alive, and 15 couples were still living together.

The subjects' ages at separation and placement ranged from two months to 61 months, clustered, by design, in the four age-at-separation groups previously described. Overall length of placement in the nurseries ranged from 12 months to 50 months, with just over three years as the mid-point. As might be expected, the younger the child at placement, the longer his stay was likely to be, though in a few cases this relationship was violated (e.g., a Two who stayed just 12 months and a Four-plus who stayed over 50 months).

TABLE 1

THE TWENTY CASES, BY SEPARATION AGE AND RESIDENTIAL NURSERY

Age Group at Separation	Case	Nursery	Sex	Age at Interview (Years)
The Ones...............	A	N	m	19
	B	N	f	19
	C	S	f	21
	D	N	m	19
	F	O	m	20
The Twos	G	S	f	23
	H	N	m	21
	J	N	f	21
	K	E	f	21
	L	E	m	22
The Threes.............	M	E	f	20
	P	E	m	22
	Q	S	m	24
	R	N	f	23
	T	E	m	23
The Four-Pluses	V	N	m	23
	W	E	m	24
	X	E	m	21
	Y	S	m	26
	Z	S	f	26

While all of these young adults returned to their families during their growing-up years, two of the Ones and one Four-plus spent four or more years in a boarding school, a training school, or an institution for deprived children subsequent to their wartime placements, and one other Four-plus, before returning to her family, finished out the war years in a series of nonrelative family billets. In summary, three of the Ones, all of the Twos, all of the Threes, and three of the Four-pluses, that is, 16 of

however, in a house owned by the maternal grandparents, and the grandfather was described as an attentive and indulgent father surrogate. Also among the Ones is F, whose father's date of death is unknown. By the time of the interviews, his mother was remarried, with a "new family," and F was completely alienated from her.

the 20, grew up with their families without interruption after their wartime nursery school stay.

REASONS FOR THE ABSENCE OF A CONTROL GROUP

Finally, I must comment on the absence of a control group in this study. A control group in an investigation of this type and size should, ideally, be matched with the persons being studied, like them on all relevant variables except the independent variable of early childhood separation and placement in a wartime residential nursery. But children who were not evacuated and stayed in London with their families were exposed for many years to the horrors of aerial attack upon London, and children who were evacuated with their mothers experienced the difficulties of being billeted in someone else's house, often as unwelcome guests, often with many changes of billet.

In addition to these two variations, there was another fundamental difference between possible "controls" and the persons studied. In the case of the nursery school children, the parents *had* decided—admittedly under the force of circumstances—to place their children in a nursery. Our earliest interviews with parents suggested that this fact possibly had multiple and dynamic implications reflecting on the parents as personalities and as members of a family group, and especially on their feelings about parental roles. Any control group would have had to have been matched on this criterion, too. Young adults in such a control group would have to have parents who had decided to place their children for their safety, but for some reason did not. Ignoring this variable would have meant that the children's growing-up years in their own families were spent with parents whose orientations to parental roles, at least in the children's preschool years, were probably different in crucial, although difficult to specify, ways.

We discovered one city where an evacuation nursery was planned and applications were filed, but the scheme was not realized. This seemed at first to answer our needs for a control group, but it became clear that growing up in this city after the war was not really similar to growing up in any of the London boroughs in which our 20 persons lived. At this point we abandoned the search for controls.

The plan for study, then, provided four comparison age-at-separation groups and three comparison nursery groups. It seemed to me that the basic questions we asked could be answered by rating against assumed norms for an urban population. Other controls, such as the blind analyses of some of the data, were built into our procedures for study.

METHODS OF DATA COLLECTION AND ANALYSIS

I used a direct approach with these 20 adults. I explained that I was a visiting American interested in the care of small children who had had to live away from their parents. Since, for their physical safety, they all had been evacuated during the war, I thought that some things could be learned about such early childhood care if I had a chance to talk with them, primarily about how they were getting along now. Many of them replied in essence that if their participation would help children, they would help us. There was only one exception, a Four-plus who was married and the mother of two children. She completed a first session with my interviewer colleague, Leslie Bell, of The London School of Economics, and then, ostensibly because she was moving and starting a new job, etc., could not arrange a second appointment with me. Confronted with our time limits, she readily agreed to our getting a substitute for her. Our substitute, a Four-plus mother of one child, six months pregnant with her second, was an alumna of the same nursery school. She and all the others kept every appointment, in one case as many as five.

The questions we asked about the adjustment of these young adults were formulated in the light of the literature on early childhood separation. This literature predicts that damage would be manifest in five areas: First, *feeling life* would suffer—apathy, inability to express feelings, narcissism, depression, and/or low self-esteem would be more apparent than their opposites on each continuum. Second, assessment of *inner controls* would reveal extremes of impulsiveness or overcontrol; lack of manifest anxiety or an excess of this; antisocial proclivities or overconforming rigidity; and/or extremes in orientations to pleasure, achievement, and short-term goals. Third, *relationships with people* would be characterized by lack of emotional attachment, social isolation, shallowness, short duration, receptive dependency, distrustfulness, noninitiating passivity, and/or sexual inappropriateness. Fourth, *performance in key social roles*, as, for example, son, daughter, husband, wife, parent, employee, friend, would be characterized by lack of involvement and/or inadequacy. Fifth, *intellectual functioning* would tend to be low and/or unstable. (Chart 1)

INTERVIEW METHODS

To provide data for rating each of the 20 adults on a five-point scale for each of 24 items dealing with the five major variables, Leslie Bell and I interviewed and tested the young adults, interviewed their parents, and consulted collateral agency records. A case folder on each participant was then submitted for rating to James Robertson and his wife, of the Tavistock and Hampstead Clinics, respectively.

Using a minimum of structure for the interviews, we asked for certain face-sheet data and facts about the chronology of living arrangements, and then for material on work history, leisure-time interests, most recent school experience, and family life (both family of origin and marital family). We cut across these life areas with our questions about the areas of predicted failure listed above. In addition to the interview, each person was asked to tell stories in response to 14 Thematic Apperception Test (TAT) cards, and ten, five men and five women, completed the California Psychological Inventory.[18] The number of interview sessions with each person, the hours for each session, and the informal situations in which we met varied considerably. We saw 14 subjects interacting with their own parents, four with spouses and own children or fiances. We had an informal dinner, tea, or a pub snack and bitters with about half

CHART 1
CASE RATING SHEET

_____(Case)_____   (Rater)_____

1. Feelings (Write X on one of 5 dashes, or circle ? for "Don't know")
    a. apathetic (lacking feelings)   __ __ __ __ __ ? vital (alive)
    b. repressive (unable to express)   __ __ __ __ __ ? spontaneous· (free)
    c. narcissistic (self-centered)   __ __ __ __ __ ? altruistic (outgoing)
    d. pessimistic (depressive)   __ __ __ __ __ ? optimistic (happy)
    e. low self-esteem   __ __ __ __ __ ? high self-esteem
2. Inner controls (X one of 5 dashes, or circle ? for "Don't know")
    a. impulsive, acting out   __ __ __ __ __ ? overcontrolled
    b. no anxiety, guiltless   __ __ __ __ __ ? anxiety laden, guilty
    c. antisocial   __ __ __ __ __ ? over conforming
    d. low achievement orientation   __ __ __ __ __ ? high achievement orien-
                                                          tation
    e. high pleasure orientation   __ __ __ __ __ ? low pleasure orientation
    f. short-term goals   __ __ __ __ __ ? long-range goals
3. Relationships with people (For relationship with mother, write m; father, f; sib, s; husband or fiance, h; wife or fiancee, w; child(ren), c; employer, e; friend, fr; other, o. Write appropriate letter, wherever evidence permits.)
    a. emotionally unattached   __ __ __ __ __ ? emotionally attached
    b. Socially isolated   __ __ __ __ __ ? socially belonging
    c. shallow   __ __ __ __ __ ? deep
    d. short-term   __ __ __ __ __ ? long-term
    e. receptive (dependent)   __ __ __ __ __ ? giving
    f. hostile, distrustful   __ __ __ __ __ ? friendly, trusting
    g. passive, non-initiating   __ __ __ __ __ ? aggressive, initiating
    h. sexually inappropriate   __ __ __ __ __ ? sexually appropriate
4. Role performances (For role of son, s; daughter, d; husband, h; wife, w; parent, p; employee, e; friend, fr; recreation time, r; citizen, c.)
    a. uninvolved, unmotivated   __ __ __ __ __ ? involved, identified in
    b. sees self as inadequate in role __ __ __ __ __ ? sees self as adequate
    c. seen as inadequate by others in role __ __ __ __ __ ? seen as adequate by others
5. Intellectual functioning (X one of 5, or circle ? as in 1 & 2 above.)
    a. low functioning (manifest)   __ __ __ __ __ ? high level functioning
    b. uneven functioning   __ __ __ __ __ ? stable functioning

of them. With 15, we walked from office to home or from either to the underground station. Observation as well as tests and interviews seemed important as sources of data.

---

[18] The CPI's had not been analyzed when the case folders were submitted for rating. Therefore, the CPI data are not included in this report.

We also arranged visits with the parents of all but two of the 20.[19] We hoped that their memories would provide us with useful data on the children's earliest days, their leavetaking, and homecoming, but these hopes were rarely fulfilled. Asked to tell what her son was like when he returned home, one harried East End mother of six replied, "He'd had a haircut," and nothing more could be evoked. A less pressed and better educated mother had more vivid recollections of her own reactions at her son's departure than of his. After the bus left, she said, "I went cycling all day long—not to be back in this empty house." Home visits to the parents did, however, provide independent evidence of the young adults' current adjustment. In addition, these were invaluable opportunities to observe family life and the behavior of parents and siblings together. But if any early damage had occurred, we got essentially no evidence from the parents to describe it.

A final source of information was the records of social and medical agencies and the nurseries themselves. Nine of the 20 adults grew up in the East End. The district office of the Children's Department that had full records on all dependent and delinquent children in its area screened the nine names provided and made folders available. These folders amplified details of the material previously given by the young adults and their parents, but in no case did they reveal any inaccuracies. Specifically, four of the nine had told me in the interviews of episodes that led me to believe the Children's Department would have a file on their family, but the other five described no such episodes. These five were unknown to the Children's Department. Records on the other four essentially corroborated what they had told me: in one case a bicycle theft at age 11, and in the others facts about the dependency or sexual or other delinquencies of siblings in their families. Records from another social agency and from two medical facilities similarly substantiated what our subjects or their parents had said. All this confirming evidence suggests the validity of the interview data. It seems that an American visiting for a year is a safe recipient of London secrets. Or, perhaps an opportunity to talk honestly about one's self in our times is still all too rare to miss.

---

[19] In F's case, he was the only one of the 20 alienated from his mother. For this reason we did not arrange an interview with her, but drew as extensively as possible upon medical and social agency collateral material. The other parents not interviewed were Z's, who was the late substitute for the Four-plus we "lost." We did, however, interview Z's husband, and obtained a picture of Z's relationships with her parents and sibling that was documented by recent photographs. Although Y's parents were separated (the father moved out when Y was about 17), they still saw each other and we interviewed them both.

ANALYSIS CONTROL

As another control on the data and their analysis, each respondent's TAT stories were sent for blind analysis to George A. De Vos, a psychologist on the University of California faculty and a specialist in projective tests and in the fields of personality and culture, and delinquency. He was given no more information about each case than age and sex. Although he knew of the problem for investigation, he knew nothing about the sources of cases, their separation ages, or which might be "controls" or "experimental" cases.

Since ratings of case material may, of course, prove unstable even when made consensually, as the Robertsons worked, by co-rating, a table of random numbers was used to draw five cases for rerating. Norma Haan, of the Institute of Human Development, University of California, Berkeley, rerated them. There were two women and three men; one One, two Twos, one Three, and one Four-plus; one from Nursery N, two from Nursery E, and two from Nursery S. The analyses were examined for agreement in the same dichotomous intervals that were used as the basis for findings in this report, and the ratings agreed on a case-by-case basis in a range from 69 percent to over 90 percent. For the five variables, agreement was 76 percent on *feelings,* 75 percent on *inner controls,* 76 percent on *personal relationships,* 92 percent on *role performance,* and 80 percent on *intellectual functioning.*

One procedure for analyzing the ratings is to compare them with a typical metropolitan population. It was arbitrarily assumed that clinicians would rate a typical population on five-point scales in a 5 percent–20 percent–50 percent–20 percent–5 percent distribution. Thus, references to this metropolitan population are to persons for whom 50 percent of the ratings fall in the central interval, with lower and upper quartiles below and above. We tested the observed rating frequencies against this expected distribution (Table 2). Our findings include comparisons of the four age-at-separation groups, on each of the five psychosocial variables studied, and contrasts of the three nursery groups.

FINDINGS

We are now ready to consider some of the findings and to offer a few interpretations and some questions for further study. We found:

1. Although these 20 young adults may have been seriously damaged by their early childhood separation and residential nursery experiences, most of them give no evidence in young adulthood of any extreme aberrant reactions. There are no ratings at the extremes for 12 of the 20, and 15 have fewer than 10 percent of their total ratings at the

extremes.[20] To this extent, the data support assumptions about the resiliency, plasticity, and modifiability of the human organism rather than those about the irreversibility of the effects of early experience.

2. Where there is evidence in individual cases of aberrancy in the adjustment of these young adults, in almost every case the data on their families seem sufficient to explain it. Although our design called for the inclusion only of persons from intact families without gross pathology, as the families became better known, so did their disabilities. In the final section of this paper, the nature of some of these families, in relation to their surrender of preschool children, is described. At this point, however, it should be noted that, far from permitting the reversibility of early damage, growing up in some of these families might well have given reinforcement to it; and that, seen against their family and neighborhood backgrounds, a few of these young adults give vivid testimony to the strengths that are either inherent in them or were initially developed during years that included their nursery experiences.

3. The data do support the prediction that children placed in residential group care during the first year of life will show evidence of damage in their young adult years. Every test shows that this age group fared the worst of the four groups. (Details on the Ones appear later in this paper.) The family data, however, indicate parenting problems in this group that cannot be ignored in explanations of these young adults' adjustment.

4. None of the evidence from the Four-plus group supports the prediction that separation and group care starting at this period are followed by enduring damage that is evident in young adulthood.[21]

5. The Twos fared quite well, better than the Threes, differing from our metropolitan population on only one of the five psychosocial variables. Possible explanations for the difference between these two age-at-separation groups are offered later, since this fact raises questions about the assumed linear relationship between age at separa-

---

20 More specifically, there were no ratings at the lowest extreme on *intellectual functioning* for any of the 20, no ratings at the extremes of *feelings* or *inner controls* for 19 cases, on *role performance* for 14 cases, on *relationships* for 12 cases. Compare Yarrow's summary statement of findings—albeit largely "clinical impressions"—on the social and personality disturbances of institutionalized children: ". . . characteristics described are usually at the extreme end of the scale, reflecting exaggerated pathology or a complete lack of capacity, rather than a relative deficiency." Yarrow, *op. cit.*, p. 468.

21 This finding is not a function of shorter periods of separation from family for this age group, since V was in the nursery for 50 months, and two others, Z and X, had subsequent periods of separation from family of five and seven years.

tion (and group residential care) and the extent of enduring damage. In other words, these findings do not support the assumption that the earlier the child is separated, the more permanent is the damage to the child.

With these basic findings as a background, some facts about work and love in the total group are relevant. When interviewed, 17 of the 20 were gainfully employed in the London labor market, two were married women and mothers who had good employment histories, and the twentieth was a university student in her last year of training as a teacher. In four or five cases, at most, could job histories be characterized as unstable. Occupations for the men ranged from an industrial engineer who was graduated from Oxford to a dustman. Half of the 12 young men were employed at trades for which they had begun apprenticeships on leaving school at age 15, and five were employed in unskilled jobs. The unmarried women's jobs were file clerk, typist, switchboard operator, waitress, and tailor. Work seemed important to the young people, and it

TABLE 2

DISTRIBUTION OF RATINGS ON FIVE-STEP SCALE, BY PSYCHOSOCIAL VARIABLE AND
AGE GROUP

Age Group	Five-Step Frequencies					Dichotomies for Testing*		
Variable 1: Feelings						Low	Normal & Above	Probability
I	—	20	5	—	—	20	5	p < .001
II	1	5	14	5	—	6	19	n.s.
III	—	15	8	1	—	15	9	p < .001
IV	—	2	17	5	—	2	22	n.s.
Variable 2: Inner Controls (a)						Low	Normal & Above	Probability
I	—	15	5	5	1	15	11	p < .001
II	—	7	16	7	—	7	23	n.s.
III	—	5	11	10	—	5	21	n.s.
IV	—	6	21	3	—	6	24	n.s.
Variable 2: Inner Controls (b)						Normal & Below	High	Probability
I	—	15	5	5	1	20	6	n.s.
II	—	7	16	7	—	23	7	n.s.
III	—	5	11	10	—	16	10	n.s. (p = .10)
IV	—	6	21	3	—	27	3	n.s.
Variable 3: Relationships						Low	Normal & Above	Probability
I	21	47	13	3	—	68	16	p < .001
II	7	37	75	9	—	44	84	p < .02
III	17	48	66	4	—	65	70	p < .001
IV	—	29	70	9	—	29	79	n.s.
Variable 4: Role Performance						Low	Normal & Above	Probability
I	9	9	8	1	1	18	10	p < .001
II	—	12	21	9	—	12	30	n.s.
III	5	9	22	1	—	14	23	n.s.
IV	—	8	21	10	—	8	31	n.s.
Variable 5: Intellectual Functioning						Low	Normal & Above	Probability
I	—	5	2	1	—	5	3	p < .02
II	—	1	5	1	2	1	8	n.s.
III	—	3	4	3	—	3	7	n.s.
IV	—	1	7	2	—	1	9	n.s.

* Tested against expected distributions of 5%, 20%, 50%, 20%, 5%, or, as dichotomized, 25% and 75%, with values smaller than those required for .05 level considered non-significant (n.s.).

was an obvious source of satisfaction to most of them. It was manifestly a drain and merely a means of income for only four, and one of these had applied and been accepted at a university after three and a half years of secretarial work, which she had found tedious. Out of a total of 43 ratings made by the Robertsons and Mrs. Haan on involvement and feelings of adequacy at work, "normal and above" accounted for 35 ratings, or 81 percent. To this extent, the group made an occupational investment and a socially responsible contribution.

Love seems more difficult than work for a research person to assess. (The data on *feeling life* and *relationships,* to be presented shortly, bear on this topic.) Two of the women and one of the men were enjoying marriage and had parented a total of seven children. Another six of the 20 had set dates for their marriages. Three had what American teenagers call "steadies." Only four seemed at the time of interviews to be "unattached" by plan, and four others were between attachments. In a country where, as of 1959, the average age at marriage for men was 25 years, and for women, 23 years,[22] this group of 19- to 26-year-olds seems well on schedule.

RATINGS ON VARIABLES BY AGE AT SEPARATION

Analysis of ratings on the five variables is, however, more revealing.

1. *Personal relationships* present some problems in three age groups, but not for the Four-pluses. That is, ratings on this variable differ significantly from the normal metropolitan population for the Ones, the Twos, and the Threes, but not ratings at the very bottom extreme for the Twos.

2. *Feeling life,* for the Ones and the Threes is less vital, spontaneous, and outgoing than it is for more normal groups, such as the Twos and the Fours.

3. The evidence that is available on *intellectual functioning* fails to indicate retardation or instability for any group but the Ones.

4. The *role performance* ratings indicate that all but the Ones are performing key social roles with involvement and feelings of adequacy that lie within the expected distribution.

5. Problems with *inner controls* fail to appear in the pattern predicted by the separation literature for any group but the Ones. The Twos and the Four-pluses are rated within a normal distribution for inner controls. The Ones alone present a group picture of somewhat greater impulsiveness. The Threes also show a group tendency to differ, approaching the .10 level of significance, but in the direction of above normal control and conformity.

---

[22] *The Registrar General's Statistical Review of England and Wales for the Year 1959,* Part II (London: Her Majesty's Stationary Office, 1960), Table L, p. 72.

In summary then, the ratings indicate that relationships are some problem for all but the Four-plus group. The other variables present a scattering of age-differentiated findings that principally involve the Ones, who emerge as the lowest rated group on all variables. The Four-pluses pass on all tests, and the Twos are a better adjusted group than the Threes.

RATINGS BY NURSERY

There are also findings on these young adults as alumni of the three quite different wartime nurseries. For this analysis, the Ones were eliminated because Nursery E is unrepresented and Nursery N is over-represented in this age group. This leaves only 15 cases, but there are 176 to 277 ratings for each nursery group (Table 3). Examination of these ratings by nursery group reveals that the graduates of the somewhat firm, if not stern, and suppressive small Welsh Nursery E appear as young adults to be essentially no better or worse adjusted than the graduates of the psychologically sophisticated and much larger Nursery N. The group that is clearly the best off is the one from the day nursery school evacuated as a unit—Nursery S, with its faith in God, King, and denial and its rather inspirational, repressive, and possessive approach to the children.

TABLE 3

COMPARISON OF THREE NURSERY GROUPS BY SUMMATED FREQUENCIES OF RATINGS ON FIVE-STEP SCALE

Nursery	Rating Frequencies					Total
N 4 cases	11 6%	54 31%	78 44%*	31 18%	2 1%	176 100%
E 7 cases	19 7%	116 42%	126 45%*	16 6%	—	277 100%
S 4 cases	— —	18 8%	175 78%*	32 14%	—	225 a 100%

* 50% of ratings expected in "normal" central step.
a There are a larger number of ratings per case for Nursery S than for other two nurseries because the three married adults in the study, all parents, were in this group. They thus had more "relationships" and "roles" to rate, and therefore more ratings.

SOME QUESTIONS AND INTERPRETATIONS

A study of only 20 persons, though relatively intensive, cannot provide a sound base for contributions to agency program planning. Rather, such a study may help sharpen questions about assumptions that underlie practice. Therefore, I shall further examine three issues: the superior adjustment of Nursery S graduates, the better adjustment of the Twos than of the Threes, and the matter of family background, especially among the Ones.

SUPERIOR ADJUSTMENT OF NURSERY S GROUP

The procedure of group residential placement following a period of day care, where children come to know the other children involved and the adults in charge, is unusual. At a day care nursery school, teachers and working mothers meet to discuss child-rearing and child-care problems, and some awareness of each others' values is communicated. Continuity in way of life and in personal relationships for the children between their day care and their residential group is provided for. "For the infant and young child," as Yarrow says, "changes result in a loss of environmental predictability. The degree of stress involved is likely to vary with the degree of unpredictability."[23] The Nursery S placement plan seems to reduce the unpredictability of residential care. Whether this arrangement alone induces results such as the superior adjustment of Nursery S children would seem to warrant further study.

SUPERIOR ADJUSTMENT OF THE TWOS

Why should the Twos have fared better than the Threes? The range and average number of years they were separated are similar, mid-points of just under three years. In both age groups, coincidentally, there are three persons who had older siblings present at their residential nursery, and in each group there is one sibling who was the elder sibling at the nursery. During the study the data suggested that younger siblings fared well to the detriment of elder sibs, but later analysis failed to support this proposition any more than it supported the proposition that children placed as sibling units do better than children placed apart from their siblings. Developmental theory suggests that 2-year-olds are closer to the autonomy phase, to use Erikson's term,[24] than are 3-year-olds, who are beginning to be more involved in Oedipal alignments with parents. The Threes also seem cognitively better equipped to understand—and misunderstand—the whys of separation than are the Twos. These developmental differences probably contributed significantly to the findings of this study, but we have no data available that help to indicate just how.[25]

---

[23] Yarrow, *op. cit.*, p. 481.

[24] Erik H. Erikson, *Childhood and Society* (New York: W. W. Norton & Co., 1950), pp. 222–26.

[25] Findings that the Threes included some of the most overcontrolled and overconforming of the young adults studied suggest that identifications occurred in the course of early development among these persons although the parent figures present were not their own parents. The extent to which these more rigid ego controls were patterned after nursery staff adults, or developed in response to the institutional children's groups with whom they spent their early years—from about three years until school age—is a nice question for study. Are children who begin residential group life

Another plausible explanation, however, involves the manifest disturbances in three of the five families in each of these two age groups. Did earlier removal of the Twos than of the Threes give them a sounder base for coping with familial strife upon their return home? Since, in the families of both age groups there are unevacuated younger siblings who seem more troubled than the once-separated persons in this study, questions about the families as causal agents are appropriate. The inference is that separation from such troubled families at age 2 may be preferable to separation at age 3 because by that time greater damage has been inflicted on the child. This proposition might be tested on sibling groups in institutional or foster family care.

HOME LIFE OF THE ONES

If the Twos fared better than the Threes because of earlier separation, why then did the Ones not fare better still? They were the earliest separated of all and from troubled parental situations in every case. As young adults, however, the Ones fared the worst of the four age groups. But here the issues of when the damage first occurred, its irreversibility, and its reinforcement seem hopelessly confounded. When did it first occur? Nursery N's longitudinal records, written while the children were in residence, describe three of the Ones. They tell vividly of A's slow motor, language, and social development (because of congenital defect, birth injury, or separation?) ; of B's growth from a peaked, birdlike two-month-old at arrival into a willful, active child; of D's excellent physical development and voracious eating, and other not unusual behavior. Except for A's retardation, which is of unknown origin, there is no evidence of gross pathology in any of these records. Only a nursery staff member's memories of F as a wild, unmanageable under-five foreshadow reports on his later markedly regressive behavior at about age eight. During the intervening years he had returned home to what is probably the most aberrant family situation among the 20 persons studied.

Why are the Ones the worst off as young adults? They were not only the earliest separated, but also, except for C, the earliest to return to their own parents. What can be said about the families in which the Ones grew up? I present just a few observations on four of the families to indicate why I question whether the Ones are the most damaged group by far because they were irreversibly scarred during early separation, or whether their multiple adjustment problems were induced or reinforced by their post-nursery school lives in their relationships with such parents as these.

---

at about age three, among age-mates with whom they pass through the Oedipal period, more likely to be overcontrolled and conforming than children who do not spend these years in group residential life or who begin it much earlier or much later?

THE YOUNG ADULT ADJUSTMENT | 357

A's mother, widowed since A was 12, lives in a tiny East End flat, sharing a bedroom with the boy, now 19, her only child. She had kept her husband waiting as a suitor for 12 years before they married, ostensibly because of her relationship with her own mother. She reminisced, "But from the moment we were married, it was wrong from the first time." The symbiotic bond between Mrs. A and her son today follows upon Nursery N's early descriptions of her regular weekend visits. But despite requests that she take him home because he was such a slow developer, she did not do so until Nursery N closed down. The role of mother to infant and pre-school child seems to have been impossible for this simple, immature woman to have performed effectually, as was the role of wife. She could not engage in either of the differing kinds of mutuality required for each role.

For Mrs. A, her son in his infant and pre-school years was a body to be fed and protected by someone else. A spoke of his growing-up years in terms of illnesses, outpatient visits to the hospital, and physical impediments to relationships with his peers. Mrs. A's attentions in those years were constantly focused on an unable body. Mrs. A still devotes herself to feeding and protecting this body, although A at 19 is a large six-footer.

B grew up with her immediate family in a house owned and occupied by maternal grandparents. A brief excerpt from Nursery N's wartime records reads: "When Mrs. B arrived, B started to cry immediately. Her mother picked her up but B cried more and more. Perhaps the ill baby who vomited so easily could not stand the mother's rocking; perhaps B felt her mother's anxiousness. B got restless each time her mother came to see her. . . . It was hard to feel the disappointment of the kind, shy woman who never complained."

Leslie Bell's impressions of Mrs. B, almost 20 years later, were that she was "very naïve and unintrospective in her observations of her children," and that her early difficulties in feeding B before she placed her in Nursery N at 2 months could not have been a matter merely of her being simple. Even though she is deeply indebted to Nursery N, Mrs. B still feels B became spoiled and willful there, and accounts for the difficulties in their relationship with this idea.

C's mother, an extremely intelligent woman, was outspokenly troubled by her inability to reach or understand her daughter from her birth to the present day. Mrs. C returned to work soon after C's birth and placed her in a wartime nursery at five months. In talking of C's undemonstrativeness, Mrs. C said that she had not had a mother herself and that, consequently, she found it difficult to show her feelings and to give physical affection. C was kept at boarding school until she was nine. Her father died when she was 11, but she remembers most vividly his scolding her for not getting better school reports. The distance from each other that characterizes the members of this family seems to be a model for C's own underlying remoteness from people.

D's parents, superficially warm, had three repeatedly delinquent children with approved school (correctional institution) histories. D, the youngest, seemed to have escaped such a career by acceding to his obese and hypochondriacal mother's demands and by avoiding a close relationship with his father. Mr. D emerged quite accurately in the blind analysis of D's TAT stories as "a rather passive individual who has borderline conformity to the law . . . a corrupter of the young." In the D family, one finds again parents interested in feeding the child's body but too preoccupied with themselves to be able to give much more than food. The fact that D does not more closely resemble Bowlby's descriptions of the "affectionless character"[26] may be because he was in placement for 40 months so early in his life. His older siblings, who spent more of their earliest days with these same parents, have far more aberrant histories than D.

Are the shallowness and the restricted nature of the young adult relationships of these Ones and the flatness of their feeling lives an irreversible result of infant separation and early group care? Or have these parents contributed appreciably during the children's growing-up years to these conditions? The available facts provide no basis for conclusive answers.

They do, however, suggest that parents who voluntarily place a child away from home in the first year of life, albeit in a program sanctioned by society and in a time of national crisis, often have limited or distorted feeling lives and relationship capacities for caring for their children. Even in the families of some of the children separated at an older age, parental roles seem ego-alien. Therefore, the effects of separation cannot be considered apart from the family life from which the children were separated and, in the case of the group under study, to which they were returned.

CONCLUDING COMMENTS

With these facts in mind, the good adjustment made by many of these young adults—who grew up in a time of war and unsettling postwar years—is worth pondering. As a group, they attest to the plasticity of human personality and, perhaps, also reflect favorably on their early nursery parent substitutes. Finally, they assure us that, at least from about age 2, early childhood separation and preschool residential care are not themselves *sufficient* antecedents to a seriously troubled or troublesome young adulthood.

---

[26] John Bowlby, *Forty-four Juvenile Thieves: Their Characters and Home Life* (London: Ballière, Tindall, & Cox, 1946).

HANS H. STRUPP

21 | *A Multidimensional Comparison of Therapist Activity in Analytic and Client-centered Therapy** [1]

"In science we need flexible minds and rigid concepts, but in psychoanalysis we have rigid minds and flexible concepts" (13, p. 233). This statement by a leading analyst, which is equally applicable to other forms of psychotherapy, epitomizes a growing awareness among research-minded psychotherapists that the fluidity of concepts, the ambiguities of language, and the idiosyncratic frames of reference espoused by competing schools represent serious barriers against furthering our knowledge of the psychotherapeutic process. From numerous quarters in recent years has come the cry for simpler concepts, for operational definitions, and for identifying the common denominators underlying all psychotherapeutic procedures. This trend implies, among other things, that differences in theory are meaningless if they fail to carry over into practice, and that focus upon the actual operations may be more fruitful for testing theoretical differences than prolonged controversy about the uniqueness of a given system.

The analysis of therapeutic protocols has occupied the time of researchers for some years, but rarely has an attempt been made to go outside a school of thought and to compare the techniques of, say, a nondirectivist with those of an analyst. Yet, such comparisons will inevitably play a part in future attempts to evaluate the relative effectiveness of competing approaches to psychotherapy.

This paper presents a preliminary descriptive analysis of two varieties of psychotherapeutic techniques: insight therapy with reeducative goals based on psychoanalytic principles, and client-centered therapy. The analysis is mediated by a multidimensional system, designed to quantify the common denominators in the verbal operations of therapists irrespective of their theoretical orientation. The data obviously do not permit an

* From Hans H. Strupp, "A Multidimensional Comparison of Therapist Activity in Analytic and Client-centered Therapy," *Journal of Consulting Psychology*, 21 (4), 301–308, 1957. Copyright 1957 by the American Psychological Association, and reproduced by permission.

1 This research is part of a larger project which is supported by a research grant (M-965) from the National Institute of Mental Health, of the National Institutes of Health, U.S. Public Health Service. Grateful acknowledgment is made to Winfred Overholser, M.D., under whose general direction this work was carried out, and to Leon Yochelson, M.D., project consultant. In addition, I am greatly indebted to my former research associate, Rebecca E. Rieger, A.M., who contributed materially to the execution of this study. A slightly different version of this paper was presented at the 1956 Annual Meeting of the American Psychological Association in Chicago.

evaluation of the respective merits of short-term analytic and client-centered therapy.

THE TWO CASE HISTORIES

The first case history, published by Wolberg (12, pp. 688–780),[2] comprises nine treatment sessions with a retired business woman, a widow in the middle years of life, who had become progressively depressed, and retreated from her customary social contacts. Concerning his technique, the therapist (Wolberg) mentions that the work proceeded almost entirely on a characterologic level, and that the effect of treatment was mostly of a reeducative nature, despite the fact that he interpreted some of the patient's defenses. A follow-up indicated that the results of treatment had been durable.

The second case history is that of Mary Jane Tilden, counseled by Rogers in a series of 11 interviews (9, pp. 128–203). Unfortunately, the author was not aware that this case is available in its entirety, which necessitated the selection of reasonably complete interviews from the beginning, middle, and terminal phases of treatment from the published portions.

Miss Tilden was described as a 20-year-old attractive young woman brought to the clinic by her mother, who complained that the patient was sleeping all the time, brooding, and ruminating. Miss Tilden seemed to be withdrawing progressively—she had given up her job and lost interest in her social life. Miss Tilden was treated by non-directive therapy. Rogers felt that the 11 counseling hours were followed by a period of improved adjustment; nevertheless, the evaluation of final outcome remained somewhat in doubt since, shortly after a year had elapsed, there seemed to be a recurrence of the earlier symptomatology.[3]

THE SYSTEM OF ANALYSIS

The system of analysis whose development and operational characteristics have been delineated in another publication (10), yields five measures relative to any therapist communication. There are two sets of categories *(Type of Therapeutic Activity* and *Dynamic Focus),* and three intensity scales *(Degree of Inference, Initiative,* and *Therapeutic Climate).* These components may be briefly characterized as follows:

Type of Therapeutic Activity.—The categories specified the outer form

---

[2] This case, particularly the therapist's activity, has been more fully discussed (11).
[3] Although one cannot be sure, this case may pertain to that period in the evolution of client-centered therapy in which Rogers (7) detects "vestiges of subtle directiveness."

or structure of a therapeutic intervention and provide a gross analysis of the therapist's techniques. The major categories were:

00 Facilitating Communication (Minimal activity) .
10 Exploratory Operations.
20 Clarification (Minimal interpretation) .
30 Interpretive Operations.
40 Structuring.
50 Direct Guidance.
60 Activity not clearly relevant to the task of therapy.
70 Unclassifiable.

Sixteen subcategories served to refine the primary rating.

Degree of Inference.—This intensity scale was based on the conception that inference is an integral part of all therapeutic communications and that it is always present to some degree. Each communication was rated by means of a five-point scale ranging from low to high inference. Scale points were defined *a priori* rather than via empirical judgments, but examples of typical communications were used to define each scale point.

Dynamic Focus.—Dynamic Focus referred to the frame of reference adopted by the therapist at a particular juncture, and characterizes the manner in which he focuses the therapeutic spotlight. Two major sectors were used to differentiate whether the therapist "goes along" with the patient (A) or whether he introduces a different focus (B) . Communications assigned to Sector B were further analyzed in terms of five subcategories:

B-1 Requests for additional information.
B-2 Focus on dynamic events in the *past*.
B-3 Focus on dynamic events in the *present*.
B-4T Focus on dynamics of the therapist-patient relationship (analysis of the transference).
B-4 Focus on the therapist-patient interaction in terms of the therapist's role as an expert, authority, etc.

Initiative.—The second intensity scale measured the extent to which the therapist assumes responsibility for guiding the patient's communications in a given channel. Initiative was conceived as ranging from low to high, and ratings were made on a four-point continuum. As in the case of *Degree of Inference,* scale points were defined by reference to appropriate examples.

Therapeutic Climate.—Emotional overtones discernible in a communication were quantified by means of a bipolar scale: $0 =$ neutral; $+1 =$ mild degree of warmth; $+2$ strong degree of warmth; -1 mild degree of coldness; -2 strong degree of coldness. A "warm" communication is one in which the therapist empathizes, shows understanding, or supports; a "cold" communication is one in which the therapist rejects, withdraws support, or punishes.

PROCEDURE

Seven of the nine Wolberg interviews and three representative interviews from the Miss Tilden case were scored jointly by two raters from the printed scripts. Two of the Wolberg interviews were rated independently by the same raters to obtain a measure of rater agreement.

RESULTS

RATER AGREEMENT

Table 1 presents results based on a unit-by-unit analysis of two interviews scored independently by two raters. Agreement on a unit (therapist communication) means that both raters assigned it to the same category (on *Type* and *Focus,* respectively), or that they gave it an intensity score (on *Degree of Inference* or *Initiative,* respectively) no more than one-half step apart. For the last two scales, product-moment coefficients were computed in addition.

TABLE 1
AGREEMENT BETWEEN TWO INDEPENDENT RATERS[a]

System Component	Wolberg Interview VII (N = 114)	Wolberg Interview IX (N = 154)
Type	80.7%	80.5%
Degree of Inference..............	86.0% (r = .86)	94.0% (r = .885)
Dynamic Focus...................	80.7%	85.7%
Initiative	87.7% (r = .87)	93.5% (r = .93)
Therapeutic Climate[b].............	—	—

a All percentages and correlation coefficients are significant beyond the .01 level.
b Nonzero scores too infrequent.

THE WOLBERG CASE

The therapist's activity, as mirrored by the multidimensional system of analysis, is presented in Figures 1, 2, 3, and 4. Within each interview, frequencies have been converted into percentages. In the case of *Degree of Inference* and *Initiative,* the designation Level 1, 2, and 3 signifies that scores have been grouped; Level 3 refers to the most intense scores. Chi squares computed for each component of the system were significant beyond the .01 level, indicating that the fluctuations in therapist activity for the interview series are not attributable to chance.

The therapist's techniques show systematic variations on all components over the course of therapy.[4] The initial interview is devoted largely to an exploration of the patient's problem; the next two interviews reveal an intensification of therapeutic activity, both in terms of inferential operations and *Initiative;* Interviews IV and VII emerge as interpretive ones, the intervening sessions as less "dramatic"; data for the remaining sessions point to a phasing out of interpretive activity, but *Initiative* remains at a relatively high level.

The therapist's interpretations are geared to the patient's current interpersonal relations, with relatively little emphasis on the therapist-patient relationship or on genetic antecedents. Throughout treatment, but especially in the second half, the therapist stands out as a person who, in the role of an expert, gives guidance, states opinions, and engages in procedures which may be labeled reeducative. He is clearly more active than passive, both in terms of frequency of intervention and in directing the course of therapy. Wolberg's own descriptive label "insight therapy with reeducative goals" appears to be corroborated by the quantitative analyses.

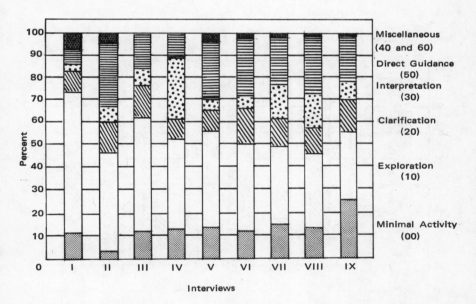

FIGURE 1. Therapist activity in the Wolberg case in terms of *Type of Therapeutic Activity.* (Interviews: I, $N = 108$; II, $N = 79$; III, $N = 108$; IV, $N = 174$; V, $N = 123$; VI, $N = 85$; VII, $N = 114$; VIII, $N = 130$; IX, $N = 154$. Total number of therapist interventions: $N = 1,075$.)

---

[4] *Therapeutic Climate* had to be omitted because there were very few nonzero scores.

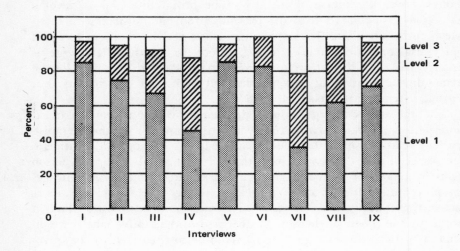

FIGURE 2. Therapist activity in the Wolberg case in terms of *Degree of Inference*.

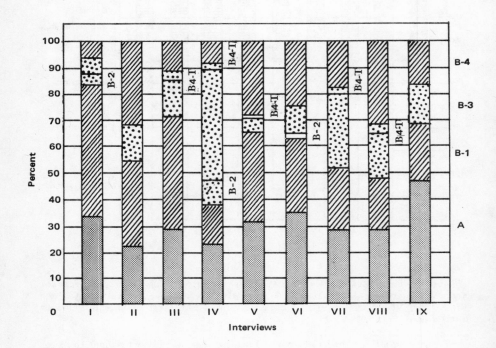

FIGURE 3. Therapist activity in the Wolberg case in terms of *Dynamic Focus*.

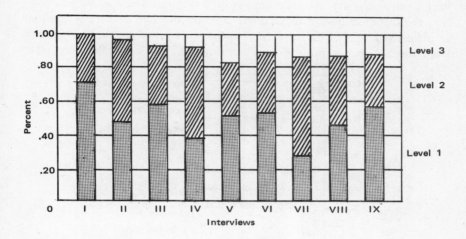

FIGURE 4. Therapist activity in the Wolberg case in terms of *Initiative*.

The most noteworthy single result is perhaps the *phasing* of therapeutic activity. It seems as if the therapist gradually prepares the patient for more inferential formulations which he advances in the fourth session. Then he waits for a consolidation of insight before renewing his interpretive efforts in Interview VII. Thereafter, he diminishes his interpretive activity while maintaining a degree of therapeutic pressure till the end.

THE CASE OF MISS TILDEN

The analysis comprises three selected interviews; they are, however, separated in time and they presumably represent different stages of therapy.

Reference to Figures 5, 6, 7, and 8 indicates that the profiles of therapist activity are quite similar from interview to interview. As might be expected, reflections of feeling account for a large percentage of all interventions (75%); interpretations are virtually absent; explorations are used minimally in the initial session and are almost nonexistent later on; direct guidance is equally rare. The data on *Degree of Inference* and *Initiative* corroborate these findings: Neither maximal *Degree of Inference* nor maximal *Initiative* is used to any appreciable degree, but the initial interview is relatively more inferential than the final one. (In this instance, chi square exceeded the .01 level of probability; all others failed to reach the .05 level.) In most of his interventions, the therapist accepts the patient's focus; only very rarely does he assume the role of an expert or an authority.

INTERTHERAPIST COMPARISONS

While the preceding analyses have shown that Wolberg's technique varies systematically over the course of treatment whereas Rogers' does not, the question may still be asked, how do the two therapists compare at different stages of therapy? To explore this problem, three interviews from the beginning, middle, and terminal phases of the Wolberg series

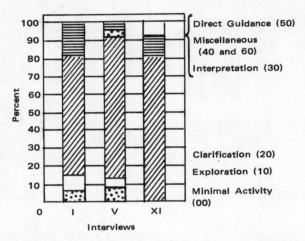

FIGURE 5. Therapist activity in the Miss Tilden case in terms of *Type of Therapeutic Activity*. (Interviews: I, $N = 57$; V, $N = 23$; XI, $N = 53$. Total number of therapist interventions: $N = 133$.)

were selected and compared with the Miss Tilden case. Since the distributions of the categories within *Type* and *Dynamic Focus* vary so greatly for the two therapists, the only meaningful comparisons concern the continua of *Degree of Inference* and *Initiative*. The results of this analysis are presented in Table 2.

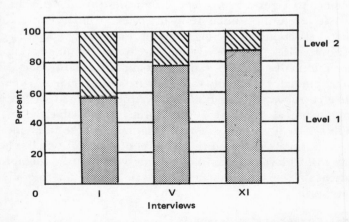

FIGURE 6. Therapist activity in the Miss Tilden case in terms of *Degree of Inference*.

In the case of *Degree of Inference,* a significant chi square indicates that Wolberg's technique is significantly more inferential than Rogers'; with respect to *Initiative,* Wolberg exerts stronger guidance in the middle and terminal interviews, but not in the initial one. The latter finding is accounted for by the fact that Wolberg employs a great many exploratory questions of a diagnostic character in his first session, which in terms of *Initiative* receive scores similar to the reflection-of-feeling technique, which Rogers employs throughout.

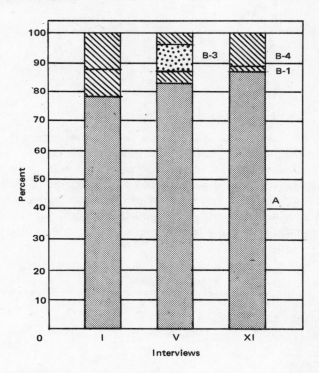

FIGURE 7. Therapist activity in the Miss Tilden case in terms of *Dynamic Focus.*

DISCUSSION

A multidimensional system of analysis has been applied to the therapist's communications in two forms of therapy in an effort to measure aspects which may be common to both. With respect to the Miss Tilden case, the system of analysis yields data which are substantially in agreement with other analyses which have been performed on interviews conducted by non-directive counselors. By and large, these results also agree with Rogers' recommendations on therapeutic technique. Wolberg's technique, too, is in agreement with his descriptive account but, to my

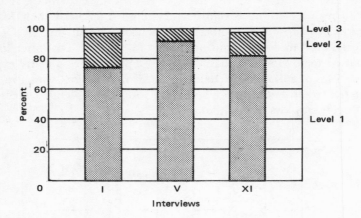

FIGURE 8. Therapist activity in the Miss Tilden case in terms of *Initiative*.

knowledge, no comparable quantitative studies have been published. While not crucial, such evidence attests indirectly to the validity of this system of analysis. Of at least equal importance, however, is the tentative demonstration that the method facilitates the comparative treatment of therapeutic techniques—a treatment which is quantitative and highly objective, and which does not prejudge a particular communication as desirable or undesirable on *a priori* grounds.

TABLE 2

CHI-SQUARE COMPARISONS OF THERAPIST ACTIVITY IN INITIAL, MIDDLE, AND TERMINAL INTERVIEWS

	Wolberg I (N = 108) vs. Rogers I (N = 57)	Wolberg IV (N = 174) vs. Rogers V (N = 23)	Wolberg IX (N = 154) vs. Rogers XI (N = 53)
Degree of Inference	19.32[b]	9.39[a]	4.66*
Initiative	.19	22.79[b]	9.85[a]

* Significant between the .02 and .05 level.
a Significant at the .01 level.
b Significant at the .001 level.

To be sure, the present two case histories are comparable only in superficial respects and they do not lend themselves to a rigorous evaluative comparison. However, they suggest a number of questions which appear to be basic to all psychotherapy research. Consider the following two points.

We know that both patients entered psychotherapy seeking alleviation of their emotional problems. Did their difficulties have any common basis? What was the relative degree of their disturbance? Even if both had been diagnosed as "depressed," or by any other label, we would know but little about the common denominators of the underlying dynamics. As Kubie (6) has pointed out, the time is ripe for fresh attempts to identify the common principles of the "neurotic process." It is clear that studies in which patients are matched with experimental "controls" remain largely meaningless unless this Herculean research task can be accomplished.

Secondly, what transpired in the therapeutic sessions that led both therapists to evaluate the outcome as "successful"? Both therapists are highly experienced men in their field; both had a rationale for their respective procedures which on the evidence of this study differed quantitatively (*Degree of Inference* and *Initiative*) and perhaps qualitatively (*Type* and *Dynamic Focus*). Rogers, in keeping with his theory, consistently reflected the patient's feelings, whereas Wolberg, combining analytic principles with reeducative techniques, attempted to effect therapeutic changes in his patient mainly by means of interpretation and guidance. But even if the patients could be equated it would not be possible to attribute differences in therapeutic outcome (whose measurement is another staggering problem) to variations in technique as long as relevant factors in the therapist's personality are left out of account. Certainly, Wolberg was more "directive" (by Rogerian standards). But both therapists conveyed an attitude of respect for their patients and implied their right to self-direction; both appeared to be warm, accepting and noncritical; both encouraged the patient's expression of feelings; and both, by their therapeutic performance, seemed to engender a feeling of greater self-acceptance in their patients. These attitudes on the part of the therapist—he may have them in common with the mature person who can also be a good parent[5]—are as yet largely unexplored by objective research, but they may be the touchstone of *all* therapeutic success, regardless of the theory.[6] Given the "basic therapist personality" it may still be possible that some therapeutic techniques or combinations of techniques catalyze the therapeutic process whereas others are relatively

---

[5] I have in mind Fromm's "productive character" (5).

[6] There is increasing evidence that the therapist's attitude may "cut across" theoretical orientations. For a comprehensive statement of the client-centered position, see Rogers' discussion (8, pp. 19–64). On the other hand, Wolberg's transcript offers evidence that respect for the patient, his capacities, his right to self-direction, and his worth as a human being can be conveyed even when the therapist makes interpretations. Fiedler's studies (2, 3, 4) suggest that "experts," irrespective of whether they subscribe to the analytic, Adlerian, or client-centered viewpoint, create highly similar "ideal therapeutic relationships" but, as Bordin (1, pp. 115–16) has pointed out, Fiedler's findings cannot be regarded as evidence for or against the question of the importance to be attached to differences among theories.

inert; contrariwise, no amount of training in technique may compensate for deficiencies in the therapist's "basic attitudes." To approach these problems by research is difficult, but by no means impossible.

It seems that altogether too little attention has been paid by researchers to the therapist and his contribution to the therapeutic process. In keeping with this conviction, I have focused upon one facet—the therapist's techniques—and attempted to abstract common denominators from the therapist's verbal operations. The isolation and measurement of common denominators in varying therapeutic techniques appears to be a needed research task which must be expanded by research on the therapist's personality, from which technique seems to be inseparable.[7]

SUMMARY

In an effort to compare the therapist's activity in two forms of psychotherapy, a multidimensional system for analyzing therapeutic communications has been applied to two published case histories: a case treated by short-term therapy based upon psychoanalytic principles, and a case treated by client-centered therapy.

The therapist's activity in analytically oriented therapy showed statistically significant variations over the course of treatment in terms of *Type of Therapeutic Activity, Degree of Inference, Dynamic Focus,* and *Initiative.* The data point to an intensification of therapeutic activity from the first to the fourth interview, at which time a number of relatively more inferential interpretations were advanced. In the seventh session, a similar intensification occurred, followed by a phasing out to the end of treatment. Interpretations dealt principally with the patient's current interpersonal situation; in addition, the therapist's verbalizations were designed to achieve a degree of reeducation in the patient.

As predictable from theory, the client-centered therapist's activity consisted principally of reflections of feeling. This therapeutic technique was sustained, with minor fluctuations, throughout treatment.

Intertherapist comparisons showed that the analytically oriented therapist used techniques which were generally more inferential and which showed greater *Initiative* than those of his client-centered counterpart. While the initial interviews did not differ significantly in terms of *Initiative,* the approach of the two therapists was nevertheless divergent on other dimensions.

The primary implications of this preliminary comparison relate to the comparative study of therapeutic techniques, which is considered one of

---

[7] A three-year investigation, currently nearing completion, deals with the techniques, therapeutic formulations, and attitudes of more than 200 therapists who responded as vicarious interviewers to a sound film of an initial interview.

the most important frontiers of research in psychotherapy. The isolation and measurement of common denominators in the techniques of therapists adhering to different schools should lead to more definitive studies of the therapist's personality, particularly of those attitudes which, wittingly or unwittingly, he brings to bear upon the therapeutic interaction.

REFERENCES

1. BORDIN, E. S. *Psychological counseling.* New York: Appleton-Century-Crofts, 1955.
2. FIEDLER, F. E. The concept of an ideal therapeutic relationship. *J. consult. Psychol.,* 1950, 14, 239–45.
3. FIEDLER, F. E. A comparison of therapeutic relationships in psychoanalytic, nondirective, and Adlerian therapy. *J. consult. Psychol.,* 1950, 14, 436–45.
4. FIEDLER, F. E. Factor analyses of psychoanalytic, nondirective, and Adlerian therapeutic relationships. *J. consult. Psychol.,* 1951, 15, 32–8.
5. FROMM, E. *Man for himself.* New York: Rinehart, 1947.
6. KUBIE, L. S. Some unsolved problems of psychoanalytic pschotherapy. In Frieda Fromm-Reichmann & J. L. Moreno (eds.), *Progress in psychotherapy 1956.* New York: Grune & Stratton, 1956. Pp. 87–102.
7. ROGERS, C. R. Significant aspects of client-centered therapy. *Amer. Psychologist,* 1946, 1, 415–22.
8. ROGERS, C. R. *Client-centered therapy.* Boston: Houghton Mifflin, 1951.
9. SNYDER, W. U. (Ed.) *Casebook of nondirective counseling.* Boston: Houghton Mifflin, 1947.
10. STRUPP, H. H. A multidimensional system for analyzing psychotherapeutic techniques. *Psychiatry,* in press.
11. STRUPP, H. H. A multidimensional analysis of technique in brief psychotherapy. *Psychiatry,* in press.
12. WOLBERG, L. R. *The technique of psychotherapy.* New York: Grune & Stratton, 1954.
13. WOLFF, W. *Contemporary psychotherapists examine themselves.* Springfield, Ill.: Charles C Thomas, 1956.

Selected References

ALLEN, RUTH, "A Study of Subjects Discussed by Elderly Patients in Group Counseling," *Social Casework* (July, 1962).

APPELBERG, ESTHER, "Verbal Accessability of Adolescents," *Child Welfare* (February, 1964).

BEHER, JEROME, "Male Adolescent Inmates' Perceptions of Helping Persons," *Social Work* (April, 1965).

BERNSTEIN, ROSE, & CYR, FLORENCE E., "A Study of Interviews With Husbands in a Prenatal and Child Health Program," *Social Casework* (November, 1957).

BRIM, ORVILLE G., FAIRCHILD, ROY, & BORGATTA, EDGAR, "Relations Between Family Problems," *Marriage and Family Living* (August, 1961).

BROYLES, J. ALLEN, "The John Birch Society: A Movement of Social Protest of the Radical Right," *Journal of Social Issues* (April, 1963).

BONJEAN, CHARLES, "Community Leadership: A Case Study and Conceptual Refinement," *American Journal of Sociology* (May, 1963).

COPPERMAN, MICHAEL, "Residential Mobility of a Group of Public Welfare Clients," *Social Casework* (July, 1964).

DOWNING, RUTH, "A Cooperative Project of an Elementary School and a Family Agency," *Social Casework* (November, 1959).

DUNKEL, MARY, "Homelessness as a Major Problem of Hospitalized Children," *Social Service Review* (March, 1963).

FRINGS, JOHN, "Experimental Systems of Recording," *Social Casework* (February, 1957).

GARCEA, RALPH, "A Family Agency Deals with the Problem of Dropouts," *Social Casework* (February, 1962).

GOTTESFELD, HARRY, "Professionals and Delinquents Evaluate Professional Methods with Delinquents," *Social Problems* (Summer, 1965).

GRUSKY, OSCAR, "Authoritarianism and Effective Indoctrination: A Case Study," *Administrative Science Quarterly* (June, 1962).

GYARFAS, MARY GORMAN, "Learning Disability in Boys: An Exploration of Family Pathology," *Social Service Review* (December, 1961).

HANSON, ROBERT, "The Systematic Linkage Hypothesis and Role Consensus Patterns in Hospital-Community Relations," *American Sociological Review* (June, 1962).

JACOBSON, SHIRLEY, & KLERMAN, GERALD, "Interpersonal Dynamics of Hospitalized Depressed Patients' Home Visits," *Journal of Marriage and the Family* (February, 1966).

JONASSEN, CHRISTEN, "Functional Unities in 84 Community Systems," *American Sociological Review* (June, 1961).

JONASSEN, CHRISTEN, "Toward an Operational Definition of Community Welfare," *Social Problems* (Fall, 1962).

KADUSHIN, ALFRED, "The Effect on the Client of Interview Observation at Intake," *Social Service Review* (March, 1957).

KADUSHIN, CHARLES, "Social Distance Between Client and Professional," *American Journal of Sociology* (March, 1962).

KIRSCH, JANET, "The Effect of Music Therapy on Mentally Ill Patients," *Social Casework* (April, 1962).

KITSUSE, JOHN, "Societal Reaction to Deviant Behavior: Problems of Theory and Method," *Social Problems* (Winter, 1962).

LEHRMAN, PAUL, "Argot, Symbolic Deviance and Subcultural Delinquency," *American Sociological Review* (April, 1967).

MEYERHOFF, BARBARA, & LARSON, WILLIAM R., "Primary and Formal Aspects of Family Organizations: Group Consensus, Problem Perception, and Adolescent School Status," *Journal of Marriage and the Family* (May, 1965).

PARNICKY, JOSEPH J., & BROWN, LEONARD N., "Introducing Institutionalized Retardates to the Community," *Social Work* (January, 1964).

PERRY, JOSEPH, "The Mother Substitutes of Employed Mothers: An Exploratory Inquiry," *Marriage and Family Living* (November, 1961).

PILIAVIN, IRVING, & BRIAR, S., "Police Encounters with Juveniles," *American Journal of Sociology* (September, 1964).

RADIN, NORMA, & GLASSER, PAUL, "The Use of Parental Attitude Questionnaires with Culturally Disadvantaged Families," *Journal of Marriage and the Family* (August, 1965).

RUBINGTON, EARL, "Organizational Strains and Key Roles," *Administrative Science Quarterly* (March, 1965).

SHERMAN, JAMES, "Use of Reinforcement and Imitation to Reinstate Verbal Behavior in Mute Psychotics," *Journal of Abnormal Psychology* (June, 1965).

SPEIGEL, IRVING, "An Exploratory Research in Delinquent Subcultures," *Social Service Review* (March, 1961).

SUDNOW, DAVID, "Normal Crimes: Sociological Features of the Penal Code in a Public Defender Office," *Social Problems* (Winter, 1965).

WARD, DAVID, & KASSEBAUM, GENE, "Homosexuality: A Mode of Adaptation in a Prison for Women," *Social Problems* (Fall, 1964).

WETZEL, RALPH, "Use of Behavioral Techniques in a Case of Compulsive Stealing," *Journal of Consulting Psychology* (October, 1966).

WHITMER, CARROLL A., & CONOVER, C. GLENN, "A Study of Critical Incidents in the Hospitalization of the Mentally Ill," *Social Work* (January, 1959).

Bibliography

CAMPBELL, D. T. and STANLEY, J. C., "Experimental and Quasi-Experimental Designs for Research on Teaching," Gage, N. L. (editor), *Handbook of Research on Teaching.* Chicago: Rand-McNally, 1963, pp. 171–246.

EATON, JOSEPH W., "Science, Art, and Uncertainty in Social Work," *Social Work* (July, 1958), pp. 3–10.

EDWARDS, ALLEN L., *Experimental Design in Psychological Research* (rev. ed.). New York: Holt, Rinehart and Winston, 1960.

FESTINGER, LEON, "Laboratory Experiments," in *Research Methods in the Behavioral Sciences,* Leon Festinger and Daniel Katz (eds.). New York: The Dryden Press, Inc., 1953, pp. 136–172.

FRENCH, JOHN R. P., JR., "Experiments in Field Settings," in *Research Methods in the Behavioral Sciences,* Leon Festinger and Daniel Katz (eds.). New York: The Dryden Press, Inc., 1953, pp. 98–135.

GREENWOOD, ERNEST, *Lectures In Research Methodology For Social Welfare Students,* University of California Syllabus Series No. 388. University of California, Berkeley, 1960.

KERLINGER, FRED N., *Foundations of Behavioral Research: Educational and Psychological Inquiry.* New York: Holt, Rinehart and Winston, Inc., 1967.

LEWIS, OSCAR, *The Children of Sanchez.* New York: Random House, 1961.

SUCHMAN, EDWARD A., *Evaluative Research: Principles and Practice in Public Service and Social Action Programs.* New York: Russell Sage Foundation, 1967.

TRIPODI, TONY; FELLIN, PHILLIP; MEYER, HENRY J., *The Assessment of Social Research: Guidelines For The Use of Research in Social Work and Social Science.* Itasca, Ill.: F. E. Peacock Publishers, Inc., 1969.

THOMAS, EDWIN J., "Field Experiments and Demonstrations," in Polansky, Norman A. (editor), *Social Work Research.* New York: University of Chicago Press, 1960, Chapter 14.

————, "Selecting Knowledge from Behavioral Science," in *Building Social Work Knowledge.* New York: National Association of Social Workers, 1964.

WEINBERGER, ROSLYN and TRIPODI, TONY, "Trends in Types of Research Reported in Selected Social Work Journals: 1956–1965," University of Michigan School of Social Work, mimeographed (May 1968).

Index

BOOK MANUFACTURE

Exemplars of Social Research was typeset, printed by offset and paper-back bound at Webb Publishing Company. Cloth binding was by A. J. Dahl Company. The paper is Perkins & Squier Company's Glatfelter Old Forge Wove. Internal design was by the F. E. Peacock Publishers, Inc., art department. Cover design was by Earl E. Hilland. The type in this book is Baskerville with Lydian Light display.